W9-DII-610

6 50

THE BEST PLAYS OF 1954–1955

THE BURNS MANTLE YEARBOOK

Illustrated with photographs, and with

Drawings by HIRSCHFELD

from "Peter Pan

THE BEST PLAYS
OF 1954–1955

EDITED BY LOUIS KRONENBERGER

DODD, MEAD AND COMPANY

NEW YORK   1955   TORONTO

EDITOR'S NOTE

IN editing this thirty-eighth volume in the *Best Plays* series, I am once again under very pleasant obligations. Once again I am indebted to my wife, Emmy Plaut, for help that is more fairly called collaboration. For editorial help I am greatly indebted to Phyllis Terry. For the use of photographs I must thank the Editors of *Life* magazine and Doris O'Neill; for the use of its tabulation of Hits and Flops, I must thank *Variety* and Mr. Abel Green. Particular thanks are due, for their several reports, to Miss Cassidy, Mr. Tynan, M. Josset, Mr. McLaughlin, Mr. Nichols and Mr. Sherwood; and for very kindly granting the use of their sketches, to Boris Aronson, Cecil Beaton, William and Jean Eckart, Eldon Elder, Mordecai Gorelik, Oliver Messel, Jo Mielziner, and Motley.

Nor can I conclude without saying once more what a pleasure it is to be associated in this project with Mr. Hirschfeld.

LOUIS KRONENBERGER

CONTENTS

THE BEST PLAYS OF 1954–1955

SUMMARIES OF THE SEASONS

THE SEASON ON BROADWAY

THE '54-'55 season didn't make history, but it often did make news. Most of its headlines will scarcely survive as footnotes, but in their own day they paced a season that while lacking real vitality showed considerable liveliness. Sometimes the liveliness had less of an on-stage than of a backstage, or even smoking-car, quality. For a brief spell the work that gained Mr. Tennessee Williams both the Pulitzer and the Critics Circle awards was less well known as a play about a cat than as containing a dirty joke about an elephant; while such were the season's wrangles that the author of *The Boy Friend* was locked out of rehearsals by his producers, and whoever would have chronicled the road try-out of *Silk Stockings* needed the credentials of a war correspondent. But the liveliness was not just from episodes like these, or from Miss Bankhead's caperings in *Dear Charles* or the downstage bubble bath in *Lunatics and Lovers*. The season had its genuine excitements and explosions; not all its wars were fought out of vanity, and in its search for novelty it sometimes stumbled on merit. Furthermore, for the second year straight Broadway, if not overpoweringly virtuous itself, was the cause of virtue in others: for even more than during the previous season Off-Broadway proved adventurous; even more it achieved modest effects of style and sensibility and wit that Broadway itself fell short of.

Real achievement, genuine stature, is indeed what Broadway fell short of most; what Broadway concerned itself with was seldom at a very high level. But to give the level its due, it involved, if not pure, then much clouded or diluted or adulterated talent; much fitful power and intermittent vivacity. Deplorably much in the season's playwriting might be false or synthetic or unsustained; but, compared with even ten years ago, there was far less that was blatantly unprofessional or downright bad. High production costs may have not yet taught producers and backers what is basically vulgar or counterfeit, but at least they are learning what is merely cheap or highflown. Thus if Broadway still offers not too many unforeseen triumphs, there are much fewer plainly predestined fiascos. So far, it is no more than a negative achievement: the fine imposing dramatic structures are still to come, but slum clearance seems at least under way.

3

And if we are to be architectural, it was chiefly on the Brownstone Era that Broadway cast its eye last season. The season's sharpest trend was toward good old-fashioned theatre, toward rousing second acts, toward stately, plump Recognition Scenes. At times, in all this return to theatre, the ancestor might be Ibsen as well as Sardou, the subject matter our own Age of Violence rather than mid-Victorian trapdoors and trances. One phenomenon of our current stage is to saturate our most pressing anxieties in escapism; to fumigate our real horrors with macabre make-believe; to forestall our private nightmares at three in the morning by having us undergo them publicly and wakingly at ten at night. It is at least a new wrinkle, and may become, in time, The New Catharsis.

What with these backward glances and violent gestures and beclouded talents, the business of choosing the ten best plays has once again a somewhat maddening charm. There are once again so few plays that would qualify at a really stiff level, there are so many more that have qualifications at a somewhat relaxed one. But the faults in the weaker contestants must be held fatal where the virtues are never really impressive. Thus, a *Rainmaker* has at its best a good brisk humor, but is even at its best nothing better than very high-grade corn. *The Flowering Peach,* at its worst, is both unfocused and dull, but it reaches at its best where a *Rainmaker* fails to. Musicals, also, can be a troublesome factor. A *Damn Yankees* contained lively tunes and wonderful George Abbott pacing, not to speak of Gwen Verdon; a *House of Flowers* offered much, by way of music and dancing and décor, that had charm. But one cannot set pace to paper, or convey fragrance even by scenting the page; and since in neither musical were the book and lyrics outstanding, neither musical ended in the Best Ten. Unless the title of these yearbooks is to be changed to *Best Productions,* and *Best Productions* boasts movie cameras for the dance sequences and record players for the tunes, the Ten Best must qualify on a basis of their texts.

As in the preceding season, drama fared better than comedy. This holds true even if by drama one all too often only means "theatre," since by comedy one would equally often only mean farce. There were also, as in the preceding season, times when drama and comedy merged—or clashed—in the same play. What was perhaps most rewarding about the season's drama was not, unfortunately, any galaxy of fine plays; but rather that there was something presentable at every artistic level from prose tragedy downward—through prose drama, problem drama, journalistic

drama, to "theatre," thriller, and whodunit. If the two most competent of these seven exhibits were those at the two lowest levels,
that should cause no surprise, since sheer competence constituted
their one problem and their only goal. But by providing at least
one respectable play at every dramatic level except poetic tragedy,
Broadway might claim to function, however minimally, as a living
theatre should; and since all these plays had elements of excitement, Broadway might boast an awareness of what living theatre is.
In plain words, all that this comes down to is that there was roughly
something for every taste; but those plain words are yet too un-
approachably grand to apply to the bulk of Broadway seasons.

As it happens, the play espousing the highest artistic level was
the first to open and much the quickest to close. Alone of our seven
stages of drama, Graham Greene's *The Living Room* proved a commercial failure. All the same, it alone had any real distinction; had
a quality austere enough, undeviatingly serious enough, enough im-
bued with a tragic vision of life, to merit unalloyed respect. *The
Living Room* began, indeed, where most theatre successes leave off;
and though it clearly went downhill, it never once turned off its own
steeply rocky road.

Mr. Greene told of a young Catholic girl—in love with a middle-
aged married man—who, on her mother's death, is sent to live with
elderly relatives in a kind of religious Bleak House. The girl is so
disturbed by her awareness of the other woman and her sense of
the Other World, and gets so little spiritual help from the priestly
great-uncle she appeals to, that she commits suicide. It is a common enough triangle story, but it is treated in religious rather than
sociological or psychological terms. The eye of God rather than
of neighborhood gossips is upon it, and the problem is not simply
of the conscience but of the soul. The play's Catholic-convert
author is deeply perturbed himself by so tragic and vast a theme,
and stands ready with no facile answers. Blinkered faith and clear-
eyed rationalism he alike denounces; beyond his own blindly
clutched and self-tormenting Jansenism, his spiritual cupboard
seems bare. No God from on high, let alone any theatrical god
from the machine, ultimately intervenes or for that matter glibly
brings light. One real value of *The Living Room,* on a too frivolous
Broadway, was that it brought darkness to light places.

If, after its impressive first half, the play sharply declines, it is
from a compulsion to prolong the suffering without knowing how to
dramatize it. The fine fiction craftsman, who treated a comparable
story in *The Heart of the Matter,* somehow in his first play could
not channel his anxious emotions: hence, well before the suicide—

and for a whole scene after—he merely hacked at his theme. But however over-extended the play may be in clawing its way toward spiritual understanding, a fair part of it has urgency and distinction. Its black-bordered script bestowed real dignity on a Broadway that is much too fond of greeting cards.

The Living Room perished after 22 performances; a much happier fate befell the season's only other play to reveal any comparably turbulent intensities. Mr. Williams' *Cat on a Hot Tin Roof* was both crowned with honors and enriched with controversy. And even those who question its ultimate achievement must freely concede its frequent power. And concede, too, the honest anger, the organic heat—in a theatre of largely rented emotions—in Williams' reaction to life. Here is a playwright with an expertly instinctive sense of theatre—technically *Cat* shows much that is original—who has also a gashed and troubled vision of the world. He flays life in full view; whatever his need of a bridle, there can be no doubt of how he handles a whip.

Something not far from the nightmarish distempers the scene and story of *Cat;* a father dying of cancer under the illusion that he has just been proved free from it; his family at greedy odds over the disposition of the estate; his favorite son an alcoholic who refuses to sleep with the wife he hates—the wife who has intimated a homosexual attachment between him and his now-dead closest friend. Guilts gnaw and concealments rankle, resentments mount and accusations multiply; words are now bitten off, now bellowed, now spewed forth in profane accents with obscene intent; and at least once, between father and son, words are exchanged with the force of hammerblows.

It is an inward fury that relieves itself in a centrifugal rhetoric; and even the commentator on the play tends to turn rhetorician. Yet the commentator may use rhetoric not just to characterize what Mr. Williams has done, but also to criticize it. What must be communicated is the sense of something excessive, of an author wallowing first in the emotions he writes out of, and then in the situations those emotions beget. However unchanneled in treatment, *The Living Room* remains austere in tone: *Cat* is lush. It frequently, to be sure, bites and stings; it has so harsh a style that the *Little-Foxes*-like episodes of financial conniving have almost an air of comic relief. And the big encounter between father and son, turned by its blurted-out ugly truths into a kind of self-recognition scene, has the pulverizing charge of true drama.

The intensity of this scene is unrivaled in the season's playwriting. But it also helps to expose much else in Williams' own play.

Against such compulsive drama, much else in *Cat* seems merely effective (or, as in the final curtain, bogus) theatricalism. Mr. Williams' two pre-eminent gifts are oftener in conflict than in concert: his sense of theatre sensationalizes his vision of life—the more so since this playwright overfond of stage effects is no less overfond of words. And the attendant danger is most acute in a play about disturbed people and disordered lives, where severity of treatment would seem particularly judicious. There is too much emotionalism in the play. There is too much theatricalism—less should explode and more uncoil. There is too much—or, at any rate, too unmarshaled—material: is *Cat* chiefly about a family or about a marriage or about a man? And the sense of excess alienates; in the face of so much that is disturbing, one at best is fascinated, one is never in any vital sense disturbed.

When we drop a step to the level of problem drama, we encounter the season's overwhelmingly most harrowing play. In telling of a sweet little girl who commits three ugly murders, Maxwell Anderson's *Bad Seed* has only begun to ladle out its horrors. For slowly the girl's mother learns the truth about her daughter; and while grappling with this, learns that her own mother was a mass murderess also. Nor does the play rest content with what seems a bleakly tragic conclusion; it contrives an additional ironic turn of the screw.

In its catalogue and crescendo of horrors, *Bad Seed* has a number of gripping scenes and chilling moments. The horror grows, moreover, through the play's quasi-realistic tone, its reassuringly middle-class atmosphere. As a literate shocker, *Bad Seed* is successful; while even as a problem play, with the mother confronting the pathology of her child, no Ibsen could have raised a graver issue. (The accompanying idea of inherited evil is, of course, less an honest problem than a mere added *frisson*.) But, sticking to the legitimate dilemma, though *Bad Seed* goes through all the paces of problem drama, we somehow grasp that it is written with no real concern for its theme. In that sense, it isn't even the kind of matinee play that honestly reduces a problem to words of one syllable. Here the approach, at times, seems almost cynical—in the way the play makes its bag of horrors positively bulge, in the way it merely seems to deal in pain for pain's sake. The misfortune of the play is that it succeeds on unattractive terms; that something so hard-hitting should betoken neither art nor life, that something so grim can only be classified as entertainment.

One step further down, at the level of stage journalism, was *Inherit the Wind*. Flashing back to 1925 and the famous Tennessee

"monkey trial" of John T. Scopes, the play juggled some wonderfully theatrical material. There was all the vivid local color of the
little town where once the embattled fundamentalist stood and
started a ruckus heard round the world. Far more significantly, in
the famous clash between Clarence Darrow and William Jennings
Bryan, history supplied more electrical drama than most even very
gifted dramatists could invent; and in Bryan's subsequent collapse,
it supplied a twist few playwrights would dare resort to. Accordingly the second act of *Inherit the Wind*—helped by excellent performances from Paul Muni and Ed Begley—is first-rate theatre.
Aside from the second act, however, the play suffers from not really
being a play; from constituting too shapeless a transcript of actual
events; from seeming too flat where the material is borrowed, and
too fictional where it is contrived. What *Inherit the Wind* possesses
is frequent good theatre and journalistic color; what it lacks is sustained drama and an artistic tone.

Another step down, to *Anastasia,* and we are at the level of unabashed theatre, of old-fashioned romantic melodrama. This piece
of highfalutin about a waif-like girl who insists she is a Russian
princess who fled the Bolsheviks, had the nice counterfeit ring of
the stage's gaudiest era. To judge by the welcome it received, you
might have thought a fine new playwright had arrived instead of a
foolproof old plot. To be fair, however, the big scene between the
tremulous claimant and her presumable grandmother, the Empress
Dowager, is the kind of thing that made the theatre famous.
Though nothing else in the play approaches this scene—indeed, the
villains quite lack polish and the love story sadly lacks glow—the
evening as a whole was fun. Inviolably trashy, it put Czarist Russia
in the running with Graustark.

The new step down is very firm and steady: Joseph Hayes' *The
Desperate Hours* was a well-executed thriller, all the better for not
aspiring to be anything more. Mr. Hayes offered an up-to-date old-
fashioned scare piece about escaped convicts who take refuge in a
respectable household while waiting for their getaway money to
arrive. The situation has its obviously psychological and sociological aspects, but in *The Desperate Hours* they pretty much lurk
in corners. It is pure excitement that is stationed at the front door
and pure suspense that guards the back. What does enhance the
melodrama—by seeming to diminish it—is the sense of normal
middle-class life suddenly swimming in nightmare. All twists and
turns, but with no serious detours or downhill stretches, *The Desperate Hours*—though perhaps lacking an ultimate icy tingle for the

spine—did a better-sustained job with thrills than any other of the season's dramas did with soberer emotions.

The bottom step is firm and steady too: in *Witness for the Prosecution* Agatha Christie contrived a nice tidy whodunit (during a stage era when there aren't even many untidy ones). If, after the British fashion, it's not always tense, it is agreeably literate instead. Classically rendered, with no faddish horrors or avant-garde grisliness, it provides, in particular, an engrossing trial scene, and it most ably represents its famous author in the last five minutes. For not till the play seems over does Miss Christie really exhibit her mettle.

In addition to coming off respectably at each of these levels, the season offered various dramas, or near-dramas, or comedy-dramas with less to be said for them. One of these, Christopher Fry's *The Dark Is Light Enough*, seems to me, for all its shortcomings, worthier of the Best Ten than an *Anastasia;* and Fry's description of it as a "winter comedy" may help explain its being best included among the dramas. Certainly in stage terms it most succeeds where it has some of the clang of costume drama; and in plot terms it adheres, however topsy-turvily, to the line of heroic drama. Only it is heroic drama that gradually beats its swords into similes, and whose principal activity is the search for philosophic truth. As a result, the play is not very dramatic; which is rather a pity, since it doesn't cut very deep philosophically, either. Fry's sharp words —as they jab at such standard themes as love and compassion and loyalty—suggest not so much a scalpel as an embroidery needle. Indeed, he is so unsimple with words that he can never be really complex about things or people.

Yet Fry here is concerned, as hardly before, with the soberer side of life—or, at any rate, of language; and is capable, as very often before, of elaborate and whaleboned wit, of metaphysical elegances, of quick theatrical thrusts, of sudden aphoristic insights. And if an embroidery needle is not a scalpel, at least it is not a stencil cutter. The play, moreover, is better than it seemed in production (where Tyrone Power was woefully miscast), and doubtless better in book form than on the stage. At least Mr. Fry's merits, however overrated, are individual ones: even where he does not write successfully, he writes like himself. Most of his colleagues in the theatre have no self to write like; haven't even, as Mr. Fry has, a self to parody.

Robert Anderson's *All Summer Long*, which was the first drama of the season, told on the surface a much different story from Mr. Anderson's *Tea and Sympathy*. But this chronicle of life in a Midwestern household whose physical foundations are being eroded and whose human foundations are neglected and ignored, yet centers in a comparably sensitive and bewildered young boy who finds understanding in an unhappy brother, as Tom Lee did in his housemaster's unhappy wife. But where Tom, in *Tea and Sympathy*, was caught up violently in action, the hero this time, in a play that might almost have been called *Tea and Apathy*, had inaction to struggle against; and Mr. Anderson, deprived of melodrama, was driven into sentimentality. With much less theatricalism and considerably more honesty of purpose, *All Summer Long* yet fell infinitely shorter of effect. The play drifted much like the people it wrote about; the hero had sensibility but little imagination or humor; and for a lack of surface vigor there was no compensating depth.

Another early production was the only new drama offered during its disappointing second season by the Phoenix Theatre. Robert Ardrey's *Sing Me No Lullaby* was a socio-political play about a reunion of friends who had been young, eager and in some cases radical during the '30s; in the '50s, along with idealists who have been driven into negativism is an ex-Leftist who has been hounded into nothingness. Jobless and despondent, he plans to leave the United States the one way possible—by being smuggled to the Russians he despises; and it is only when this appalling scheme comes to light that the others are flayed into action. Seeking to portray a timid, jittery contemporary America, the play unhappily worked with viewpoints rather than people; and its central figure, who might have emerged a figure of tragedy, proved merely a mouthpiece for protest.

Horton Foote's *The Traveling Lady* seems chiefly notable, in retrospect, for Kim Hunter's fine performance in the title role—a sort of warm-up for her even finer one in *Bus Stop*. Writing of small-sized small-town people groping among their crotchets and habits and heartache, Mr. Foote could at times be touching; but in general displayed the same lack of drive, the same sense of muddle, the same ungifted garrulity, as his characters.

Sharper in approach, *Mrs. Patterson*—the story of a poverty-beset, gaudily daydreaming Negro girl—fell almost flatter in production. Eartha Kitt's darting, prickling performance as the heroine staved off a tedium that it could not in the end avert—a tedium to be regretted, since a sound theme miscarried not through genteel or timid treatment, but from a want of imaginative voltage and emotional poignancy. A play like *Mrs. Patterson* should be full of moments that are like bright stains; what stood out glaringly was the number of dull stretches.

Another failure—this one half-doomed to fail—was William Archibald's dramatization of Henry James' *The Portrait of a Lady*. For stage purposes, James' novel employs too broad a canvas, has too subterranean a flow, treats of too complexly simple a heroine. Not to come off a waxwork, it needs the prose, the unified tone, the countless small insights that give it distinction in book form. Its one chance for the stage would be to treat only its central story, which in Mr. Archibald's version is not even arrived at until the second act. To fit the stage, everything in Mr. Archibald's version had to be sliced paper-thin; the effect, though never cheap, was vague and dim—was Henry James glimpsed from a train window through a drizzle.

In *Fragile Fox* Norman Brooks wrote a competent but routine thriller about World War II. Treating, in the italics of melodrama, of a company thrown into the Battle of the Bulge under a craven, drunken, much-loathed captain, it banged through three acts with a variety of theatrical weapons, sometimes recalling the war, oftener recalling other war plays.

There also appeared, in the spring, a sort of running-mate for *Anastasia,* Jacques Deval's *Tonight in Samarkand.* A melodrama about kismet, about the inescapableness of one's fate, its choice of a doom-dodger was a lady tiger-tamer; and it dramatized her dodging to the blare of circus music and against the color of circus life. For a while all this generated a nice, garish, old-fashioned excitement with a minimum of metaphysical frills. A blonde girl symbolized death but no more abstrusely than a headwaiter symbolizes dinner. Unfortunately, from having no deeper values and from moving to a predestined end, the show in time started dragging its feet; and the third act seemed almost as tiresome as the first act was exhilarating.

There was variety enough to the season's comedy, extending as it did from the erotic to the macabre, from Victorian drawing rooms to hotel bathrooms. But it was considerably less interesting, on the whole, than the drama. In *Bus Stop* it provided what seemed to me the season's most generally satisfactory play; elsewhere comedies might be novel in conception, or fitfully fresh or individual in treatment, or intermittently gay, or powdered with wit or dusted with fancy. But their good qualities were almost never sustained, and their good qualities were very seldom distinguished. At times even hack writers of drama, catching fire from what they write about, are driven to communicate what they really feel. But Broadway's popular comedy writers are never so much taken out of themselves;

and suffer, moreover, not only from carefully calculating their laughs but from enrolling in current schools of humor. In play after Broadway play there is no want of basic wit; but there is such a want of grace, tact, restraint, there is such a display of cleverness without taste, there is such a barrage of mere gags, such brassiness of tone, that every fine point and subtle reward of comedy is forfeited. Most Broadway comedy lacks what can only be called breeding; and this tells the more when, as in a *Reclining Figure,* it invades a world where skulduggery wears a velvet glove. This is no complaint— perhaps it is necessary to say—against low humor. There is nothing much better than good low humor, or much less in need of defense. The trouble with most current Broadway comedy is that it attempts something rather higher—and at *that* level cannot, even in terms of tone, live up to its pretensions.

Comedy's opening gun was *Dear Charles,* an over-aggressive sex comedy that Tallulah Bankhead should have thought twice about appearing in, and very possibly did. For, however labored and tasteless, it had just enough useful lines and situations to let Tallulah get going and steadily evoke the charm of something caged and carnivorous. Not for several weeks after, not till *Reclining Figure,* did any comedy emerge with more formidable aims. Concerned with an eccentric, difficult art collector who falls for a fake Renoir, Harry Kurnitz's play got in a good many licks at the expense of 57th Street's dealers, whom it represented as double-dealers; and of their competitiveness, which it portrayed as conspiracy. Mr. Kurnitz contributed much nimble wisecracking and a last act with a welcome air of madness; but the play for two acts had no sustained animation, and was almost everywhere brash where it might better have been elegant. Writing of 57th Street, Mr. Kurnitz quite caught Broadway's tone while missing its tempo.

A week later, in *The Tender Trap,* Max Shulman and Robert Paul Smith had a nice theme for smart popular comedy, and a certain knack for making it lively. Their gaudy thesis that almost any New York bachelor who bathes regularly and has a steady job can lead the life of Don Juan just by answering the doorbell was amusing in itself and produced fitful amusement as it proceeded. But on different grounds *The Tender Trap* exhibited somewhat the same mistake as *Reclining Figure:* it failed of the right tone, it asked for something civilized in approach, something assured and quietly disdainful; what it got was too farcical and breezy.

A feeling for tone was infinitely more marked in Noel Coward's *Quadrille:* the difficulty there was a glaring lack of almost everything else. Coward's yarn of a marchioness and an American rail baron who pursue their eloping spouses only in the end to elope themselves, was Victorian in spirit as well as in setting; it scented its sinfulness in lavender, bodiced its escapades in whalebone; and it gave the Lunts the chance to play things to the hilt. The only trouble is that there was no blade. The play's light volleys of wit came from a Coward turned mild and middle-aged, who only plays doubles and no longer will go to the net.

Three blatantly American comedies also left something to be desired. Indeed, Theodore Reeves' *Wedding Breakfast,* with its story of two New York sisters, its double-entry playwriting, is about equally comedy and drama. Or rather, unequally—for it is the romance between salesgirl and bookkeeper that is comedy and that, at a broad popular level, succeeds; while the story of the college graduate with a magazine job—who loves but at first looks down her nose at a young Buffalo hardware merchant—rather shabbily fails. Mr. Reeves' misfortune here is to get just serious enough to make the situation ring false; and to dispose, in terms of movie romance, of what he seems to present as problem drama. The character of a girl who has risen above her background and whose cultural aspirations are as valid as her intellectual snobbery is distressing; the position of a girl who in rejecting philistine values embraces priggish pretensions, is well worth studying. But Mr. Reeves first threw his heroine to the wolves by reducing her to caricature, and then let his story go to the dogs with a trumped-up ending.

Of the three American comedies, N. Richard Nash's *The Rainmaker* exhibited, at its best, the greatest freshness. When it chronicled the home life of a Western farm family, and the efforts of a plain girl's father and brothers to get her married, it had a bright, brisk air and an engagingly humorous smack. But with the arrival, during a drought, of a garrulous con man who swears he can change the weather and who stays long enough to change the girl, the play lost its appeal. After the rainmaker, there indeed came the deluge: for this was a symbolic character out of playwriting's dead past, whose spouting and philosophizing were a bore and whose love scenes seemed rather an offense.

In *Lunatics and Lovers* Sidney Kingsley turned, for the nonce, from drama to farce. His scene was a Broadway hotel suite, his characters were crooks, crackpots, flunkeys, cops, distraught wives and girls on the town. His method was a slambang sequence of exits and entrances, phone calls and doorbells; his comic stock-in-trade was lowdown talk, quenchless lust, drunken careenings, and on-stage bubble baths. Attempting nothing startlingly new, aspiring toward nothing uncomfortably lofty, Mr. Kingsley contrived

some funny scenes, some entertaining characters, and a nice unin-
hibited coarseness. In a play so constantly frenzied and mobile,
there could be no really sustained comedy; and in fact there were
numerous ups and downs and starts and stops. Nor was *Lunatics
and Lovers,* for all its emphatic raffishness, quite to the gutter born.
The siren, in the end, lost out to the wife; the tough guy, it tran-
spired, was custard-filled: despite its atmosphere of sinfulness, the
play struck few real blows for sin.

Not till Christmas week brought Clifford Odets' *The Flowering
Peach* was there, if no very different amount of achievement, at least
one of inherent talent. Mr. Odets set himself to retell, in his own
fashion, the story of Noah: to make his scene a kind of historical
no man's land—so long as there is any land; to make his people
oftener slangily modern than imposingly ancient—not so much Biblical, indeed, as bohemian. What they most are, perhaps, is time-
lessly racial, with a Jewishness surviving from the ark on Mount
Ararat to the borscht-belt in the Catskills, and with a Jewish family
sense only intensified by family feuds. The family itself is far from
godly—Noah drinks, Ham wenches, Shem loves money. But Noah
is a stern patriarch who, if hooted at when first he warns of the
Flood, is yet at all times feared and in crises obeyed. A real despot
in fact, it is only through the Flood that Noah comes to learn humility.

This softening of Noah, this small-scale, half-humorous taming
of a Lear, is as much as the play can claim by way of theme or of
final affirmation. The final scene of the play is touching, it has the
charm of something newborn and childlike and also ageless and lay-
ered deep in time; but it seems a little pat and prettified for all that,
it somehow hasn't the rest of the play behind it. Perhaps this
springs from Mr. Odets himself having had no strong sense of what
the rest of the play should be. Understandably, he was beguiled
by the notion of an untraditional free-hand treatment of Noah. It
enabled him to scramble chronology, dabble in philosophy, insinuate
folklore, while always having for solid substance the verities of family life. And Odets indeed succeeds in terms of particular scenes,
of bright brief exchanges, of those matings of the vernacular and
the rhetorical, those metaphors of the cosmos and the kitchen, that
have always inspired him. The play opens even more engagingly
than it concludes, and has bright spots betweenwhiles. But it can
only indicate, it cannot maintain, distinction. Its garbling of eras
is merely diverting; but its juggling of levels, its failure to achieve
a fused vision, is a real weakness. As storytelling, too, the play

runs aground. There is too much meandering, too wordy philosophizing, too repetitious family squabbling.

If *The Flowering Peach* was a highly uneven product of talent,
Paul Vincent Carroll's *The Wayward Saint* was an almost consistently disappointing one. The play, on Broadway, was cursed
by a ponderous production; but only here and there were there the
truly imaginative touches and humorous outbursts to be required
of a good fantasy and expected of a Carroll. Far too much seemed
merely cute, far too much of the writing was machine-made Irish
lace, and far too many familiar jokes about the Irish and the clergy
assumed the actual status of leitmotivs.

It was not indeed until March, until the arrival of *Bus Stop,* that
comedy could take much pride in itself. One's chief critical obliga-
tion with *Bus Stop* is to define its limits; for within those limits the
play, I think, very genuinely succeeds. The limits are perhaps im-
plicit in the very title: a chronicle about a busload of people cannot
but smack of formula or cling to surfaces; it will almost certainly
mate averageness and picturesqueness in about equal proportions;
it will almost certainly dramatize the feeling of loneliness in a crowd.
Indeed, it will do something more; for a bus—as opposed, say, to
even a boarding house—must evoke a peculiar sense of anonymity
and feeling of homelessness. Yet *Bus Stop,* if a minor, is an attractive play, a sound blend of sentiment and humor, a nice contrast
between the itinerant, peripheral figures who are the central ones in
Inge's own universe, and the more integrated ones who, in juxta-
position, restore balance as well as add poignancy.

The play doesn't lose in humanity, and it certainly gains in humor,
by treating chiefly a raw young cowboy's rambunctious courtship
of a soiled young Kansas City nightclub singer. This has a rowdy,
positive quality that is theatrically very useful to the largely static
form, the largely Chekhovian mood of the play; it gives a sense of
motion to what is becalmed, and of lustiness to what is basically
sentimental. Indeed, the humor of *Bus Stop*—or rather the way
the naturalistic brooder in Inge is absorbed into the humorist—has
a real value; even Mr. Inge's tendency to make sex the root of all
trouble, to confuse deep yearnings in mankind's bones with every
inconvenient stirring of the flesh, is here gone at with humor. Po-
tentially, *Bus Stop* is less significant a play than *Picnic:* actually it
is not just more successful, it is more persuasive. Meaning to dig
much deeper, *Picnic* seemed in the end all surfaced glare; about
Bus Stop, for all its outward humors, there was at least a suggestion
of inner glow.

Following *Bus Stop,* comedy more or less slunk out of sight.

Leslie Stevens' *Champagne Complex* after it—as Ronald Alexander's *The Grand Prize* before—exhibited a gift for amusing lines, but little to attach them to. And Roald Dahl's *The Honeys,* a reasonably grisly farce about two wives who decide it would help matters if they bumped off the ghastly twin brothers they are married to, had good wacky moments and amusing intervals. But, unlike an *Arsenic and Old Lace, The Honeys* couldn't parlay murder into three-act merriment, largely because it never made murder the basis for daffy complications. It just hammered away at its one idea; and in time even death can cease to seem hilarious.

As in any season, one could berate comedy with what crimes were committed in its name—the worst of them, *Black-Eyed Susan,* showing how much could be achieved, with a minimum of effort, in the way of truly dazzling vulgarity. In general, however, there were hardly more outrageously bad comedies last season than outstandingly good ones. Since the war years, when almost anything found a way of getting produced and at times of even showing a profit, there has been a steady decline in the palpably fourth-rate. I suspect this is oftener a matter of economics, of the appalling rise in costs, than one of taste: but perhaps economics, with time, becomes an influence on taste. For years, every April and May stood host to enough dreadful comedies to become known as the Silly Season. Of late there are too few such comedies to constitute a "season"; and such as there are will as likely benumb you in December as in May.

For the second season in a row, Broadway disgraced itself (no lesser word will really do) in the matter of revivals. Since the Old Vic *Midsummer Night's Dream* was offered by Sol Hurok, who is strictly speaking not a Broadway producer, and was installed at the Met, which is by no form of reasoning a theatre, it can be said that not for two seasons had Broadway offered a single theatrical classic. Fortunately the situation may argue a blacker eye for Broadway than a future for Ben Jonson or Molière, since an interest in revivals is part of the recent very rewarding growth in Off-Broadway production. There is no sense being merely airy about a situation where finances are so vital; but increasingly, on Broadway, revivals are a matter of stars and name casts, and of indifference to ensemble playing or possibly even what is played. Probably the only long-term Broadway solution would be a repertory company that combined sane methods with high standards—a company generously financed, moreover, on a basis of very-slowly-arrived-at financial independence. Failing that, it is perhaps better to look to Off-

Broadway for the classics, for there they can be done from the out-set *con amore* and eventually with real skill and style. For one example: already last season, on a sort of arena stage in a former tiny lower-East-Side synagogue, a production of Chekhov's *The Three Sisters* indicated how much can be done with right feeling alone. There were inevitable limitations and even crudities; but this *Three Sisters*, in an admirable new translation by Stark Young, seemed to me the most sensitive in approach, the most Chekhovian in feeling, of any Chekhov seen in years. Furthermore, Off-Broadway will not only stage revivals oftener than Broadway, it will be more adventurous in what it revives. Broadway recognizes, at best, only four writers of classics: Shakespeare, Ibsen, Chekhov and Shaw.

The sanctity of these four perhaps explains the record of the Phoenix Theatre, an organization with, uniquely, one foot on Broadway and one foot off. During its first season the Phoenix revived Shakespeare and Chekhov; during its second, Ibsen and Shaw. Of the two, the Shaw came off the better; but the point is less that neither was very impressive than that both seemed much too ortho-dox. The moral to this was supplied by the Phoenix itself which, having one Monday night given a single reading to Webster's *The White Devil,* woke up the next morning to find itself famous. Surely, for organizations like the Phoenix, audacity is by and large the best policy.

Broadway itself revived Rodgers and Hart's *On Your Toes,* to discover too late that it had perhaps confused the whole uneven musical with the ballet that gave it distinction—"Slaughter on Tenth Avenue." Not to be niggardly, Broadway also brought back *Abie's Irish Rose,* though not for long.

Unlike the season before, there were no one-man shows and there was only one woman's—Libby Holman's *Blues, Ballads and Sin Songs.* The trouble with it was that it insisted on *being* a one-woman show, for which Libby lacked the showmanship, rather than a straight recital, for which she still has, if not the vocal power, at least some of the vocal sex.

But as one-man shows died down, triple bills bobbed up. One first bobbed up as *3 for Tonight,* Paul Gregory's stage novelty of the season; it consisted—with Hiram Sherman as master of cere-monies—of the dance team of Marge and Gower Champion, singer Harry Belafonte, and a large chorus. Mr. Sherman was friendly, the Champions were deft, Mr. Belafonte had personal appeal, and the chorus was well trained at vocal tricks. The evening added up to slick entertainment, indeed to very high-styled hick stuff; though, along with lacking distinction, it was short on perkiness and zip.

The second triple bill, *All in One,* attempted a sort of higher vaudeville—a short Leonard Bernstein operatic satire, an early one-act Tennessee Williams play, and dancer Paul Draper. Draper's tap dancing was, as always, crisp and stylish. Bernstein's *Trouble in Tahiti* was rather thin satire about a snarled middle-class marriage, enriched by one very funny scene; Williams' *27 Wagons Full of Cotton*—featuring a brilliant performance by Maureen Stapleton— was as rowdy as Erskine Caldwell and rather crueler, and showed that from the outset life, for Williams, had dirty fingernails. Though not a wholly satisfactory evening, *All in One* indicated the sort of superior offbeat entertainment that Broadway could greatly gain from.

Musically, it was a busier and a brighter season than usual.* Things got engagingly under way with *The Boy Friend,* which proved much the same surprise hit on Broadway that it had been in London. Sandy Wilson's witty spoof of musical comedy during the '20s managed to hold up as evening-long entertainment by blending burlesque with nostalgia; it also avoided trouble by concentrating entirely on the musicals of the '20s and ignoring the mores. The sappy sentiment of *The Boy Friend* recalled the kind of musicals that were the ladyfingers of an age of hooch. Yet, for all its squealing ingénues, its mincing idiocies, its piercingly obvious repartees, *The Boy Friend* managed to be likable—and even touching—as well as funny. Mr. Wilson, fondling every insipidity of an era that he witnessed from his pram, gave the whole show— tunes, lyrics, dialogue—a sort of nitwitted charm.

Bound to become a musical in time, *Peter Pan* sensibly became one in time for Mary Martin to play Peter. She made as plausible a boy as probably a grown-up lady can; she danced and sang and dueled well, and she flew enchantingly through the air. With Cyril Ritchard delightfully lacing gusto with style, and giving a grandly baroque air to Captain Hook; and with Jerome Robbins—who is more genuinely imaginative than Barrie, and far less saccharine— contriving gay dances, *Peter Pan* had many production virtues. If, for all that, it never quite came off as a musical, it was partly from having uninspired music, partly from a certain lack of follow-through

---

* I omit with regret from this report Gian-Carlo Menotti's *The Saint of Bleecker Street* because—unlike Menotti's earlier works that appeared on Broadway—*The Saint* is unequivocally opera. Performing an opera in a Broadway theatre no more makes it a musical play than (to borrow a phrase from Swift) being born in a stable makes a man a horse.

as entertainment.   Though their marriage was celebrated with festive splash, Barrie and Broadway are hardly an ideal couple.

The season's two most disappointing musicals were its two most ballyhooed ones—*Fanny*, which was leadenly lavish, and *Silk Stockings*, which ran shrieking from whatever might show the least distinction.   *Fanny*—telling of a French girl who finds herself pregnant after her lover goes off to sea, and of her marriage to a widower who craves a child—was a ticklish Gallic compound of sentiment and hard sense.   It needed delicately simple treatment; what it got was wildly incongruous overproduction, with undersea ballets and full-rigged ships crossing the stage.   There was a nice sentimental score by Harold Rome, some colorful dancing and pleasant acting; but these, set beside its sluggish grandeurs, seemed incidental merits.   Quantity had ousted quality; the heaping portion been substituted for the proper food.

Silk Stockings, adapted from *Ninotchka*—that tale of a fanatical Soviet woman commissar who, on a mission to Paris, responds to French living and American love—had its pleasant things, too.   There were some nice Cole Porter tunes, a few gaily satiric episodes, a lively Moscow jam session, some good performers.   But for a musical with so promising a theme, *Silk Stockings* remained stubbornly uninspired, devoutly unadventurous.   The result was formula stuff, a kind of glazed mediocrity; and, in the desire for the common touch, something that proved a touch too common.

Two rather offbeat musicals—*House of Flowers* and *Plain and Fancy*—were considerably more attractive.   *House of Flowers*, with its West Indian yarn of high-toned rival bordellos, was genuinely individual, with tropical color and fragrance and profusion.   Against Oliver Messel's wonderful sets, it provided—to Harold Arlen's appealing score—vivid Negro dancing and a playfully rococo Truman Capote book.   Unfortunately, what made it fresh and flowerlike also made it droop and fade; what conferred a unified tone also created a monotonous effect.   In the nose-in-the-air gentility of its bordello girls it had a satiric theme its book somehow failed to exploit; and it gradually sank into the languor of a tropical afternoon.

At the other extreme from tropical sinfulness, *Plain and Fancy* featured Amish respectability.   Against this it set a sophisticated young New Yorker and his acidly vivacious girl friend.   The contrast was amusing, the Amish folkways were refreshing, the whole thing had a nice country smell of good ripe apples.   What limited *Plain and Fancy* as a musical was its not very infectious music and its not very frequent dancing: the show had more regional tang than social gaiety; smelled more of apples that go into pie than into cider.

Ray Walston, Stephen Douglass and Gwen Ver

"Damn Yankees"

The season was to bring down its curtain on an ineffective musical version of an old play-and-movie favorite, *Seventh Heaven*. Fortunately, just before this doleful last trump sounded for '54-'55 came the explosive, joyous blare of *Damn Yankees*. All about a rooter for the Washington Senators who sells his soul to the Devil in order to take the pennant from the Yankees, it banged away, with the notion that all music aspires toward a brass band's exuberance, all locomotion toward a fire engine's clanging speed. It had pleasant Richard Adler tunes and Bob Fosse dances; in Ray Walston it had a fine stylish Devil, and in Gwen Verdon what was by all odds the musical-comedy delight of the year—a vivacious redhead who can dance superbly, and be as hilarious about sex as she can be seductive. If there was anything in a fairly controversial season not subject to controversy, it was Miss Verdon's ability to please.

THE SEASON IN CHICAGO

By Claudia Cassidy

Drama Critic, Chicago *Tribune*

LOOKING back, even for annual surveys, can be disconcerting. You can wonder if being a drama critic in Chicago is a dog-in-the-manger job. It doesn't amount to much any more, either in the volume of work or the quality of stimulation, and you have to have another, livelier job to survive. It could be you cling to this peculiar post to keep anyone else from getting it, unless you can rationalize the grip in terms less suicidally selfish.

Concerts and the dance flourish, even opera is staging a comeback. But theatre jogs along in its rut of about twenty shows a season, most of them old, few of them exciting. There are, of course, variable, sometimes amusing overtones. In the voice, say, of a visitor who finds on our boards a show he saw elsewhere three years ago and remarks reminiscently, "That wasn't bad, as I remember. Not bad at all." In the decision of a Jean Arthur half an hour before curtain time that she is "too exhausted" to risk opening "Saint Joan" here, whereupon certain critics hastily warned not to come remember that because they felt duty-bound to see her they had relinquished their tickets to the sold-out bow of Maria Meneghini Callas in "La Traviata." Or even—I'm still talking about overtones—in the caprices of producers, who apparently want not just to be rich, but, simultaneously, to be loved.

Now when a producer has a brand-new hit he apparently feels about it the way people feel about a brand-new baby—expansive, and eager to show it off. Come see it, he says, at once. This is most hospitable, and possibly rewarding, if the critical visitor writes a glowing and persuasive piece for home consumption. But if two or three seasons later what is allegedly the same show comes touring, and the critic is tactless enough to note traces of mildew in the corn, that producer makes manifestations.

They are not the same every season, which is mildly diverting. When "The King and I" arrived, three and one half years after the New York premiere, some of the newspapers observed that it was not the same show, being less subtle to the ear and less lustrous to the eye. This time the management did not issue proclamations about

23

withholding Broadway courtesies from such ungrateful malcontents, nor did it plant a minor actor to emit diatribe at a Drama League luncheon, perhaps having discovered that to such things the critic, unless paid to make his own speech, doesn't go.

No, this time it was another, more expensive story. The management bought space in offending newspapers to reprint in underscored full the review of a local lawyer whose vehicle is the Chicago Daily Law Bulletin. Herewith the underscored portions: "Once again I am fed up with the 'I saw it in New York' patron critics who are unable to judge a local production objectively. . . . This is a magnificent musical play skillfully directed and for the most part expertly performed. . . . The show is very colorful with fine lyrics and interesting characterizations. Pay no attention to the killjoys who talk about the New York production."

As it turned out, "The King and I" flourished while Yul Brynner headed the cast. When he left after seventeen weeks the musical had what it called a "net gross" of more than $800,000, plus another $100,000 in advance sales. The understudy, Leonard Graves, stepped in, and the bottom fell out. The musical stuck it out eight weeks more, then looked for greener fields.

In contrast, "Wonderful Town" was cause for rejoicing. Repolished to a knowing glitter, it had a brilliant opening night, with Carol Channing shooting the works to win what turned into a vociferously loyal audience.

The most distinguished plays were "Tea and Sympathy," with Deborah Kerr, and "The Caine Mutiny Court-Martial," returning after a brief 1953 stopover on the way to New York. Both could have extended limited engagements. By the time "Picnic" arrived it had turned into an exhibition, and "The Fifth Season" was not improved by substituting Joseph Buloff for Menasha Skulnik. The most uncomfortable night of the season was spent trying not to watch Diana Barrymore in a horror called "Pajama Tops," cut-rated for the snicker trade.

Not all went according to schedule. Ruth Draper was welcomed, yes. Eartha Kitt turned out to be an actress in "Mrs. Patterson." But Tallulah Bankhead could not sell "Dear Charles," nor could the first downtown booking of Geraldine Page lure them into "The Rainmaker." Edith Piaf and Harry Mimmo deserved bigger houses than they drew in the otherwise negligible "Continental Revue," and Olsen and Johnson found no water at the television well of "Pardon Our Antenna." If you rue the starving theatre's waste of talent, you might have shaken a disturbed head to see William Marshall's powerful performance in "Oedipus Rex"—had you taken the trouble

Eartha Kitt in "Mrs. Patterson"

to pursue a homeless local troupe, the Playwrights Theatre Club, to one of half a dozen improvised and frustrating stages.

One interesting glint appeared on the horizon of too little and too late. "The Tender Trap" was rescued after the New York closing, recast with Kent Smith, K. T. Stevens and Russell Nype, along with Janet Riley and Joey Faye, and sent in to lure those who enjoy comedies about nothing in particular, blithely done. It has not been a bonanza, but it is a lively meal ticket, and it may encourage similar gestures. In fact, one such gesture, less brisk on the draw, brings us "The Teahouse of the August Moon" on Labor Day, 1955, approximately one month after it has found its way to Tokyo's Kabuki Theatre.

Meanwhile, as of the 1954-55 season, twenty shows ran 159 weeks in six downtown theatres. It must interest the landlords to know that one of them was not the Great Northern, which a season ago ran second to the flagship Shubert with 35½ weeks of booking.

The record:

Harris Theatre: 48 weeks—"Time Out for Ginger," 18 this season, 38 in all; "Mrs. Patterson," 7; "Oh, Men! Oh, Women!," 16; "The Tender Trap," 7 so far.

Shubert Theatre: 45 weeks—"Wonderful Town," 20; "The King and I," 25.

Erlanger Theatre: 28 weeks—"Picnic," 4; "The Fifth Season," 16; "Dear Charles," 4; "The Rainmaker," 4.

Blackstone Theatre: 24 weeks—"Twin Beds," 1 this season, 2 in all; "Pajama Tops," 8; "The Caine Mutiny Court-Martial," 5; "Tea and Sympathy," 10.

Selwyn Theatre: 10 weeks—"Pardon Our Antenna," 6; Ruth Draper, 2; "Continental Revue," 2.

Civic Opera House: 4 weeks—"A Midsummer Night's Dream," 2; "South Pacific," 2; Ethel Waters, 1 performance.

THE SEASON IN LONDON

By Kenneth Tynan

Dramatic Critic, London *Observer*

The New Plays

IT is a vexing truth that, ever since the great Ibsen challenge of the nineties, the British intellectuals have been drifting away from the theatre. They still perk up at the mention of Giraudoux and Brecht, but they do not take the plays of Eliot and Fry very seriously, and of a native prose playwright who might set the boards smoldering they see no sign at all. The 1954-55 season was mostly devoted to what Walter Kerr calls "the secondary theatre," and especially to one department of it—the genteel or Loamshire play. Its setting is either a town house in Belgravia or a country house in Loamshire. Except when someone must catch a cold or be murdered, the sun always shines. The characters belong to a social class derived partly from romantic novels and partly from the playwright's vision of the leisured life he will lead when the play is a hit. Joy, in these surroundings, becomes a giggle, sorrow a whimper; the thunder of denunciation dwindles into "Oh, really, Daddy!" and "Oh, stuff, Mummy!" There is no shortage of British playwrights; indeed, there are hundreds of them, but they are all writing the same play. Nor is there a dearth of actors; the land is alive with them, but they are all playing the same part.

Perhaps Loamshire's greatest triumph is the crippling of creativeness in directors and designers. After all, how many twists can you impart to a tea party? And how can a designer spread his wings in "Rodney Curzon's Mayfair flat" or "The library at Charles Trevannion's country house near Dymsdyke"? We still have a couple of directors capable of staging a masterpiece, and a handful of designers fit to dress something less submissive than a clothes horse. But they are the end, not the beginning, of a tradition.

These cries are wrung from me by a series of crypto-Loamshire first nights. Alan Melville's "Simon and Laura" was an arid backstage joke about a bickering theatrical couple (living in Belgravia) who revive their fortunes by starring in a TV show about marital bliss. "Book of the Month" was the dusty sepulcher of a good idea:

27

a Tory M.P.'s daughter (living in Berkshire) writes a prurient best-seller about her own family. "All for Mary" developed an original farcical theme, the incidence of chicken pox among English tourists in the French Alps, so roguishly that it became a minor plague. Agatha Christie fell below her best in "Spider's Web," a country-house murder story complete with sliding panels and a mortally slugged dope-smuggler: the clues were too blatant, and people who emerged from "Witness for the Prosecution" murmuring "How clever she is!" tended to emerge from its successor murmuring "How clever I am!" Rex Harrison and Lilli Palmer repeated their Broadway success in "Bell, Book and Candle," John van Druten's flimsy comedy about witch covens in Knightsbridge; Miss Palmer's Satanic compact and powder compact managed a charmingly peaceful coexistence. But the most opulent Belgravia-type play was "The Night of the Ball." Its author, Michael Burn, preserved the unities of time and place and might claim to have invented a new unity, that of tedium. Sir Richard throws a party in order to propose to a pretty widow; unknown to him, the widow is being pursued by an ex-lover, who, unknown to anyone, is being pursued by Sir Richard's niece. Enough plot here for three plays by Pinero, but not enough dramatic skill for three pages. Gladys Cooper, as a peppery peeress, gave a performance resplendent enough for a face cream advertisement.

After these trivia it is good to turn to Terence Rattigan's "Separate Tables," much the most satisfying British play of the season; or rather, the most satisfying two plays, for this is a double bill, set in a shabby-genteel seaside hotel—a clever device which enables the author to use the same supporting characters in both halves of the evening. The overriding themes are loneliness and desperation. In the first, less plausible play, a drunken left-wing journalist re-meets his fading, narcissistic ex-wife; she revives his self-torturing love for her, and by curtain-fall they are gingerly reunited. The second play aims higher, focusing on a bogus major who has lately been convicted of assaulting women in a local cinema. His foible, we painfully learn, is the result of fear, which has made him a hermit, a liar and a pervert. The revelation kindles sympathy in a broken, over-mothered spinster, who befriends him. Love unbridled, says Rattigan in the first play, is a destroyer; and so, he adds in the second, is love bridled. Both situations are unfolded with Rattigan's unique talent for withholding vital information until the crucial moment of suspense, when it drops quivering into place. The quartet of leading characters are beautifully observed; it is in his treatment of the lesser roles—a comic maid, a whimsical schoolmaster, a tyrannical matriarch—that the author moves down to the level of stereo-

Lynn Fontanne, Alfred Lunt, Brian Aherne and Edna Best in "Quadrille"

type. Margaret Leighton plays the two principal women rather externally: her mousy spinster, gangling and pink-knuckled, verges on caricature. It is Eric Portman who commands the stage, volcanic as the journalist and even better as the major, speaking in nervous spasms and walking with shoulders protectively hunched. Miss Leighton shows that she dislikes the woman in the first piece and pities the girl in the second. Mr. Portman makes no such comment: simply the thing he is shall (and does) make him live.

Philip King, formerly known as a farce writer, brought off a neat right and left when two of his plays opened in London on successive nights. The more ambitious, "Serious Charge," dealt with small-town gossip, aimed at that most vulnerable target, the English male virgin—in this case a young clergyman, living with his mother. A repulsive young spiv accuses the vicar of indecent assault, and the village believes him. Unfortunately (English censorship being what it is) the miscarriage of justice had to be avoided, which meant a last act of melodramatic falsification in which the villain confessed. Mr. King's other play, a parlor farce called "Sailor, Beware!", touched a note of authentic back-street poetry; and in Peggy Mount, a new-comer who played a heavyweight mother-in-law, London found a comedienne fit to be floodlit. Miss Mount positively scorches the earth, charging as she cleans, swooping as she dusts; even out of sight she intimidates, like the distant thunder of hooves. The savage impatience of her acting has no rival in my memory.

In "Misery Me!", which deserved to run much longer than it did, Denis Cannan embarked on a full-scale satire of the contemporary condition. His setting is a spectacularly moth-eaten tavern in Arcadia; the host's wife is in labor, and against this background of impending birth Mr. Cannan sets a comedy of impending death. A glum intellectual, intent on suicide, meets an even glummer young woman, chased by two armed lovers, a Communist and a millionaire. Both try to hire the would-be suicide as their trigger man, and we have the fine satiric tableau of two great powers forcing weapons onto a man bent only on self-destruction. They discover that hatred is their natural state at the same moment as the young people discover that theirs is love. Mr. Cannan's is a true mid-century voice, which suspects politics and is in no mood for war; and its stream of mind, as Johnson said of Burke, is perpetual. The trouble was that the characters, perfectly "seen" as symbols, did not come into focus as human beings; concentrating on essences, Mr. Cannan forgot about surfaces.

Among the importers, France fared best. The thrill of "Time Remembered," a translation of Anouilh's "Léocadia," resided in its bouquet, a wry, château-bottled fragrance. A nubile milliner is engaged by an elderly duchess (Margaret Rutherford) to revive her nephew from the apathy induced by the death of his adored Léocadia. The sleeping prince is duly awakened; but the milliner's brisk, candid questioning uncovers the fact that, far from being a paragon, Léocadia was a screaming bore. The tale unfurls in the heart as lightly and crisply as a Japanese water-flower, and the production was full of playful artifice. The familiar Anouilh heroine (known in the trade as Little Orphan Anouilh) was played by Mary Ure with a cool assurance amazing in a professional debut; but Paul Scofield's elegant sulking dominated the show. Nothing in our theatre speaks more tellingly of grief than the broken music of this actor's voice.

When spring ended, Christopher Fry's adaptations of Anouilh's "L'Alouette" and Giraudoux's "La Guerre de Troie n'aura pas lieu" were already on tour; and the Arts Theatre Club, to which the Lord Chamberlain's veto does not extend, was completing a predominantly French season. Obey's "Sacrifice to the Wind" was presented in a double bill with Eugène Ionesco's "The Lesson," a votive offering to Dadaism in which a goatish old professor vents his lunacy on a young female pupil; a crazy, destructive exercise in naked theatricalism. Julien Green's "South," movingly directed by Peter Hall, gave the Turgenev treatment to a Southern plantation on the eve of the Civil War; this noble, savagely moral play about sexual unease automatically came under the censor's ban. During the winter the Arts also staged the Ruth and Augustus Goetz version of Gide's "The Immoralist" (banned out of hand) and "The Rules of the Game," an early and acridly misogynistic Pirandello. Add to these the superb revival of "Saint Joan" (discussed below), and you have a record of astonishing quality.

Two Broadway arrivals were damply received. Maxwell Anderson's "The Bad Seed" contains some leaden prose and a highly tendentious theory about hereditary evil; yet, judged as sheer dramatic vivisection, it works. The audience is jabbed with acid, and the sting is real. What we need from cast and director is the strictest Hitchcock realism; what we got from the London production was amateur operatics. As the mother, a nice, harassed housewife, Diana Wynyard combined traditional English "hostess" acting, with its rambling downward inflections and moaning tremolo, with totally irrelevant echoes of Shirley Booth in "Come Back, Little Sheba." Thankfully, Carol Wolveridge brought a transfixing purity of attack to the part of the eight-year-old murderess, a Wordsworthian child rejoicing in intimations of mortality. Joseph Hayes' "The Desperate Hours" was housed in a theatre much too large for it; and, in all, the most prosperous new American piece was Thornton Wilder's "The Matchmaker," a reworking of his earlier play, "The Merchant of Yonkers." This had the raciness of Labiche and a touch of the vigor of Jonson. To New York in the eighties come Horace Vandergelder, a merchant in search of a wife; Mrs. Levi, a professional matchmaker with an eye for a husband; and the merchant's two clerks, on a stolen spree. The real hero, however, is none of these, but New York itself, before it scraped the sky, a roaring village of brownstone and beer halls. This vision so enchants Mr. Wilder that he forgets his plot and bases the last scene on a stupid and useless female impersonation. Even so, Tyrone Guthrie's production, matchlessly vital, had the impact of a musical from which the music had been discarded as superfluous. And Ruth Gordon flew at the name part like a bat out of hell, her flaming hair redoubling her resemblance to a small but unmanageable forest fire. The evening belonged, by right of magic, to this malevolent pixie.

The Revivals

At the top of the list comes Peter Ashmore's production of "Hedda Gabler," the best tribute to Ibsen since Michael Benthall staged "The Wild Duck" in 1948. British playgoers normally shun Ibsen's grim galoshes and abiding rain; aware of this, Mr. Ashmore's designers (Motley) made the Tesman villa a costly pleasance baked in sunlight. The centerpiece was Peggy Ashcroft's Hedda, a performance which made it quite clear that the woman's destructiveness sprang not from passion but from sexual frigidity. Most Heddas rage like tigresses; this one was scaled down to suburbia, and nothing of the part's ironic comedy was missed. Miss Ashcroft's display was a monument to *nymphomanie de tête,* which might roughly be rendered as the nymphomania of Hedda. Another unique performance was that of the Irish actress Siobhan McKenna as Shaw's "Saint Joan." The beaming, pink-nosed girl of the opening scenes had undergone, by the end, an annealing; all that was mortal about her was peeled away, and sheer soul burst through. "God is alone" had tears flowing everywhere in the house, and one left convinced that this was the richest portrait of saintliness since Falconetti in "La Passion de Jeanne d'Arc."

The Old Vic started badly on the second leg of its five-year plan to present all the plays in the First Folio of Shakespeare. "Macbeth" was a bellowing-match, with every word spat in the audience's face; in "Love's Labour's Lost" Paul Rogers' Armado, aghast in a fog of rhetoric, came off best in a strained evening. "The Taming of the Shrew" was absurdly over-directed; somebody aptly described Ann Todd's Katherina as "the rudest girl in Eastbourne," and as Petruchio (a part heaven-sent for Groucho Marx), Paul Rogers presented a charmless vignette of Ivan the Terrible. "Richard II" was lucidly played by the Gielgudesque John Neville, who rightly refused to make the king an effeminate. This was very nearly the "young hot colt" of whom York speaks; Mr. Neville overweened, rejoicing in the manipulation of power, and failed only in pathos, which he signally lacks. "As You Like It," a pale pastel production by Robert Helpmann, was unexpectedly followed by a twin triumph: the two parts of "Henry IV," directed by Douglas Seale. For me the Henries, great public plays in which a whole nation is on stage, are the summits of Shakespeare's achievement; more than anything else in English drama they deserve the name of epic. The strange, irregular rhythm wherein societies die and are reborn is captured as no playwright before or since has ever captured it. There is no true villain in these plays, no Iago or Claudius on whom the audience can pin its righteous indignation. Hotspur is on the wrong side, yet he is a hero; Prince John is on the right side, yet he is perfidious enough to have staggered Hitler. Only a few plays in world drama preserve this divine magnanimity. And the Henries, which have no star parts, precisely fitted a company deficient in star quality. The tavern scenes, writhing with squalor and visual wit, were a perfect setting for Paul Rogers' Falstaff, a gorgeous explosion of vocal fireworks; and John Neville's Pistol went off with a splendid bang. Eric Porter gave us more of the king's guilt than his grandeur, and Robert Hardy's Hal was soft-centered; but, in general, these two productions set the Old Vic firmly on the right, realistic track.

Stratford-on-Avon struck a bad patch. Sir John Gielgud's production of "Twelfth Night" nipped the play with an astringent frost, leaving an impression for which the polite word would be "formal" and the exact word "mechanical." A frosty charm was sought and achieved. Vivien Leigh concealed her stock in trade, brittle vivaciousness, beneath a dazzling vocal monotony. This Viola did not, as she promised, speak "in many sorts of music": she commanded but one, a music recognizable to sheltering travelers as that of steady rain on a corrugated tin roof. Sir Laurence Olivier's sun peeped fitfully through the chintz curtains of the production. His Malvolio was a self-made snob, aspiring to "the quality" but always being let down by lower-class vowel sounds; this was, in fact, Malvolio seen from his own point of view instead of from Sir Toby's. Yet the sketch remained an outline; accomplished and diverting, but scarcely the substance of Sir Laurence's vocation. The second Stratford production, "All's Well That Ends Well," was very stately and extremely dull. What the company (and English classical acting in general) needs is someone to set the tone for it, some actor or director to bang a tuning fork of reality against the text. Joyce Redman, as Helena, was allowed to roam at large in the dangerous pastures of vocalized "poetry," pitching her voice to a lifted sweetness three tones higher than audibility demanded, and ignoring the basic Shakespearean rule: take care of the sense, and the sounds will take care of themselves.

Some of the meatiest revivals of the season came from the left-wing company called Theatre Workshop, operating in East London. Under the dynamic direction of Joan Littlewood, these impoverished idealists staged "The Good Soldier Schweik," "Arden of Feversham" and a modern-dress "Volpone," as well as a plethora of pinkish tubthumpers from Hungary and Mexico. It is a significant comment on British theatre that this group alone was chosen to represent Britain at the 1955 Paris Festival of International Drama.

The Musicals

Little of native growth. "The Talk of the Town," a spectacular revue, had pace of production, taste in its dressing, and evidence of something more than automatic writing in its sketches. "Jokers Wild" was the latest in the series of extravaganzas starring the sexagenarian Crazy Gang; most of its ideas were borrowed from the brilliant, surrealist Paris revues of Robert Dhéry, and vulgarized in the borrowing. Bud Flanagan, his face a great cheese melting, was deeply and ruminatively merry; a marvelous clown on the brink of being ruined by uncritical audiences.

The one-man show called Maurice Chevalier returned to delight us with its momentous innocence. M. Chevalier once wrote that "an artist carries on throughout his life a mysterious and uninterrupted conversation with his public"; but this democratic view of the artist's job was bluntly denied by "An Evening with Beatrice Lillie." Miss Lillie converses not with her public but with herself; she reproduces on stage the grievous lunacy with which most of us behave when absolutely alone. For her the theatre is a heritage; for M. Chevalier it is a Rotarian convention. Since both have genius, both are right.

Three Broadway musicals went well. The score of "Can-Can" showed Cole Porter at half-pressure, except for "It's All Right with Me," which had all of the master's wan bedside wit. Otherwise, the world of "Trilby" became the world of pork pie, and memory dwells chiefly on Michael Kidd's dances, boisterous ecstasies of flung limbs and flashed skirts which smack of the most callipygous excesses of ergot poisoning.

"Wonderful Town," the ironic snook cocked by Leonard Bernstein, Adolph Green and Betty Comden at Greenwich Village in the thirties, was an instant success. The Bernstein score reminded us that to be lyrical was not necessarily to be sentimental; but the casting was less happy. Pat Kirkwood robbed Ruth of the caustic intellectual dignity Rosalind Russell gave her in New York; and on the whole it was in the teeth of its British interpreters that the show triumphed.

Perhaps the most sonorous popular hit was "Kismet." This Persian panorama had all that could legally be looted from Bakst, Flecker, Borodin, Minsky, and Aladdin. I would linger over Joan Diener's meditative vamp and Doretta Morrow's fervent heroine, were it not for Alfred Drake, whose London debut showed us the supreme professionalism of American theatre at its best. His performance was a radiation of controlled pride; pride in flexible fingertips, bestriding legs and a baritone voice which pierced without effort to the dome of an enormous theatre. Were we throughout "Kismet" on a level much lower than that of "Wonderful Town"? We were indeed; but such was Mr. Drake's impact that we forgot to ask such questions. He rounded off a mixed and mostly miserable season.

THE SEASON IN PARIS

By André Josset

Playwright; and Secretary-General of the International Theatre
Institute, UNESCO

OUR summer-bronzed faces matched those on the stage of the
Théâtre de l'Empire on the night of September 30, 1954.

It was the opening of the season, and the extraordinary American
Negro company played *Porgy and Bess* before a packed audience.
Its success was considerable, even though language is still a barrier
—but a barrier which is being lowered from day to day, as we shall
see more precisely when I discuss the International Festival of Paris.

In October, unfortunately, unlucky days followed lucky ones.
The Man Who Came to Dinner, a play which also came from the
United States, had a very tepid welcome. This brings up once
again the question of the choice of subjects for works to be presented in foreign countries. The central character of *The Man
Who Came to Dinner* is a sort of phenomenon absolutely unknown
in France, hence the interest taken in the comedy was unfortunately
nil, and the Théâtre Antoine, which had put it on, was hastily
obliged to produce *La Main Passe* (The Dealer Passes) by Feydeau,
to try to repair the catastrophe; and the old comedy showed once
more, and brilliantly, all the vitality it still contains.

Then our excellent and admirable Maurice Chevalier, whose hair
is silver but whose talent is still intact, gave a large recital all by
himself in the immense Théâtre des Champs Elysées. His program
consisted of new songs, satiric or full of sweetness, which were enriched by his great talent for pantomime, his personal charm, the
air of sympathy that surrounds him, and the truthfulness of the
sketches themselves. He thus achieved a considerable personal
triumph and his one-man festival lasted about a month and a half.

A play about Lord Byron called *Comme les Dieux* (Like the
Gods) then appeared at the Théâtre de l'Oeuvre, made illustrious in
the past by the famous Lugné-Poé, who brought the great Scandi-
navian masterpieces to France. There were, therefore, veritable
gods listening in silence to the performance of this play by a modern author, which must have been quite intimidating. Nevertheless,
the play was received with some favor, despite or perhaps because

36

of the incestuous love of Byron for his beautiful sister Augusta. We were surprised not to note any perceptible sensuality: the intellect alone was given the task of making us understand that these two souls loved each other in carnal fashion.

I go on at once to the presentation in Jean-Louis Barrault's theatre, the Théâtre Marigny, of Chekhov's *The Cherry Orchard*.

This production had been awaited with great curiosity and I hasten to say that this curiosity was satisfied. I emphasize this intentionally, for afterwards I was indignant at the revolting reception given another production of Jean-Louis Barrault, *A Sleep of Prisoners* by Christopher Fry; an incomprehensible reception, save from the point of view of sheer ferocity which satisfied long-repressed instincts so far held back by the successes of a producer who has been playing the role of a lion-tamer. These cries of collective fury are not rare in the theatre, and that evening Jean-Louis Barrault was their victim. But let us return to *The Cherry Orchard*, which ran for several months.

Everyone knows the subject of this masterpiece of delicacy and despair, in which the Russian soul is depicted in a way that has become classic and even quite traditional. A giant "nitchevo" covers the whole play with its rather terrifying shadow. The characters, save the vulgar buyer of the Cherry Orchard, allow themselves to slide slowly into the depths of an abyss in which they will perhaps find rest.

Misfortune, renunciation and poetic resignation are the beds in which these beings who find living so difficult on earth lie down to die. Beneath his dialogue with its light touches, Chekhov's great plaint murmured like the wind in the leaves of the beech trees. Madeleine Renaud, in the principal role, Jean-Louis Barrault, Jean Desailly, Simone Valère, Nathalie Nerval (of Russian descent), played to perfection this discreet and tragic intermezzo.

I shall pass over two or three productions which were as ephemeral as they deserved to be, and go on at once to a lovely production by the Comédie Française of Molière's *Les Amants Magnifiques* (The Magnificent Lovers). Enchantment was awaiting us and stayed from the first rise of the curtain until the end, which produced an ovation. Molière's play, however, was slender—a simple impromptu quickly written for a sort of fairy-tale ballet to be spoken and sung, in which Louis XIV wished to amuse himself by playing one of the roles. Molière did not wish this inimitably graceful little impromptu to be included among his works, but, much to our good fortune, posterity did not respect his wish.

A plot, to which no one paid much attention, yet managed to

amuse a gala Parisian audience. But their delight was in the staging, in the décor and the extraordinary costumes of Suzanne Lalique, in the brilliance of the colors, in the charming realism of animals mingling with human beings and dancing in the ballet at their side. Jean Meyer, the producer, had brought forth a masterpiece. The great actress Annie Ducaux played the role of the Queen. Robert Hirsch, who began his career as a dancer in the ballet of the Opéra de Paris, and who then went on to the Comédie Française, was one of the two or three revelations of the evening, an actor of delightful, bouncing humor. I have said enough to show that *Les Amants Magnifiques* was one of the three great successes of the Comédie Française during the season of 1954-1955.

On the Butte Montmartre, in the very old little theatre once run by Charles Dullin, l'Atelier, we were shown a novelist's play entitled *Caterina*, which unfortunately did not last because, even though its dialogue was honest and sharp, it did not hold up after a promising beginning.

On October 29th we were back at the Comédie des Champs Elysées to see a little play by Jean Anouilh, *Cécile ou l'Ecole des Pères* (Cécile, or, The School for Fathers). *Cécile*, quite curiously, played together with an Oscar Wilde play. I very much liked the two plays, deliciously performed as they were, but the general effect seemed a bit thin and I am not quite sure that the evening was a success.

On the last day of October I went off to the Théâtre des Mathurins where *Electre ou la Chute des Masques* (Electra, or, The Fall of the Masks) was being given—a play by Marguerite Yourcenaar. I believe that this author lives in New York, and I owe her particular gratitude for the great joy her book *Les Mémoires d'Hadrien* (The Memoirs of Hadrian) gave me; I have read and reread it with interest that has always been compensated. It would be difficult to resurrect the Roman Empire and the Emperor Hadrian and the unforgettable Antinoüs and the latter's death, with a more gripping power of evocation. Arriving at the theatre, I therefore hoped to feel similar emotions. Unfortunately, it seemed to me that either the performance was inadequate to the text, or that the text itself was insufficient for the stage.

A production composed of old works by Henri Monnier ought to have struck me as being in a somewhat melancholy vein. However, Henri Monnier is the inventor of the extraordinary Monsieur Prud'-homme, the incarnation of the hilarious stupidity of a certain type of nineteenth-century bourgeois, at the time when a National Guard had grown up composed of shopkeepers and members of the middle

Ricardo Montalban, Gloria DeHaven, Kurt Kasznar and Robert Clary in "Seventh Heaven"

class dressed in uniform. These good people gave us a show which brought bursts of laughter, and their statements, as invented by Henri Monnier, were charged with explosive humor. I will cite one: when M. Prud'homme receives his National Guard saber for the first time, he swears an oath to the Republic, and adds: "I will use this saber to defend our institutions, and, if need be, to combat them!"

At the Théâtre Saint Georges arrived one of the successes of the season, Graham Greene's *The Living Room,* presented and played by Jean Mercure, one of our three or four best producers. America probably knows this play, and for that reason I shall not describe it. It had considerable success with the Parisian public, and the success is lasting, for the play is still running at the moment I write these lines.

As it does each year, the Théâtre National Populaire of Jean Vilar managed to attain the highest beauty: this time, indeed, the experience was almost sublime. The bill was Corneille's tragedy *Cinna,* which is hardly ever given any more, save at times by the Comédie Française.

Jean Vilar likes, wherever possible, to do without décor and to play on a bare stage before dark or light draperies, or against dark backgrounds which set off the striking colors of the costumes. Jean Vilar also likes to highlight the psychology of the passions of his characters. For *Cinna* he had built an enormous broad staircase silhouetted against the sky. On the steps were two soldiers at attention, at once disciplined and savage, representing the power of the Roman Empire. Vilar played the Emperor Augustus with a company he chose personally, whose principal members change almost every year.

I admired the feeling for naturalness and human truth which flowed from this performance. An aura at once tragic and familiar enveloped Corneille's work. The living beings created by Corneille moved about on the stage, fought, loved and suffered with the naturalness of clear, evident things. We were happy to see these seventeenth-century characters freed of their traditions, and we had the strange feeling of knowing that their hearts beat close to ours.

Port-Royal, a play by Henry de Montherlant, was presented on December 8th at the Comédie Française. The public, like myself, was not very much informed about the religious doctrine of Jansenius and the very grave consequences it had for the community of nuns of the convent of Port-Royal des Champs, under Louis XIV. One would have thought that it would be very difficult for the producer, Jean Meyer, and for the actors, to put on this severe, lofty, and rather static work. And yet *Port-Royal* has been and continues to be one of the greatest successes of the season, with a considerable box office.

To what should this success be attributed? To the fact, I believe, that the public—saturated with facile works that were carelessly written, were sometimes vulgar, and in any case, were *small*— wanted better-written works of greater range.

On the 10th of December the Théâtre Hébertot presented *La*

Condition Humaine (Man's Fate), adapted by Thierry Maulnier from the famous novel by André Malraux. It was a succession of rich and colorful scenes laid in Shanghai at the beginning of the struggle between the Chinese Nationalists and the Communists— scenes of great energy and cruelty, in a production that was well defined and full of talent.

Next, a play by Jean Anouilh, written during the Second World War, was revived on December 13th at the Théâtre de l'Atelier. This was the *Rendez-vous de Senlis* (Rendezvous at Senlis), a work that is ravishing, bizarre and cruel, as Anouilh's works usually are. It had a fine four-months run.

Just after this production came the opening on December 19th, at the Théâtre Sarah Bernhardt, of Arthur Miller's very important play *Les Sorcières de Salem* (The Crucible). Raymond Rouleau had produced the play with extraordinary firmness and color. There was great curiosity to see Yves Montand, the great popular singer, play the major role in a play for the first time in the theatre. He distinguished himself with more than the usual honors, and the intensity of his personality and his stage presence were unanimously noted. Arthur Miller's play had a very great success and lasted until the opening of the Festival of Paris, that is, until the middle of this past May.

A play by Peter Ustinov, adapted from the English text, then appeared at the Théâtre Fontaine, and this very pretty theatre had the luck to have *The Love of Four Colonels* performed by the Grenier-Hussenot company, in a very intelligent and original adaptation.

I should also put Jules Roy's *Les Cyclones* (The Cyclones) among the successes, together with a charming comedy by Marc-Gilbert Sauvajon, *Adorable Julia,* treating of the domestic life of a married couple who also happen to be well-known actors.

The theatre-in-the-round made its first appearance in Paris, in a tiny theatre situated in Montmartre. The play was Marcel Achard's circus piece, *Voulez-vous jouer avec moâ?* (Do you want to come and play with me?), which in French is a traditional phrase said by clowns. It was full of Achard's melancholy poetic charm.

Two other great productions, *Macbeth* at the Théâtre National Populaire, and *Volpone* at Jean-Louis Barrault's Théâtre Marigny, had, on the other hand, only a relative success. To say nothing of *Macbeth, Volpone* had been before the war one of the great successes of Charles Dullin. This time we found that the play had been put on in too cool a fashion, although, in my opinion, the décor was responsible for this so-called coldness. Jean-Louis Barrault had composed a frightening and cynical character for the old miser, tottering at the edge of the tomb and clinging frantically to the good things of this world. Fernand Ledoux, onetime member of the Comédie Française, played the role of Volpone with a great deal of power and sobriety, but, like *Macbeth,* this play did not last very long.

The immense theatrical variety in Paris brings us now to two plays at opposite worlds from one another, *La Petite Maison de Thé* (The Teahouse of the August Moon) by John Patrick, and *L'annonce faite à Marie* (The Tidings Brought to Mary), Paul Claudel's admirable mystical tragedy.

Beyond appreciating the humorous qualities of *The Teahouse of the August Moon* and its ravishing décor, the audience gave enormous approval to a little goat which, on opening night, showed that it was a great actress.

Paul Claudel's great cathedral, a monument both terrible and sublime, got a bad reception, and, from the critics, one that was even outrageous. The production was under indictment, for the text is destined, I believe, to live through the ages. The President of the French Republic had come to honor the performance with his presence, but this did not help. A few days later, Paul Claudel died, and France gave him a national funeral at Notre-Dame. It is a pity that his last days should have been saddened by this reception of his masterpiece.

A frightening Italian comedy by Dino Buzatti made us shiver on the night of March 11th at the Théâtre La Bruyère. The play was called *Un cas intéressant* (An Interesting Case). Its subject is a sort of slow descent into Hell, Hell being represented by a medical and surgical clinic. The hero of the play has auditory hallucinations; he suddenly hears terrifying metallic howlings in the great silence which surrounds him. It is then that he decides to consult a great professor who specializes in brain cases. Is the patient truly ill, or is this only a delusion, or does the surgeon know that the illness is incurable and still dare to operate? All this is not expressed very clearly. In any case, the unfortunate victim starts that slow descent of which I have spoken above: he begins by occupying a room on the fifth floor of the clinic, but descends with implacable regularity to the lowest and darkest floor.

The operation has naturally not been successful, and little by little, death is dragging the hero down. This fall from floor to floor is made still crueler by the lies of the doctors trying to reassure the patient that his decline is altogether natural, and will not prevent him from one day leaving the place, free and cured. It is then that death imposes silence on both the executioners and the condemned man.

The play is written in a simple, realistic style which only makes its anguish more striking. It weighed so heavily on audiences that it only ran for a month.

Jean Renoir, the great film director, offered us on March 18th at the Théâtre de la Renaissance a play written by himself, *Orvet* (Adder), starring Leslie Caron. I must say that this charming, dreamy, ironic and human work did not receive the critical welcome it merited. Despite this, *Orvet* is still playing successfully. Leslie Caron has shown herself in this play to be an actress of astonishing power.

Jean Giraudoux's *Intermezzo* on March 21st faced the test of a revival after twenty years. The danger was the greater because the play had been produced originally in an absolutely unforgettable fashion by Louis Jouvet. Jean-Louis Barrault and his company brilliantly accepted the challenge set to them by the memory of a great theatrical producer, by changes in public taste, and most of all by the terrible gulf that separates the years before 1939 from those after 1945. The text had not at all aged, though its reflection of a happy epoch may sometimes have seemed a bit too graceful. It was not without a certain melancholy that we listened to this play, but its success was enormous.

The Comédie Française presented Racine's *Athalie,* a verse play full of blood, violence, passion, ambition and innocence. Racine's lovely poetry surrounds this sanguinary drama, thanks to choruses of young girls who recite and sing the prettiest verses in the French language, which some people, however, have called "vulgar doggerel"; for myself, I have always been fascinated by these choruses. Marvelous décor and very beautiful costumes enhanced this revival of a 300-year-old masterpiece.

On May 11th, at the Salle Luxembourg, the Comédie Française also revived a play by the writer of this article, *Elizabeth, la Femme sans Homme* (Elizabeth, Woman without a Man). It had been first produced twenty years earlier at the Théâtre du Vieux Colombier.

Finally, we arrive at what is perhaps the summit of the theatrical season, with the International Theatre Festival, which opened in the middle of May. As of the time of writing, Ireland, Finland, Italy, Yugoslavia and China had put on their performances and had a great deal of success.

I would particularly mention Yugoslavia and Italy; the latter offered a comedy by Eduardo de Filippo, *Ces diables de Fantômes* (These Wretched Ghosts). De Filippo is a Neapolitan playwright and actor who has had great success in the films as well as the theatre. He enchanted the audience as much by his pantomime as by his text, so that everyone present thoroughly understood the story of the play, though it was performed in Italian.

But the sensation of the Paris Festival as of this writing is the Chinese company from the Pekin Opera, which had a veritable triumph.

Theirs was truly a quite extraordinary performance in its color and strength, its strangeness and grace. The professional Chinese companies that we had seen previously never approached the perfection and originality of the Pekin Opera. The word "Opera" is perhaps not quite accurate, for the program was composed of many elements.

I remember particularly a sort of mime-drama, which takes place at night in an inn, in which a general is attacked with a saber by the innkeeper; both are supposed to be fighting in absolute darkness, although the stage is brilliantly lighted. This conflict was intensely comic, and its thousand details delighted the audience.

There was also a charming tableau that is almost impossible to describe: an old fisherman with a long white beard stops his boat on the bank of a great river and takes on board a young and ravishing passenger dressed in sky-blue silk; then, after much delightful humor, he takes her over the river against the current. There was naturally no décor at all, no boat, no river, but the two characters pantomimed so well that the river, the sky, the canoe were intensely real.

Now we are awaiting the company from the U.S.A., with *Medea* and *The Skin of Our Teeth*. Thus far, the Paris Festival has had considerable success, and has made great progress over last year. Twenty-one countries are participating in it; and I believe that this sort of expression is of capital importance for the future of world theatre.

THE SEASON IN CALIFORNIA

By Luther Nichols

San Francisco Drama and Book Critic

HOW was the theatre year 1954-55 in California?
There are several answers to that. In terms of the artistic and entertainment qualities of the professional shows seen here, the season was sometimes mile-high. In terms of the meaningful content of those plays, it was, as usual, mole-low. Commercially, it was better than average. Speaking of this vulgar aspect of the year, Manager William Zwissig of San Francisco's Curran and Geary Theatres confided that "One show made all the difference between a fair season and a good one." That was "Teahouse of the August Moon," which cracked all records for unbroken runs by nonmusical shows in both San Francisco and Los Angeles.

Most encouraging developments took place in the field of home production—but more of that anon.

It's always hard to keep a résumé of the West Coast season from reading like Dead Sea history to those on the East Coast. We can't escape the fact that our year is often dressed in hand-me-downs from earlier Broadway seasons. Some of the articles retain their stylish look. But many appear a trifle worn and shapeless.

There were two notable exceptions to this, two occasions when we slipped off our self-pity and Cinderella rags and went to the ball in glittering attire of our own making. These were the West Coast productions of "Three for Tonight" and "Peter Pan."

"Three for Tonight" was another Paul Gregory-Charles Laughton brainchild. It certainly kept the gloss on their reputation for unusual and exciting shows. Marge and Gower Champion danced and Harry Belafonte and the Voices of Walter Schumann (not a ventriloquist's act, but a choral group) sang. American folk scenes and musical traditions were evoked. And before you knew it the audience was rocking, crying and stomping like sinners at an oldtime revival meeting. "Three for Tonight" marched triumphantly on to New York.

Big event of the 1954-55 San Francisco-Los Angeles Civic Light Opera season was the world premiere in the former city of a musical version of Sir James Barrie's fit of whimsey, "Peter Pan." It hardly threw off stardust as first seen here. Mary Martin, wired, flew—

though not with the greatest of ease.   And Cyril Ritchard was delightfully unsure as to whether Captain Hook should be played as a figure in a Restoration comedy or as a mortgage holder in a 19th-century melodrama.   Both stars were enchanting, and both were voted, with Helen Hayes, best stage performers of the year by the San Francisco critics.

Jerome Robbins worked heroically to get "Peter Pan" in shape, and so he did by the time it left for New York's Winter Garden.

This and other Civic Light Opera attractions were profitable enough to make Director Edwin Lester and his sponsors glow like so many fireflies.   Last year's losses were forgotten as "The King and I" arrived and Yul Brynner filled the huge S.F. Opera House with his dynamic personality and with satisfied customers.   Patricia Morison made a sweet, if sometimes inaudible, English schoolteacher. The show did a nice $102,000 in its final week.   "Porgy and Bess" was a teeming, noisy hit of the CLO season in the Blevins Davis-Richard Breen revival, with Cab Calloway as Sportin' Life and a cast that changed faces as often as a revolving door.   A reprise of "Brigadoon" found the misty Highland magic evaporating, though William Johnson sang well.

As a "bonus" show, the CLO sponsored the West Coast appearance of London's touring Old Vic Company in its song-and-dance production of "A Midsummer Night's Dream."   It was a Shakespearean extravaganza to delight the eye; one of the most opulent spectacles ever seen here.   And the ear was not neglected by Felix Mendelssohn's score.   But even Moira Shearer, Robert Helpmann and Sterling Holloway didn't persuade us it was anything more than a lovely phantasmagoria.

There is a feeling—it amounts to a resentment—out this way that many shows lose their integrity somewhere on the road.   An old complaint is that actors learn all too quickly which moments get the laughs or the bated breath, and begin to play them to the audience rather than to each other.   They gain an easy confidence that anticipates lines.   There are motions, but no emotions.   Call it "long-runitis" or what you will, it leads to spoiling the evening for many Pacific Coast theatregoers.

Such was the case, many felt, with "Teahouse of the August Moon."   Burgess Meredith did very well as Sakini except when mistaking the role for a prize theatrical Guernsey to be milked for laughs.   Scott McKay counterbalanced this tendency, however.   And though there was some grousing that the show re-employed parts of "Mister Roberts" and "The King and I," there was no doubt of its smashing popularity.

The same kind of acting superfluity went on in "Picnic" when

Tallulah Bankhead in "Dear Charles"

William Inge's Broadway wonder arrived. Ralph Meeker gave an impression of posturing for a series of photos for *Strength and Health* magazine rather than attending to his role. At any rate, the piece had become a trifle musclebound and was unable to lift Californians out of the heavy torpor that seems to overcome them in the presence of latently good straight drama.

A milder sort of narcissism seized Franchot Tone as he went through an erratic interpretation of a psychiatrist in "Oh, Men! Oh, Women!" But all agreed that Edward Chodorov had turned out a neatly tooled comedy.

Eddie Bracken successfully avoided the pitfalls of overacting in "The Seven Year Itch," and the George Axelrod comedy, for this and other reasons having to do with its being a lot of fun, stayed around San Francisco for nine weeks.

"Time Out for Ginger" was further light and agreeable marma-
lade—with which, as you can see, the season was thickly spread.
Melvyn Douglas applied it in this.

And then there was "Dear Charles," which Tallulah Bankhead
held up as a center pole holds up a tent. I mean no disparagement
of the international team of authors who gave her the material to
hold up; it's just that Miss Bankhead is the sort of actress of whom
you say a year later, "What *was* that play she was in?"

"Tea and Sympathy" brought Deborah Kerr to the West Coast
stage for the first time, and the red-haired movie star was at once
acclaimed as capable and pretty in plays as she is in pictures. Robert Anderson's play, however, had a more equivocal reception. Some
thought it tapered into melodrama and the inconsequential; most
thought it a remarkably fine and sensitive work. It seemed to depend
on whether you regarded it merely as a treatment of homosexuality,
or as a universally rousing plea for what Sartre calls "engagement"
—for individual action beyond tea and sympathy if we are ever to
right the wrongs we see.

Now come the revivals. I'll try not to detain you long. Leonard
Sillman's "New Faces" made a brief return; Frank Fay's rabbit in
"Harvey" seems to be getting more visible and mechanical with each
revisit; Jerome Cowan showed up in "The Moon Is Blue," which
did a surprising four and a half weeks in San Francisco, and "The
Caine Mutiny Court-Martial" came again in a second-company version that had Paul Douglas overcoming his Mt. Rushmore solidity
to make a fairly convincing neurotic as Captain Queeg.

A revival that deserves separate mention was that of Helen Hayes
in "What Every Woman Knows." With the old Barrie play the
new Huntington Hartford Theatre was opened in Hollywood in September, 1954. The amiable, art-loving Hartford spent a reported
$1,000,000 converting a radio station into what is possibly the most
beautiful theatre in America, and the only one with a café-bar. This
was the first opening of a new legitimate house on the Pacific Coast
in twenty-seven years.

Following Miss Hayes, whose spirited performance made the Barrie
play seem in a much gayer and less varicose vein than it was, the new
Hartford showplace presented "Sailor's Delight," an innocuous
English comedy by Peter Blackmore, with Eva Gabor as its bright-
est feature. After that there were ominous spells of darkness. It
became apparent that a playhouse needs something to play. At this
writing, it looks as though the elegant structure is, at least tempo-
rarily, the theatre's loveliest white elephant.

In contrast to the Hartford Theatre's fate was the lively response

Helen Hayes in "What Every Woman Knows"

elicited by a series of shows presented at Los Angeles' Carthay Circle
Theatre by the team of Jack Present, Harry Zeven and Joseph Just-
man. They offered "Anniversary Waltz" (MacDonald Carey and
Marsha Hunt), "Oh, Men! Oh, Women!" (Franchot Tone), "The
Shrike" (Dane Clark) and "The Fifth Season" (Joseph Buloff).
"Fresh productions and fresh casts, instead of tired road companies
playing against crumbling sets, and a limit of four weeks to each
show, so that people know they must see it in that time"—these
were reasons given by the Carthay producers for their spanking
season and $75,000 advance sale.

The Greek Theatre (we're still in Los Angeles) enclosed starlit,
outdoor engagements of such shows as "Three for Tonight"; "Wonderful Town," with Carol Channing in the Rosalind Russell role;

the New York City Ballet, and the fine José Greco and his Spanish Dancers. Careful production and the romantic natural beauty of the setting kept Manager James Doolittle's enterprise in the black without subsidy.

At the Biltmore, in addition to most of the same shows already mentioned that came through San Francisco, Los Angeles playgoers saw "The Solid Gold Cadillac." It was only moderately successful without a big name in its cast.

In California it never rains, but it did drizzle one-man shows rather steadily. Agnes Moorehead re-created some "Great Moments in Literature"; Ethel Waters put on a warm-hearted song revue; Charles Laughton read deliciously; Edith Piaf found audiences no longer so nostalgic for her vibrant recollections of Paris, and Josephine Baker discovered pretty much the same thing. It was not a good year for singles.

Anyone for doubles, then? This logical—or biological—step was taken by Hume Cronyn and Jessica Tandy when they opened their husband-and-wife show, "Face to Face," for its big-city tests in San Francisco and Los Angeles. A well-selected and tastefully read sort of literary vaudeville, it did not, unfortunately, draw well.

Welcome visitors were the Dublin Players, who returned to San Francisco with four famous plays from their repertoire, of which the most popular was O'Casey's "Juno and the Paycock."

A Los Angeles production that ran for twenty weeks at the tiny Las Palmas Theatre before coming to San Francisco was Danny Dare's musical revue, "That's Life." It introduced some fresh faces; perhaps too fresh for Northern Californians, who seemed to cotton more to their own Straw Hat Revue Theatre. The latter group suspended operations for the year, but is due for a comeback.

Exotic spices sprinkled into the year's gumbo were the Kabuki Dancers of Japan and two companies of Yiddish actors.

In all, I would say that the happiest thing about the 1954-55 California theatre season was the continued upsurge of the "do-it-yourself" spirit out here. The Gregory-Laughton productions, the Civic Light Opera, the Huntington Hartford Theatre and the Carthay Circle series are among the more professional examples of this.

There were also strong indications that regional self-realization was being achieved in such semiprofessional groups as the Actor's Workshop and Interplayers of San Francisco, and the Players' Ring, Stage Society, Hollywood Repertory Theatre and Negro Ebony Showcase Theatre in Southern California.

The Actor's Workshop, among producing groups I have seen, merits a special citation. Headed by Jules Irving and Herbert Blau, the group outshone even its hit of last season, "Death of a Salesman," with a production of another Arthur Miller play, "The Crucible," that simply electrified audiences. It was quite the most forceful attack on the emotions seen here all year on any stage. After running many weeks at the Workshop's theatre, it was moved downtown for a continued record run at the Marines' Memorial Theatre. Dedicated to ensemble playing, the Actor's Workshop company has now developed to a point where it makes most touring professional pick-up companies look like Sunday boaters compared to its well-drilled crew. The group has proven, among other things, that a sound regional theatre can grow from nothing, that "serious" drama can make a profit, and that unions, if correctly approached, can help rather than obstruct a low-budget theatrical effort. In short, it's an ANTA dream come true.

Among the more interesting regional productions of the year were a new play, "Caricature," by Irving Phillips, put on by Ebony Showcase, and a Bohemian revel called "Poets' Follies of 1955," co-produced by Weldon Kees and Michael Grieg in San Francisco. The latter was an experimental revue that threw all the arts into uneasy conjunction in the theatre. It had everything from professional strip teasers to poetry readings by prominent local writers, from jazz and dance interpretations to T. S. Eliot and cybernetics. Whatever else it was, it was neither orthodox nor dull.

The Interplayers presented a version of "The Shrike" that had crowds of eager patrons and indignant psychiatrists lined up halfway down the block, and also staged an original satire of promise in George Hitchcock's "Kan-Chen-Chomo." It dealt with human cupidity.

And, finally, the Pasadena Playhouse had its usual active season. There were several "premieres," including a first production of Irving Phillip's comedy, "Mother Was a Bachelor," with Billie Burke; a West Coast first of "The Prescott Proposals," with Judith Evelyn, and a world premiere of "In the Spirit," with Alan Mowbray living up to the title as the play's author, director and star.

Much, I fear, has gone untouched in this back-skipping through the season. Apologies to the neglected. I only hope to make the main point that the drama did not languish out here; that, indeed, we Westerners do not have to hold hat in hand when talking of our own productions in the presence of Easterners. The struggle is not for complete independence—we would sorely miss those Broadway imports—but for ever greater self-expression and more work for our own theatre artists. That struggle is far from won. But last year held evidence of growing potential, and if the buds go untrampled this coming season there may be more auspicious things to report in 1956.

OFF BROADWAY

By Garrison P. Sherwood

OFF Broadway theatre this year had considerably more quality than heretofore. Of the four non-featured supporting actors named in the Clarence Derwent Awards, three appeared in Off Broadway productions. And Proscenium Productions, at the Cherry Lane, received an Antoinette Perry Award and citation from the Cultural Division of the French Embassy for their delightful production of Anouilh's "Thieves' Carnival." It is safe to say that Off Broadway is making a very real contribution to the New York theatre scene. It may no longer be dismissed lightly or considered a lark.

Let us look at some of these productions. There is first the rather special case of the Phoenix Theatre. It is without question Off Broadway geographically and spiritually but it uses Broadway talent. (Perhaps we should say that it has a foot in both worlds.) It began its season with Robert Ardrey's "Sing Me No Lullaby," which for all its faults attracted a great deal of attention. The last act alone made it worthy of production. Next came "Sandhog," a ballad in three acts by Earl Robinson and Waldo Salt, and it, too, proved to be interesting. This was followed by two revivals—neither of them brilliant—Shaw's "The Doctor's Dilemma" and Ibsen's "The Master Builder." The Phoenix wound up the season with a delightful revue, "Phoenix '55," which proves—if proof be needed—what a fine comedienne is Nancy Walker. The Phoenix also presented, on Monday evenings, a series of what they termed "Sideshows," one of which, John Webster's "The White Devil," was an exciting dramatic production admirably staged by Jack Landau (who also staged "The Clandestine Marriage," mentioned below). There is talk of "The White Devil" being put on for a run in 1955-56.

The Players Theatre at the Provincetown gave us an excellent production of Robinson Jeffers' "The Cretan Woman," with Jacqueline Brookes performing the lead role very creditably. They then did a splendid stylized version of David Garrick's "The Clandestine Marriage," with Frederic Warriner giving a truly distinguished performance.

The Blackfriars put on two very interesting productions, "Bam-

52

Margaret Truman in "Autumn Crocus"

boo Cross" by Theophane Lee and "Slightly Delinquent" by Leo
Thomas. This group gives us consistently good plays well presented.

Originals Only produced "The Chair" by Tom Hill and Don
Stuart, which was fairly successful, following this with an interesting
revival (originals only?) of Tennessee Williams' "A Streetcar Named
Desire."

The Theatre de Lys was host to various groups and producers,
housing stimulating work, especially in terms of acting. This theatre's season started off in June with a sorry little item called "Home-
ward Look" by Effie Young and Ernest Pagano. Even the presence
of such fine talent as Vicki Cummings and Roddy McDowall could
not help it. July saw three one-act plays by Paul Green entitled

Robert Helpmann and Moira Sh

Midsummer Night's Dream"

"Chair Endowed," "The No 'Count Boy" and "Supper for the Dead." These did not fare well. Later in the fall—October—a revue brought a change of pace. "I Feel Wonderful" was its title, and it had music and lyrics by Jerry Herman and sketches by Barry Alan Grael. It was fresh and entertaining, without a tedious number in it. An odd, but interesting, play, David Z. Goodman's "High Named Today," held forth in December. In February the Artists Theatre took over the de Lys with James Merrill's "The Immortal Husband." There was much to recommend this play, though I found it pretty confusing. Anne Meacham, who played the lead, is an actress of unusual interest. Late in the season at the de Lys was Patricia Joudry's "Teach Me How to Cry," written with tenderness and simply and sincerely played.

The Cherry Lane housed a new and very promising group known as Proscenium Productions. If they can continue their fine work, they have the makings of a splendid repertory company. Here is a group, under Warren Enters' direction, that brings us real authority and genuine style and ensemble playing. Mr. Enters has a sure touch and knows his job thoroughly. Their first production, Congreve's "The Way of the World," was a delight, well staged and handsomely costumed. The company played together as though they had been playing together for years. The same may be said for Anouilh's "Thieves' Carnival"—one of the delights of the season, on or off Broadway.

Mention must be made of "Twelfth Night" and "The Merchant of Venice," put on at the Jan Hus Auditorium by a group calling themselves The Shakespearewrights. These productions were interesting, lively and perfectly suited to the wide-open platform which serves as their stage. The costuming was exceptional and the acting, capital. No Broadway production could have pleased its patrons more.

Down at the Fourth Street Theatre David Ross produced and directed two revivals. The first, "The Dybbuk," in October was so successful that the engagement was extended several times; the second, Chekhov's "The Three Sisters," translated by Stark Young, proved to be one of the best revivals of this play ever seen in New York.

To the small President Theatre, uptown, Ben Bagley brought his "Shoestring Revue." Put together on just what its title implies, it turned out to be a gem in its way. At its poorest it was good and at its best it was hilarious and delightful, full of youthful spirit. Beatrice Arthur, Arte Johnson, Chita Rivera and others went on to bigger if not better things even before the show closed. Certainly

Gloria Vanderbilt Stokowski in "The Swan"

one of the high spots of the revue was Mel Larned's "Wabash 4-7473."

As this is being written a new group, The Masquers, has just put on a thoroughly successful revival of "Billy Budd." The acting is superior and the production has been admirably set and directed. Here is another reason for Off Broadway. It gives us these good plays for which there is a definite audience but which, for various reasons—mostly economic—can't quite stand the rigors of Broadway.

This leaves just enough space to mention the usual revivals put on by Equity Library, which somehow did not come up to their usual standard, and the Greenwich Mews productions of "Major Barbara," William Branch's eloquent "In Splendid Error" and "Juno and the Paycock." And there was the Broadway Chapel Players group, who did a fine revival of Obey's "Noah," as well as William Alexander Percy's "In April Once," done with professional excellence.

There were others, but these, I believe, most fairly represent the season—a season that on the whole had much to shout about and has established Off Broadway theatre more firmly than ever as an interesting and stimulating supplement to Broadway.

THE SEASON IN TELEVISION

By Robert McLaughlin

Radio and TV Editor, *Time* Magazine

TELEVISION has in abundance all the essential requirements of a theatre. There is an instantly available audience numbering in the tens of millions. There is a large and technically skilled behind-the-scenes staff. There are dedicated and wealthy sponsors, willing to pour hundreds of thousands of dollars into a single production. There are readily available all of the great writers of the world, living and dead.

As a result, during the height of the season, the TV networks fill the nation's screens with more than 200 dramatic shows each week. Some run for as little as fifteen minutes; a few as long as one-and-a-half hours; most are presented in thirty- or sixty-minute segments. They include melodramas, love stories, farces, musicals, situation comedies, documentaries, excursions into history. The majority of these shows—whether live or filmed, whether made in Hollywood or Manhattan—are dreadful.

Running through this huge effluvium of dramatic garbage is a thin trickle of creative talent. The men responsible for television's few quality programs operate under an unwritten but generally accepted TV rule: for every five or six plays that are satisfactory to the commercial sponsor (*i.e.*, romantic in tone, trivial in content, upbeat in ending) they are allowed to put on one play that is artistically satisfying to them. From the operation of this rule have come most of the best TV dramas, ranging from adaptations of Chekhov, Ibsen, Pirandello and Shakespeare to original work by such veteran TV dramatists as Horton Foote, Reginald Rose, Paddy Chayefsky and Robert Alan Aurthur.

Yet the season's outstanding original play, "Patterns," was written by a relative newcomer, Rod Serling. Produced by Kraft TV Theater, Serling's drama dealt with what sociologists call the "pecking order" that is established in every well-run barnyard and through which each rooster learns to get and keep his place in the line of command. In "Patterns" the barnyard was a large U.S. corporation and Everett Sloane played the cock-of-the-walk with a nervous-eyed and lethal authority. The play found its tension in the reluctant

59

clash for the No. 2 position between Richard Kiley, an eager-beaver young engineer, and Ed Begley, an aging and ulcerous vice president.

The final scene was an authentic shocker: with Begley discredited and dead, young Kiley closed with Sloane to damn him as an insensitive monster. But, instead of bringing off the classic denunciation speech, Kiley found himself caught up in Sloane's soaring vision of an ever-expanding, if morally pointless, economy. Despite some wounded editorial outcries from the *Wall Street Journal* that business was never like this, "Patterns" won resounding praise from critics and audience. The play was triumphantly repeated with the same cast and the same scalpel-like effect just four weeks after its first performance.

Only three other TV originals caused anything like the same excitement—Robert Alan Aurthur's "Man on a Mountaintop" and two melodramas by Reginald Rose, "Twelve Angry Men" and "Crime in the Streets." Aurthur's play, showcased by Philco-Goodyear Theatre, pointed to the dangers of intellectual force-feeding in the young. Steven Hill played a child prodigy who had become ingrown instead of grown-up and now, huddling hermit-like in a hall bedroom, was convincingly regressive as he thumbed comic books with more pleasure than he had ever pored over Hegel. This specialized theme was given a more universal resolution when Hill was slowly weaned to reality through the generous love of a young girl; if the ending had rather too much patness, the painful ascent from the pit of infantilism was brilliantly shown.

Reginald Rose dealt much more with surface fireworks. In "Twelve Angry Men," produced by Studio One, Rose started out with an old idea (what happens inside a jury room) but turned it into exciting verbal swordplay. Franchot Tone got a baleful malevolence into his part as a juryman determined to hang the defendant, while Robert Cummings was bland and believable as the quiet man who changes everyone's mind. "Crime in the Streets," on Elgin Hour, had the bite of a good documentary as well as the challenging bark of theatricality. Sounding as if it had been scribbled down at white heat by an indignant social worker, the play was one long snarl from an urban slum. As a teen-ager bent on homicide, sullen John Cassavetes lounged through his role with all the prowling ease of a puma and not even his last-minute redemption could rub out the memory of his anarchic rage against society.

Eva Marie Saint is probably televiewers' favorite actress, as well as their own discovery, but this season they saw her only in three plays—the best of them, Paddy Chayefsky's "The Middle of the Night." Not top-grade Chayefsky, it nevertheless had tender moments in telling of a young girl's escape from the shambles of an adolescent marriage to the safe harbor of an older man's love. "Class of '58" was by Louis Peterson and dealt also with the storms and tumults of adolescence in following a day-long crisis in the life of a college freshman (Jack Mullaney) whose inchoate angers at the world and himself had got him dropped from school. On a happier note was David Shaw's "Sing Me Hearts and Flowers," a show-business comedy that chronicled the rise and separation of a TV team not too unlike Martin & Lewis. Joey Adams was brash and demanding as the wise-guy comedian, while Singer Johnny Desmond smoldered as the vocalist who was forced more and more to double as a straight man. Shaw's writing and the better-than-competent acting made Adams & Desmond equally believable whether showing their ineptitude as entertainers at the start of their careers or in punching over a funny routine when they were supposed to have arrived at stardom. All three of the above shows were on Philco-Goodyear Theatre.

At the season's end, two extremely effective plays by Wendell Mayes appeared within a period of three weeks on Pond's Theater. The first, "No Riders," was an hour-long story, almost without dialogue, that told of a truck driver's abandonment of the boozy, slattern wife who was forever mourning the death of their only child. On his last trip, the driver picks up a hitchhiker—a Mexican boy as innocent of English as the truck driver is of Spanish—and there grows between them the wordless affection of the mutually despairing, for the boy is as orphaned and bereft as the man. The play ends in guarded optimism: the truck driver returns home with the boy to find his wife making a desperate effort to fight off the bottle and restore some coherence to her life.

Mayes' second play, "Hang Up My Guns," showed the same economy with words and the same ability to make a phrase infinitely suggestible. The time was 1925, the place, somewhere in the Tennessee hills. The play opened with a double murder in a country store and the prime suspect was Odie Cox, the illiterate scion of a gaggle of moonshiners. Odie's Goliath of a father and two giant brothers come down from the mountain to hire diminutive lawyer Harry Townes for the defense. Here he comes, says one character of the lawyer, "like a little old mouse running interference for three grizzly bears."

Author Mayes and his lawyer protagonist find hillbillies sad and defenseless rather than loud and funny. Winning acquittal for Odie meant carrying the case to the Supreme Court but it was almost easier than persuading his family that they were living in the Twen-

Hiram Sherman, Harry Belafonte, Marge and Gower Chan

for Tonight"

tieth Century. The patriarchal head of the clan is allowed one homicidal rage and one fine speech lamenting the old days before he grudgingly concedes that the past is dead.

Revivals culled from every corner of the world's theatrical library are what keep TV drama going. This season rummaged deeper than ever into the shelves, and Omnibus may have come up with the most surprisingly effective revival of all: Sophocles' "Antigone." With Philip Bourneuf as Cleon and Beatrice Straight as the burning Antigone, the holocaust in ancient Thebes had more suspense, tension and clash of strong personalities—as well as more biting language—than TV screens had witnessed all year.

Few of the other revivals strayed back beyond 1900. Best of Broadway set out each month to dazzle viewers with hit shows and superlative casts, and at least succeeded in demonstrating that TV was capable of handling farce: Monty Woolley re-created his stage role in "The Man Who Came to Dinner" and it was his dominant and domineering personality that kept the comedy on the rails. The satellite roles were ably filled by Zasu Pitts, Merle Oberon, Joan Bennett, Reginald Gardner, Bert Lahr—a cast that must have made many a Broadway producer envious. The cast was also the thing in "Arsenic and Old Lace," where the comic chores were neatly dispatched by Helen Hayes, Billie Burke, Boris Karloff and Peter Lorre. The same rule of thumb held for the Producers' Showcase version of Clare Boothe Luce's "The Women." Even though considerably bowdlerized for family audiences, the play packed excitement as Ruth Hussey, Shelley Winters, Mary Astor, Nancy Olsen and Cathleen Nesbitt struggled for control of the manless screen.

Hallmark Hall of Fame brought Maurice Evans on for his annual presentation of Shakespeare—this time, "Macbeth." Evans is perhaps too slight physically for the role but, as always, he spoke the ringing lines with feeling and clarity. Judith Anderson's brooding intensity riveted the eye during the sleepwalking scene but the remainder of the cast, and especially the three Weird Sisters, were drowned in Highland mist.

Lux Video Theatre devoted itself mostly to sugarplums in the form of remakes of saccharine movies but offered a change of diet in two tart and appetizing instances—"The Heiress" and "Sunset Boulevard." Both were one-woman shows, with Marilyn Erskine touching the heart as the defeated Catherine Sloper in "The Heiress" and Miriam Hopkins having some big ravaged moments as the faded film star who still hears the clamor of her public.

"Darkness at Noon," presented by Producers' Showcase, made its

TV appearance under the highest political auspices. After Lee J. Cobb broke under the torture of David Wayne and Oscar Homolka and cried his *mea culpa* to the "people's court," the TV producers apparently had the uneasy feeling that not all their audience might be bright enough to grasp precisely what had happened. Any possibility that the show might be actually pro-Communist propaganda was neatly disposed of by a film trailer in which the nation's Vice President, Richard Nixon, carefully explained that "Darkness at Noon" was an anti-Communist play and that its lesson was that America "must be forever on guard against all its enemies, foreign and domestic."

Television, like Broadway, seems most at ease when serving up big, colorful musicals. This was the season of the TV spectacular— NBC's splashy, ninety-minute attempts to stun viewers with songs, dances, old plots and TV color. Since color sets throughout the nation numbered only 10,000, the addition of the rainbow to TV made not a bit of difference to most viewers.

The spectaculars had everything—and often too much of everything. Stars like Betty Hutton, Ann Sothern and Judy Holliday did their best to turn the shows into fascinating romps and they were bolstered by such diverse talents as France's Jeanmaire and Jacques Tati and Britain's Jeannie Carson and Jack Buchanan. Yet few of the shows turned out to be solidly satisfying from beginning to end. Almost all had something—a skit, a dance, a well-remembered song well sung—but too often the spectaculars foundered in a sea of musical comedy eyewash.

One happy exception was "Babes in Toyland," which struck just the right Christmassy chime and featured Jack E. Leonard as a superb villain forever foiled by Wally Cox, Dave Garroway, Dennis Day and a sensationally fine pair of clowns from England, the Coroli Brothers. Of the others, "Naughty Marietta" came closest to the mark with a swirl of exciting dances and a bravura handling of the love story by Alfred Drake and Patrice Munsel.

But TV's top musical came straight from Broadway. Mary Martin's "Peter Pan" threw a web of enchantment over an estimated 65 million viewers, and a gratified NBC announced that the show will become an annual TV Christmas feature. The entire cast—and, notably, Mary Martin, Cyril Ritchard and Cathy Nolan—were so *right* for television that most viewers could scarcely credit the report that "Peter Pan" was only a lukewarm Broadway success.

Not strictly a musical—in fact, not strictly anything fish, flesh or fowl—was the "Diamond Jubilee of Light," a two-hour program produced by Hollywood's veteran David O. Selznick and combining film, live drama and topical comment into a not especially unified, but vastly entertaining whole. The filmed segments included a lively excerpt from "Tom Sawyer"; an old and entrancing Robert Benchley short on the care and feeding of infants, and the dramatization of an inspirational-type John Steinbeck novelette. In the live numbers, comedian George Gobel made his first and lasting conquest of the TV audience with a brilliantly delivered monologue on electronic "brains"; Lauren Bacall and David Niven co-starred in a surprisingly successful adaptation of Irwin Shaw's memorable *New Yorker* story, "The Girls in Their Summer Dresses," while Helen Hayes and Thomas Mitchell gave a professional tug to viewers' heartstrings in a Max Shulman playlet. This form of TV extravaganza, for which there is no precise name—although "vaudeville" might do —may well be television's wave of the future. At any rate, for sheer entertainment the "Diamond Jubilee of Light" was topped last season only by "Peter Pan."

THE SEASON IN PICTURES

PHOTOGRAPHS

BARBARA BEL GEDDES AND BURL IVES IN "CAT ON A HOT TIN ROOF"

OUTSTANDING BROADWAY PERFORMANCES OF 1954-1955

TANI AND DRAN SEITZ IN "FANNY"

GEOFFREY HOLDER IN "HOUSE OF FLOWERS"

SKETCH BY WILLIAM AND JEAN ECKART FOR THE DUAL SET FOR "WEDDING BREAKFAST"

ELDON ELDER'S SET DESIGN FOR SKETCH ENTITLED "UPPER BIRTH" IN THE REVUE, "PHOENIX '55"

COSTUME SKETCHES BY MOTLEY FOR "PETER PAN"

PAUL NEWMAN, MALCOLM BRODRICK AND KARL MALDEN IN "THE DESPERATE HOURS"

ERNEST CLARK, HENRY CRAIG NESLO AND FRANCIS L. SULLIVAN IN "WITNESS FOR THE PROSECUTION"

DON AMECHE, HILDEGARDE NEFF AND GRETCHEN WYLER IN "SILK STOCKINGS"

GEORGE TOBIAS, JULIE NEWMAN, FORREST GREEN, TONY GARDELL AND DICK HUMPHREY IN "SILK STOCKINGS"

SKETCH FOR BORIS ARONSON'S SET FOR "BUS STOP"

SKETCH BY OLIVER MESSEL FOR THE SET FOR "HOUSE OF FLOWERS"

NANCY KELLY AND PATTY MCCORMACK IN "BAD SEED"

SHEILA BOND, BUDDY HACKETT AND DENNIS KING IN "LUNATICS AND LOVERS"

COSTUME SKETCH BY CECIL BEATON FOR "QUADRILLE"

JO MIELZINER'S SET DESIGN FOR "ALL SUMMER LONG"

CECIL BEATON'S SET FOR "QUADRILLE"

Barbara Bel Geddes and Burl Ives in "Cat on a Hot Tin Roof"

PATRICIA JESSEL
as Romaine in
"Witness for the Prosecution"

MAUREEN STAPLET
as Flora Meighan in
"27 Wagons Full of Cot

PAUL MUNI
as Henry Drummond in
"Inherit the Wind"

ED BEGLEY
as Matthew Harrison Brady in
"Inherit the Wind"

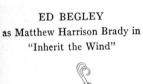

RAY WALSTON
as the Devil (Applegate
"Damn Yankees"

EUGENIE LEONTOVITCH
as the Dowager Empress in
"Anastasia"

CYRIL RITCHARD as Captain Hook in "Peter Pan"

PERFORMANCES 1954-1955

NANCY WALKER
in "Phoenix '55"

BURL IVES
as Big Daddy in
t on a Hot Tin Roof"

KIM STANLEY
as Cherie in
"Bus Stop"

GWEN VERDON
as Lola in
"Damn Yankees"

NASHA SKULNIK
as Noah in
he Flowering Peach"

JULIE ANDREWS
as Polly in
"The Boy Friend"

Photographed for LIFE by Gene Cook, © TIME, Inc.

Tani and Dran Seitz in "Fanny"

Photo by Zinn Arthur

Geoffrey Holder in "House of Flowers"

Sketch by William and Jean Eckart for

the dual set for "Wedding Breakfast"

Eldon Elder's set design for sketch entitled "Upper Birth" in the revue "Phoenix '55"

Costume sketch by Motley for "Peter Pan"

Costume sketch by Motley for "Peter Pan"

Michael Rennie and Karl Malden in "The Desperate Hours"

Cardin, Henry Craig Nesto and Francis L. Sullivan in "Witness for the Prosecution"

Photographed for LIFE by Cornell Capa, © TIME, Inc.

Don Ameche, Hildegarde Neff and Gretchen Wyler in "Silk Stockings"

Sketch for Boris Aronson's set for "Bus Stop"

Sketch by Oliver Messel for the
set for "House of Flowers"

Nancy Kelly and Patty McCormack in "Bad Seed"

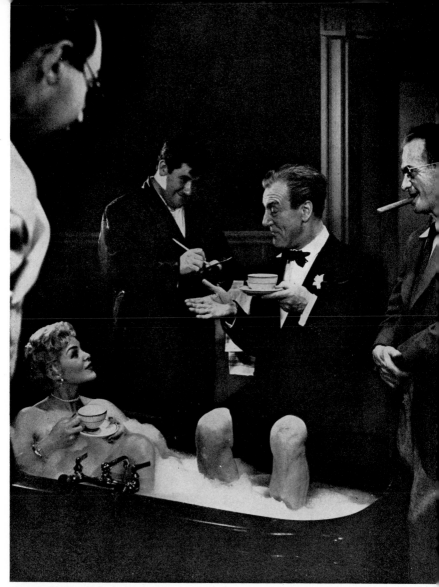

Sheila Bond, Buddy Hackett and Dennis King in "Lunatics and Lovers"

Costume sketch by Cecil Beaton for "Quadrille"

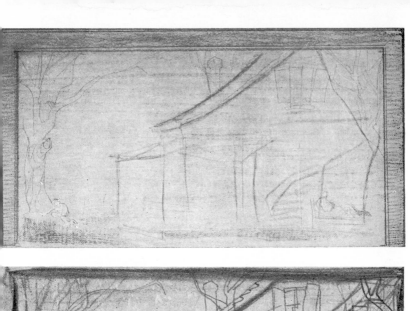

Jo Mielziner's set design for "All Summer Long"

Cecil Beaton's set for "Quadrille"

Sketch by Mordecai Gorelik for the set for "The Flowering Peach"

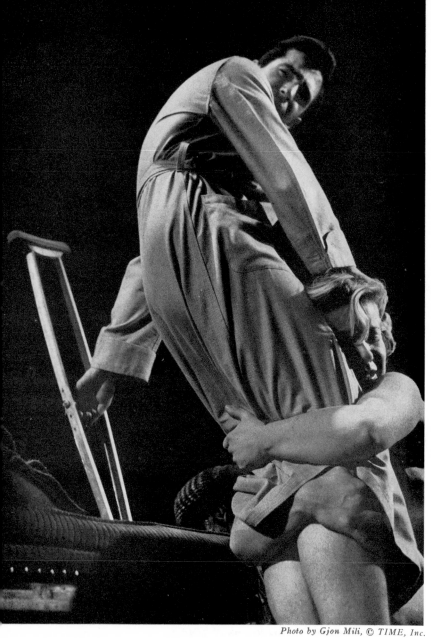

Ben Gazzara and Barbara Bel Geddes in "Cat on a Hot Tin Roof"

Kim Stanley in "Bus Stop"

Photo by Eileen Darley, GRAPHIC HOUSE, Inc.

THE TEN BEST PLAYS

THE BOY FRIEND *

A New Musical Comedy of the 1920s

BOOK, MUSIC AND LYRICS BY SANDY WILSON

[SANDY WILSON, *author, composer and lyricist, traded his given name of Alexander for the nickname Sandy, honoring his Scottish ancestry. He attended Harrow and graduated from Oxford, where he wrote his first show. He contributed revue material to "Slings and Arrows" and "Oranges and Lemons," as well as fashioning two complete revues, "See You Later" and "See You Again." He did the 1953 Edinburgh Festival Revue before writing "The Boy Friend," his first book show and the first of his things to be done in New York.*]

THE place and time are the French Riviera around 1926, when a musical-comedy drawing room would very likely boast a chic French maid 'alloing into a phone of the period. The drawing room is in Mme. Dubonnet's finishing school near Nice, and Hortense the maid, waving a feather duster over her lace-capped hair, is interrupted by her young charges while phoning the *costumier* about their carnival costumes.

Maisie, Dulcie, Fay and Nancy, all given to extreme animation, wag their bottoms and bandboxes and get hushed by Hortense: "Mamselles, Mamselles, 'ave you forgotten who you are?" "Forgotten who we are?" they breathily squeak. "Of course not." And they show they haven't by prancing and preening through their song: "Perfect Young Ladies"—their cloche hats down almost to their pretty noses, their belts and hemlines almost meeting at their knees. Hortense relieves them of their boxes, and swishes out herself, leaving the girls to their giggles and excitement over tonight's carnival.

Dulcie can't wait for the evening: "My frock is a dream."

FAY—So is mine! And rather daring too! I'm sure Madame Dubonnet will be furious.

MAISIE—Not she! I bet you she'll turn up in something frightfully shocking! (*They all laugh.*)

DULCIE—Do you think we shall be allowed out late?

MAISIE—Who cares? I intend to dance the whole night through!

FAY—Do you, Maisie? Who with?

MAISIE—Anyone who asks me!

DULCIE—Don't take any notice of her, girls. She'll dance all night with Bobby Van Husen, that terribly rich and good-looking American who's staying at the Negresco! (*Laughter.*)

MAISIE—Oh, no, I shan't! He bores me! (*She goes to the windows.*)

NANCY—Oh, isn't she the limit!

DULCIE—No wonder they call her Madcap Maisie!

It is Maisie, standing at the windows, who sees Polly Browne (pronounced P*o*ly) coming across the tennis court with a letter. The girls all greet Polly. Polly, a sweet girl in a simple frock, without a speck of jewelry, her blonde prettiness framed by marcelled dips over her forehead, has a gentle manner quite unlike her friends' flapper pertness. Polly listens patiently to Fay's and Dulcie's goings-on about their carnival costumes till Maisie stops them with: "Oh, be quiet, chaps. You know we'll all be jealous of Polly when she gets hers. What are you going as, Polly?

POLLY—I'm going as Pierrette.

FAY, DULCIE, MAISIE AND NANCY—Pierrette! How divine!

MAISIE—Now do tell us your secret, Polly.

POLLY—What secret?

MAISIE—Well, if you're going as Pierrette, who's going to be Pierrot?

"Oh—" hesitates Polly, her hands nervously fingering the letter, "I still want it to be a secret." She reads from the letter, however, that "he" says he's motoring down overnight—and should be there any moment. The girls are thrilled, and dying to know how he signs his letter . . . "Oh, do tell us about him, Polly," beg the girls, and the music obligingly starts so Polly may sing to them "The Boy Friend":

> Any girl who's reached the age
> Of seventeen or thereabout

Has but one desire in view.
She knows she has reached the stage
Of needing one to care about;
Nothing else will really do.
DULCIE—
Childhood games are left behind,
FAY—
And her heart takes wing,
MAISIE—
Hoping that it soon will find
GIRLS—
Just one thing.
POLLY—
We've got to have
We plot to have
For it's so dreary not to have
That certain thing called the Boy Friend.
POLLY AND GIRLS—
We scheme about
And dream about
And we've been known to scream about
That certain thing called the Boy Friend.
At the end of the second chorus, the Boys burst on, singing:

"Life without us is quite impossible
And devoid of all charms.
No amount of idle gossip'll
Keep them out of our arms."

Polly and the Girls admit they're blue without that certain thing called the "Boy Friend," and the Boys and Girls do a fast-stepping dance. When the dance and song are finished, Dulcie neatly clears the stage by saying: "Boys, boys, you know you're not allowed on the premises. You must leave at once." Yanking the action back to the main plot, Dulcie continues: "But you still haven't told us much about *him*, Polly." Fay joins in: "Not even his Christian name."

Madame Dubonnet's operatic singing off-stage before her entrance, gets Polly out of this tight spot. Madame, a striking-looking lady, her dress well fringed, the very essence of French sophistication, enters carrying a bouquet and a spare rose or two. *"Tiens! Tiens! mes enfants,"* she addresses them; then, to show she speaks both languages, reprimands them in English, and waves them off to the classroom. They all curtsy and depart—except Polly, who is stopped by Madame.

Madame Dubonnet wants to know if Polly is going to the ball, and when Polly hesitantly shows Madame her letter from Paris, Madame quickly inquires: "Then why is this letter postmarked from Nice?" "Nice? Oh! Oh dear!" cries Polly, bringing out her hanky.

MME. D. (*returning the letter*)—Do not worry, little Polly. Your secret is safe with me. *Voilà!* But just tell me one thing.

POLLY—Y-yes, Madame?

MME. D.—How does it happen that one so sweet and charming as you has to pretend to have a—how do you say?—boy friend and write herself love letters?

POLLY—It's because of my father, Madame.

MME. D.—Your father, *hein?*

POLLY—Yes. You see, when he dies, I shall be extremely wealthy, and he thinks that every man who makes advances to me is just after my fortune.

"So," says Madame, "he forbids you to have a boy friend?" That is why Polly must invent one? Polly stammers she's afraid so. "I see," says Madame. "Poor little rich girl! Well, I too have had a letter today—from your father. He is coming here this morning." "Daddy?" cries Polly. "Coming here?" He has been nearby on a business trip, and when he arrives Madame intends to have a word with him on Polly's behalf. Polly dries her eyes, just as Maisie pops in through the French windows: "Oh, *excusez-moi*, Madame," chirps Maisie. "*Je n'avais pas aucune idée que vous êtes ici.*" "That is all right, Mademoiselle Merryweather. I was about to go. (*To* POLLY.) *Soyez gaie, ma petite,* and trust in me." And Madame glides out.

Maisie is dying to know what Madame was telling Polly, and upon hearing that Polly's father is arriving any minute, she gasps: "What a thrill! Is he handsome as well as being rich?" "You wait and see," says delightful Polly as she exits laughing. Maisie calls to her to wait, she has to look for her missing dorothy bag. And she searches for the bag among the sofa pillows, giving handsome, blazer-decked Bobby Van Husen a chance to sneak in the window and take her unawares. His "Guess who?" draws a squeal from Maisie: "Bobby! You're crazy to come here! If Madame Dubonnet found out, I would be asked to leave under a cloud!" Bobby refuses to leave until Maisie promises one thing.

Maisie—Oh, and what is that, may I ask?

Bobby—Oh, you know as well as I do.

Maisie—Do I?

Bobby—Of course you do. I want you to promise to dance every dance at the ball tonight with me.

Maisie—That's out of the question.

Bobby—Oh, come on, Maisie, be a sport. You know there's no one else I want to dance with but you.

Maisie—Really? I don't believe it.

The music starts and Bobby sings "Won't You Charleston with Me?" while Maisie with coy reluctance listens, then wildly joins Bobby to "shake a leg" to "that old vodeodo." After the Charleston, and a kiss, Bobby confidently leaves, with Maisie waving him off: "Good-by!" she calls, then doing a double take: "Oh, he's gone! Bobby, Bobby, wait for me," and she runs through the windows after him, leaving the way clear for Hortense to show in Percival Browne.

Hortense leaves the pompous, gray-haired millionaire, to announce his arrival to Mme. Dubonnet. When Madame enters the room, she gives a vivid start, but then, all correctness, introduces herself. Percival is equally correct. Madame listens pleasantly to Percival's wishing he could see more of his motherless daughter . . . "but I'm so taken up with business, you know."

Mme. D.—Yes. I understand, Monsieur. But I am sure you would not put it before your daughter's happiness.

Percival—Polly's happiness? But she's perfectly happy, isn't she? She never complains in her letters.

Mme. D.—Oh, no, I am sure she does not. But there are certain things, Monsieur, which a young girl cannot discuss by post.

Percival—Oh? Such as what?

Mme. D.—Her heart, Monsieur.

Percival—Am I to take it, Madame, you are referring to love? I sincerely hope that nothing of that sort is allowed to occur in your school.

Mme. D. (*laughing*)—No, no. I do not encourage it on the premises, but—well, *les jeunes filles seront les jeunes filles, n'est-ce pas?*

Percival—I don't follow you, Madame.

Mme. D.—Surely you have not forgotten all your French, Monsieur Browne—or should I call you *mon petit* Percy?

Percival—What! (*Recognizing her.*) Good heavens! It can't be—!

Mme. D.—*Mais oui, mon cher,* it is. Do you not remember—your little Kiki!

Percival—Kiki. This is impossible! Most awkward—!

Mme. D.—But this is no way to greet an old friend. After all we have been to each other? Have you forgotten Armistice night in Maxim's, when you—?

Percival—Yes, Madame, I have. Completely forgotten!

Mme. D.—But surely not, *chéri!* I wore a red dress, and—you were in uniform. I called you my Tiny Tommy, and we drank champagne. Later on we danced and the orchestra played a waltz which was all the rage in Paris. Let me see, how did it go?

The lights dim appropriately, as the orchestra shows how the waltz went, with Madame singing "Fancy Forgetting." Percival loosens up enough to do a ramrod version of a waltz with Madame, his hand behind her head, his manner reminiscent of all ballroom dance teams. They conclude their song:

> "Though the years go by
> And our youth is gone,
> Memories don't die,
> Like a song they linger on.

> "So just when I thought you'd remember it too
> Fancy, just fancy you forgetting."

Madame is about to kiss Percival when the girls are heard close by, so she offers to show him the school instead. *"Allons,"* says Madame. "This way . . . *mon petit chou!"* "Oh!" says the ever-startled Percy.

Enter the giggling girls with Polly. Dulcie urges the girls to leave Polly alone to wait for her father, whom the girls breathily call "him." Left alone, Polly sadly tears up her letter, drops it out of the window, turns away with a sob, and sits down on the sofa, at the exact moment that Tony, in messenger's uniform, a large box under his arm, appears at the French windows. His cough and *"excusez-moi"* startle Polly. Tony apologizes. "I'm afraid I came in the wrong way. This is the Villa Caprice, isn't it?"

Polly—Yes.

Tony—Well, I have a package here for Miss Polly Browne.

Polly—Really? How funny!

Tony—Funny? Why?

Polly—Because I'm Polly Browne.

Tony—Well, it's a very pretty name.
Polly—Oh, thank you.
Tony—And you live up to it.
Polly—Oh!

Tony promptly apologizes for forgetting himself, and gives her the box, assuring her that she and her costume will be the prettiest at the ball. It is love at first sight. Tony turns to go.

Polly—You're—you're English, aren't you?
Tony—Yes, as a matter of fact, I am.
Polly—You don't seem like a messenger boy somehow.
Tony—Don't I? Well, to tell you the truth, I don't usually do this sort of thing, but just at the moment, I'm afraid I'm rather on my beam ends.
Polly—Oh, what a shame! And at Carnival Time, too.

Polly hesitantly offers her extra ticket to Tony. . . . "Oh dear, you must think me terribly forward."

Tony—No, I don't. I think you're terribly—
Polly—Yes?

Tony starts the number "I Could Be Happy with You," Polly joins in, and together they sing:

> I could be happy with you,
> If you could be happy with me.
> Polly—
> I'd be contented to live anywhere.
> What would I care,
> As long as you were there?
> Tony—
> Skies may not always be blue
> Polly—
> But one thing is clear as can be.
> Tony—
> I know that I could be happy with you,
> My darling,
> Both—If you could be happy with me. . . .

They dance, at the end of which Tony places Polly on a hassock. From this perch she whistles him on in his tap dance. For the final chorus, she steps down and they perform in the style of the old three-a-day, ending up with Polly once more on the hassock and Tony's arm about her.

POLLY—Then you will come to the ball?
TONY—Well, I'll try. I'll have to see about a costume.

But how can he let her know? Polly thinks out loud: "I'll be on the Plage at three o'clock this afternoon—beside the bandstand." Tony agrees to be there, and says, "Good-by till then!" When he leaves, suddenly it dawns on her: "And I don't even know his name."

Madame Dubonnet enters with Percival, and simultaneously the girls drift on to witness Polly's meeting with her father. From his arms she cries out how happy she is.

PERCIVAL—Are you, my dear? I'm very glad to hear it!
MAISIE—Has he arrived yet, Polly?
POLLY—Yes, he's arrived! He's really arrived!

The Boys of the chorus then arrive to join in the reprise of "The Boy Friend," and it all ends with Rockette kicks, and Hortense on the sofa waving a feather duster above the heads of the dancers.

ACT II

The Plage that same afternoon has the sea for a backdrop, the promenade in the forefront, and a palm tree somewhere about. The Girls are dressed for swimming in one-piece bathing suits, their hips swathed with bandannas, their heads tied with bandeaux. The Boys lend tone in white flannels, and Boys and Girls sing and dance: "Sur La Plage."

Lord Brockhurst, a jolly, jumpy, monocled British aristocrat, enters accompanied by his austere Lady. Lord B. has his eye on the Girls, while Lady B. longs for Bognor, all the more as she sees the effect of the Riviera on her husband. How can he go around ogling girls after "their loss"?

LORD B.—Now, now, Hilda, don't take on so! After all, Tony isn't dead, is he?
LADY B.—He might as well be. Sometimes when I think of the disgrace, I would rather he were.
LORD B.—Oh, come now! After all, the boy has done nothing wrong.

LADY B.—Nothing wrong? Disappearing from Oxford in the middle of Hilary term, ruining a brilliant career! Why, they won't even consider him for the constituency now!

Lord B. has difficulty keeping his mind on his son's penniless plight when Dulcie, Nancy and Fay prance by. Though he is forced to find his wife a sheltered chair, he manages a quick pinch before he goes after it.

Dulcie asks: "Well, who's for a dip?" The others are ready, but Polly—clad in chiffon and carrying a picture hat—strolls on, and confesses she is about to meet "him." The girls exit giggling, while Polly anxiously waits half a second for Tony.

He arrives, wearing the correct flannels and blazer, and full of good news: he will be able to have a costume from Monsieur Gaston's. Polly is overjoyed. Tony confesses to being nervous, because, after all, he is just a messenger boy and she is one of the Villa Caprice rich young ladies.

POLLY—Rich? Oh, I'm not rich. You see—I just work there as Madame Dubonnet's secretary.

TONY—Do you honestly? Then we're not so different after all.

POLLY—No.

TONY—I'm so glad. I thought you would only like the grand life—you know, big cars, diamonds and champagne.

POLLY—Oh no. I'm quite content with simple things.

TONY—How ripping. So am I . . .

The lights dim as Tony starts to sing of the simple life he longs for. Polly sits listening, her eyes straight ahead on some distant point.

> "All I want is a room
> In Bloomsbury.
> Just a room that will do
> For you and me.
> One room's enough for us.
> Though it's on the top floor.
> Life may be rough for us
> But it's a trouble we'll ignore.
> On a wint'ry night
> I'll light a fire,
> Everything I shall do
> As you desire. . . ."

Julie Andrews and

"The Boy Friend"

They are sure:

> "In our attic
> We'll be ecstatic
> As lovebirds up in a tree.
> All we want is a room in Bloomsbury."

Tony soft-shoes as Polly mimes all the domestic things she'd be doing in that attic room. What with cooking, knitting and sewing, she will keep pretty busy. When the song is over, and they are about to kiss, Hortense arrives. She is horrified that one of her charges should think of kissing a messenger boy. Polly quickly takes her aside to explain: "Dear Hortense, don't betray me. I know he is just a messenger boy; but he is doing it because he is poor, and I'm sure that in reality he is as well born as I am." "Perhaps so," Hortense admits. "But he has no right to make advances to a young lady like yourself in his present condition." Polly pleads with Hortense not to let anyone know. . . . "I am so happy to have an admirer who isn't just interested in my wealth. Surely you must know how I feel?" Hortense softens: "But if Madame Dubonnet should find out—" Polly cries: "Oh, she won't. That is, unless *you* tell her," and Hortense promises that she won't.

Hearing the gay laughter of her friends, Polly urges Tony to leave: she can't risk the chance of being seen with him. "All right, Polly," says Tony. "Let's nip over to the promenade." They take so long nipping, what with Polly's last-minute reminder to Hortense, that Dulcie and Fay and the Boys have difficulty not bumping into them. Dulcie still wonders out loud: "I say, wasn't that Polly?" Fay is sure it was. . . . "I recognized her frock."

The Girls next discover Hortense—who has been right under their noses all this while. They wheedle, they tease, they implore her to tell them about Polly and her beau; they even try to bribe her with things like sachets and crocheted flowers. *"Taisez-vous,* mademoiselles," says Hortense. "It is not seemly to be so curious about a young man!" Marcel slyly suggests that Hortense isn't so prim as she pretends. Dulcie and Fay and Nancy all rush to her defense: "Of course she isn't! After all, she is French." "Yes, I am," says Hortense. "And I am very proud of it, too." And Hortense sings her song: "It's Nicer in Nice," with its quota of "oo la la's"; then she finishes her dance in a daring attitude, supported by the Boys.

When warned of Madame Dubonnet's approach, the Boys and Girls and Hortense swiftly leave, so Madame can vamp Percival in private. She is attired for this, and a swim, in a slinky black bathing suit, a black turban, and a casual white cape. She waves a long cigarette holder. Still Percival is very reluctant: he doesn't want to swim, and tries to keep "Kiki" at arm's length. Madame is clearly coming off the winner as she goes off to find him a suit. Percival, still on his dignity, must now deal with his skittish fellow-Briton, Lord Brockhurst. That jolly old boy thinks Percy knows the ropes with these French women. . . . "I'm a stranger here, you see, and what's more—(*Whispers.*)—I've got the wife in tow. She's not a bad sort really, but—*she doesn't understand me.*"

PERCY—I'm afraid I can't assist you in your domestic affairs.

LORD B.—I don't want assistance in my domestic affairs. It's foreign affairs I'm talking about! (*Laughing as before.*) Now come on, old chap, we Englishmen abroad must stick together, you know.

PERCY—Yes, of course.

LORD B.—Now, what about this little lady you were dallying with just now? She seems a sporty little filly!

PERCY—Sporty little filly! Really, sir, I must ask you to control your language. That lady is a highly esteemed member of the community.

LORD B.—Oh yes, yes, I'm sure she is. They manage these things so much better in France.

PERCY—She is, sir, a head mistress.

LORD B.—I say! you *are* in luck, aren't you?

Madame Dubonnet returns in triumph to a Percy who peevishly refuses the suit she offers. Lord Brockhurst is dying to get into the act, and is beginning to have some luck with Madame when Lady B. enters, brings him up sharp—"Hubert! Remember we are British!" —and drags him off.

Percy continues to be stuffy till Madame cries out in exasperation: "Oh, you are what you call—a damp blanket! You spoil all the fun." "It's high time," Percy reminds her, "you realized that things are very different from what they were." Rather resignedly Madame seats herself and sings—smack at the audience—"You Don't Want to Play with Me Blues"—to which Percy does a rigid, finger-snapping solo, joining deadpan in the refrain:

> Oh dear,
> I've got the you-don't-want-to-play-with-me blues.
> Don't-want-to-play-with-me blues.

MME. D.—
> It's clear
> I've got the you-don't-want-to-stay-with-me blues

PERCY—
  Don't-want-to-stay-with-me blues.
MME. D.—
  I am so good
  At spreading mirth and joy.
  But it's no good
  With such a sulky boy.

  I try
  To play the games the other fellows all choose
PERCY—
  The other fellows all choose . . .

Madame sings and the Girls dance in, lively as ever, making Percy's dance seem all the prissier.

At the end of the number, Percy, Madame and the Girls quickly leave. Maisie now has her innings with Bobby. Tossing her head and highly flirtatious, she tries to make him jealous. . . . "Because I want to have a good time while I'm young," she wiggles: "After all, I am only seventeen." "But I can give you a good time," protests Bobby: "It's not as if I hadn't got plenty of cash." "Money," remarks Maisie, "isn't everything," and starts waving at the other boys as they pass, promising to dance with them. "Maisie!" cries Bobby. "Listen to me!" "Listen to all of us!" cry Marcel, Pierre and Alphonse, as they go into the song: "Safety in Numbers," with Maisie joining in to remind them:

  Now listen, boys, you should recall
  I've often said I love you all
BOYS—
  You love us all?

MAISIE—
  Yes, I love you all

  It's time you learned
  That I'm no fool
  Where love's concerned
  I stick to this rule . . .

and, jamming a yachting cap over her curls, she struts and shouts and does some high kicks to drum beats:

> "There's safety in numbers,
> That's what I believe
> The girl who knows
> A lot of beaux
> Is never likely to grieve.
> The lady who slumbers
> Is left high and dry.
> But I'm awake
> And never miss
> The chance to take
> Another kiss
> There's safety in numbers
> And the more the merrier am I. . . ."

At the end she does a Harriet Hoctor toe dance and adagio with the Boys.

When the coast is clear, Tony signals Polly to come back. They plan to meet at the Café Pataplon at nine P.M. "Yes, and it's going to be a wonderful evening," says Tony fondly. In fact, "it's just the first of lots of wonderful evenings—isn't it?" Polly expects so. "But why shouldn't it be?" he asks. "Remember what you said this morning?" "What did I say?" Polly inquires.

> "I could be so happy with you
> If you could be happy with me . . ."

Polly remembers:

> "I'd be contented to live anywhere.
> What would I care
> As long as you were there?"

At the end of the reprise, she gives Tony permission to kiss her—at which point Lord and Lady Brockhurst come on and see them. Lady B. becomes highly agitated; a crowd quickly gathers; a gendarme conveniently strolls by. Tony sees the English couple and tells Polly, "I—I've got to hop it, Polly—quickly." He can't explain now, "I'll—I'll see you tonight"—and off he starts as Lord Brockhurst calls for the gendarme to "Stop that man!" As Tony is pursued, poor Polly hears Marcel say: "It is the rich milord Brockhurst and his wife. They seem to be chasing a thief."

POLLY (*in soliloquy*)—A thief! Oh no, it couldn't be. (*Music.*) And yet they are rich. And he is penniless—he told me so himself—

oh dear, he must have known all along that I am not a working girl but a millionaire's daughter. Oh dear! He's just like all the rest. (*She breaks down.*)

DULCIE (*running over to her*)—Polly? Did he steal something from you today?

POLLY—Yes, Dulcie, he did.

DULCIE—Not your gold bangle?

POLLY—Not my gold bangle. Something much more precious.

MME. D. (*coming to* POLLY)—What is the matter, *ma petite?* You look quite pale.

HORTENSE (*joining them*)—I think I can explain, Madame. That man was Monsieur . . .

POLLY—No, Hortense! You promised!

MME. D.—But what is it, Polly?

POLLY—It's nothing, Madame. I'm just a little disappointed, that's all. You see, I shan't be going to the Carnival Ball after all . . .

And Polly and the crowd sing the reprise of "I Could Be Happy with You" in sorrow, though the sunlight breaks through as the curtain falls.

ACT III

On the terrace of the Café Pataplon that night, the Carnival is in progress amidst gaiety, giggles and drink. Lord Brockhurst staggers more than usual, and Hortense is all done up in her version of the simple peasant Sunday-best. The Girls and Boys hear from Hortense that Polly is determined not to come to the ball. "Oh, what a frost!" exclaims Maisie. "Now we shall never know who her boy friend is." But Madame, in sequins and plumed headgear, makes such a sensational entrance that Polly, for the moment, is forgotten.

Percival Browne, in dinner jacket and cocked hat, says he feels like a fool. Madame assures him he looks *"ravissant"* and urges him to have some champagne. Percy now begins to feel better, but says, "I'd feel happier if I knew how Polly is. She seemed so miserable this afternoon."

MME. D.—She is in love, *pauvre petite!*

PERCIVAL—In love? Do you honestly believe that?

MME. D.—Yes, *mon vieux,* I do. It takes a woman to understand these things.

PERCIVAL—I'm beginning to believe you're right. Perhaps Polly misses her mother more than I realized.

MME. D.—Every girl needs a mother when she is young.

PERCIVAL—I have been selfish, Kiki. I have neglected Polly. When she needed comfort, I was far away. So she turned instead to you. For that I shall always be grateful to you.

Music starts up, *their* music, and Madame Dubonnet says, "It was nothing. You know, sometimes I feel as if little Polly were like my own daughter." "She could be, Kiki, she could be—" murmurs Percy, starting to waltz with Madame.

MME. D.—Do you remember the dear old waiter with the red nose?

PERCIVAL—And the fat lady behind the counter who went to sleep and snored?

MME. D.—And you said—(*Music finis.*) you said you wanted the night to go on forever.

PERCIVAL—Kiki, give me that champagne.

MME. D.—So you are beginning to remember.

PERCIVAL—Yes, Kiki, I am beginning to remember. (*Music.*)

After a toss of his champagne glass, Percy and Madame do an intense bit of dancing to "Fancy Forgetting," with Percy ending the dance in a back-breaking embrace. They depart.

Bobby and Maisie take over. Bobby has reached the point of proposing to Maisie, who registers her delight with another wiggle, but insists on time to think it over. . . . "Until—until midnight tonight. I'll let you know then. I promise." And Maisie joins her girl friends, who, oddly enough, have all been proposed to. "Poor boys!" they all happily say. "We've got them on tenterhooks." And they all copy Maisie, refusing to give their answer till midnight. "At midnight? But it is so long to wait!" wails Marcel. Pierre decides: "They are just torturing us, *ces jeunes filles.*" Bobby agrees, knowing Maisie put them up to it. Philosophically he suggests how to pass the time: "We can dance." And Bobby and Maisie start "The Riviera":

BOBBY AND MAISIE—
   When trouble troubles you
   The only thing to do
   Is dance, you simply gotta dance.
BOYS AND GIRLS—
   And if you've had a tiff,
   You'll soon forget it, if

You dance, you simply gotta dance.
Here in the South of France
They've got a new step.
It's quite the cutest dance
Invented to step,
So do step.
GIRLS—
Wriggle your hips and kick up your heels
BOYS—
You'll be surprised how lovely it feels
GIRLS—
Everybody's doing the Riviera.
BOYS—
Waggle your fingers, wiggle your toes,
Just how it started nobody knows.
BOYS AND GIRLS—
Everybody's doing the Riviera.
Multimillionaires and their little pets do it
Even maiden ladies who wear lorgnettes
Have taken to it.

Tell ev'ryone to give out the news.
This is the way to shake off the blues.
Ev'rybody's doing the Riviera.

The five couples then show how it's done, in a snappy dance, that turns into a strenuous snake line. After this excitement is over, Hortense, drawn to the champagne, sees Tony. She stops him before he can get away, and gets his promise that if she can persuade Polly to come, he'll be at the ball. Tony then dances off with the parcel he's carrying, and Hortense goes in search of Polly.

The Boys and Girls come merrily on, followed by Lord Brockhurst, wild for fun. When Dulcie slaps her Boy, and is left behind, Lord Brockhurst considers this an opening. Dulcie is fed up with boys. "With boys?" says Lord Brockhurst. "Well, then, why not try something older?" "Something older?" wonders Dulcie in her cracked squeak. "Yes, like me, for instance," says Lord Brockhurst and starts:

"It's Never Too Late to Fall in Love"

LORD B.—
I may be too old to run a mile

DULCIE—
  Run a mile.
LORD B.—
  Yes, run a mile,
  But there's one thing I still do very well.
  I may be too old to climb a stile
DULCIE—
  Climb a stile?
LORD B.—
  Yes, climb a stile,
  But there's one thing at which I still excel.
  Although my hair is turning gray,
DULCIE—
  Yes, it's rather gray,
LORD B.—
  I still believe it when I say
DULCIE—
  Well, what do you say?
LORD B.—
  It's never too late to have a fling,
  For autumn is just as nice as spring,
  And it's never too late to fall in love.
DULCIE—
  Boop a Doop, Boop a Doop, Boop a Doop.

Lord B. repeats more such sentiments, echoed by Dulcie with shivers and shakes. The Boys and Girls come in to lend a cheery: "Whack a Do, Whack a Do, Whack a Do," and then Dulcie has her innings:

  The modern artists of today
  May paint their pictures faster
  But when it comes to skill I say
LORD B.—
  You can't beat an old master.

  It's never too late to bill and coo
DULCIE—
  At any age one and one make two
LORD B.—
  And it's never too late to fall in
DULCIE—
  Never too late to fall in

LORD B.—
  Never too late to fall in
DULCIE—
  Love.

After Dulcie squeaks "Love," the two do their encore of song and dance. Lady Brockhurst comes on her happy husband just as he is about to get a kiss: "Hubert!" Lord Brockhurst knows when he's licked: "Oh Lord, the wife!" Then he tells Dulcie to run along like a good girl, and as she blows him a kiss and obeys, he can't resist an exuberant kick.

As Lord Brockhurst settles his Lady at a table and orders champagne to quiet her, all the Boys and Girls assemble just in time for Polly's sad, pretty entrance as Pierrette. "So she's come to the ball after all. Poor child," says her father. "How sad she looks." Madame takes over, and leads Polly to a table. Lady Brockhurst, recognizing her as the girl who was with Tony, wishes to speak to her, but Polly is surrounded by her solicitous friends. Lady B. is further prevented by a roll of drums announcing a "Carnival Tango" that Dancers Pepe and Lolita perform with whip cracks in the Valentino manner.

When it is over, Hortense edges up to Madame to whisper of Mamselle Browne: ". . . I fear she is wishing to leave the ball already, but if you can persuade her to stay, I do not think she will regret it." Madame promises to do what she can, and, approaching Polly and Percy, says: "You do not wish to dance, Polly?"

PERCIVAL—I have already asked her myself, but she prefers not to.
MME. D.—Never mind. The night is still young. Let you and I have a little talk together.
POLLY—Very well, Madame. (PERCIVAL goes upstage.)
MME. D.—You know, Polly, when I look at you in that sweet costume, you remind me of a song I knew when I was a child.
POLLY—Do I? Can you sing it?
MME. D.—Yes, I think so.

And Madame sings with operatic gestures: "Poor Little Pierrette" as Polly sits and looks straight ahead with great sweetness. In the final choruses, Polly clasps hands with Madame and adds piercing trills.

At the end of the number, there is much bustling and excitement, as all the other couples enter and stand about. Then Tony enters, dressed as Pierrot. Hortense is all excited, Madame says: "Look, Polly! Pierrot has not forgotten after all!" Polly says: "Oh!"

The orchestra plays: "I Could Be Happy with You" as Tony peers into masked face after masked face, until he finally discovers Polly. She doesn't know who he is.

TONY—Perhaps this will remind you. (*He kisses her.*)
POLLY—It isn't—it isn't.
TONY (*removing his mask*)—Yes, Polly, it's me.

Lady Brockhurst cries: "Hubert! It's Tony! We've found him at last." The parents embrace their son, as Percival asks indignantly: "And who, may I ask, is this young man?" Lord Brockhurst draws on his forgotten dignity: "This, sir, is my son, the Honorable Tony Brockhurst." Polly can say nothing more than: "Oh." But Lady Brockhurst would like to know who the young woman is. "This, madam, is my daughter. And I am Percival Browne." Tony is amazed, but willing to forgive Polly her deception.

It is now time for Percival to announce that Madame Dubonnet has consented to be his wife and for the Girls to announce to the Boys that "After due consideration we have come to the conclusion that the answer is unanimously—yes!"

Everyone Charlestons to the chorus of "The Boy Friend," and the curtain comes down as they all sing "I Could Be Happy with You."

THE LIVING ROOM *

A Drama in Two Acts and Four Scenes

BY GRAHAM GREENE

[*Following his graduation from Oxford University* GRAHAM GREENE *worked briefly on the Nottingham "Journal." Later he became sub-editor of the London "Times" and while working there wrote his first novel in 1906. It was in this year that he became a Catholic and married a Catholic girl. His first really successful novel was "The Orient Express," which Hollywood shaped into a movie, as it did his "This Gun for Hire," "Confidential Agent," "The Third Man" and others. His works all reflect his concern with his status as a Roman Catholic writer. British reviewers hailed "The Living Room" as "the best first play of a generation."*]

THE scene is the living room of an ordinary South Kensington house. The room, strangely enough, is at the top of the house, of an unusual shape, low-ceilinged, and oddly furnished. And at one end of the room (opposite the door that opens on the landing) is a small flight of steps leading to a closed door.

Mary, the maid of all work, enters looking for someone; then clomps down the many steps to answer the ring of the door bell. All this goes on while running water can be heard through the closed door at the top of the small flight of steps.

Once again Mary enters: With her, this time, is Michael Dennis, a man in his middle forties with a lean, anxious look. At his side is a twenty-year-old girl, Rose Pemberton, who has the look "of being not quite awake, a bewildered tousled-pillow face, a face which depends for its prettiness on youth. . . ." The couple is left alone, to stand stiffly, and a bit apart, as the maid goes for her mistress, Miss Browne.

Michael, to make conversation, comments on the oddness of the room. He even tries the door at the top of the steps, then returns to the exact spot where he'd been standing: "Locked. The Browne family's skeleton. Browne with an E. Well, haven't you anything to say? Some joke? Something to show that we don't really care a damn?" Rose mutely shakes her head, as Michael goes on: "Well, I've delivered you safely. The reliable family friend. You are only twelve hours late. And we sent the right, considerate telegrams. The orphan is safe. But they wouldn't have worried. You were in *my hands*." Rose yearns to touch him, but Michael clasps her hand, having her stand just as before, warning her to be careful . . . "You can always trust me to be very careful. I've reached the careful age." He then asks Rose to admire his arrangements for the night before, with their rooms ostensibly at opposite ends of the corridor. Rose implores him not to go on so: "Isn't it bad enough, dar-ling . . . ?" That's a word she mustn't use, Michael warns her. "Dear," however, is safe for a married man of his age. Rose, in-sisting that anyone coming upstairs can be heard, kisses him. At this precise moment, the key in the closed door turns, and a little old lady emerges and comes down the steps. Miss Teresa Browne, "who must have passed seventy a long while ago . . . ," now walks past the two startled people, not paying the slightest attention to them. They might have not been there.

Miss Teresa continues through the door, out on the landing and down a few steps. Then she starts coming back. All the while Mi-chael and Rose worry. Rose thinks the old lady might have heard their talk, with Michael hoping: "There wasn't anything to hear." Teresa now re-enters, armed with a proper smile of greeting, and outstretched hand.

TERESA—My dear, you must be Rose. Mary never told me you'd arrived.

ROSE (*kissing her*)—And you are Aunt Helen. Or do I have to call you Great Aunt?

TERESA—I'm Aunt Teresa, dear.

ROSE—How silly of me.

TERESA—Not silly after all these years. You were only six, weren't you?

ROSE—Only six. This is Mr. Dennis, Aunt Teresa.

TERESA—I'm interested to meet you, Mr. Dennis. My niece men-tioned you often in her letters.

ROSE (*to* MICHAEL)—My mother.

MICHAEL—Of course. I hope you don't think, Miss Browne, that I've let down your trust already.

TERESA—I don't know what you mean, Mr. Dennis. Trust?

MICHAEL—We're twelve hours late. It seemed sensible to catch an early morning train instead of traveling after the funeral.

TERESA—I was so sorry not to be there, dear. But I couldn't leave your uncle and your Aunt Helen. You found a room in the village, I hope, Mr. Dennis?

MICHAEL—Oh, yes. The Red Lion.

TERESA—Mass was said for your mother this morning, dear, by Father Turner.

ROSE—Oh, I'm so sorry. I didn't know. I should have been there.

TERESA—We were all there—even my brother. We remembered you with her. Are you a Catholic, Mr. Dennis?

MICHAEL (*abruptly*)—No.

TERESA—How odd that my niece should have left you her executor.

ROSE (*with asperity*)—Why not? My father wasn't a Catholic.

"No, dear," commiserates Teresa. "Poor man." She wonders whether Mr. Dennis would like a cup of tea. He really wouldn't, but Teresa has the idea: "A laborer deserves his hire." And goes down all those stairs to see about the afternoon tea.

"Well," says Michael lamely, "we've broken the ice. That's not a good phrase, is it, for a pair of people skating like we are?"

ROSE—Darling, what are you worrying about? Me? You don't have to. I swear it. (*With a touch of bitterness.*) I loved you the night of my mother's funeral. That's an oath, isn't it, like mixing blood. For ever and ever. Amen.

MICHAEL—Oh, it's myself I'm worrying about. I'm afraid you're going to disappear. In a wood of old people. I'm afraid I'm losing you—the minutes are hurrying. What happens tomorrow? (*He moves around the room while she stays still but rather at a loss, in the center of it.*)

ROSE—You don't have to worry. You can't lose me. After all, you're the *e*xecutor.

MICHAEL—You mean the ex*e*cutor. Yes, I suppose I can always see you on business. She came from up here. (*He opens the closet door.*) It just doesn't make sense. The third floor. A bathroom leading out of the sitting room. This must have been a bedroom. (*Shuts door.*)

Miss Helen Browne, whose false, fat-woman jolliness is immediately apparent, now enters. "Young Rose," she says heartily, and kisses her niece. "My dear little sweetheart I used to call you" . . . and as she shakes hands with Michael Dennis, she adds: "Oh, you wouldn't believe what a bad little sweetheart she could be sometimes." And, without further ado, suggests that Rose give her Aunt Teresa a hand with the tea. Even though Rose has no idea where to go, this is clearly an order.

Rose looks at Michael: "I'll see you . . . ?" Helen assumes Mr. Dennis is staying for tea. And Michael, however unwillingly, must stay, just as Rose must go downstairs. Helen, firmly settling herself in the room's one comfortable chair, asks Michael—after Rose goes —all about the funeral. She's all ears, she says: "The Brownes all have long ears, like the Flopsy Bunnies. You know the Flopsy Bunnies, Mr. Dennis?" He does not. "Not dear Beatrix Potter? But of course she was my generation," says Helen Browne. "I saw her once shopping at Debenham's. Now, I'd expected you—somehow—to be an older man."

MICHAEL—I'm forty-five. (*He sits unwillingly.*)

HELEN—Catholics are much too clanny sometimes, don't you think? Dear Teresa was quite surprised when my niece chose someone who wasn't a Catholic as a trustee.

MICHAEL—I was her husband's friend, you know—his pupil, too. I owe everything to him. Even my job now—at London University.

HELEN—You'll think us rather bigoted but we never cared very much for poor John's profession. It would have been so awkward for my niece if it had been—condemned.

MICHAEL—I'm afraid you won't approve of my profession then— but I'm a mere *lecturer* in psychology. Not a professor.

HELEN—Oh, well, of course, it doesn't matter about you, does it, Mr. Dennis? We aren't concerned. And the will? We've no details yet. (*Coyly.*) Long ears again.

Michael tells of the modest sum of money that will be coming to Rose at twenty-five, until which time he and James Browne will serve as trustees. It is obvious, though she tries not to show it, that Helen feels it's for the family to handle such matters. Michael is as explicit as possible: "You see, her father appointed me a trustee before he died, and Mrs. Pemberton just let it stand. His friends were always her friends. I used to visit them every summer after his death." Helen thinks sadly: "She was the first Browne to marry a non-Catholic." Michael is amused: "The first *Browne?*" Helen is not amused: "The first of our Brownes. And you are the executor too, Mr. Dennis?" Michael quickly explains that this was the lawyers' idea, and as soon as the will is executed, he will resign both roles. Helen clearly thinks this a fine idea.

Off on another tack, Helen confides that they were a bit anxious about Rose, till Michael's wire arrived. Again, Michael explains all about the post-funeral fatigue, and the morning train. Helen mentions casually that it must have been lonely in the house for Rose. Again, Michael tells of taking a room for himself at the Red Lion. "So right of you, Mr. Dennis," says Helen. "In a village like that there'd have been a lot of silly talk if you'd stayed in the house."

"Even about a man of my age and a girl of hers?"

Helen answers: "Human nature's such a terrible thing, Mr. Dennis. Or is that very Roman of me?" Michael refuses to find it terrible . . . : "Complicated, tangled, perhaps unhappy. Needing help." But Michael's attention is much more on the room than the conversation. Finally Helen asks him why he is staring. "It looks quite a big house from outside," Michael answers, still trying to find out why this is the only living room. "A great many of the rooms are closed," is Helen's tight reply. "War damage?" Michael persists. "For one reason or another," is all he gets out of her.

Teresa, entering with a cake stand, announces tea will be ready in a moment. Michael is torn between wanting to get out and wanting to see Rose again before he goes. And is somewhat startled by Teresa's: "What a good thing you're a careful man, Mr. Dennis." Teresa goes on: "That's what you were telling Rose, wasn't it? 'You can always trust me,' you said, 'to be very careful.' I thought it was so sweetly put." "Well," he answers, "an executor has to be careful —or he goes to jail." "You should really see my brother," says Helen, "about all those legal things. Rose is too young to understand. Dear little sweetheart. Teresa, if Rose is tired, tell her to lie down. We can entertain Mr. Dennis." But Rose, entering with the tea things, refuses to be dismissed. So she and Michael are trapped into sitting silently in the stiff chairs while Helen goes for her brother. Teresa pours tea and does most of the talking: "I started a novena for you as soon as I heard of your poor mother." Rose is grateful; and when Teresa continues: "I expect you'd like to go to Mass tomorrow. It's the second of nine we've arranged for her. Mary doesn't come in till eight-thirty, but we'll wake you ourselves." Rose thanks her again.

Teresa hopes Rose won't mind sleeping in the living room, since they are so very cramped for space . . . "So many rooms are closed." Rose is willing, but Michael can't resist finding out *why* so many rooms are closed. Teresa proves quite as evasive as her sister, who prevents further talk by returning with James Browne in his wheel chair.

James is a man of sixty-five "with a face to which one is not sure whether nature or mutilation has lent strength . . ."—a shawl covers his legs, and a scarf is wound around his neck. His greeting to Rose is seemingly cheerful, and his answers to her inquiries about his health are uncomplaining . . . and "Thank God you won't play train with my chair now. Well, Mr. Dennis. I hope she hasn't been a trouble to you." Michael for the third time explains his late arrival: "The morning train seemed a better idea, Mr. Browne." "*Father* Browne, Mr. Dennis," Helen coldly corrects him. "My brother . . ." Michael realizes his mistake. James lightly says he hopes that Rose will be able to bear all the Brownes. Rose immediately reassures her uncle: "It was good of Mother to leave me to you. I'd have been lost without you." "The only Catholic Pemberton. But somehow I never think of you as Pemberton . . ." murmurs James.

Teresa, over tea, abruptly remembers a strange phone call of the previous night. When the woman at the other end heard Rose wasn't arriving till the next morning, she just hung up. Rose looks at Michael with apprehension. But Teresa, always distrait, has just as quickly forgotten all about the phone call. And now she begs her brother to keep the maid from leaving before the end of her workday, and to prevent Helen from assuming the kitchen chores . . . "The cooking tonight is *my* responsibility," says Teresa. "Isn't that so, James?" James kindly agrees that Thursday is his elder sister's cooking day. Helen, unshakable as always, decides to accompany Teresa to the kitchen.

As Helen leaves the room, she glances backward just as Rose and Michael touch hands over a teacup. She also can't help hearing Rose address Michael as "dear." "See that Mr. Dennis has a slice of my plum cake, James," she says in parting.

Rose and Michael plan stiltedly to meet the next day on business matters—this is the best they can do in front of Father Browne. But as Michael takes his leave, Rose meets him—outside James' vision—behind the wheel chair, and silently clings to him, afraid to kiss. She then goes with him into the hall, until James calls her back.

JAMES—Yes, it's a long way down, isn't it? Only the kitchen is in the place you'd expect. In the basement. Even if you don't like tea, come in and sit down. I don't see many strangers.

ROSE—Am I a stranger?

James—One can love a stranger.

Rose—Yes. (*She comes back, but her mind is away.*) Uncle, why are so many rooms closed?

James—Have you noticed? So quickly.

James wouldn't be telling her, except this is to be her home, and he knows there will be a lot to puzzle her.

Rose—I thought it was funny the way Aunt Teresa came out of there, not paying any attention . . .

James—Yes, it's funny, isn't it? Go on thinking it's funny— a bit pathetic, too. There's no harm in it. Don't let it get on your nerves. I sometimes think the young have worse nerves than we have. Age is a good drug and it doesn't lose its effect.

Rose—But you still haven't told me.

James—My dear, it's so absurd. And I should have been able to stop it. (*Right arm on chair.*) I hope you'll laugh. Please laugh. It's very funny—in its way.

Rose—Yes?

James (*nerving himself*)—You see, your Aunt Helen sleeps on the first floor in the old drawing room. Because I'm an invalid they would have insisted on the dining room for me but I told them they couldn't get me up- and downstairs to the living room, so I have what used to be a nurse's little sitting room here—next to this one— this was the night nursery in the old days. Aunt Teresa has the day nursery just opposite. You see the bedrooms are all closed.

Rose—But why?

James (*slowly and reluctantly*)—They don't like using a room in which anybody has ever died.

Rose (*not understanding*)—Died?

James (*purposely light*)—It's a habit people have—in bedrooms. So the bedrooms are all shut up—except this. It's an old house and they aren't taking any chances. They risked this one—it had been a night nursery for a long time, and children don't die very often. Anyway, they don't die of old age.

Rose—When did it all start?

James—I'm not sure. (I first noticed it when our father died.) It had seemed quite natural before when my mother's room was shut; there was nobody else to sleep in it. I only came for holidays, and they had no visitors. But when this (*He taps his rug.*) happened and I came to live here I noticed our father's room was closed too, and when I wanted a room on the second floor Teresa said—I think it was Teresa—"but that was Rose's room."

ROSE—Rose?

JAMES—Your grandmother. She was the only one of us who got married. She died here, you know, when your mother was born.

ROSE—Was that when it started?

JAMES—It may have been. Who knows when anything really starts? Perhaps when we were all children together here in this room.

Rose thinks this creepy, but James disagrees. He used to threaten laughingly to die in this room, and what would they then have for a living room, he'd say. . . . "But," James thinks, "at the last moment they'd push me into my own little room—and that could be closed, too." Rose can't understand them. . . . "Nor do I," her uncle answers. "I suppose it's the fear of death. They don't seriously mind accidents. They aren't so much worried about your poor mother—because she was still young. She needn't have died. It's the inevitable they hate. Of course, when someone dies they'll do all the right things (they are good Catholics). They'll have masses said—and then as quickly as possible they forget. The photographs are the first things to disappear." But why? Rose keeps asking. Why? Father Browne, for this answer, refers her to the psychologist, Mr. Dennis. As a priest, James has given up psychology. But this much he does know—his sisters are good people. He doubts whether "they've ever committed a big sin in their lives—perhaps it would have been better if they had. I used to notice, in the old days, it was often the sinners who had the biggest trust. In mercy. My sisters don't seem to have any trust. (*Pause.*) Are you afraid of death?" Rose doesn't think so, at least she has never thought about it. That's because it's so far away for Rose, and so close to his sisters. "Are you afraid of death, Uncle?" James has thought about it for a long time: "I used to be—twenty years ago. And then something worse happened to me. It was like God reproving me for being such a fool. When that car smash came I ceased to be any use. I am a priest who can't say Mass or hear confessions or visit the sick. I shouldn't have been afraid of dying. I should have been afraid of being useless."

Rose tells him: "But you are of use to them, Uncle?" "A priest," answers James, "isn't intended to be just a comfort to his family. Sometimes in the morning when I am half asleep, I imagine my legs are still here. I say to myself, oh dear, oh dear, what a day ahead. A meeting of the Knights of Saint Columba, and then the Guild of the Blessed Sacrament, a meeting of the Altar Society, and after that . . . It's strange how bored I used to be with all the running around."

Rose hopes that she may take her uncle out to the park, but James explains that would mean a couple of men just to get him down the stairs. Rose should marry soon, her uncle adds. He doesn't wish to use her.

Helen bustles in, and Teresa hurriedly follows, looking for Michael. On hearing he has left, Teresa announces a lady is on the phone who wishes to speak with Rose. Rose is frightened, but Teresa adds sweetly: "She says she's Mrs. Dennis. Will you speak to her, dear? She's asking all sorts of questions I can't answer." Rose protests she doesn't know her: "I've never even met her." Helen is all ears while James quietly questions Teresa. The old lady tries to be as clear as possible: "She said she tried to speak to Mr. Dennis last night at the hotel. She wasn't well. Where did you say he stayed, dear?" Rose says she doesn't know just where . . . : "In the village."

TERESA—And then she tried your house and you weren't there. She sounds a little—strange. I wish you'd come, dear. She's waiting on the telephone.

JAMES—Better have a word with her.

ROSE (*desperately*)—I can't, I don't know her. Michael will be home any moment.

JAMES—Well—perhaps. (*Leans forward, hand on table.*)

HELEN—Don't worry my little sweetheart, James. She's tired. Such a long journey. (*To* ROSE.) Your Aunt Helen will take care of it for you. (JAMES *turns slowly after* HELEN *crosses.*)

SCENE II

Michael appears early the next morning. He finds Teresa waiting for him, but no Rose. And he's told that no matter when he comes, he will find no Rose. Helen has seen to that. Teresa assumes Helen knows the reason—she doesn't. Teresa feels she's never told anything in this house. Michael tries to insist that as the executor of her mother's will, he's entitled to discuss business matters with Rose, and that Helen is not entitled to stop him. But Teresa is not so sure: "I've no idea what she can do and what she can't, Mr. Dennis. She's a terribly determined woman. I'm her elder, but she's always had her way. Even my brother—and he's a priest. Do you know, Mr. Dennis, she's so arranged this house that . . . that . . . (*her eyes are on the closet*). Well, I'm quite ashamed. I don't know what strangers think. We should have made one out of the cupboard on the landing."

Teresa daren't even take a message from Michael—even as a trustee—without permission from Helen. Michael has had enough, and says angrily: "I don't care what Miss Browne thinks. . . ." just as Helen pushes James' chair through the door. Helen is not even faintly good-humored; she is simply a strong-willed heavy woman. Michael matches her stubbornness: "I've come to see Rose." . . . James tries to introduce a light note, but realizes he hasn't a chance.

Helen starts off by saying that Mrs. Dennis had called again. Michael says yes, he knows. Helen obviously wants to find out from Michael what has been going on between him and Rose. She also wants to get rid of Teresa before going into action, but Teresa balks and appeals to James. This time James doesn't come to her help: "Better go, dear. There are too many of us as it is." After Teresa leaves, Helen reminds her brother he was to have a word with Mr. Dennis.

JAMES (*with a helpless or perhaps appealing gesture*)—Mr. Dennis is not a Catholic. I am not in the confessional. I have no authority.

HELEN—But, James, a woman can hardly ask . . .

MICHAEL—This is the second time I've been on trial today. I hope I've reached the Supreme Court. You want to ask me whether Rose and I are lovers. That's it, isn't it?

HELEN—We would never have put it so crudely.

MICHAEL—But I'm not a Catholic, as your brother says. I haven't learned to talk about "offenses against purity." In my lectures I try to be crude—it's only another word for precise.

JAMES—Forgive me, but so far you haven't been very precise.

MICHAEL—You said you had no authority. I agree with you. I'm not going to answer.

HELEN—Then we can only assume the worst.

Forearmed with information from his wife, Helen fires one question after another at Michael. Michael insists that his relationship with Rose is a business one, but suddenly stung by James': "Go on being frank. I like you better that way," Michael confesses: "I love her. Is that frank enough for you?" "Frank?" shrills Helen. "It's—it's repulsive. Seducing a child at her mother's funeral." Helen is ready to do battle, but James cuts in: "You've asked your questions, Helen. Now leave us alone." She stays on, until James says, very deliberately: "Helen, I can't bear your voice when it gets on one note. We are too near death, you and I . . ." After a pause, Helen says: "You're impossible, James," but leaves. James knew the word "death" would do the trick.

Alone with Michael, James asks him what they are to do about Rose. Michael moves restlessly about the room, at intervals stopping at James' chair.

MICHAEL—When I got home last night my wife was in bed with the door locked. Like a jury after the evidence has been heard. This morning she gave her verdict of guilty.

JAMES (*leans forward, hand on table*)—Was it a just one?

MICHAEL—Do you believe in justice? (*With angry irony.*) Of course. I forgot. You believe in a just God. The all-wise Judge.

JAMES—That kind of justice has nothing to do with a judge. (*He turns his head and follows* MICHAEL'S *movements.*) It's a mathematical term. We talk of a just line, don't we? God's exact, that's all. He's not a judge. An absolute knowledge of every factor—the conscious and the unconscious—yes, even heredity. All your Freudian urges. That's why He's merciful.

MICHAEL (*coming to a halt by* JAMES' *chair*)—I know what I seem like to you. A middle-aged man. Whose wife won't divorce him.

JAMES—That wouldn't have helped.

MICHAEL—But I mean to *marry* Rose.

JAMES—It would be better to live with her. She'd be less bound to you then.

MICHAEL—How I hate your logic.

JAMES—I sometimes hate this body cut off at the knees. But my legs won't exist however much I hate the lack of them. It's a waste of time hating facts.

MICHAEL—I believe in different facts. (*A pause.*) Father, we have our heretics in psychology too. I believe in the analysis of dreams, but sometimes I have had a dream so simple and brief that there seems to be nothing there to analyze—a shape, a few colors, an experience of beauty, that's all. Then I refuse to look further.

Michael feels he can analyze his own love and can give all the arguments: "Pride that a girl can love me, the idea that time is hurrying to an end, the sense of final vigor which comes before old age, the fascination innocence may have when you've ceased to believe in it—it's like seeing a unicorn in Hyde Park. It's true, Father, you *can* analyze every dream, but sometimes the analysis does not seem to make sense. . . ." James doesn't have to be told that the truth seems all wrong sometimes. . . . He learned that years ago in the confessional. All the same, James says: "I'd rather you

were dead. Or somebody different." "Different?" wonders Michael.
Like his grandfather, says James: "He may have visited a brothel
once in a while when he went abroad, but he believed you only loved
the person you married. He wasn't even tempted to leave his wife—
society was so strong—any more than you are tempted to commit
murder. You may be a better man, but he caused much less trouble."

Michael pleads that things hadn't turned out as he had meant
they should. He hadn't wanted a "love affair"! He had meant to
tell his wife gently about it and avoid bitterness. James accuses him
of lack of imagination even to think he could leave a woman without trouble or bitterness. Brushing aside Michael's argument that
he and his wife no longer slept together, James retorts: "You've been
companions, haven't you?" Michael repeats that he hadn't meant
to hurt anyone, or even planned anything when he went down to the
funeral. But now that marrying Rose seems out of the question,
Michael wants to know what they're to do. "You're the psychologist," James answers. . . . "Let's hear the wisdom of Freud, Jung
and Adler. Haven't they all the answers you need? You can only
get a priest's answer from me." Michael wants just that—then
he'll know what he has to fight.

James lays it on the line: "You're doing wrong to your wife, to
Rose, to yourself . . . and to the God you don't believe in. Go
away. Leave her, don't write to her, don't answer her letters if she
writes to you— She'll have a terrible few weeks. So will you. You
aren't a cruel man." "And in the end?" Michael asks. James tells
him: "We have to trust in God. Everything will be all right."

MICHAEL (*angrily*)—All right—what a queer idea you have of
all right. I've left her. Fine. So she'll always associate love with
betrayal. When she loves a man again there'll always be that in her
mind . . . love doesn't last. So it won't last. She'll grow her defense mechanisms until she dies inside them. And I'll go on as I
have for the last ten years, having a woman now and then, for a
night, on the sly, substitutes, living with a woman I don't desire—
a hysteric. She has something real for her hysteria now, but for ten
years she's invented things. Ever since our child died. Sometimes
I find myself thinking she invented even that. I wasn't there.

JAMES—Can't you even find a cure for your own wife?

MICHAEL—No. Because I'm part of her insecurity. I'm inside
her neurosis as I'm inside her house.

JAMES—So you'll burn down the house. For God's sake don't talk
any more psychology at me. Just tell me what you want.

Michael wants to be able to live with Rose and to have a family by her. And perhaps one day his wife will divorce him, and they can marry. James is ironical about this kind of marriage, sure that Rose would never settle for it. "You can't fob off a Catholic with a registrar's signature and call it a marriage. We do as many wrong things as you do, but we have the sense to know it. I don't say she wouldn't be happy—in a way—as long as the desire lasted. Then she'd leave you—even with the registrar's signature. I'm sorry for you, being mixed up like that, with one of us."

As Michael talks of his wife, sadness and horror overtakes James: "It's a terrible world." When Michael asks, can't he forget he's a priest, James reproaches himself for forgetting it twenty-two hours of the day. But when Michael asks if, as a man, James can see Rose happy in this house—"three old people and all those closed rooms"— and why are they closed?—James confesses to his sisters' fears, and gives Michael ammunition for seeking a chance to speak to Rose. James makes his last appeal: "You're a psychologist. You know how often young girls fall in love with a man your age, looking for a father." Michael is defensive about it, and James succeeds in getting under his skin with his next remark: "Rose never knew her father." Michael, revealing that James has made a fair hit, answers that he doesn't give a damn whether he's a father substitute or not: ". . . a substitute may give satisfaction for a lifetime." James quickly points out that a man of his years can't think in terms of a lifetime. "I might die before she got tired of me," argues Michael. "You might," James answers, then adds: "It's a terrible thing to have to depend on, though."

Far off, the bell rings, and Michael—recognizing Rose's step on the stairs—asks James point-blank whether he's to see Rose with or without his consent. "What are you going to say to her?" James asks. Says Michael: "I'm going to ask her to pack her bag."

When Rose enters, pleased and surprised, James tells her right off of Michael's plans. "Michael watches Rose with growing uneasiness. She is too young and unprepared." Totally without apprehension Rose says: "How lucky I never unpacked the trunk. I can be ready in a few minutes." Only the briefest flicker of remorse makes Rose turn to her uncle. . . . "You must think we are very wicked?" "No," James answers. "Just ignorant. And innocent." "Not innocent," Rose answers proudly.

Rose tells her uncle: "I know it's wrong, but I don't care. We're going to be happy." "Is he?" curtly asks James. For the first time Rose sees that Michael doesn't look happy. But when Michael explains that his wife now knows, Rose, with the unfeelingness of youth, brushes this aside: "It had to happen sooner or later. Was she very angry?" "Not exactly angry," Michael answers. Says Rose: "You've had an awful time." Michael cries: "Other people are having an awful time." "Yes, of course," Rose answers. "It's terribly sad, but we'll be all right. You'll see. And people get over everything." James doesn't care to be a witness to this conversation any longer, and demands to be taken to his room.

Michael, knowing he has won, feels anything but victorious. But Rose, returning, is only momentarily disturbed by the news that Michael's wife won't give him a divorce. . . . He and Rose wouldn't have had a real marriage anyway. "Somebody may die" is her way of passing it off.

MICHAEL—You're a Catholic. I never knew any Catholics before. Except your mother.

ROSE—Perhaps I'm only half one. Father wasn't.

MICHAEL—You never knew him, did you?

ROSE—No. But I've seen lots of photographs. He had a nose rather like yours.

MICHAEL (*with bitterness*)—I never noticed that.

ROSE—Shall I pack now? (*She begins to get her things together in a small suitcase while the dialogue continues.*)

MICHAEL—You don't mind—about the Church? You know you won't be able to go to your—what do you call it? Communion, is it?—so long as we are together.

ROSE (*lightly*)—Oh, I expect it will come all right in the end. I shall make a deathbed confession and die in the odor of sanctity.

MICHAEL—Our children will be illegitimate.

ROSE—Bastards are the best, so Shakespeare says. We did *King John* my last term at school. The nuns hurried over those bits. There was a lovely phrase for bastards—"born under the rose." I liked Faulconbridge. Oh, what an age ago it seems.

And Rose isn't shaken by the thought that her aunts won't have her in the house again. She can't bear the house—with all its closed rooms, it reminds her of something out of Poe. "What a lot of books you've read," Michael murmurs. "You aren't angry about something, are you?" Rose queries. "I'll do anything you say. Just tell me where to go and I'll go. Like Ruth. 'Your people shall be my people.' I suppose your people are all psychologists." But for all her going on and on, she has to find out what's bothering Michael. It's the responsibility—"Have you really *thought?*" he asks.

Rose cries: "I don't *want* to think. You know about things, I

don't. Darling, I've never been in love before. You have." **He**
knows his way around. . . . "Tell me what to do. I'll do it. I've
packed my bag, but I'll unpack it if you want it a different way.
I'll do anything, darling, that's easier for you. Look, tell me to come
to Regal Court, now, this minute, and I'll come." Michael is puzzled, but Rose has found out that Regal Court is where people go
to make love. Or, she adds, she is willing to take her bag and go
away for years: "Just say what you want. I'm awfully obedient."

Michael is touched and tries to bring Rose down to earth: "Dear,
it's not only you and me . . . you have to think." Rose won't have
it: "Don't make me think. I warned you not to make me think. I
don't know about things. They'll all get at me if they have a
chance. They'll say, 'Did you ever consider this? Did you ever
consider that?' Please don't do that to me, too—not yet. Just tell
me what to do." Michael, aware of the trouble he has caused, finds
it difficult to put worry aside: "You can live in the moment because
the past is so small, and the future so vast. I've got a small future.
I can easily imagine—even your uncle can imagine it for me. And
the past is a very long time and full of things to remember."

Before they go, Michael must go home to say good-by to his wife.
This Rose finds hard, and then worries that his wife may talk him
around: "She's had you so long. She'll have all the right words to
use. I only know the wrong ones." Michael harshly quiets her
fears: "You don't need words. You're young. And the young
always win in the end." They arrange to meet at Lancaster Gate
tube station in an hour. Rose is worried by Michael's reserve: "You
do still want me?" Michael tells her that of course he does. "I
wasn't much good," says Rose, "but I'm learning awfully fast."
Michael reassures her: "You've nothing to fear." As he kisses her,
he can't help saying: "You've got the whole future." Passionately
Rose answers: "I only want one as long as yours."

Michael, leaving Rose to do her packing, reckons without Helen.
When Rose goes for her promised farewell with James, Helen, frantic
and distraught, uses the guileless Teresa to trap their niece. She
half-hypnotizes Teresa into thinking she is ill (sure that Rose
wouldn't desert a sick aunt). But Helen has overplayed her hand.
When she wants Teresa to go to her bedroom, Teresa balks pitifully.

HELEN—You've got such a pretty bedroom, dear. I tell you what
I'll do. I'll send Mary to Burns Oates to get you another holy
picture for that patch on the wall where Mother's portrait used to
hang. Would you like another Little Flower?

TERESA—I'd rather have St. Vincent de Paul. But, Helen—

HELEN—In a few days you'll be up and about again.

TERESA (*desolately*)—Days?

HELEN—Come, dear. You know you can't walk by yourself. Try.

TERESA—I can. I really can. (*She rises carefully to her feet and takes a step.*)

HELEN—Careful, dear. Oh, your poor head! Take my arm. You look terrible, dear.

TERESA—*No*—no—no— (*With a frightened cry* TERESA *collapses onto the floor.* HELEN *goes to the door and calls:* Rose— Rose— *There is no real fear in her voice, but when she turns and sees her sister, she feels panic.*) Teresa! Dear Teresa! Speak to me! Please, not in here, Teresa! (*She bends down and for a moment it looks as though she is going to try to drag her sister through the door. Then she runs through the door onto the landing and cries in real fear.*) Rose! Help me, please! Please help me! Rose! *Rose!*

ACT II

Three weeks have passed. In the early evening, Father Browne's chair is drawn close to Teresa's. He has been reading to her.

TERESA—Go on a little longer. I like what you read so much better than what Helen reads. I don't understand it, but I like it. She always reads me St. Therese. She talks about *my* Little Flower, but it's her Little Flower really.

JAMES—Helen gets confused. She thinks of us two as the old ones, but she's old too. She means no harm.

TERESA—Was I really dying the other day?

JAMES—How do I know? We are all nearly dying, I hope—except Rose.

TERESA—Do you know, for just a moment I didn't want to die in the day nursery where all our toys used to be kept. I wanted to die where everybody else had died—in a real bedroom.

James, leaning forward, says encouragingly: "Why not?" But apparently this feeling was fleeting; the next moment Teresa is fuller of the old fears than ever, for, according to Helen, it was Teresa's idea to close off the bedrooms. Teresa also remembers what Helen once told her about lost souls, so now she can only think of those that can't sleep—ghosts.

JAMES—Now, now. It was wrong of me to give way about those rooms. When it began it seemed silly and unimportant. Why should I fight you over a fancy? But perhaps I should have fought you. I've been very useless, Teresa. Do you know one of my "daydreams"? I get them again now—perhaps they belong to second childhood. I dream of helping somebody in great trouble. Saying the right word at the right time. In the old days in the confessional —once in five years perhaps—one sometimes felt one had done just that. It made the years between worth while. Now I doubt if I'd know the right word if the chance came.

TERESA—I'm afraid of dying, James, even of thinking about death. Then Rose came, and I seemed to frighten *her*. It's a nice house. We aren't bad people. I don't know why there should be so much fear around.

JAMES—Perhaps your fear frightened her. Your silly fear of death.

TERESA—Is it a silly fear, James?

JAMES—No one who believes in God should be afraid of death.

TERESA—But there's Hell, James.

JAMES—Oh, we aren't important enough for that, Teresa. Hell is for the great, the very great. I don't know that anyone is great enough for Hell except Satan.

TERESA—I sound a bit braver now, but it's only because I'm back here—in the living room. It was good of Helen to hide that patch in my room with a picture, but I said *not* the Little Flower. Do you think Helen likes her because she died young? Sometimes she looks at Rose in a strange way, as though she's thinking, "I may survive even you."

"Now, now," says James. "You want to rest. Shall I read a little more?" And James tries to explain to Teresa what St. John meant when he spoke of "the dark night of the soul." Teresa, listening, guesses: "You have a dark night of your own, James." James cheerfully tries to change the subject, and to Helen's eyes, on her entrance into the room, the two look quite peaceful.

Helen wonders whether they have heard Mary return from an errand, a vague sort of errand, that Helen sent her on. To Teresa's suggestion that Rose do the tea dishes for the absent Mary, Helen snaps: "You don't expect Rose to be here, do you, dear?" And abruptly leaves.

Teresa puzzles over Rose, of whom she is so very fond. Rose was so good to her when she was ill: "I'd wake up sometimes so frightened and there she'd be, dozing in the chair by my bed. I remember

when I was a child, before Helen was born, Mother used to give me
a night light because I was so afraid. It made a sound like someone
breathing quietly. Like Rose asleep."

"She's a kind child," says James. Teresa wonders why she wasn't,
at the beginning, and what it was Helen had said about Rose's running away. James soothes her. "Don't worry. She's still here."
Teresa answers: "People don't tell me things. And there's such a
lot I don't understand." "Don't try," advises James. "It's much
better to believe only what we see, and not ask questions. Leave
questions to the psychologists. 'Is this really so?' they ask you.
'Do you really think that or just think that you think?' They aren't
any happier worrying at the truth like a dog does at a bone. The
bone is still there at the end of it all. An indestructible fragment,
the dog buries it next morning and worries at it all over again."

Neither of them is prepared for Rose storming up the steps, angrily
pushing Mary into the room ahead of her. Rose's anger doesn't
mask the noticeable change in her. She has aged perceptibly. The
frustration, decisions, and disappointments of these past weeks
have left their mark—"she has had time to think." She is not as
pretty as she was. Rose demands that Mary make a report to them
all—instead of just to Helen—on her spying activities of the afternoon. Noting James and Teresa's consternation, Rose says, referring
to Helen: "I'm sorry. I might have guessed it was her work. She
hates me." "Nonsense," James tells her. But Rose knows why:
". . . Love is normal. Love is being born and growing older and having children and dying. She can't bear that. She wants to build
a wall of closed rooms . . . and in the middle there's this *living
room*. Nobody will ever die here. Perpetual motion. Nobody will
even be born here. That's risky. I can camp here all night because
I'm young and there's no danger, but I mustn't put up a photograph
of my mother because she's dead. And a man mustn't come and
see me here because life might not stand still. We might make love
and that means getting older, running risks—in your precious mu-
seum piece of a room. Period 1902."

Helen enters on the last of this and pretends to know nothing
about Mary's afternoon, and orders her to the kitchen. When Mary
leaves, in spite of Rose's demanding to hear her report, Helen
blandly remarks: "I can't think what you are talking about." Rose
refuses to let her get away with it, and offers Helen details that Mary,
on the outside of Regal Court, couldn't possibly have known. Rose
also lets Helen know that Michael and she have been meeting three
or four times a week—"ever since you stopped my running away
for good." Rose bitterly concludes: "With your great need of help—

You could have done without me, all right—if Mary's time had not been taken up with spying."

James is outraged; Teresa cries softly. James demands of Helen how she could have done this thing. . . . Helen pontificates that Rose was about to commit a mortal sin. "Do you think you know a mortal sin when you see it?" James lashes back. "You're wiser than the Church then." Helen coolly tells him to have some common sense. "Yes, if you would have some charity," says James. Helen doesn't hesitate calling her brother a fool; she further announces: "You've heard her . . . bragging. They'd have been living together now, day in and day out, if I hadn't stopped them."

JAMES (*sharply*)—Stopped them?

ROSE—Of course we'd have been together. Of course we'd have been lovers. Oh, you talk a lot about mortal sin. Why didn't you let me go? Is this any better? Afternoons at Regal Court?

HELEN—It *is* better. It will soon come to an end—this way.

ROSE—Love ending is a good thing, isn't it? To you.

HELEN—This sort of love.

ROSE—What's the difference between this sort of love and any other? Would making love feel any different if he hadn't got a wife? (*She answers her own question in a lower voice.*) Only happier.

JAMES (*who has been waiting his opportunity*)—You said you stopped them?

HELEN—Yes. I'm not ashamed of it. I've kept her in the Church, haven't I? She can go to confession now any time she likes.

ROSE—And do it again, and go to confession, and do it again. Do you call that better than having children and living together till we die . . .

HELEN—In mortal sin.

ROSE—God's got more sense. And mercy.

HELEN—And it's another sin to trust too much to his mercy.

ROSE—Oh, they have a name for that too. I know it. The nuns taught me. It's called presumption. Well, I'm damned well going to presume.

JAMES (*to* HELEN)—What do you mean, you stopped them?

HELEN—Teresa wasn't ill.

ROSE—Not ill? She was in a faint on the floor.

HELEN—I told her she was ill. She believed it. (*Defensively.*) I had to act quickly, James. (ROSE *turns quietly away.*)

JAMES—I'd think you were a very wicked woman if you weren't such a fool.

Teresa has had difficulty in following their talk; James, wanting a word alone with Rose, first tells her to take Teresa to her room. Helen, intending to know what passes between James and their niece, refuses to budge. She also refuses to accept any blame for making Teresa ill or ruining Rose's life. James is only too conscious of his guilt: "We've ruined her between us." "Us?" says Helen. "We aren't to blame. It's that man. With all his wickedness."

JAMES—Don't blame him. Blame our dead goodness. Holy books, holy pictures, a subscription to the Altar Society. Do you think, if she had come into a house where there was love, she wouldn't have hesitated, thought twice, talked to us . . .

HELEN—And why didn't she?

JAMES—Because there was fear, not love, in this house. If we had asked her for a sacrifice, what would we have offered? Pious platitudes.

HELEN—Speak for yourself, James.

JAMES—I do. Goodness that sits and talks piously and decays all the time.

HELEN—He seduced her.

JAMES—It's a silly word, but what if he did? God sometimes diverts the act, but the pious talk He seems to leave like the tares, useless.

On Rose's return, Helen still is defiant and determined to remain. But James is now equally determined. As a priest, he orders her to leave. She goes, but not before spewing out: "The Church is well rid of a useless priest like you, James."

Rose, all defiance too, tells her uncle that since Teresa is apparently well, she's free to go away with Michael. They are just where they were before. But, "Are you?" asks James. Rose is unable to keep up the pretense. She breaks down and confesses: "Uncle, it isn't wonderful at all. It's sad, sad . . ." and as she sits on the floor by his chair, she tells him: "I'm tired—I don't know what to do. . . ." Michael isn't standing things much better, either. When they're together, Rose tells James, they're happy, but when the time to separate draws near, it's sad. Rose hesitates to tell her uncle all of this, but he wants to hear: "People don't talk to priests much—except in formulas in that coffin-shaped box of ours." Rose bursts forth: "Since my last confession three weeks ago I've committed adultery twenty-seven times. That's what Aunt Helen would like me to say, and, Father, it doesn't mean a thing. We are supposed to be talking to God, aren't we, through you, and God knows all about the clock on the mantelpiece. I don't want to confess. I want to say 'Dear God. Give us more love. Give us a life together. Don't let it be just Regal Court over and over again.' Do you understand?" James does a little, but his answer is bound to be the priest's answer, and unacceptable to Rose. She insists she is willing to live a lifetime without the sacraments but not without Michael.

James comments sadly on Rose's growing up these past weeks. Rose, searching for the answer, asks: "Do you think if I left Michael I could really love a God who demanded all that pain before he'd give Himself?"

JAMES—Why shouldn't you love God just because you don't understand Him? You love Michael now—but in ten years you'll have understood him to the last word and gesture. It takes a terrible lot of love to survive understanding.

ROSE—You make things so complicated.

JAMES—You simplify too much.

ROSE—But it's a simple situation, Father. There's nothing complicated about this—love affair. I'm not a case history.

JAMES—The trouble is you don't trust God enough. It's not only your own good you are troubled about. Michael haunts you too. "What would he do without me?" you are saying to yourself. "Am I going to hurt him rather than break a rule?" Do you imagine God doesn't see your problem and your suffering and that He doesn't suffer with you just as you suffer with Michael, only worse? You aren't a saint. He can't communicate with you, you won't let Him, He can't come to you and say, "This is such a little day of twenty-four hours, this problem of suffering is going to seem so small when you know the answer, in the long days ahead without hours or any time." You have free will and you don't trust Him, and He suffers for that too. Because He will make things so much easier if you would shut your eyes and leave it to Him.

Rose's face hardens as she listens to James. She doubts very much that He works in that fashion. . . . "Look at the world nowadays. He seems to want heroes and I'm not a hero. I'm a coward. I cannot bear too much pain. . . . When I betray Him I'm not doing any worse than Peter, am I? God died for cowards too." And she won't accept James' arguments, the Church's arguments: all she wants is a bit of human comfort. . . . "Not formulas. 'Love God. Trust God. Everything will be all right one day.' Uncle, please say something that's not Catholic." Even if he would, James has no opportunity. Helen has entered.

She has very deliberately arranged for Mrs. Dennis to come to see Rose, and now triumphantly announces her presence. Rose gets panicky and James accuses his sister: "Is this your work again, Helen? Tell her Rose is sick, not here. Tell her anything, but get rid of her." Helen insists that it is Mrs. Dennis' right. "This child has had enough to bear," pleads James. But Rose, having stood the thought of Mrs. Dennis all these weeks, decides to face her. Helen loses no time in having the woman sent upstairs and James, helplessly being pushed off, can only tell Rose: "Call me if you need me. I'll be in my room."

SCENE II

A few moments later, Mrs. Dennis confronts Rose. She comes in uneasily, conscious of the oddness of the room. But her attack on Rose, which comes almost at once, is full of malice and venom. Mrs. Dennis warns Rose not to trust Michael: . . . "There's always been trouble with his students. Reading Freud together, I suppose. The third year we were married—just after our baby died—I could have divorced him." Rose asks why didn't she? Rose wouldn't try to hold a man through forgiving him: "I wouldn't want to hold him a minute if he wanted to go somewhere else." Mrs. Dennis hears that the reason Michael had not left her was Rose wouldn't go at the time because . . . : "I was caught like him. By pity. (*Savagely.*) He pities you."

MRS. DENNIS (*maliciously*)—It didn't feel like pity—last night.
ROSE (*crying out in pain*)—I don't believe you.
MRS. DENNIS—If I'm ready to share him . . .
ROSE—You're lying. You know you are lying. What have you come here for? You're just lying to break me. You're wicked.
MRS. DENNIS—Wicked's an odd word from you. I *am* his wife.
ROSE—You can stay his wife. I only want to be his mistress.

Mrs. Dennis suddenly crumbles, changing tactics. She starts to weep and go all to pieces. She implores the upset girl not to take Michael from her, admitting that she and Michael haven't been lovers in years. The hysteria of the woman gradually increases as Rose, utterly trapped, watches in horror. Mrs. Dennis threatens to kill herself with sleeping pills, then becomes so hysterical that she gets up out of her chair and suddenly strikes the girl across the face.

The next minute she is on her knees beating the floor with her hands, crying: "You made me. . . . I wish I could die, I want to die, I want to die. . . ." Rose helplessly stands by, as the woman cries: "He wants me to. You all want me to die." Rose moans: "No. No. We only want to be happy." After threatening to go mad, too, Mrs. Dennis suddenly subsides, gets off the floor, sits down and quietly asks Rose for a glass of water. While Rose goes after it, Mrs. Dennis takes a bottle of sleeping pills out of her bag, concealing it in her hand when Rose gives her the glass. "Could you turn out the light, dear?" Mrs. Dennis asks. "It's so strong." Then, deliberately for Rose's benefit, she starts to take the pills just as Rose turns toward her. It is Rose's turn to become hysterical as she dashes to the woman's side, snatches the bottle and throws it into the far corner of the room: "Why did you do that?" she screams with the harshness of fear. "If you want to kill yourself, kill yourself at home." "I can buy more," answers Mrs. Dennis. "Buy them then. You're just blackmailing me," Rose tells her.

Rose, hearing Michael calling her, runs to the door crying: "Michael, for God's sake, Michael." He comes in, almost seeming to expect what Rose tells him: "She tried to kill herself." "Oh, no. She didn't. I know that trick of hers. You promised not to try that again. You know it doesn't work," he tells his wife. But as Rose watches the two together, "they are so unmistakably man and wife" that she can't bear to look.

Michael is gentle with Mrs. Dennis, and tries to tell her that she can live more happily without him, they hadn't been happy for such a long time: "Long before I met Rose . . ."

MRS. DENNIS—You talk so much about happiness. No. I wasn't happy. Do you think I'm going to be more happy without you? Happiness isn't everything, is it? Do you often come across someone happy at your lectures? I don't want to be alone, Michael. I'm afraid of being alone, Michael, for God's sake. . . . I forgot. You don't believe in God. Only *she* does.

ROSE (*comes back into the fight*)—Stop. Please stop. Both of you. You are making it so complicated. (*They both turn and look at her. It's as if she were the outsider. She looks from one to the other.*) We love each other, Mrs. Dennis. It's as simple as that. This happens every day, doesn't it? You read it in the papers. People can't all behave like this. There are four hundred divorces a month.

MICHAEL (*in a low voice*)—Then if there are four hundred divorces, there are hundreds of suffering people.

ROSE—But, darling, *you* aren't going to suffer, are you? You

want to live with me. You want to go away. You don't want to
stay with her. We are going to be happy.

MRS. DENNIS—You see—*she* doesn't suffer.

Michael answers angrily that Rose doesn't use suffering as a
weapon. Then, realizing that he too has been shouting, he apologizes: "This scene is making us all hysterical." "Well," Mrs. Dennis
quietly replies, "you won't have to be hysterical any more. You can
go home. I mean to the house—and pack. I won't be there. I'll
keep out of the way till you've gone." As she walks to the door,
she adds: "You can sleep there tonight. I won't be there." And
she leaves.

Michael is much disturbed; he follows her out, calling down the
stairs after her. Getting no answer, he comes back to Rose, talking
more to himself than to her: "She won't do anything. People who
talk about suicide never do anything." He asks: "Do they?" but
doesn't hear Rose's "No." And her pleading: "What are *we* going
to do?" is met by his absent-minded: "Oh, we are going to be
happy." He finds it hard to remember that he told his wife that
he and Rose were going away. Rose asks if he meant it. "Of
course," Michael answers, his mind very much on his wife. "As soon
as your aunt's better. We always said so."

ROSE—She's better now. I'm free.

MICHAEL (*slowly*)—Then—of course—we can go.

ROSE—When? Now? Tomorrow? (MICHAEL *hesitates very
slightly*.)

MICHAEL—The day after. You see—I must find out how she is.

ROSE—I wish you didn't love her so.

MICHAEL—My dear—my dear—there's no need of jealousy.

ROSE—I'm not jealous. I just can't bear you to suffer. That's
all.

MICHAEL—We'll be all right—the day after tomorrow. (*He kisses
her and goes to the door.*)

ROSE (*not knowing what to say—in a schoolgirl accent*)—À
bientôt.

MICHAEL (*his mind still on his wife*)—I wish I knew where she'd
gone. She hasn't got many friends. (*He goes out.*)

Helen, pushing the wheel chair into the room, finds the miserable
girl, alone. Very calmly she asks Rose when she plans to leave.
Rose (the phrase sounding weak even to her) says: "The day after
tomorrow."

Reminded by James to kiss her niece, Helen pecks at Rose's cheek before going out of the room, leaving no mark of affection. Rose is desperate: she had warned Michael not to make her think; now, after seeing the miserable Dennises together, she is thinking. She begs her uncle: "What am I to do?" Rose flings herself on the floor by his chair, pleading: "Tell me what to do, Father."

JAMES—When you say "father," you seem to lock my mouth. There are only hard things to say.

ROSE—I only want somebody to say, Do this, do that. I only want somebody to say, Go here, go there. I don't want to think any more.

JAMES—And if I say, leave him . . .

ROSE—I couldn't bear the pain.

JAMES—Then you'd better go with him if you're as weak as that.

ROSE—But I can't bear hers, either.

JAMES—You're such a child. You expect too much. In a case like yours we always have to choose between suffering our own pain or suffering other people's. We can't *not* suffer.

Perhaps "fools" can live happily ever after, but Rose and Michael aren't fools, and a lifetime would be a long time to remain fooled, forgetting that poor hysterical woman.

Teresa, wearing a dressing gown and paying no attention to Rose or James, comes in and goes toward the bathroom. Rose, watching, with her hand to her mouth, cries: "It's horrible, horrible, horrible." Rose moans: "I can't go on living here with them. Like this. In the room where nobody has died. Uncle, please, tell me to go. Tell me I'm right to go. Don't give me a *Catholic* reason. Help me. Please help me." James wants desperately to help: "But when I talk, my tongue is heavy with the Penny Catechism." The only hope he finds himself offering is the hope of forgetting Michael. Rose can't stand this, jumps up and swings away from him. James still can find nothing but formulas. Rose is full of hatred and contempt for prayer: "You tell me if I go with him he'll be unhappy for a lifetime. If I stay here, I'll have nothing but that closet and this—living room. And you tell me there's hope and I can pray. Who to? Don't talk to me about God or the saints. I don't believe in your God who took away your legs and wants to take away Michael. I don't believe in your church and your Holy Mother of God. I don't believe. I don't believe. I wish to God I didn't feel so lonely."

Helen comes in with orders to have the table set here for dinner.

James begs: "Couldn't we tonight—use another room?" "You know very well," answers Helen, "there isn't another room." And Helen pushes the now broken old man to the door, while ordering Rose to lay the table.

Rose is alone. "I don't believe. I don't believe," she repeats. Teresa opens the bathroom door and moves across the room, ignoring Rose's cries to speak to her. "Please, Aunt Teresa. It's Rose." But she leaves the room. Rose sits hopelessly down.

(*Her eyes rest on the bottle she has flung into a corner: she speaks with a flat, false calm:* "Won't somebody help me?" (*She gets up and goes over to the bottle. Some of the tablets have fallen out. She sits down on the floor like a child playing and begins to scoop them up. When she has them all in her hand, she makes an attempt to pray, but she can't remember the words.*)

ROSE (*cont'd*)—"Our Father who are . . . who art . . ."

(*Suddenly she plunges into a childish prayer quite mechanically and without thinking of what she's saying, looking at the tablets in her hand.*) God bless Mummy, Nanny and Sister Marie-Louise and please God don't let school start again ever.

SCENE III

The next morning: preparations are being made to seal off the living room. Mary is removing bedding and dragging furniture to the door. Michael is present, staring out the window; Father Browne sits in his chair.

The air is heavy with guilt and vain wishes. But Helen is not one to share this guilt. Full of household plans for using Teresa's room, she sends Mary on her way, while doing her best to ignore Michael. He won't have it: "For somebody so frightened of death you've done a lot of harm." She tries to turn aside these accusations and James' coldness: "Why are you blaming me for this? Why do you both pick on me? If anyone's guilty it's you. (*To* MICHAEL.) It's you who've been killing her—all these weeks at Regal Court. Killing her conscience so in the end she did—that." Michael hurls back that Helen brought the sleeping pills into the house with his wife. But James points out there would have been the window or the tube . . . if not the pills. Helen cries: "I *know* the guilty one—" "You do, do you?" Michael breaks out. "Look in your damned neurotic heart . . ." James breaks in: "I thought Freud said there was no such thing as guilt. . . ."

In his present state of guilt Michael can't bear to hear any more psychology. James knows: "Our hearts say guilty." But Helen's doesn't. Michael turns on her: "Then why don't you sleep in this room? You're so innocent. All right, then. What are you afraid of?" James backs him up. Helen immediately becomes fretful and fearful, and puts off the whole idea, saying she couldn't frighten Teresa like that. She tries her best to wriggle out of it, and is coldly dismissed by James with: ". . . the room won't harm him or me for the little while we'll be here."

The two men go over the reasons for Rose's taking her life—James explains to Michael Rose's fear of pain . . . : "your pain, her pain, your wife's pain." Michael sees himself, the psychologist, having ruined two people's minds. "Psychology may teach you to know a mind," says James. "It doesn't teach you to love." . . . and none of them loved enough. "Dennis," James now speaks urgently, "I've got to tell somebody this. You may understand. It's your job to understand." "My job," bitterly repeats Michael.

JAMES—For twenty years I've been a useless priest. I had a real vocation for the priesthood—perhaps you'd explain it in terms of a father complex. Never mind now. I'm not laughing at you. To me it was a real vocation. And for twenty years it's been imprisoned in this chair—and the desire to help. You have it, too, in your way, and it would still be there if you lost your sight and speech. Last night God gave me my chance. He flung this child, here, at my knees, asking for help, asking for hope. That's what she said: "Can't you give me anything to hope for?" I said to God, "Put words into my mouth," but He's given me twenty years in this chair with nothing to do but prepare for such a moment, so why should He interfere? And all I said was, "You can pray." If I'd ever really known what prayer was, I would only have had to touch her to give her peace. "Prayer," she said. She nearly spat the word.

MICHAEL—I went away to look for my wife. I was frightened about *her*. What do we do now? Is everything going to be the same as before?

JAMES—Three old people have lost a living room. A psychologist with his sick wife. That's all. She's fallen like a stone into a pond.

Michael wonders that James can believe in a God who lets this happen. To Michael it's a senseless creed. James is sure that at the back of his mind—though his senses feel nothing but revolt, uncertainty and despair—Faith is saying: "This is God: all goes well." James implores Michael not to talk of Him with such hatred even if he is an unbeliever. He pleads with him as he almost pleads with himself. Michael asks again: "And you believe God made the world like that?" "Yes," says James. "And I believe He shared its pain. But He didn't only make the world. He made eternity. Suffering is a problem to us, but it does not seem a big problem to the woman when she has borne her child. Death is our child, we have to go through pain to bear our death. I'm crying out with the pain like you. But Rose—she is free now. She's borne her child."

Michael thinks bitterly that the Church thinks Rose damned because of taking the sleeping pills. "We aren't the fools you think us," James answers. "Nobody claims to know what she thought at the end. Only God was with her at the end." But she was so young and simple in Michael's eyes. James assures him it was her complexity that they all loved, and her capacity for despair. "Some of us are too small to contain that terrible tide . . . she wasn't, and we loved her for that." "A stone in a pond," Michael repeats. "Everything the same as before."

But Teresa is about to change things. Suddenly she comes in peacefully with her bedclothes, intending to sleep in Rose's room. Helen, following in panic, tries to prevent her. When reasoning fails, she starts to use force. "Stop it, Helen," orders James. "Stop it. We've had enough of this foolishness. God isn't unmerciful like a woman can be. You've been afraid too long. It's time for you to rest, my darling. It's time for you to rest." Helen collapses suddenly across the bed, and Teresa, now the stronger, takes over.

"Tears, tears, tears . . ." croons Teresa, smoothing Helen's hair: "they are only good to water cabbages. It's all nonsense, my dear. Why shouldn't I sleep here? We're not afraid of the child. And there'd be no better room for me to fall asleep in forever than the room where Rose died."

BAD SEED *

A Play in Two Acts

By Maxwell Anderson

(Adapted from William March's novel *The Bad Seed*)

[*The son of a Baptist minister,* Maxwell Anderson *was born in 1888 in Atlantic, Pa. After graduating from Stanford University he joined the faculty. He worked as a newspaperman in San Francisco until he came to New York in 1919 and was editorial writer for the "World." It was here he met Laurence Stallings and together they wrote "What Price Glory?". Since then he has become one of America's most prolific playwrights. He has won a Pulitzer Prize with "Both Your Houses," 1932-33, and two Drama Critics Circle Awards, for "Winterset," 1935-36, and "High Tor," 1936-37. His other plays include "Elizabeth the Queen," "Mary of Scotland," "The Eve of St. Mark," "Storm Operation," "Joan of Lorraine" and "Anne of the Thousand Days."*]

THE scene is the apartment—in a small Southern town—of Colonel and Mrs. Kenneth Penmark and their daughter Rhoda.

The living room, with a dining bay, offers a glimpse of the kitchen at one end; at the other end is a door to the den (which contains a piano) and a door to the hall.

The apartment is light and airy, with many windows and pleasant Colonial furniture: comfortable-looking chairs, a sofa and coffee table.

Rhoda Penmark, the cleanest and neatest of braided little girls, sits primly in a chair reading a book as her father carries his suitcases to the hall door. To her father, the pretty, quaint-looking eight-year-old is just too good to be true. Everything she says to her "Daddikins" in farewell makes him purr. How she'll miss him, cries Rhoda, and she promises to write to him every single day. Christine Penmark, a gentle, gracious, pretty woman under thirty, joins them, and can't let her husband go without one more embrace—even though he's only going to the Pentagon. Kenneth promises to wire her on his plane's arrival in Washington: "Take care of each other, you two," he says.

Mrs. Monica Breedlove, their chatty upstairs neighbor and land-lady, accompanied by her brother Emory, arrives to tell Kenneth good-by. Emory tells him not to worry about his girls: "We'll keep an eye on them, and if one looks peaked, we'll send up smoke signals. . . ."

At the last minute, Christine can't help showing concern about the separation. "Don't, sweet," Kenneth soothes her. "It's just another empty month or two. We'll get through them somehow." And he follows Emory into the hall, leaving Christine to confess to Monica: "I'm not very self-sufficient."

Monica, the friendly busybody, now takes over. First on her agenda are presents for Rhoda, at the very mention of which Rhoda shows enormous interest.

Monica produces a pair of rhinestone-studded sunglasses from her brother, which Rhoda seizes, puts on, observes in the mirror, and approves of, only to ask immediately: "Where's the case?" Monica affectionately hands over the case. Next, with a preamble about this present having been hers since she was Rhoda's age, Monica draws out of her bag a gold heart and chain. The garnet that is now set in the center of the locket she intends to change for Rhoda's birthstone, a turquoise. With some urgency, Rhoda begs: "Could I have both stones? The garnet, too?" This is too much for Christine, but Monica chuckles indulgently over Rhoda's wonderfully candid ways and promises her both stones. Rhoda in return bestows on the delighted woman a great hug.

Gazing fondly at Rhoda, Monica thinks she is rather oddly dressed for a picnic. Her starched, red-dotted-swiss is hardly right for roughing it. But this is what the child chose, and since she *never* gets dirty, Christine consents to it, though she can't imagine how Rhoda manages to stay so clean.

RHODA—I don't like coveralls. They're not—

MONICA—You mean coveralls aren't quite ladylike, don't you, my darling? (*She embraces the tolerant* RHODA *again.*) Oh, you old-fashioned little dear!

RHODA (*looking at the locket*)—Am I to keep this now?

MONICA—You're to keep it till I find out where I can get the stone changed.

RHODA—Then I'll put it in my box. (*She goes to her table,*

*opens a drawer and takes out a box which once held Swiss choco-
lates. She opens it and places the locket carefully inside.*)

Leroy, the houseman-janitor, comes in carrying a pail, with a
nasal apology for being early: it's his day for window washing.
He disappears into the bedroom.

As Rhoda, her possessions stashed away, skips gaily across the
room, Monica comments on the little taps her shoes make. "I run
over my heels, and Mother had these iron pieces put on so they'd
last longer," Rhoda explains. Christine refuses the credit—it was
Rhoda's idea. "I think they're nice. They save money," says the
paragon, and Monica gushes anew. But with a difference: Monica
has noticed that Rhoda worries too much when she comes off second at anything. These presents from Emory and herself were to
make up to Rhoda for not winning the penmanship award. As
Leroy passes into the kitchen to fill his pail, Rhoda exclaims: "I
just don't see why Claude Daigle got the medal."

CHRISTINE—Rhoda, these things happen to us all the time, and
when they do we simply accept them. I've told you to forget the
whole thing. (*She puts an arm around* RHODA, *trying to soften
her.* RHODA *pulls away impatiently.*) I'm sorry. I know you
don't like people pawing over you.
RHODA—It was mine! The medal was mine!
CHRISTINE—Rhoda, forget it. Put it out of your mind.
RHODA—I won't. I won't. I won't.

Leroy passes near Rhoda and some water slops on her shoes.
When Monica admonishes him, he slops some more water near
Christine. Monica launches into an attack on the man: "Leroy,
I own this apartment house! I employ you! I've tried to give
you the benefit of every doubt because you have a family! I've
thought of you as emotionally immature, torn by irrational rages,
a bit on the psychopathic side. But after this demonstration I
think my diagnosis was entirely too mild. You're definitely a
schizophrenic with paranoid overtones. I've had quite enough of
your discourtesy and surliness—and so have the tenants in the
building! My brother Emory has wanted to discharge you! I've
been on your side, though with misgivings! I shall protect you
no longer!"

CHRISTINE—He didn't mean it, Monica. It was an accident,
I'm sure it was.

Patty McCormack and Henry Jones in "Bad Seed"

RHODA—He meant to do it. I know Leroy well.

MONICA—It was no accident, Christine! It was deliberate—the spiteful act of a neurotic child!

RHODA—He meant to do it. (*To* LEROY.) You made up your mind to do it when you went through the room.

CHRISTINE—Rhoda!

RHODA—I was looking at you when you made up your mind to wet us. (*He takes his handkerchief and cleans* RHODA'S *shoes.*)

CHRISTINE (*not wishing the man to humble himself*)—Oh, Leroy, please, please!

Ordering him to go about his work, Monica says she has kept him on, despite his having the mind of an eight-year-old, because of his wife and children.

The arrival of Rhoda's principal, Miss Fern, clears the air. This prim, once rather beautiful woman, talks to Christine as Rhoda curtsies and goes upstairs with Monica for the cupcakes Monica is contributing to the children's picnic.

MISS FERN—She does everything well. As you must know better than I.

CHRISTINE—And as a person, does she fit in well—at the school?

MISS FERN—Let me think—in what way, Mrs. Penmark?

CHRISTINE—Well, Rhoda has been—I don't quite know how to say it. There's a mature quality about her that's disturbing in a child. My husband and I thought that a school like yours, where you believe in discipline and the old-fashioned virtues—might perhaps teach her to be a bit more of a child.

MISS FERN—Yes—yes, I know what you mean. In some ways, in many ways, Rhoda is the most satisfactory pupil the school has ever had. She's never been absent. She's never been tardy. She's the only child in the history of the school who has made a hundred in deportment each month in every class, and a hundred in self-reliance and conservation on the playground each month for a full school year. If you had dealt with as many children as I have, you'd realize what a remarkable record that is. And she's the neatest little girl I've ever encountered.

CHRISTINE—Kenneth says he doesn't know where she gets her tidiness. Certainly not from him or me.

MISS FERN—And she has many good qualities. She's certainly no tattletale.

CHRISTINE—Oh?

She coolly refused, according to Miss Fern, to give state's evidence against a schoolmate, denying everything—"and looking us over with that pitying, calculating look she has at certain times." Christine knows well that look of her daughter. If all this is true about Rhoda, is she popular, Christine wants to know. Miss Fern hesitates, trying to think of some tactful answer, but without succeeding. Luckily she is saved by Monica's and Rhoda's return with picnic baskets.

Rhoda goes to Christine for a kiss on her cheek, then rushes to Monica for a final hug before leaving with Miss Fern.

Once the child has left, Christine gloomily faces the morning. With her husband away, she has the awful feeling that anything can happen.

To shake Christine out of her mood, Monica talks of their lunch guests: her brother Emory, and his criminologist friend, Reginald Tasker. According to Monica, a complete set of his works would encircle the Empire State Building. Monica says she may be a garrulous old hag, but she's not going to let Christine be lonely, and goes with her into the kitchen to figure out lunch.

With the women out of the way, Leroy returns to do the living room windows, muttering: "That know-it-all, that Monica Breedlove, she don't think nobody knows anything but her. I'll show that bitch plenty. And that young trough-fed Mrs. Penmark. She don't get enough of what she needs, and I could give it to her. Now, Rhoda's smart. That's a smart little girl. She's almost as smart as I am. She sees through me and I see through her. By damn, she's smart."

Scene II

Christine and her guests, Emory and Mr. Tasker, are at the lunch table lingering over their coffee and listening to Monica's monologue about her psychoanalysis and her life and dreams. Hearing his sister's unchecked flow of technical clichés, Emory grumbles: "I can stand anything except talk about your analysis—and analyzing of your friends—and me. I don't want to look into the bottom of my soul."

Monica—I can understand that perfectly. We're all so sensitive about these things. The truth absolutely disgusts us. Now I've come to the conclusion that Emory is a "larvated homosexual—"

Christine—Whaaat!

Emory—Thank you. What does larvated mean?

Monica—It means covered as with a masque—concealed.

Tasker—It means something that hasn't come to the surface—as yet.

Emory—You can say that again. If I'm a homosexual, they'll have to change the whole concept of what goes on among 'em.

Asked where she got this idea, Monica says from pure association, the best evidence of all. She goes into the details of Emory's life, his fishing with cronies, his preference for murder mysteries in which housewives are dismembered. She hopes she's shocked everybody with her comments on sex, until Emory asks if they could talk about something normal, like murder.

Since Reginald Tasker is the murder expert, he speaks first—about what to him was a commonplace bit of murdering by a woman who was after her victim's insurance.

Christine reacts unhappily to all this, and admits she doesn't like to hear about such things. Monica immediately tries to trace Christine's psychic block to violence of all kinds: Christine even hates the revolver Kenneth keeps in the house. Monica orders her to listen to Tasker and then to speak up, stating the first thing that comes to mind. Hearing that the murderess brought her niece. arsenic with which she was going to kill her, Christine says: "Well, I was thinking at the moment of how devoted the Fern sisters were to my father, when he was a radio commentator," . . . they had spoken of it when she had enrolled Rhoda in their school.

Emory interjects that during the last war the whole nation was devoted to her father, Richard Bravo. Told to continue, Tasker tells how his murderess gave her niece sarsaparilla to drink, then watched the child's convulsions for an hour. Christine, prompted by Monica, gives her second association, feeling it's even sillier than the first: "I've always had a feeling that I was an adopted child, and that the Bravos weren't my real parents." Monica whoops over Christine's ignorance of the widespread changeling fantasy, and asks had she always had this suspicion that she was adopted? Her dreams are Christine's only evidence.

Tasker, under Monica's prodding, finishes the crude details of the murderess' career, remarking that there had been others not so crude. . . . "There have been artists in her line, really gifted operators like Bessie Denker. Bessie never made a mistake, never left a trace, never committed an imperfect crime—"

CHRISTINE (*suddenly interested*)—Who was this?

TASKER—The most amazing woman in all the annals of homicide, Bessie Denker. She was beautiful, she was brainy, and she was ruthless. She never used the same poison twice. Her own father, for example, died of rabies, contracted supposedly from a mad dog. It just happened that all his money went to Bessie—

Christine now seems really upset, and Emory puts a finish to this talk. Tasker, consulting his watch, realizes he must go. He asks

Christine's forgiveness and she in turn asks his. . . . "I have some kind of phobia or mania. I'm quite unreasonable when I hear such things." Tasker says: "I'm sick of the bloody stuff myself and only keep on with it to make a living—so let's be friends." They shake hands, and he leaves.

Turning to the radio for the news, Emory catches the local broadcast, which is suddenly interrupted by a flash bulletin of the drowning of a child on the Fern picnic. The child's name is being withheld till the parents have been notified. Monica assures Christine: "It was not Rhoda. Rhoda is too self-reliant a child. It was—some timid, confused youngster, afraid of its own shadow. It certainly wasn't Rhoda." Emory turns the radio voice up.

RADIO—To return to local affairs, I am now authorized to give the name of the victim of the drowning at the Fern School picnic. It was Claude Daigle, the only child of Mr. and Mrs. Dwight Daigle of 126 Willow Street. He appears to have fallen into the water from an abandoned wharf on the Fern property. It is a mystery how the little boy got onto the wharf, for all the children had been forbidden to play near or on it, but his body was found off the end of the landing, wedged among the pilings. The guards who brought up the body applied artificial respiration without result. There were bruises on the forehead and hands, but it is assumed these were caused by the body washing against the pilings. . . . And now back to the national news. (EMORY *turns off the radio.*)

CHRISTINE—Poor child—poor little boy!

MONICA—They'll send the children home immediately. They must be on their way now.

EMORY—This will be the end of the picnic.

CHRISTINE—I don't know what to say to her. Rhoda is eight. I remember I didn't know about death—or it didn't touch me closely—till I was much older. A teacher I adored died. My whole world changed and darkened.

Tactful for once, Monica withdraws with Emory, so that Christine can handle her child as she chooses.

When Rhoda comes home, she is quiet and unruffled. In matter-of-fact tones, she announces Claude Daigle's death, and then asks for the lunch she missed as a result of it.

RHODA—He was drowned, so then they were all rushing and calling and hurrying to see if they could make him alive again, but they couldn't, so then they said the picnic was over and we had to go home.

CHRISTINE—I'm glad you're home!

RHODA—So could I have a peanut butter sandwich and milk? (CHRISTINE *puts her arm around her.*)

CHRISTINE—Did you see him, dear?

RHODA—Yes, of course. Then they put a blanket over him.

CHRISTINE—Did you see him taken from the water?

RHODA—Yes, they laid him out on the lawn and worked and worked. But it didn't help.

CHRISTINE—You must try to get these pictures out of your mind. I don't want you to be frightened or bothered at all. These things happen and we must accept them.

RHODA—I thought it was exciting. Could I have the peanut butter sandwich?

Christine withdraws her comforting arm and goes for the sandwich, re-entering with praise for Rhoda's control, . . . "but just the same, it was an unfortunate thing to see and remember. I understand how you feel, my darling." "I don't know what you're talking about," answers Rhoda. "I don't feel any way at all." Christine is puzzled, and Rhoda, sensing that she has somehow displeased her, grabs her mother's hand and rubs it against her cheek. This causes Christine to ask whether Rhoda has been naughty.

RHODA—Why, no, Mother. What will you give me if I give you a basket of kisses?

CHRISTINE (*feeling a great rush of affection*)—I'll give you a basket of hugs!

RHODA—I want to go out and skate on the asphalt.

CHRISTINE—Then you should, dear.

As her mother returns to the kitchen, Rhoda puts on her skates. Coming in to empty wastebaskets, Leroy sees Rhoda and mutters under his breath: "How come you go skating and enjoying yourself when your poor little schoolmate is still damp from drowning in the bay? Looks to me like you'd be in the house crying your eyes out; either that or be in church burning a candle in a blue cup." Rhoda simply stares at him, picks up her sandwich and walks on her skates to the door.

RHODA—'By, Mother!

CHRISTINE (*from the kitchen*)—Good-by, Rhoda.

LEROY—Ask me, and I'll say you don't even feel sorry for what happened to that little boy.

RHODA—Why should I feel sorry? It was Claude Daigle got drowned, not me.

SCENE III

That evening Christine allows her pajama-clad daughter to lie on the couch to hear a last story. As she reads to Rhoda, the child contentedly sips her juice, takes her vitamin pills, and asks questions about the fairy story Christine is reading, till she gradually falls asleep.

Once Christine is sure she's asleep, she puts down the book, returns the empty glass to the kitchen, then carries Rhoda to her room.

Christine whiles away the time writing a letter while waiting for her long-distance call to come through. The phone finally rings: "Hello—Yes, I did place a call to Washington, D. C. Mr. Richard Bravo—that's right—yes, Bethesda 7-1293. Daddy? I'm so glad I found you at home. I've been trying to get you all evening. Daddy—you said in your last letter that you might be coming to Tallahassee. Are you sure you're well enough to be doing such things? Well, that's not really far from here. Couldn't you come to see me? Daddy, could you make it sooner? Could you— Oh, no—we're both well. It's not that. Oh, you met Kenneth at the airport? How is he? Tell him I love him and miss him very much. But, Daddy—I must see you— No, it's nothing like that. Daddy, do you remember that recurrent dream I used to have when I was a little girl— Now I'm beginning to have it again and again. I know what the Freudians say—but even they tell you dreams can't come out of any past but your own. Daddy, is there some terrible thing about my past that I don't know? No—nobody. It's something I dream. All right— I'll be good. And remember I love you. And tell Kenneth I'm finishing my letter to him tonight, and I'll send it airmail special in the morning. And, Daddy, I will see you, won't I? All right, dear— Good night."

Christine goes back to her letter, but after writing a few lines she looks towards Rhoda's room and slowly tears the letter up.

SCENE IV

Miss Fern has come to see Christine, after a visit to the grief-stricken Daigles. Mrs. Daigle has asked her to find out if Christine has some clue to the whereabouts of the penmanship medal. It wasn't on the child's body.

As soon as Rhoda leaves her piano-playing for the cool of the arbor outside, Miss Fern says to Christine: "It did occur to me that—that Rhoda might have told you a detail or two which she hadn't remembered when she talked with me. You see, she was the last to see the little Daigle boy alive—" Christine hadn't known this.

Miss Fern—About an hour after we arrived at the estate, one of our older pupils came on Rhoda and the Daigle boy at the far end of the grounds. The boy was upset and crying, and Rhoda was standing in front of him, blocking his path. The older girl was among the trees, and neither child saw her. She was just about to intervene when Rhoda shoved the boy and snatched at his medal, but he broke away and ran down the beach in the direction of the old wharf where he was later found. Rhoda followed him, not running, just walking along, taking her time, the older girl said.

Christine—Has it occurred to you that the older girl might not be telling the truth?

Miss Fern—That isn't at all likely. She was one of the monitors we'd appointed to keep an eye on the younger children. She's fifteen and has been with us since kindergarten days. No, Mrs. Penmark, she was telling precisely what she saw. We know her well.

Christine—And that was the last time Claude was seen?

Miss Fern—Yes. A little later—it might have been about noon —one of the guards saw Rhoda coming off the wharf. He shouted a warning, but by then she was on the beach again and he decided to forget the matter. The guard didn't identify the girl by name, but she was wearing a red dress, he said, and Rhoda was the only girl who wore a dress that day. At one o'clock the lunch bell rang and Claude was missing when the roll was called. You know the rest, I think.

Christine, shocked, says all of this is very serious. But Miss Fern now makes a schoolteacher's excuses for Rhoda, though she does admit thinking that Rhoda knows something she hasn't told. ". . . I think that, like many a frightened soldier," Miss Fern carefully words this next accusation, "she deserted under fire. This is not a serious charge. Few of us are courageous when tested." "She has lied, though," says Christine. "Is there any adult who hasn't lied?" asks Miss Fern. "Smooth the lines from your brow, my dear. You're so much prettier when smiling," she majestically adds. Christine determines to question Rhoda.

Christine now has a question for Miss Fern. Why wasn't she asked to contribute along with the others to the floral tribute that the entire school sent to Claude's funeral? Miss Fern avoids a direct answer, but Christine forces the issue.

CHRISTINE—You make excuses for Rhoda—and then you admit that you didn't ask me to help pay for the flowers—and the reasons you give for not asking me are obviously specious. Does this mean that in your mind, and in the minds of your sisters, there is some connection between the drowning and Rhoda's presence on the wharf?

MISS FERN—I refuse to believe there is any connection.

CHRISTINE—And yet you have acted as if there were.

MISS FERN—Yes, perhaps we have.

CHRISTINE—This is a terrible tragedy for Mrs. Daigle, as you say. She has lost her only son. But if there were any shadow over Rhoda—from what has happened—I shall have to live under it—and my husband, too. As for Rhoda—she would not be happy in your school next year.

MISS FERN—No, she would not. And since she would not, it would be as well to make up our minds now that she will not be there.

CHRISTINE—Then there is a shadow over her—and you have decided that she will not be invited to return to the Fern School?

MISS FERN—Yes. We have made that decision.

Rhoda doesn't play the game, according to Miss Fern. She has no sense of fair play. At the same time, Miss Fern makes clear that she has no thought of the child's being involved in Claude's death.

The painful effect of this conversation on Christine is followed by something equally painful: The Daigles have come to call.

Mr. Daigle tries ineffectually to restrain his drunken wife's outburst, but the minute she comes in the room the distracted, harried creature ticks off Christine as a "superior person," and the daughter of that wealthy Richard Bravo. Then she takes a sideswipe at Miss Fern's snootiness. Miss Fern looks down on her, cries Mrs. Daigle, because she used to work in a beauty parlor: "I was that frumpy blonde. Now I've lost my boy and I'm a lush. Everybody knows it."

After indulging in maudlin admiration of Christine's looks and taste, Mrs. Daigle slithers drunkenly round to the point of her visit. She wants to know about Claude's medal: Miss Fern wouldn't tell her a thing. Miss Fern protests she truly doesn't know. Undeterred, Mrs. Daigle cries: "You know more than you're telling. You're a sly one—because of the school. You don't want the school to get a bad name. But you know more than you're telling, Miss Butter-Wouldn't-Melt Fern. There's something funny about the whole thing. I've said so over and over to Mr. Daigle. He married quite late, you know. In his forties. 'Course I wasn't exactly what the fellows call "a spring chicken," either. We won't have any more children. No more."

Mr. Daigle—Please, Hortense. Let me take you home where you can rest.

Mrs. Daigle—Rest. Sleep. When you can't sleep at night, you can't sleep in the daylight. I lie and look at the water where he went down. There's something funny about the whole thing, Christine. I heard that your little girl was the last one who saw him alive. Will you ask her about the last few minutes and tell me what she says? Maybe she remembers some little thing. I don't care how small it is! No matter how small! You know something, Miss Fern dyes her hair. She knows something and she won't tell me. Oh, my poor little Claude! What did they do to you? (Christine *goes to* Mrs. Daigle *and puts her arm around her.*)

Christine—I will ask Rhoda, Hortense. Oh, if I only knew!

Mrs. Daigle—Somebody took the medal off his shirt, Christine. It couldn't come off by accident. I pinned it on myself, and it had a clasp that locks in place. It was no accident. You can wear such simple things, can't you? I never could wear simple things. I couldn't even buy 'em. When I got 'em home they didn't look simple— He was such a lovely, dear little boy. He said I was his sweetheart. He said he was going to marry me when he grew up. I used to laugh and say, "You'll forget me long before then. You'll find a prettier girl, and you'll marry her." And you know what he said then? He said, "No, I won't, because there's not a prettier girl in the whole world than you are." If you don't believe me, ask the girl who comes in and cleans. She was present at the time.

Mr. Daigle—Hortense—Hortense!

Mrs. Daigle—Why do you put your arms around me? You don't give a damn about me. You're a superior person and all that, and I'm—oh, God forgive me! There were those bruises on his hands, and that peculiar crescent-shaped mark on his forehead that the undertaker covered up. He must have bled before he died. That's what the doctor said. And where's the medal? Who took the medal? I have a right to know what became of the penmanship medal! If I knew, I'd have a good idea what happened to him.—I don't know why you took it on yourself to put your arms around me. I'm as good as you are. And Claude was better than your girl. He won the medal, and she didn't. I'm drunk. It's a pleasure to stay drunk when your little boy's been killed. Maybe I'd better lay down.

Poor Mr. Daigle guides his wife to the door, apologizing as he goes, over Mrs. Daigle's: "Oh, who cares what they think?"

Miss Fern takes her reserved, ladylike farewell, thanking Christine for bearing with her and the Daigles. Promising to do what she can with Rhoda, and much moved by the tragic figure they've just seen, Christine embraces Miss Fern, crying: "She will have to live with it till she dies!" Miss Fern agrees, and goes.

After checking on Rhoda in the arbor, Christine answers the phone and Kenneth. Happy to speak to her husband, she reassures him that in spite of the accident Rhoda is her usual self; and says nothing of her worries, nothing about Miss Fern. Christine just asks him to call her as often as possible and tells him how much she loves him.

It is now Monica's turn to barge in, but this time she hasn't come to gossip, but to take Rhoda's locket to be fixed. Christine goes to Rhoda's table and gets the locket; in doing so, her fingers touch something else. She takes this out, too, but conceals it from Monica.

After Monica leaves for the jeweler, Christine looks with horror at the medal in her hand. She still has it in front of her when Rhoda comes in.

Confronted with the evidence, Rhoda warily makes conversation while gaining time to think.

CHRISTINE—All right, Rhoda. Answer my question. And remember I'm not as innocent about what went on at the picnic as you think. Miss Fern has told me a great deal. So please don't bother to make up a story for my benefit. (RHODA *is silent, her mind working.*) How did Claude Daigle's medal get in your drawer? It certainly didn't get there by itself. I'm waiting for your answer.

Rhoda is silent, then starts insisting she had nothing to do with the medal's being there. Christine, controlling herself, checks over the guard's report of Rhoda's being on the wharf. Rhoda's time for being there is earlier than the guard's; she says the guard was wrong, and that she told Miss Fern so. . . . "He hollered at me to come off the wharf and I did. I went back to the lawn and that's where I saw Claude. But I wasn't bothering him."

CHRISTINE—What did you say to Claude?

RHODA—I said if I didn't win the medal, I was glad he did.

CHRISTINE (*wearily*)—Please, please, Rhoda. I know you're an adroit liar. But I must have the truth.

RHODA—But it's all true, Mother. Every word.

When Christine gives her the monitor's report of seeing her grab the medal from Claude, Rhoda tells of a game she and Claude had rigged up, to explain how it came into her possession.

Christine asks why she hadn't told Miss Fern. This produces a whimper: Miss Fern doesn't like her and would think bad things about her. Why hadn't she given the medal to heartbroken Mrs. Daigle, Christine next asks. For a moment, after Christine describes the sad state Claude's mother's in, Rhoda is quiet. Then she bursts out: "It was silly to want to bury the medal pinned on Claude's coat. Claude was dead. He wouldn't know whether he had the medal pinned on him or not." Sensing Christine's revulsion, Rhoda swiftly gushes: "I've got the sweetest mother. I tell everybody I've got the sweetest mother in the world," but she adds: "If she wants a little boy that bad, why doesn't she take one out of the orphan's home?" Christine shrinks from her: "Don't touch me! Get away from me! Don't talk to me. We have nothing to say to each other." "Well, okay," says Rhoda, turning away. "Okay, Mother."

Christine says sharply to Rhoda: ". . . when we lived in Baltimore, there was an old lady upstairs, Mrs. Clara Post, who liked you very much."

RHODA—Yes.

CHRISTINE—You used to go up to see her every afternoon. She was very old, and liked to show you all her treasures. The one you admired most was a crystal ball, in which opals floated. The old lady promised this treasure to you when she died. One afternoon when the daughter was out shopping at the supermarket, and you were alone with the old lady, she managed to fall down the spiral back stairs and break her neck. You said she heard a kitten mewing outside and went to see about it and somehow missed her footing and fell five flights to the courtyard below.

RHODA—Yes, it's true.

CHRISTINE—Then you asked the daughter for the crystal ball. She gave it to you, and it's still hanging at the head of your bed.

RHODA—Yes, Mother.

CHRISTINE—Rhoda, did you have anything to do, anything at all, no matter how little it was, with Claude getting drowned?

Rhoda, looking her straight in the eyes, says she had nothing to do with Claude's getting drowned; and when told that the Ferns don't want her back at the school next year, tosses off another: "Okay."

With a view to asking Miss Fern to come back, Christine calls the school, but she hasn't yet got there. Christine isn't prepared to leave a message. As Rhoda tries to figure out what her mother will tell Miss Fern, Christine exclaims: "No! It can't be true! It can't be true!" She turns to Rhoda, looks at her hard, then gathers her in her arms.

ACT II

As Rhoda goes to the kitchen to open an excelsior-filled carton containing a present from her father, Monica says how she yearns for a little girl just like her. Christine replies with the news that this perfect little girl isn't wanted at the Fern School next year. Monica immediately condemns the Ferns for being too small-minded to appreciate such a child.

Having rhapsodized over Rhoda, Monica next invites her to dinner. Christine is delighted: Reginald Tasker is coming for cocktails to advise her on some writing she plans to do, and it will be a help to have Rhoda out of the way.

It is unfortunate for Leroy that he chooses this moment to bring back a garbage pail, for he's at once put to work cleaning up the excelsior in the kitchen. A moment later Christine, having had a wire from her father announcing his imminent arrival, goes upstairs with Monica to get a room ready for him.

Leroy finds this a fine opportunity to taunt Rhoda, who at first pays no attention, but a little later snaps: "Go empty the excelsior. You talk silly all the time. I know what you do with the excelsior.

Thomas Chalmers, Evelyn Varden, Nancy

You made a bed of excelsior in the garage behind that old couch, and you sleep there where nobody can see you."

LEROY—I been way behind the times heretofore, but now I got your number, miss. I been hearing things about you that ain't nice. I been hearing you beat up that poor little Claude in the woods, and it took three of the Fern sisters to pull you off him. I heard you run him off the wharf, he was so scared.

McCormack and Henry Jones in "Bad Seed"

RHODA—If you tell lies like that you won't go to heaven when you die.

LEROY—I heard plenty. I listen to people talk. Not like you, who's gabbling all the time and won't let anybody get a word in edgewise. That's why I know what people are saying and you don't.

RHODA—People tell lies all the time. I think you tell them more than anybody else.

LEROY—I know what you done to that boy when you got him out

on the wharf. You better listen to me if you want to keep out of bad trouble.

Rhoda listens to Leroy's account of how she murdered Claude with a stick because he wouldn't hand over the medal, and calmly tells him that what he figured out never happened, that he should go away with his excelsior. Leroy can't faze her until he says it's impossible to wash off blood, that the police have a special powder that will show up the little boy's blood on her stick, and turn it a pretty blue color. "You're scared of the police yourself," Rhoda angrily yells back.

Whereupon, Christine enters. Finding her daughter all worked up, she orders the smirking Leroy not to speak to her again, or she'll report him. This time Rhoda says it was all her fault, that she started it. Leroy meekly leaves.

Leroy, however, has said something to ruffle Rhoda's calm. She asks her mother if the police really have a blue powder that uncovers bloodstains. Christine doesn't know, but offers to ask either Mr. Tasker or Miss Fern. At the name of her principal, Rhoda deliberately puts on a crying scene that doesn't fool Christine in the least. Having failed to make the intended impression, Rhoda casually decides it's time for dinner with Monica. She makes a fine impression on Reginald Tasker, who comes in as she goes out, a radiant smile on her face.

Tasker is pleased, too, that any minute he may be seeing Richard Bravo. He wonders why Christine doesn't ask her father rather than himself for pointers on mystery-story writing. Christine's answer is that her problem is a very modern psychological one, which can only have been solved very recently. What Christine asks him is: "Do children ever commit murders? Or is crime something that's learned gradually, and grows as the criminal grows up, so that only adults really do dreadful things?"

TASKER—Well, I have thought about that, and so have several authorities I've consulted lately. Yes, children have often committed murders, and quite clever ones too. Some murderers, particularly the distinguished ones who are going to make great names for themselves, start amazingly early.

CHRISTINE—In childhood?

TASKER—Oh, yes. Just like mathematicians and musicians. Poets develop later. There's never been anything worth while in poetry written before eighteen or twenty. But Mozart showed his genius at six, Pascal was a master mathematician at twelve, and some of the great criminals were topflight operators before they got out of short pants and pinafores.

CHRISTINE—They grew up in the slums, or among criminals, and learned from their environment?

The doorbell rings before Tasker can answer. Richard Bravo and his daughter greet one another with great affection. The men are then introduced to one another and exchange compliments on their work. When Tasker asks Bravo why he doesn't return to the criminology racket, Bravo says: "Well, all compliments aside, my latest books didn't sell as well as the early ones—and the war came along. Now I write filler." "You've written some things that won't be forgotten," says Tasker, "and now your daughter is going to try her hand." Christine quickly says it's all to take care of empty evenings with Kenneth away.

Tasker was rather stumped, he tells Bravo, by Christine's last question—whether criminal children are always the product of environment. Bravo unhesitatingly answers: "Nothing difficult about that, little one. They are. Look, can't I have some of this wicked mixture you're lapping up—" Christine gets him a drink, but keeps to the subject. Bravo repeats they are *always* products of their environment.

TASKER—I couldn't prove you're wrong, of course. But some doctor friends of mine assure me that we've all been putting too much emphasis on environment and too little on heredity lately. They say there's a type of criminal born with no capacity for remorse or guilt—born with the kind of brain that may have been normal among humans fifty thousand years ago—

BRAVO—Do you believe this?

TASKER—Yes, I guess I do.

BRAVO—Well, I don't.

TASKER—I've been convinced that there are people—only a few, and certainly very unfortunate—who are incapable from the beginning of acquiring a conscience, or a moral character. Not even able to love, except physically. No feeling for right or wrong.

BRAVO—I've heard such assertions, but never found any evidence behind them. If you encounter a human without compassion or pity or morals, he grew up where these things weren't encouraged. That's final and absolute. This stuff you're talking is tommyrot.

Christine wants to know whether these people of Tasker's look like brutes. Sometimes they do, Tasker says, but often they present a more convincing picture of virtue than normal people. Bravo finds no sense in discussing this until the evidence is properly examined.

TASKER—Well, I'd like to go into it with you, Mr. Bravo. This clinic I frequent came long ago to the conclusion that there are bad seeds—just plain bad from the beginning, and nothing can change them.

CHRISTINE—And this favorite murderess of yours—the one you were speaking of the other day—is she an instance?

TASKER—Bessie Denker—was she a bad seed? Well, she may have been, because the deaths started so early in her vicinity. Bessie earned her sobriquet of "The Destroying Angel" in early childhood.

CHRISTINE—Oh, then she began young?

TASKER—Yes. The name wasn't applied to her till much later, when the whole story of her career came out, but Bessie was lethal and accurate from the beginning. One of her most famous murders involved the use of the deadly amanita, a mushroom known as "the destroying angel," and some clever reporter transferred the term to her.—In fact, it was a colleague of Mr. Bravo's, unless I've missed something—

BRAVO—It may have been—I don't know.

CHRISTINE—How did she end?

TASKER—Well, Mr. Bravo knows more about it than I do—

Bravo wants to change the subject, but Christine wants to know the rest of the story. Tasker says that's the mystery: by the time the authorities caught up with her, Bessie had disappeared with her sizable fortune. A similar beauty emerged in Australia under the name of Beulah Demerest. "How could she—kill so many—and leave no trace?" asks Christine. "You wrote a famous essay," says Tasker to Bravo, "listing all her methods—you must know it better than I do—"

BRAVO—Not at all. I've dropped all that—haven't read the recent literature.

CHRISTINE—Did she ever use violence?

TASKER—Forgive me, sir, I'll make it short. She made a specialty of poisons—studied not only drugs and toxins but the lives of those she wished to kill. It's practically impossible to prove murder when the victim dies of rattlesnake venom in Western Colo-

rado. Too many diamondbacks about. And tetanus can be picked
up in any barnyard. She made use of such things.—It all came to
a sudden end—she was indicted again and took off for parts unknown—leaving no—but wasn't there a child, a little girl?

BRAVO—Never heard of one. That must be a recent addition
to the myth.

CHRISTINE—I wanted to ask one more question. Was she ever
found out here?

TASKER—Not in this country. Three juries looked at that lovely,
dewy face and heard that melting, cultured voice and said, "She
couldn't have done it."

CHRISTINE—She wasn't convicted?

TASKER—"Not guilty." Three times.

CHRISTINE—You think she was one of these poor deformed children, born without pity?

TASKER—Personally, I do.

CHRISTINE—Did she have an enchanting smile?

TASKER—Dazzling, by all accounts.

CHRISTINE—She was doomed?

TASKER—Absolutely. Doomed to commit murder after murder
till somehow or other she was found out.

Christine feels Bessie would have been better off if she'd died
young, and Tasker agrees that she and society would both have
been better off.

After this cheerful conversation, Tasker takes his leave, so that
father and daughter can be together.

Christine talks first of Kenneth, and their unhappy change of
summer plans, but Bravo comes to the point and asks what is bothering her. Christine says she's less worried now that he is here:
his very presence makes her feel so safe and comfortable. And
finding it almost impossible to say what's on her mind, Christine
first talks of the amateur psychiatrist Monica, whom her father
will soon meet, and then speaks of her recurring adoption dream.
Monica, she says, calls it one of the commonest fantasies of childhood, but lately that hasn't proved much of a comfort—on account
of Rhoda. "What about her?" asks Bravo.

CHRISTINE—She terrifies me. I'm afraid for her. I'm afraid of
what she may have inherited from me.

BRAVO—What could she have inherited?

CHRISTINE—Father—Daddy—whose child am I?

He says: "Mine." Christine begs to know if she really is. She must be sure of the truth, for Rhoda's sake and her own. Bravo asks what Rhoda has done. Christine can't say definitely but is full of fear. "It cannot be inherited," mutters Bravo, "it cannot."

All at once Bravo staggers slightly, putting out his hand for support. He tells his worried daughter to get him a glass of water: every so often, he has a trace of fibrillation and becomes dizzy, but he's perfectly well. Christine promises to ask no more questions, and Bravo thinks that's just as well. No more questions are needed: Christine now knows the answer.

Bravo tells her what a lucky man he always has been, and his greatest piece of luck was a little girl named Christine, who changed his once barren and futile life for him. But Christine knows now he found her somewhere, and doesn't even need Bravo to tell her it was a very strange place. A place she keeps seeing in her dream —though, Bravo tells her, she was less than two at the time she was actually there.

CHRISTINE—I dream of a bedroom in a farmhouse in a country-side where there were orchards. I sleep in the room with my brother, who is older than I—and my—is it my mother?—comes to take care of him. She is a graceful, lovely woman, like an angel. I suppose my brother must have died, for afterwards I'm alone in the room. One night I awake feeling terrified and for some reason I can't stay in that house. It is moonlight and I somehow get out the window, drop to the grass below and hide myself in the tall weeds beyond the first orchard. I don't recall much more except that toward morning I'm thirsty and keep eating the yellow pippins that fall from the tree—and when the first light comes up on the clouds I can hear my mother some distance away calling my name. I hide in the weeds and don't answer. Is this a dream? Is it only a dream?

BRAVO—What name did she call?

CHRISTINE—It isn't Christine. It—it is—could it be Ingold?

BRAVO—You remember that name?

CHRISTINE—Yes, it comes back to me. "Ingold! Ingold Denker," she was calling. You've concealed something from me all these years, haven't you, Daddy? I came out of that terrible household. You found me there.

Bravo does everything he can to console his daughter—it's so long ago, he tells her, and can't touch her now; she has been so loving and sweet, and known nothing but love and sweetness. Kenneth loves her, and Christine has made him happy, and Rhoda's a perfect, sound little girl, too.

CHRISTINE—Is she, Father? Is she?
BRAVO—What has she done?
CHRISTINE—She's—it's as if she were born blind!
BRAVO—It cannot happen. It does not happen.

Monica breezes in with a fulsome greeting for Bravo. When Rhoda follows her, she sings the child's praises to the grandfather. Bravo picks up Rhoda, then puts her down and peers into her face. All the while Monica raves over Bravo's works of twenty years ago. He answers lightly: "I've finally met my public," and is relieved to follow her upstairs to his room. After he and Monica leave, Christine goes to the kitchen to prepare dinner.

Christine suddenly catches a glimpse of Rhoda sneaking out with a bundle wrapped in newspaper. Rhoda says blandly that she's throwing some things away in the incinerator. "Let me see it!" demands Christine. She tries to take the bundle from Rhoda, who suddenly snatches it back and attempts to run away. The package tears, revealing Rhoda's shoes. Christine wrests it out of Rhoda's hands and pushes Rhoda violently from her. The child falls into a chair, staring at her mother with cold, fixed hatred. "You hit him with one of the shoes, didn't you?" cries Christine. "Tell me! Tell me the truth!" she demands. "You hit him with those shoes! That's how those half-moon marks got on his forehead and hands! Answer me! Answer me!" Rhoda, after a moment, does answer— with complete contempt: She hit him, what else could she do? When pressed for details, she swiftly shifts to tears and compliments, trying to play on Christine's emotions. Then she cold-bloodedly gives her agonized mother the whole story, blow by blow, ending with: "He tried to pull himself back on the wharf after he fell in the water. But I wouldn't have hit him any more, only he kept saying he was going to tell on me. Mommie, Mommie," Rhoda now begs, "please say you won't let them hurt me!" Christine puts her arms around the child, promising that nobody will hurt her, while desperately wondering what in the world she can do. Rhoda makes her grandstand plea for a barrel of hugs, but Christine is incapable of responding and tells her to run along and read, and to promise to tell no one what she has told Christine. Answers Rhoda: "Why would I tell and get killed?"

Now that she knows so much, says Christine, Rhoda might as well tell her what happened to old Mrs. Post in Baltimore. Rhoda admits that she pushed the old lady. Christine now begs Rhoda **to** burn the shoes in the incinerator as quickly as possible.

RHODA—What will you do with the medal, Mother?
CHRISTINE—I must think of something to do.
RHODA—You won't give it to Miss Fern.
CHRISTINE—No, I won't give it to Miss Fern.

SCENE II

Next morning after breakfast, after Rhoda has very charmingly taken a phone message for her grandfather, Leroy comes in and, finding Rhoda alone, picks up where he left off.

This time he has hit on the right weapon: the tapping shoes that he disliked. At first Rhoda says she never had any such shoes; then she says they hurt her so badly that she gave them away; then she just accuses Leroy: "You lie all the time, all the time." "How come I've got those shoes then?" teases Leroy. Rhoda snaps to attention, but when Leroy says that he took them from the apartment, she once more relaxes with her book. "It's just more lies," she says calmly. "I burned those shoes. I put them down the incinerator and burned them. Nobody's got them."

That was smart of her, Leroy concedes; but what if he was in the basement and heard those shoes come rattling down the pipe? Rhoda waits, frightened, while Leroy crows that he rescued enough of those shoes to send her to the electric chair. With deadly calm Rhoda asks him to return them. When he refuses, her cold fury quickly puts a stop to Leroy's laughter. He quickly tells Rhoda that he's only been fooling, that he hasn't any shoes but his own. As he goes towards the door, Rhoda shouts that she wants them back. "I was just fooling at first," says Leroy, staring at her, "but now I really believe you did kill him with your shoes." "You've got them hid, but you'd better get them and bring them back here! Right here to me," says Rhoda menacingly.

Christine overhears this as she comes in. After first playing innocent, Rhoda says that Leroy has her shoes. Leroy says he hasn't, then reminds Christine of the telephone message for Mr. Bravo, and leaves.

Bravo and Monica come in, and Bravo at once goes after his call. He finds out that if he gets a taxi right away, he can just make a necessary plane connection. He intends, however, to make Christine's apartment his headquarters for the next few weeks. His farewell to Rhoda consists of telling her to patent her smile. His farewell to his daughter is something else. Putting his arms around Christine, he tells her: "You are the bright thing in my life, Christine. It was you I lived for. You I loved. No matter what happens I want you to remember that. Don't worry. It will come out well." Promising to come back soon, he kisses her, and leaves. "What a trouper," says Monica.

Rhoda, hearing the Popsicle man's bell downstairs, goes for some money, and comes back wtih money and matches. Asked what they're for, Rhoda guesses she just wasn't thinking. Christine takes them away.

When the two women are alone, Monica, noticing how poorly Christine looks, prescribes a combination of vitamin pills and sleeping pills, and tries to buoy her up with how much both she and Emory love her. Christine puts her head on the table and sobs. She welcomes Monica's arms about her, but before she can speak, a drunken Mrs. Daigle appears at the door for a little talk with Rhoda.

Rhoda returns, licking her Popsicle; and after parking it with Monica, she goes to Mrs. Daigle to be kissed.

MRS. DAIGLE—You were with Claude when he had his accident, weren't you, dear? You're the little girl who was so sure she was going to win the penmanship medal, and worked so hard. But you didn't win it after all, did you, darling? Claude won the medal, didn't he? Now tell me this: would you say he won it fair and square or he cheated? These things are so important to me now he's dead. Would you say it was fair Claude had the medal? Because if it was fair, why did you go after him for it?

RHODA—I want my Popsicle.

MONICA—Rhoda, if you're going shopping with me, you'll have to come now. Mr. Pageson is going to show us his collection.

And Monica whisks Rhoda out the door.

"Well, I must say!" exclaims Mrs. Daigle, adding sarcastically that she had no wish to interfere with Rhoda's social life. She had only planned to hold the child in her arms and ask her a few simple questions, sure that Rhoda knows something she hasn't told them. When Mrs. Daigle lapses into mild abuse, Christine takes advantage of it to ask her not to come back again.

The distraught woman suddenly stops at the door, crying: "Oh, my God, oh, my God, it's time to go home!" She sobs on Christine's shoulder: "Oh, Christine, Christine, you know something! You know something, and you won't tell me!"

After she has gone, Christine—needing desperately to speak to Kenneth—puts in a call. While waiting for it to come through, Christine rehearses what she will say: "Kenneth darling, Kenneth, my dear love, what can I say to you? That our daughter is a—" She can't; she cancels the call.

Seeing that Mrs. Daigle has gone, Monica comes back, apologizing for having removed Rhoda from the woman's clutches. She has also relaxed discipline a bit and let Rhoda go out for another Popsicle. Christine finds this odd of Rhoda, but is momentarily distracted by the neatly labeled vitamin pills and sleeping pills that Monica gives her.

A few seconds later a fire breaks out in the garage: cries of "Fire! Fire!" come through the window. Delicately finishing her Popsicle, Rhoda comes in the door, quite at sea as to what the shouting is all about—she doesn't even think it sounds like "fire." She goes, unruffled, into the den and, closing the door, plays "Clair de lune."

Outside, the excitement climaxes in a crash and a man's screams of terror and pain. Monica runs to the window, and cries: "There's a man on fire!" Christine gets there just in time to see the human torch. "It's too late," she cries. "He fell just before he got to the pond!" Half fainting, Christine slips to her knees.

CHRISTINE—I should have known it was coming! I should have known! Why am I so blind?

MONICA—Thank God Rhoda was in the den playing the piano, and heard none of this!

CHRISTINE—The fire was in the garage! Where Leroy was!

MONICA—There's nothing we can do.

CHRISTINE—This time I saw it! I saw it with my own eyes.

She becomes hysterical, while Monica pleads with her to make sense. Emory and Reginald come in, report as tactfully as possible that the excelsior Leroy was sleeping on must have caught fire, then go downstairs to meet the ambulance.

Christine, listening to Rhoda's piano-playing, screams to her to stop that music. Out of the den comes a wide-eyed and innocent Rhoda, inquiring solicitously: "Is Mummy sick, Monica?" Christine yells: "Don't let me get my hands on her." And as Monica begs to know what could Rhoda have done, Christine says: "It's not what she's done—it's what I've done."

Thinking it will be easier for Christine if she takes Rhoda home for lunch, Monica leaves, saying she'll keep the child till Christine is calmer.

Shivering in her chair, Christine moans: "She killed him— But she's my little girl and I love her— Oh, my baby—my baby!" She buries her head in her arms and weeps.

SCENE III

After dinner, Christine knits calmly, while Rhoda, in pajamas, works on her jigsaw puzzle. Christine reads the night's story and gives Rhoda her new kind of pills from Monica. There will be eight in all, but Rhoda makes no objection because she knows Monica likes her.

"Do you love me, Mommy?" Rhoda asks. "Yes," Christine answers. Making conversation and at the same time taking inventory, Rhoda asks if Christine knows about Leroy. "Yes," says Christine. Next, Rhoda wants to know what Christine did with the medal.

CHRISTINE—I drove out to Benedict today to see Miss Fern. And then I made an excuse to go on the pier alone—and dropped the medal in the deep water there.

RHODA—Mommy, Leroy had my shoes, and he said he was going to give them to the police and then tell them about me—and they'd put me in the electric chair. So—I had to—

CHRISTINE—You don't need to say any more.

After she has taken all eight of her pills, Rhoda says: "There. That's all. Don't let them hurt me, Mommy." Christine promises they won't and the child says good night.

Christine reads till Rhoda is asleep, then puts down her book. "Rhoda, dear. Rhoda, dear—you are mine, and I carried you, and I can't let them hurt you. I can't let them take you away and shut you up. They'd put you in some kind of institution. Nobody can save you from that unless I save you. So sleep well, and dream well, my only child, and the one I love. I shall sleep too."

(*She gathers* RHODA *up in her arms gently, and carries her into the bedroom. After a moment she returns and opens a drawer in a spice cabinet, takes out a revolver and goes to the den. There is a shot and a fall.*)

A few days later, Monica comes from the kitchen with coffee for Kenneth, Emory and Reginald. A grief-stricken Kenneth feels the world completely empty without Christine. Emory can understand that, feeling much the same himself.

No matter how hard they try to account for Christine's death, no one has a clue. Kenneth, however, is sure there was a reason. . . . "Christine didn't do things without a reason.—Her father died suddenly, you said?"

TASKER—He'd had a series of attacks and the news of Christine's death seemed to have been too much for his heart.

EMORY—She had some worry or other and I think it was connected with her father.

TASKER—I think she brooded over the Daigle boy's death and about the death of Leroy.

Tasker definitely rules out insanity.

Kenneth, choking back his sobs, doesn't know how he's going to live, or if he wishes to.

As the piano starts up in the den, Monica says Kenneth still has a lot to be grateful for. . . . "If we hadn't heard the shot, you'd have lost Rhoda too." And she calls the child from the den.

RHODA—Did you like it, Daddy? I played it for you.

KENNETH—Oh, Rhoda, my Rhoda, there's a little of Christine left. It's in your smile!

RHODA—I love you, Daddy! What will you give me for a basket of kisses?

KENNETH—For a basket of kisses? (*He looks at her.*) Oh, my darling—I'll give you a basket of hugs! (*His arms go round her.*)

WITNESS FOR THE PROSECUTION *

A Murder Mystery in Three Acts

BY AGATHA CHRISTIE

[AGATHA CHRISTIE (Agatha Mary Clarissa Christie) *was working as a dispenser in a Red Cross Hospital and thought it would be fun to write a detective story. It must have been, for she has written over fifty of them. She was born in Devonshire and many of her stories have been turned into pictures and plays. "The Murder of Roger Ackroyd" was one of her several well-known motion pictures and her book "Murder on the Nile" showed up on Broadway as "Hidden Horizon" in 1946. However, Broadway remembers her best for her play "Ten Little Indians" done in 1944 and which ran for 426 performances.*]

IN the Temple Chambers of Sir Wilfrid Robarts, Q.C., a clerk is answering the telephone: "Sir Wilfrid Robarts' chambers. Oh, it's you, Charles. No, Sir Wilfrid's in court. Won't be back just yet. . . . Yes, Shuttleworth case. . . . What—with Myers for the prosecution and Banter trying it? He's been giving judgment for close on two hours already. . . . No, not an earthly this evening. We're full up. Can give you an appointment tomorrow. . . . No, couldn't possibly. I'm expecting Mayhew, of Mayhew and Brinskill, you know, any minute now. . . . Well, so long."

As the clerk sorts papers on Sir Wilfrid's desk, he is irritated by the presence of Greta, the office girl. Her constant sloppiness annoys him: Greta wishes to make tea well before the tea hour; there is also an error in her typing. "Just one word," says adenoidal Greta. "Anyone might do that." The clerk's icy rejoinder is: "The word you have left out is the word *not*. The omission of it entirely alters the sense." This only seems rather funny to Greta. "Counsel's Chambers are no place to be funny in," says the tight-lipped clerk. "The law, Greta, is a serious business and should be treated accordingly." He dismisses her to make tea.

CLERK—Mr. Mayhew, of Mayhew and Brinskill, will be here shortly. A Mr. Leonard Vole is also expected. They may come together or separately.

GRETA (*excited*)—Leonard Vole? Why, that's the name—it was in the paper . . .

CLERK (*repressively*)—The tea, Greta.

GRETA— . . . asked to communicate with the police as he might be able to give them useful information . . .

The clerk gets rid of her, and continues checking his papers, till Greta ushers in Mr. Mayhew, a middle-aged solicitor. Accompanying him is Leonard Vole, a likable, friendly young man of twenty-seven. To Mr. Mayhew, the clerk is most deferential, and hurries out to fetch Sir Wilfrid from the robing room.

Although Mayhew placidly seats himself, he can understand Leonard's general restlessness. But he won't let Leonard accept a cup of tea from Greta, who has returned to stare at him. There is no nonsense in Mr. Mayhew's voice as he cuts Leonard short: "No, thank you," he tells Greta. Getting a smile from Leonard, she quickly vanishes.

In the midst of his pacing, Leonard tells Mayhew that this all seems like a dream—that it all seems so silly. Mayhew rather sharply questions such an attitude. Explaining himself, Leonard says: "I mean I've always been a friendly sort of chap—get on with people and all that. I mean, I'm not the sort of fellow that does—well, anything violent. (*A pause.*) But I suppose it will be—all right, won't it? I mean you don't get convicted for things you haven't done in this country, do you?" "Our English judicial system," states Mayhew, "is, in my opinion, the finest in the world." Leonard finds cold comfort in this when he remembers a recently rectified miscarriage of justice: A Mr. Beck was finally pardoned after languishing for years in prison, "pardoned" for something he'd never done. "The important thing," Mayhew says, "was Beck was set at liberty." "Yes, it was all right for him. But if it had been murder, now—" Leonard collapses into a chair at this thought: "If it had been murder it would have been too late. He would have been hanged." Trying to calm him, Mayhew goes over the details of Leonard's background: "You are, at present, I understand, out of a job?" Leonard is embarrassed: he thinks this has to do with paying the solicitor's fee. Such a thought in turn disturbs Mayhew, who had only wanted to have his facts straight. Leonard thereupon answers readily enough: he is unemployed at present; has been unemployed, in fact, for a couple of months. Before that he was a mechanic for three months, and before that . . . As Mayhew listens to this chronicle of past jobs, he turns a bit sharp. Was Leonard discharged? he asks.

Not at all, Leonard tells him airily. He had words with the foreman, so he quit. The job before that became a bit awkward because it involved the affections of the boss' daughter, but the parting was amicable. Before *that*, he was selling egg beaters on commission. "Indeed," breathes Mayhew. "And a rotten job they were, too," Leonard adds. "I could have invented a better egg beater myself. (*Catching* MAYHEW's *mood.*) You're thinking I'm a bit of a drifter, sir? It's true in a way—but I'm not really like that. Doing my army service unsettled me a bit—that and being abroad. I was in Germany. It was fine there. That's where I met my wife. She's an actress. Since I've come back to this country I can't seem somehow to settle down properly. I don't know really just what I want to do. . . . I like working on cars best—and thinking out new gadgets for them. That's interesting, that is. And you see—" At this point Sir Wilfrid Robarts makes an imposing entrance.

Sir Wilfrid greets his friend Mayhew and comments on today's trial; he acknowledges the introduction to Leonard and asks him to sit down. Leonard does so at once. After inquiries about Mayhew's family's health, the talk goes right back to today's courtroom. Sir Wilfrid is glad to say he won the case.

MAYHEW—It always gives you satisfaction to beat Myers, doesn't it?

SIR WILFRID—It gives me satisfaction to beat anyone.

MAYHEW—But especially Myers.

SIR WILFRID—Especially Myers. He's an irritating gentleman. He always seems to bring out the worst in me.

MAYHEW—That would appear to be mutual. You irritate him because you hardly ever let him finish a sentence.

SIR WILFRID—He irritates me because of that mannerism of his. It's this— (*clears throat and adjusts imaginary wig*) that drives me to distraction, and he *will* call me Ro-barts—Robarts! But he's a very able advocate, if only he'd remember not to ask leading questions when he knows damn well he shouldn't. But let's get down to business.

A sense of urgency has made Mayhew bring Leonard Vole to Sir Wilfrid. Leonard bluntly puts it: "My wife thinks I'm going to be arrested. (*Looks embarrassed.*) She's much cleverer than I am—

so she may be right." "Arrested for what?" asks Sir Wilfrid. Leonard is even more embarrassed to say: "For murder."

Mayhew gives Sir Wilfrid a concise account of the murder of Miss Emily French, the reports of which Sir Wilfrid had read in the press. "She was a maiden lady," Mayhew says, "living alone but for an elderly housekeeper, in a house at Hampstead. On the night of October fourteenth her housekeeper returned at eleven o'clock to find that apparently the place had been broken into, and that her mistress had been coshed on the back of the head and killed." He turns to Leonard: "That is right?" "That's right," Leonard answers; and then continues: "It's quite an ordinary sort of thing to happen nowadays. And then, the other day, the papers said that the police were anxious to interview a Mr. Leonard Vole, who had visited Miss French earlier on the evening in question, as they thought he might be able to give them useful information. So of course I went along to the police station and they asked me a lot of questions."

Sir Wilfrid asks quickly: "Did they caution you?" Leonard is vague as to whether they did or not. "Oh, well," says Sir Wilfrid, having exchanged glances with Mayhew, "can't be helped now." "Anyway," Leonard continues, "it sounded damned silly to me. I told them all I could and they were very polite and seemed quite satisfied and all that. When I got home and told Romaine about it— my wife, that is—well, she got the wind up. She seemed to think that they—well—that they'd got hold of the idea that *I* might have done it. So I thought perhaps I ought to get hold of a solicitor— (*to* MAYHEW) so I came along to you. I thought you'd be able to tell me what I ought to do about it." He says this with an anxious look at both men.

Mayhew asks Leonard to tell Sir Wilfrid how he made Miss French's acquaintance. Apparently it was through his rescuing some of her dropped parcels from the middle of Oxford Street. She was grateful out of all proportion, Leonard said: ". . . anyone would think I'd saved her life instead of parcels." Never expecting to see her again, it so happened that a few days later he sat behind her in a theatre: "She looked around and recognized me and we began to talk, and in the end she asked me to come to see her." "And you went?" asks Sir Wilfrid. "Yes," Leonard replies. "She'd urged me to name a day specially and it seemed rather churlish to refuse. So I said I'd go on the following Saturday." He knew nothing about her except that she lived alone with a housekeeper and eight cats, in a beautifully furnished house.

SIR WILFRID—Had you reason to believe she was well off?
LEONARD—Well, she talked as though she was.

SIR WILFRID—And you yourself?

LEONARD (*cheerfully*)—Oh, I'm practically stony broke and have been for a long time.

SIR WILFRID—Unfortunate.

LEONARD—Yes, rather. Oh, you mean people will say I was sucking up to her for her money?

SIR WILFRID (*disarmed*)—I shouldn't have put it quite like that, but in the essence, yes, that is possibly what people might say.

LEONARD—It isn't really true, you know. As a matter of fact I was sorry for her. I thought she was lonely. I was brought up by an old aunt, Aunt Betsy, and I like old ladies.

SIR WILFRID—You say old ladies. Do you know what age Miss French was?

LEONARD—Well, I didn't know, but I read it in the paper after she was murdered. She was fifty-six.

SIR WILFRID—Fifty-six. You consider that old, Mr. Vole, but I should doubt if Miss Emily French considered herself old.

LEONARD—But you can't call it a chicken, can you?

SIR WILFRID—Well, let us get on. You went to see Miss French fairly frequently?

He went once or twice a week, but never with his wife. Leonard frankly admits that Miss French wouldn't have been pleased had he brought her. "You see," Leonard says, "she got rather fond of me." He objects when Sir Wilfrid suggests he means she was in love with him: "Oh, good Lord, no, nothing of that kind. Just pampered me and spoiled me, that sort of thing."

SIR WILFRID (*after a moment's pause*)—You see, Mr. Vole, I have no doubt part of the police case against you, if there *is* a case against you, which as yet we have no definite reason to suppose, will be why did you, young, good-looking, married, devote so much of your time to an elderly woman with whom you could hardly have very much in common?

LEONARD (*gloomily*)—Yes, I know they'll say I was after her for her money. And in a way perhaps that's true. But only in a way.

SIR WILFRID (*slightly disarmed*)—Well, at least you're frank, Mr. Vole. Can you explain a little more clearly?

LEONARD—Well, she made no secret of the fact that she was rolling in money. As I told you, Romaine and I—that's my wife—are pretty hard up. I'll admit that I did hope that if I was really in a tight place she'd lend me some money. I'm being honest about it.

SIR WILFRID—Did you ask her for a loan?

LEONARD—No, I didn't. I mean, things weren't desperate. (*He becomes suddenly rather more serious as though he realized the gravity of that.*) Of course, I can see—it does look rather bad for me.

Sir Wilfrid wants to find out why Miss French never had Leonard bring his wife. And Leonard, it seems, had kept her out of the picture so Miss French's interest in him woludn't lessen; so Miss French might be willing to finance an invention of his. He admits it's hard to explain, but he hadn't really sponged and at no time had he ever taken money from her.

Asked about the housekeeper, Leonard describes her—her name is Janet Mackenzie—as a regular old tyrant. . . . "Fairly bullied poor Miss French. Looked after her very well and all that, but the poor old dear couldn't call her soul her own when Janet was about. (*Adds thoughtfully.*) Janet didn't like me at all."

SIR WILFRID—Why didn't she like you?

LEONARD—Oh, jealous, I expect. I don't think she liked my helping Miss French with her business affairs.

SIR WILFRID—Oh, so you helped Miss French with her business affairs?

Leonard tells breezily of helping her with her investments, and filling in forms and things like that. Sir Wilfrid then asks Leonard an extremely serious question, and demands a truthful answer: did Leonard at any time convert any of these securities to his own use? Before Leonard can make an indignant denial, Sir Wilfrid asks him to think before answering: "Because, you see, there are two points of view. Either we can make a feature of your probity and honesty— or, if you swindled the woman in any way, then we must take the line that you had no motive for murder, since you had already a profitable source of income. You can see there are advantages in either point of view. What I want is the truth. Take your time if you like before you reply." Leonard solemnly says: "I assure you, Sir Wilfrid, that I played dead straight and you won't find anything to the contrary. Dead straight."

Gratified, Sir Wilfrid proceeds to the night of the murder itself. Mayhew supplies the date: October fourteenth. Leonard cheerfully describes his visit to the lady: it was prompted by his finding a new gadget he thought might interest her, and by the fact that Friday was Janet's night off and that Miss French might be lonely. Sir Wilfrid notes with disapproval that Leonard knew it was Janet's night out, but lets him get on with his story. "Well," continues Leonard, "I got there at a quarter to eight. She'd finished her supper but I had a cup of coffee with her and we played a game of double demon. Then at nine o'clock I said good night to her and went home."

SIR WILFRID—You told me the housekeeper said she came home that evening earlier than usual.

LEONARD—Yes, the police told me she came back for something she'd forgotten and she heard—or she says she heard—somebody talking with Miss French. Well, whoever it was, it wasn't me.

SIR WILFRID—Can you prove that, Mr. Vole?

LEONARD—Yes, of course I can prove it. I was at home again with my wife by then. That's what the police kept asking me. Where I was at nine-thirty. Well, I mean some days one wouldn't know where one was. As it happens, I can remember quite well that I'd gone straight home to Romaine and we hadn't gone out again.

He lived in a tiny flat behind Euston Station, but didn't suppose anyone saw him return there. "Why should they?" Leonard says. All Sir Wilfrid means is that it would have been an advantage if they had. "But surely you don't think—" protests Leonard. "I mean, if she were really killed at half past nine—my wife's evidence is all I need, isn't it?" Sir Wilfrid and Mayhew just look at each other. Mayhew takes over to ask if he can be sure his wife will say he was at home at that time. Leonard is sure she will.

MAYHEW—You are very fond of your wife and your wife is very fond of you?

LEONARD (*face softening*)—Romaine is absolutely devoted to me. She's the most devoted wife any man could have.

MAYHEW—I see. You are happily married.

LEONARD—Couldn't be happier. Romaine's wonderful—absolutely wonderful. I'd like you to know her, Mr. Mayhew.

After knocking, Greta brings in the evening papers, points out something in one of them for Sir Wilfrid, and leaves. Mayhew tries to find out more about Leonard's walk home on the night of the murder—for which he has no witnesses. Leonard doesn't think that matters, what with Romaine. . . . "The evidence of a devoted wife unsupported by any other evidence may not be completely convincing, Mr. Vole," adds Sir Wilfrid.

And he reminds Leonard that it's not he, but the jury, that has to be convinced. Having thus chastened Leonard, Sir Wilfrid next—with the item from the newspaper—flabbergasts him: "You are aware, are you not, that Miss French left a will leaving you all her money?" Leonard was not aware, can hardly believe it. She had never said a word on the subject. Mayhew asks him if he's quite sure. "Absolutely sure," Leonard insists. "I'm very grateful to her —yet, in a way I rather wish now that she hadn't. I mean it—it's a bit unfortunate as things are, isn't it, sir?" It supplies Leonard with a very adequate motive, Sir Wilfrid answers, "if he knew about it," which he says he didn't.

What with how matters stand, Sir Wilfrid feels that Leonard should face the probability of being arrested. Both he and Mayhew assure him in the friendliest way that they will do everything they can to help him, and to look after his wife, who (Leonard is sure) will be in a terrible state. Leonard can't believe that he may actually stand in the prisoner's box. Nor can he see why the police don't think it was a burglar: the newspaper reports speak of a forced window, smashed glass, and things strewn all around. "The police must have some good reason for not thinking that it was a burglary," comments Mayhew.

When the Clerk announces the "gentlemen," Sir Wilfrid goes out to speak to the police, while Mayhew, patting Leonard's shoulder, advises him to make no further statements. Sir Wilfrid returns with a diffident Inspector, who very courteously produces a warrant for his arrest. Inspector Hearne warns Leonard that anything he says may be used in evidence. "Okay," says Leonard, looking nervously at Sir Wilfrid, "I'm ready." With a polite "good afternoon" and a proper word about the weather, Inspector Hearne hopes that "we haven't inconvenienced you, Sir Wilfrid." "I am never inconvenienced," Sir Wilfrid answers.

After the door closes on Leonard and the police, Sir Wilfrid and Mayhew agree that the young man is in a worse mess than he seems to realize. "How does he strike you?" Mayhew asks.

Sir Wilfrid—Extraordinarily naïve. Yet in some ways quite shrewd. Intelligent, I should say. . . . But he certainly doesn't realize the danger of his position.

Mayhew—Do you think he did it?

Sir Wilfrid—I've no idea. On the whole, I should say *not*. (*Sharply.*) You agree?

Mayhew—I agree.

Sir Wilfrid—Oh, well, he seems to have impressed both of us favorably. I can't think why. I never heard a weaker story. God knows what we're going to do with it! The only evidence in his favor seems to be his wife's—and who's going to believe a wife?

MAYHEW (*with dry humor*)—It has been known to happen.

SIR WILFRID—She's a foreigner, too. Nine out of the twelve in a jury box believe a foreigner is lying, anyway. She'll be emotional and upset, and won't understand what the prosecuting counsel says to her. Still, we shall have to interview her. You'll see, she'll have hysterics all over my chambers.

Perhaps, Mayhew suggests, Sir Wilfrid would rather not accept the brief. "Who says I won't accept it?" booms Sir Wilfrid. "Just because I point out that the boy has an absolute tomfool story to tell." But it's a true one, Mayhew feels. Sir Wilfrid thinks it must be a true one. . . . "It couldn't be so idiotic if it wasn't true. . . ." But it was Leonard's manner of blurting things out that made it believable. Mayhew thinks he has a good personality. Good for the jury, Sir Wilfrid thinks.

Greta now enters excitedly to say that Mrs. Vole is outside, and to add her personal opinion that Leonard didn't do it. "Why not?" demands Sir Wilfrid. "He's far too nice," says Greta. "That makes three of us," Sir Wilfrid remarks to Mayhew. And to Greta: "Bring Mrs. Vole in."

As Greta goes for Mrs. Vole, Sir Wilfrid adds: "And we're probably three credulous fools, taken in by a young man with a pleasing personality."

Mrs. Vole does not have a pleasing, easy personality. She's an attractive but strangely ironic foreigner. Sir Wilfrid is quite put off to find there are no tears, no flutterings, no helplessness. Having expected Mrs. Vole to be upset, Sir Wilfrid finds her calmness downright disconcerting. When she is told of Leonard's arrest, she doesn't turn a hair. All Sir Wilfrid can do is commend her for her "fortitude." "The great thing," he tells her, "is to be calm and to tackle all this sensibly." This suits Romaine Vole perfectly, she wants nothing hidden from her, she wishes to "know the worst."

In between compliments to Romaine, Sir Wilfrid tries fishing for information about Leonard's friendship with Miss French. He comes up with an empty hook.

SIR WILFRID—You yourself did not object at all to your husband's friendship with this old lady?

ROMAINE—I do not think I objected, no.

SIR WILFRID—You have, of course, perfect trust in your husband, Mrs. Vole. Knowing him as well as you do—

ROMAINE—Yes, I know Leonard very well.

SIR WILFRID—I can't tell you how much I admire your calm and your courage, Mrs. Vole.   Knowing as I do how devoted you are to him . . .

ROMAINE—So you know how devoted I am to him?

SIR WILFRID—Of course.

ROMAINE—But excuse me, I am a foreigner.   I do not always know your English terms.   But is there not a saying about knowing something of your own knowledge?   You do not know that I am devoted to Leonard, of your own knowledge, do you, Sir Wilfrid? (*She is smiling.*)

SIR WILFRID (*slightly disconcerted*)—No, no, that is of course true.   But your husband told me.

ROMAINE—Leonard told you how devoted I was to him?

SIR WILFRID—Indeed, he spoke of your devotion in the most moving terms.

ROMAINE—Men, I often think, are very stupid.

Sir Wilfrid tries to find out whether Romaine knew anything of Miss French's will.   She answers yes—from the afternoon papers. Asked if Leonard knew nothing, Romaine answers: "Is that what he told you?"   "Yes," says Sir Wilfrid.   And he adds: "You don't suggest anything different?"   "No," says Romaine silkily.   "Oh, no. I do not suggest anything."   To Sir Wilfrid's assurance that Miss French undoubtedly regarded Leonard as a son, Romaine inquires: "You think Miss French looked upon Leonard as a son?"   Having thus flustered Sir Wilfrid, she now startles him: "What hypocrites you are in this country."

To each question about Leonard's whereabouts on the evening of October fourteenth, Romaine answers just as Leonard said she would, but her tone and manner of answering sow confusion.   Asked what she means by all this, Romaine ever so sweetly answers: "That is what Leonard wants me to say, is it not?"   "It's the truth," Sir Wilfrid answers.   "You said so just now."   Romaine wants to make sure: "If I say: yes, it is so, Leonard was with me in the flat at nine-thirty—will they acquit him?   Will they let him go?"   Mayhew, thoroughly puzzled, says: "If you are both speaking the truth, then they will—er—have to acquit him."   "But," Romaine answers, "when I said that—to the police, I do not think they believed me." Instead of being distressed, she seems almost satisfied.   "What makes you think they did not believe you?" inquires Sir Wilfrid.   Romaine, with sudden malice, answers: "Perhaps I did not say it very well?"

Sir Wilfrid says: "Perhaps your husband's position is not quite clear to you?"

ROMAINE—I have already said that I want to understand fully just how black the case against—my husband is. I say to the police: Leonard was at home with me at nine-thirty—and they do not believe me. But perhaps there is someone who saw him leave Miss French's house, or who saw him in the street on his way home? (*Looks sharply and rather slyly from one to the other.* SIR WILFRID *looks inquiringly at* MAYHEW.)

MAYHEW (*reluctantly*)—Your husband cannot think of, or remember anything helpful of that kind.

ROMAINE—So it will be only his word—and mine. (*With intensity.*) And mine. (*Rises abruptly to her feet.*) Thank you, that is what I wanted to know.

They beg her not to go—there are so many things to discuss. Romaine, now openly mocking, brings up the oath she will have to swear on the witness stand, and causes further confusion by even casting doubt on her love for Leonard.

SIR WILFRID—You are aware, Mrs. Vole, that you cannot by law be called to give testimony damaging to your husband?

ROMAINE—How very convenient.

SIR WILFRID—And your husband can—

ROMAINE (*interrupts*)—He is not my husband.

SIR WILFRID—What?

ROMAINE—Leonard Vole is not my husband. He went through a form of marriage with me in Berlin. He got me out of the Russian Zone and brought me to this country. I did not tell him, but I had a husband living at the time.

SIR WILFRID—He got you out of the Russian sector and safely to this country. You should be very grateful to him. (*Sharply.*) Are you?

ROMAINE—One can get tired of gratitude.

SIR WILFRID—Has Leonard Vole ever injured you in any way?

ROMAINE (*scornfully*)—Leonard? Injured me? He worships the ground I walk on.

SIR WILFRID—And you? (*Again there is a duel of eyes between them. Then she laughs and turns away.*)

ROMAINE—You want to know too much.

Wishing to clear up some of these ambiguities, Mayhew asks coldly what happened on the evening of October fourteenth. As if by rote, Romaine monotonously repeats: "Leonard came in at twenty-five minutes past nine and did not go out again. I have given him an alibi, have I not?" Sir Wilfrid says: "You have, Mrs. Vole," adding, "You're a very remarkable woman, Mrs. Vole." "And you are satisfied, I hope?" says Romaine as she sweeps out the door. Sir Wilfrid is damned if he's satisfied, nor Mayhew either. Convinced she is up to something, Sir Wilfrid would like to know what. Mayhew wonders what will happen if they put her in the witness box. "God knows!" answers Sir Wilfrid.

MAYHEW—The prosecution would break her down in no time, especially if it were Myers.

SIR WILFRID—If it's not the Attorney General, it probably will be.

MAYHEW—Then what's your line of attack?

SIR WILFRID—The usual. Keep interrupting—as many objections as possible.

MAYHEW—What beats me is that young Vole is convinced of her devotion.

SIR WILFRID—Don't put your trust in that. Any woman can fool a man if she wants to and if he's in love with her.

MAYHEW—He's in love with her, all right. And trusts her completely.

SIR WILFRID—More fool he. Never trust a woman.

ACT II

Six weeks later, Leonard is on trial at the Old Bailey. Before a bewigged presiding judge, and a jury of his peers, he has pleaded "Not guilty." As was expected, Mr. Myers, Q.C., in wig and gown, is for the prosecution.

The Judge himself speaks before Mr. Myers opens the trial: "Members of the jury, the proper time for me to sum up the evidence to you and instruct you as to the law is after you have heard all the evidence. But because there has been a considerable amount of publicity about this case in the press, I would just like to say this to you now. By the oath which each of you has just taken, you swore to try this case on the evidence. That means on the evidence that you are now going to hear and see. It does not mean that you are to consider also anything you have heard or read before taking your oaths. You must shut out from your minds everything except what will take place in this court. You must not let anything else influence your minds in favor of or against the prisoner. I am quite sure that you will do your duty conscientiously in the way that I have indicated. Yes, Mr. Myers."

Mr. Myers rises and addresses the court: "May it please you, my lord. Members of the jury, I appear in this case with my learned friend Mr. Barton for the prosecution, and my learned friends Sir Wilfrid Robarts (he pronounces it Ro-barts) and Mr. Brogan-Moore appear for the defense. This is a case of murder. The facts are simple and up to a certain point are not in dispute. You will hear how the prisoner, a young and, you may think, a not unattractive man, made the acquaintance of Miss Emily French, a woman of fifty-six. How he was treated by her with kindness and even with affection. The nature of that affection you will have to decide for yourselves. Dr. Wyatt will tell you that in his opinion death occurred at some time between nine-thirty and ten on the night of the fourteenth of October last. You will hear the evidence of Janet Mackenzie, who was Miss French's faithful and devoted house-keeper. The fourteenth of October—it was a Friday—was Janet Mackenzie's night out, but on this occasion she happened to return for a few minutes at nine twenty-five. She let herself in with a key and upon going upstairs to her room she passed the door of the sitting room. She will tell you that in the sitting room she heard the voices of Miss French and of the prisoner, Leonard Vole."

Leonard cries out: "That's not true. It wasn't me." Myers continues: "Janet Mackenzie was surprised since, as far as she knew, Miss French had not expected Leonard Vole to call that evening. However, she went out again and when she returned finally at eleven she found Miss Emily French murdered, the room in disorder, a window smashed and the curtains blowing wildly. Horror-stricken, Janet Mackenzie immediately rang up the police. I should tell you that the prisoner was arrested on the twentieth of October. It is the case for the prosecution that Miss Emily Jane French was murdered between nine-thirty and ten P.M. on the evening of the fourteenth of October, by a blow from a cosh and that that blow was struck by the prisoner. I will now call Inspector Hearne."

The matter-of-fact Inspector is sworn in, and in unexcited tones tells of receiving an emergency call, of finding Miss French's body, and of the disorder in the room where she was found. Inspector Hearne tells that an attempt had been made to force the window with some implement, possibly a chisel. He tells also how glass was strewn about the floor as well as on the ground outside the window.

MR. MYERS—Is there any particular significance in finding glass both inside and outside the window?

INSPECTOR—The glass outside was not consistent with the window having been forced from outside.

MYERS—You mean that if it had been forced from the inside there had been an attempt to make it look as though it had been done from the outside?

SIR WILFRID—I object. My learned friend is putting words into the witness's mouth. He really must observe the rules of evidence.

But Myers leads up to his point: "In any other case where the windows have been forced from the outside, have you found glass on the outside of the window some distance below, on the ground?" "No," answers the Inspector. "No," says Myers, and gets on with his case, to the Inspector's finding no fingerprints save those of Miss French herself; those of Janet Mackenzie; and those of the prisoner. The Inspector is next asked to repeat the statement Leonard made when arrested. The Inspector repeats: "Okay, I'm ready." His tone makes Leonard's nervous statement sound cocky.

"Now, Inspector," continues Myers, "you say the room had the appearance of a robbery having been committed?"

SIR WILFRID—That is just what the Inspector did not say. If your lordship remembers, that was a suggestion made by my friend—and quite improperly made—to which I objected.

JUDGE—You are quite right, Sir Wilfrid. At the same time I'm not sure that the Inspector is not entitled to give evidence of any facts which might tend to prove that the disorder of the room was not the work of a person who broke in from outside for the purpose of robbery.

SIR WILFRID—My lord, may I respectfully agree with what your lordship has said? Facts, yes. But not the mere expression of opinion without even the facts on which it is based.

MYERS—Perhaps, my lord, if I phrased my question in this way my friend would be satisfied. Inspector, could you say from what you saw whether there had or had not been a bona fide breaking in from outside the house?

SIR WILFRID—My lord, I really must continue my objection. My learned friend is again seeking to obtain an opinion from this witness.

JUDGE—Yes, Mr. Myers, I think you will have to do a little better than that.

MYERS—Inspector, did you find anything inconsistent with a breaking in from outside?

INSPECTOR—Only the glass, sir.

MYERS—Nothing else?

INSPECTOR—No, sir, there was nothing else.

JUDGE—We all seem to have drawn a blank there, Mr. Myers.

Myers brings out that the jewels Miss French was wearing were left untouched, nor had anything else been taken. Next Myers asks: "Do you produce a jacket, Inspector?" And a jacket is placed in evidence. This was found by the Inspector in the prisoner's flat, and sent to Mr. Clegg at the lab to be tested for possible bloodstains. "Lastly," says Myers, "Inspector, do you produce the will of Miss French?" "I do, sir," answers Inspector Hearne. As far as the Inspector can ascertain, this will of October eighth left a net amount of eighty-five thousand pounds to the prisoner.

Mr. Myers sits down.

Sir Wilfrid takes on the Inspector, and in a moment has him agreeing that a burglar, when breaking in, almost always wears gloves. "So the absence of fingerprints in a case of robbery would hardly surprise you?" "No, sir," says the Inspector. He also concedes that the chisel marks made while trying to force the window were on the outside. But, the Inspector adds, the marks could have been made from inside or out, because the adjacent windows were casements, and it would have been simple to open one, lean out and force the catch of the other. "Tell me," says Sir Wilfrid, "did you find any chisel near the premises, or at the prisoner's flat?" At the prisoner's flat, the Inspector found one—but it didn't fit. "According to my learned friend," Sir Wilfrid drives on, "Janet Mackenzie said that curtains were blowing. Perhaps you noticed that fact yourself?" "Well, yes, sir," answers the Inspector, "they did blow about." Sir Wilfrid's point is that probably the burglar had forced the window from the outside; and that as the window swung back in a strong wind, some of the glass might easily have fallen on the outside.

Next Sir Wilfrid has the Inspector deplore with him the recent rise in crimes of violence. But when Sir Wilfrid proceeds to conjure up some young thugs intent on assaulting and robbing Miss French, Myers objects: "I submit that it is impossible for Inspector Hearne to guess at what went on in the minds of some *entirely* problematical young criminals who may not even exist." Sliding on to his next point, without apparently noticing the objection, Sir Wilfrid emphasizes that Leonard had always protested his innocence. "Yes, sir," says the Inspector. Then Sir Wilfrid puts a knife in the Inspector's hands—a good, sharp-edged French vegetable knife that Mrs. Vole had first brought to the Inspector's attention at her flat. Having emphasized the knife's sharp edge, Sir Wilfrid now asks the Inspector: "And if you were cutting—say, ham—carving it, that is, and your hand slipped with this knife, it would be capable of inflicting a very nasty cut, and one which would bleed profusely?" Myers objects: "That is a matter of opinion, and medical opinion at that."

SIR WILFRID—I withdraw the question. I will ask you instead, Inspector, if the prisoner, when questioned by you as to the stains on the sleeve of his jacket, drew your attention to a recently healed scar on his wrist, and stated that it had been caused by a household knife when he was slicing ham?

INSPECTOR—That is what he said.

SIR WILFRID—And you were told the same thing by the prisoner's wife?

INSPECTOR—The first time. Afterwards—

SIR WILFRID (*sharply*)—A simple yes or no, please. Did the prisoner's wife show you this knife and tell you that her husband had cut his wrist with it slicing ham?

INSPECTOR—Yes, she did.

MYERS (*rises*)—What first drew your attention to that jacket, Inspector?

INSPECTOR—The sleeve appeared to have been recently washed.

MYERS—And you were told this story about an accident with a kitchen knife?

INSPECTOR—Yes, sir.

MYERS—And your attention was drawn to a scar on the prisoner's wrist?

INSPECTOR—Yes, sir.

MYERS—Granted that that scar was made by this particular knife, there was nothing to show whether it was an accident or done deliberately?

SIR WILFRID—Really, my lord, if my learned friend is going to answer his own questions, the presence of the witness seems to be superfluous.

MYERS (*resignedly*)—I withdraw the question. Thank you, Inspector.

The Inspector stands down, and the police surgeon, Dr. Wyatt, takes his place on the witness stand. Dr. Wyatt tells of his examination, at eleven P.M., October fourteenth, of Miss French's body. He places her death at somewhere between nine-thirty and ten P.M., and as caused by a blow on the head with something like a cosh. Asked if Miss French had struggled with her murderer, Dr. Wyatt says no, she was apparently taken quite unawares. With this, Myers rests. Sir Wilfrid rises and asks the doctor to tell just where this blow had been struck. . . . "There was only one blow, was there not?"

DR. WYATT—Only one. On the left side, at the asterion.

SIR WILFRID—I beg your pardon? Where?

Dr. Wyatt—The asterion. The junction of the parietal, occipital and temple bones.

Sir Wilfrid—Oh, yes. And in layman's language, where is that?

Dr. Wyatt—Behind the left ear.

Sir Wilfrid—Would that indicate that the blow had been struck by a left-handed person?

Dr. Wyatt—It's difficult to say. The blow appeared to have been struck directly from behind, because the bruising ran perpendicularly. I should say it is really impossible to say whether it was delivered by a right- or left-handed man.

Sir Wilfrid—We don't know yet that it was a *man*, Doctor. But will you agree, from the position of the blow, that if anything it is more likely to have been delivered by a left-handed person?

The Doctor thinks it possible but cannot be sure. Next, Sir Wilfrid has Dr. Wyatt concede that blood would inevitably have got on the hand and arm that struck the blow, and in all likelihood only on that hand and arm. Dr. Wyatt further agrees that no great strength was needed to strike such a blow. "It would not necessarily be a man who had struck the blow. A woman could have done so equally well?" "Certainly," says Dr. Wyatt, neatly paving the way for Myers' next witness, Janet Mackenzie.

Janet, who was Miss French's housekeeper, is a dour Scotswoman. Even before she testifies, her look in the prisoner's direction tells of her loathing for him. Mr. Myers first brings out Janet's long and loyal service to Miss French.

Janet describes her late mistress as a "warmhearted body—too warmhearted at times, I'm thinking. A wee bit impulsive, too. There was times when she'd have no sense at all. She was easily flattered, you see." Myers now wishes Janet to tell how often the prisoner visited Miss French.

Janet—To begin with, once a week, but later it was oftener. Two and even three times he'd come. He'd sit there flattering her, telling her how young she looked and noticing any new clothes she was wearing.

Myers (*rather hastily*)—Quite, quite. Now will you tell the jury in your own words, Miss Mackenzie, about the events of October fourteenth.

Janet—It was a Friday and my night out. I was going round to see some friends of mine in Glenister Road, which is not above three minutes' walk. I left the house at half past seven. I'd promised to take my friend the pattern of a knitted cardigan that she'd admired.

When I got there I found I'd left it behind, so after supper I said I'd slip back and get it as it was a fine night and no distance. I got back to the house at twenty-five past nine. I let myself in with my key and went upstairs to my room. As I passed the sitting-room door I heard the prisoner in there talking to Miss French.

MYERS—You were sure it was the prisoner you heard?

JANET—Aye, I know his voice well enough. With him calling so often. An agreeable voice it was. I'll not say it wasn't. Talking and laughing they were. But it was no business of mine so I went up and fetched the pattern, came down and let myself out and went back to my friend.

MYERS—Now, I want these times very exact. You say that you re-entered the house at twenty-five past nine.

JANET—Aye. It was just after twenty past nine when I left Glenister Road.

MYERS—How do you know that, Miss Mackenzie?

Janet—By the clock on my friend's mantelpiece, and I compared it with my watch and the time was the same.

When, later, Janet came home for the night, she found Miss French —with her head beaten in—lying on the floor of the sitting room. "Everything was tossed hither and thither, the broken vase on the floor and the curtains flying in the wind." After Janet called the police, she searched the house and found no one, and found nothing else in disorder.

Myers has Janet tell what she knows of the prisoner. The one thing she knows is that he needed money. "Did he ask Miss French for money?" Myers asks. "He was too clever for that," says Janet. "Did he help Miss French with her business affairs—with her income tax returns, for instance?" Yes, says Janet, he did and there was no need of it: "Miss French had a good, clear head for business." But in the matter of wills, it seems, Miss French was most erratic. She would make them and tear them up, at one time leaving her money to help old people, the next time to help cats and dogs. Her last will was drawn on October eighth: "I heard her speaking to Mr. Stokes, the lawyer," says Janet, "saying he was to come tomorrow, she was making a new will. He was there at the time—the prisoner, I mean, kind of protesting, saying No, no. And the mistress said, 'But I want to, my dear boy. I want to. Remember that day I was nearly run over by a bus. It might happen any time.' "

MYERS—Were you aware, Miss Mackenzie, that Leonard Vole was a married man?

JANET—No, indeed. Neither was the mistress.

SIR WILFRID—I object. What Miss French knew or did not know is pure conjecture on Janet Mackenzie's part.

Myers asks Janet to support her opinion with facts.

JANET—There was the books she ordered from the library. There was the Life of Baroness Burdett Coutts and one about Disraeli and his wife. Both of them about women who'd married men years younger than themselves. I knew what she was thinking.

JUDGE—I'm afraid we cannot admit that.

JANET—Why?

JUDGE—Members of the jury, it is possible for a woman to read the Life of Disraeli without contemplating marriage with a man younger than herself.

Mr. Myers now formally concludes his part of Janet's testimony.

Sir Wilfrid rises for the cross-examination. He uses a courtroom kindliness that catches Janet very neatly. She frankly acknowledges that the previous will had been made out to her, and that the present one, which left the bulk of the fortune to Leonard, provided her with only an annuity. "It will be a wicked injustice if he ever touches a penny of that money," she cries.

Sir Wilfrid worms out of Janet the possibility that she kept Miss French from having friends; that the friendship with Leonard Vole made her angry because she didn't want Miss French imposed on; and that she disliked the way Miss French depended on Leonard. Sir Wilfrid speaks of the prisoner's influence on Miss French and of her affection for him. Janet admits to this, but won't concede that if Leonard had asked Miss French for money she would have given it to him. Sir Wilfrid then moves on to the night of the murder, when Janet said she heard Leonard and Miss French talking together.

Janet, it turns out, couldn't hear their words, just their voices and laughter. Though she stoutly maintains that it was Leonard's voice she heard through the closed door, Sir Wilfrid clouds her testimony by getting her to admit that she had applied for a hearing apparatus. "So," says Sir Wilfrid, "your hearing isn't very good, is that right? (*Lowers his voice.*) When I say to you, Miss Mackenzie, that you could not possibly recognize a voice through a closed door, what do you answer? (*Pause.*) Can you tell me what I said?" "I can no' hear anyone if they mumble," answers Janet.

Sir Wilfrid's next attempt is a dismal failure. He tries to attribute the voices Janet heard to actors on the wireless, only for her to say that the wireless was away being repaired that week. He winds up his cross-examination with the thought that had Leonard married Miss French, he might have had Janet dismissed. She says: "He would have used his influence; oh, yes, he would have done his best to make her get rid of me."

SIR WILFRID—I see. You felt the prisoner was a very real menace to your present way of life at the time.

JANET—He'd have changed everything.

SIR WILFRID—Yes, very upsetting. No wonder you feel so bitterly against the prisoner. (*End of cross-examination.* MYERS *rises.*)

MYERS—My learned friend has been at great pains to extract from you an admission of vindictiveness towards the prisoner . . .

SIR WILFRID (*without rising, and audibly for the benefit of the jury*)—A painless extraction—quite painless.

Myers now makes little headway with Janet, but asks one question more before finishing: "You say you recognized Leonard Vole's voice through the closed door. Will you tell the jury how you knew it was his?" Says Janet: "You know a person's voice without hearing exactly what they are saying." Myers thanks her, and she leaves the stand.

For his next witness, Myers has Thomas Clegg of the New Scotland Yard Lab. Clegg says that the blood found on the prisoner's washed jacket sleeve was type "O." Miss French's blood type was "O." Sir Wilfrid, when his turn comes, simply reveals that Leonard Vole's blood-bank donor's card proves that he too is type "O." Myers asks Clegg: "Blood group 'O' is a very common one, is it not?" "Oh, yes," says Clegg. "At least forty-two per cent of people are in blood group 'O.' "

The last witness for the prosecution proves a stunning surprise: it's Romaine—but Heilger, not Vole. Because—as she says—her husband is still alive, her marriage to Leonard is not valid. Sir Wilfrid rises and indignantly protests: "My lord, I have the most serious objection to this witness giving evidence at all. We have the undeniable fact of marriage between this witness and the prisoner, and no proof whatsoever of this so-called previous marriage." But Myers has Mrs. Heilger's marriage certificate to show the Judge, who examines it and accepts it. Leonard cries out: "Romaine! What are you doing here—what are you saying?" The Judge says: "I must have silence. As your counsel will tell you, Vole, you will very shortly have an opportunity of speaking in your own defense."

And he will have to, for under Myer's questioning, Romaine says that Leonard returned home at ten minutes past ten. Agonizingly Leonard protests and is hushed up by Mayhew. Cowed, shrinking, Leonard covers his face with his hands, saying almost inaudibly, "I—I don't understand."

Romaine goes on: "He was breathing hard, very excited. He threw off his coat and examined the sleeves. Then he told me to wash the cuffs. They had blood on them." Asked what she did, she repeats: "I said, 'What have you done?' " Myers asks: "What did the prisoner say to that?" "He said," Romaine answers, " 'I've killed her.' " Leonard goes into a frenzy, requiring the Warden to control him. The Judge warns Romaine, who answers: "I am to speak the truth, am I not?"

To the question why she had changed her story, Romaine cries with sudden passion: "Because it is murder. I cannot go on lying to save him. I am grateful to him, yes. He married me and brought me to this country. What he has asked me to do, always I have done it because I was grateful." "Because you loved him?" asks Myers. "I never loved him," says Romaine. She passionately agrees that because of this gratitude she at first was going to give him his alibi, but she felt that it was wrong, because it was murder. . . . "I cannot come into court and lie and say that he was there with me at the time it was done. I cannot do it. I cannot *do* it."

MYERS—So what did you do?

ROMAINE—I did not know what to do. I do not know your country and I am afraid of the police. So I write a letter to my ambassador, and I say I do not wish to tell any more lies. I wish to speak the truth.

MYERS—This *is* the truth—that Leonard Vole returned that night at ten minutes past ten. That he had blood on the sleeves of his coat, that he said to you, "I killed her." That is the truth before God?

ROMAINE—That is the truth.

Sir Wilfrid, in a cold fury, asks her, "Is it the truth?" "Yes," says Romaine.

SIR WILFRID—I suggest to you that on the night of October fourteenth Leonard Vole was at home with you at nine-thirty, the time that the murder was committed. I suggest to you that this whole story of yours is a wicked fabrication, that you have for some reason a grudge against the prisoner, and that this is your way of expressing it.

ROMAINE—No.

SIR WILFRID—You realize that you are on oath?

ROMAINE—Yes.

SIR WILFRID—I warn you, Mrs. Heilger, that if you care nothing for the prisoner, be careful on your own account. The penalty for perjury is heavy.

Passing over Myers' protests at these theatrical outbursts, Sir Wilfrid mixes Romaine up on what she said about the blood on the jacket cuffs, then suggests that her memory as to other parts of her story is equally untrustworthy. Romaine insists she lied previously on Leonard's orders.

SIR WILFRID—The question is whether you were lying then or whether you are lying *now*. If you were really appalled at murder having been committed, you could have told the truth to the police when they first questioned you.

ROMAINE—I was afraid of Leonard.

SIR WILFRID (*gesturing towards the woeful figure of* LEONARD *in the dock*)—You were afraid of Leonard Vole—afraid of the man whose heart and spirit you've just broken. I think the jury will know which of you to believe. (*Sits down.*)

MYERS (*rising*)—Romaine Heilger. I ask you once more, is the evidence you have given the truth, the whole truth and nothing but the truth?

ROMAINE—It is.

MYERS—My lord, that is the case for the prosecution.

The Judge calls on the defense. Sir Wilfrid rises, and addressing his lordship and the members of the jury, acknowledges there is a case of strong circumstantial evidence the prisoner must answer. . . . "You have heard the police and other expert witnesses. They have given fair, impartial evidence as is their duty. Against them I have nothing to say. On the other hand, you have heard Janet Mackenzie and the woman who calls herself Romaine Vole. Can you believe that their testimony is not warped? Janet Mackenzie—cut out of her rich mistress' will, because her position was usurped, quite unwittingly by this unfortunate boy . . . Romaine Vole—Heilger—whatever she calls herself, who trapped him into marriage, whilst concealing from him the fact that she was married already. That woman owes him more than she can ever repay. She used him to save her from political persecution. But she admits no love for him. He has served his purpose. I will ask you to be very careful how you believe her testimony, the testimony of a woman who, for all we know, has been brought up to believe the pernicious doctrine that lying is a weapon to be used to serve one's own ends. Members of the jury, I call the prisoner, Leonard Vole.

Leonard is sworn in, to be his own sole witness. Sir Wilfrid has him repeat his friendly, homely statements about Miss French's reminding him of his Aunt Betsy who was such a dear. Next he assures Sir Wilfrid that Miss French indeed knew of his marriage.

SIR WILFRID—So there was no question of marriage between you.

LEONARD—Of course not. I've told you, she treated me as though she was an indulgent aunt. Almost like a mother.

SIR WILFRID—And in return you did everything for her that you could.

LEONARD (*simply*)—I was very fond of her.

Asked to tell in his own words what happened on the night of October fourteenth, Leonard tells of having nothing to do that night, so, armed with a new cat brush as a present, he paid a call on Miss French. He got there before eight, played a game of double demon with the lady, and left without seeing Janet Mackenzie. "Did you know Janet Mackenzie was out?" asks Sir Wilfrid. "Well," says Leonard, "I didn't think about it." Leonard says he left just before nine, and got home at nine twenty-five. "And your wife," says Sir Wilfrid, "I will call her your wife—was at home then?" "Yes, of course she was," Leonard exclaims. "I—I think she must have gone mad. I—" And there was no washing of jackets that night; Romaine washed it the next morning, Leonard tells Sir Wilfrid. "She said it had got blood on it from a cut on my wrist." He displays the mark on his wrist to the court. Leonard testifies he was stunned to read of the murder in the next evening's paper. . . . "The papers said it was a burglar," says Leonard. "I never dreamed of anything else." But wanting to help in every way possible, he voluntarily went to the police when they broadcast that they wanted to interview him.

Sir Wilfrid next guides Leonard to Miss French's will, of which Leonard swears he knew nothing. As for Romaine's testimony, Leonard not only can't understand it, but it just wasn't true. Sir Wilfrid stresses his arriving home at nine twenty-five and having supper with his wife. Concluding, Sir Wilfrid asks: "Are you right- or left-handed?" "Right-handed," says Leonard. "I'm going to ask you just one more question, Mr. Vole," says Sir Wilfrid, then dramatically asks him: *"Did you kill Emily French?"* *"No, I did not,"* answers Leonard in clear tones.

As prosecutor, Mr. Myers gives Leonard a rough time of it. He starts with the money angle and hangs on to it. Leonard cultivated Miss French for her money. Leonard was desperate for money. Leonard was unemployed. Using Leonard's own word "worried," Myers drives on: "You were worried about money, you met a wealthy woman and you courted her acquaintance assiduously." "You make it sound all twisted," protests Leonard. "I tell you I liked her." Why did Leonard help Miss French with her income tax forms when Janet Mackenzie reports she was well able to deal with them herself? "Well," says Leonard, "that's not what she said to me. She said those forms worried her terribly." Myers wonders why Leonard never took Romaine to see Miss French. Leonard says: "Oh, I don't know. She didn't like women, I don't think." "She preferred," suggests Myers, "shall we say, personable young men? And you didn't insist on bringing your wife?"

LEONARD—No, of course I didn't. You see, she knew my wife was a foreigner and she—oh, I don't know, she seemed to think we didn't get on.

MYERS—That was the impression you gave her?

LEONARD—No, I didn't. She—well, I think it was wishful thinking on her part.

MYERS—You mean she was infatuated with you?

LEONARD—No, she wasn't infatuated, but she, oh, it's like mothers are sometimes with a son.

MYERS—How?

LEONARD—They don't want him to like a girl or get engaged or anything of that kind.

MYERS—You hoped, didn't you, for some monetary advantage from your friendship with Miss French?

LEONARD—Not in the way you mean.

MYERS—Not in the way I mean? You seem to know what I mean better than I know myself. In what way, then, did you hope for monetary advantage? I repeat, in what way did you hope for monetary advantage?

Leonard tries to describe the invention he wished Miss French to finance. Myers now introduces a new topic: why was Leonard making inquiries about foreign cruises? Leonard, in the company of a strawberry blonde, visited a travel bureau. Leonard defiantly announces that he had been feeling fed up; this was make-believe and fun, and he had enjoyed it. Myers comments on the remarkable co-incidence of Miss French's death a few days later, and of Leonard's being her heir. Myers quotes Leonard's timetable for the night of October fourteenth, and Romaine's contradictory testimony of Leonard's arriving home at ten minutes past ten. Myers, over Leonard's protesting shouts, ruthlessly presses on.

MYERS—Can you suggest any reason why this young woman, who has been passing as your wife, should deliberately give the evidence she has given if it were not true?

LEONARD—No, I can't. That's the awful thing. There's no reason at all. I think she must have gone mad.

MYERS—You think she must have gone mad? She seemed extremely sane and self-possessed. But insanity is the only reason you can suggest.

LEONARD—I don't understand it. Oh, God—what's happened—what's changed her?

MYERS—Very effective, I'm sure. But in this court we deal with facts. And the fact is, Mr. Vole, that we have only your word for it that you left Emily French's house at the time you say you did, and that you arrived home at five and twenty minutes past nine, and that you did not go out again.

LEONARD (*wildly*)—Someone must have seen me—in the street—or going into the house.

MYERS—One would certainly think so—but the only person who *did* see you come home that night says it was at ten minutes past ten. And that person says that you had blood on your clothes.

Leonard breaks down, crying and protesting that Myers is twisting everything he says. "You came home at ten past ten," Myers pounds away. Leonard cries he didn't, he's got to be believed. "You killed Emily French," says Myers. "I didn't do it," cries Leonard, "I didn't kill her. I've never killed anybody. Oh, God! It's a nightmare. It's some awful, evil dream."

ACT III

Returing after court to Sir Wilfrid's chambers, Mayhew and Sir Wilfrid hold a not-too-cheerful post-mortem of the day's proceedings. In particular, they rant at Romaine's beastly behavior. Only the office girl's unshaken confidence in Leonard renews Sir Wilfrid's hope and determination: he'll get him off but God knows how!

Mayhew and Sir Wilfrid are well aware that without any corroborative testimony, Leonard's own statements are insufficient. Everything is against him: his fingerprints, the will, the travel-agency business, his unconvincing cruise story. This last, however, Mayhew and Sir Wilfrid can understand. (Sir Wilfrid's wife plans trips she never intends to take; and Mayhew's wife has the real estate bug, all of her projects being castles in the air.) But getting back to the hard facts of the trial, both men agree that Janet Mackenzie's obvious prejudice against Leonard may help with the jury. Sir Wilfrid works himself up to feel that Janet Mackenzie is capable of anything, might stop at *nothing*. As the horrified Mayhew says: "Good Lord. Do you mean . . . ?" a clerk enters to announce a very strange visitor: "A common young woman with a free way of talking," who says she has something that might help Leonard Vole. Grasping at any straw, Sir Wilfrid resigns himself to seeing her.

The woman turns out to be a flamboyant, cheaply dressed cockney, with crude make-up and a mass of tousled yellow hair. Looking sharply from Mayhew to Sir Wilfrid, she shrills: "Here, what's this? Two o'yer? I'm not talking to two of yer." She is introduced to Leonard's solicitor and counsel for defense. Peering at Sir Wilfrid, the woman relaxes: "So you are, dear. Didn't recognize you without your wig. Lovely you all look in them wigs. Havin' a bit of confab, are you? Well, maybe I can help you if you make it worth my while."

In court today, she watched that "Jezebel" give her evidence, and now she's ready to produce hers, for a price. The woman demands a hundred quid for the letters in her hand, but Sir Wilfrid spars, hoping for a look at them before he offers any sum at all. Mayhew offers ten pounds; after cockney screams of derision, the price is finally put at twenty. In exchange for her money, the woman hands over letters in Romaine Vole's handwriting.

The letters, as the men read them, seem incredible. "How did you get hold of these?" Sir Wilfrid demands of the woman. "That'd be telling," she answers. "What have you got against Romaine Vole?" he next asks. Suddenly, dramatically, the woman jerks a gooseneck lamp so that the light falls on her slashed, disfigured face. Shocked beyond belief, Sir Wilfrid asks: "Did *she* do that to you?" No, says the woman, it was the chap Romaine had stolen away from her. Sir Wilfrid, moved, asks: "Did you go to the police about it?" "Go to the p'lice? Me? Not likely. 'Sides, it wasn't 'is fault. Not really. It was hers, all hers. Getting 'im away from me, turning 'im against me. But I waited my time. I follered 'er about and watched 'er. I know some of the things she's bin up to. I know where the bloke lives who she goes to see on the sly sometimes.

That's how I got hold of them letters. So now you know the whole story, mister. Want to kiss me?" Sir Wilfrid shrinks back from the outthrust face. "I don't blame yer," says the woman. Deeply sorry for her, Sir Wilfrid gives her five pounds more.

Eagerly turning back to the letters, the men don't notice the woman quietly slipping out of the door, and by the time they look up, she has disappeared. They have neither her name nor her address, but in spite of such handicaps, Sir Wilfrid is full of fight. Having something to go on at last, they have to plan their procedure, and go into a huddle as the curtain falls.

Scene II

Next morning at the Old Bailey, the court is surprised and Mr. Myers thoroughly annoyed that Sir Wilfrid wishes to introduce new evidence.

Judge—When exactly, Sir Wilfrid, did this evidence come to your knowledge?

Sir Wilfrid—It was brought to me after the court was adjourned last night.

Myers—My lord, I must object to my learned friend's request. The case for the prosecution is closed, and . . .

Judge—Mr. Myers, I had not intended to rule on this question without first observing the customary formality of inviting your observations on the matter. (Myers *subsides*.)

Sir Wilfrid—My lord, in a case where evidence vital to the prisoner comes into possession of his legal advisers at any time before the jury have returned their verdict, I contend that such evidence is not only admissible, but desirable. Happily there is clear authority to support my proposition, to be found in the case of the King against Stillman, reported in 1926 Appeal Cases at page 463. (*Opening law report*.)

Judge—You needn't trouble to cite the authority, Sir Wilfrid. I am quite familiar with it. I should like to hear the prosecution. Now, Mr. Myers.

Myers—In my respectful submission, my lord, the course my friend proposes is, save in exceptional circumstances, quite unprecedented. And what, may I ask, is this startling new evidence of which Sir Wilfrid speaks?

Sir Wilfrid—Letters, my lord. Letters from Romaine Heilger.

Judge—I should like to see these letters to which you refer, Sir Wilfrid. (*The letters are handed up, and the* Judge *reads them*.)

MYERS—My friend was good enough to tell me only as we came into court that he intended to make this submission, so that I have had no opportunity to examine the authorities. But I seem to remember a case in, I think, 1930, the King against Porter, I believe . . .

JUDGE—No, Mr. Myers, the King against Potter, and it was reported in 1931. I remember the case well. I appeared for the prosecution.

MYERS—And if my memory serves me well, your lordship's similar objection was sustained.

JUDGE—Your memory for once serves you ill, Mr. Myers. My objection then was overruled by Mr. Justice Swindon—as yours is now, by me.

Romaine Heilger, recalled to the witness stand, starts violently when Sir Wilfrid asks: "Mrs. Heilger, do you know a certain man whose Christian name is Max?" She knows no one by that name, and further denies ever writing him a letter, or that it was one letter in a series written over a considerable period of time. As Sir Wilfrid pounds away, she becomes agitated, and cries that what he says is all lies. Says Sir Wilfrid: "You would seem to have been on *intimate* terms with this man." At this, Leonard yells his protest, until he is requested to remain quiet in his own interests. "I am not concerned with the general trend of this correspondence," says Sir Wilfrid. "I am only interested in one particular letter." He reads: " 'My beloved Max. An extraordinary thing has happened. I believe all our difficulties may be ended. . . .' " Romaine, in a frenzy, refuses to listen, then shrieks that it was stolen, then refuses to listen to anything at all. Suggesting that it is *she* who has lied, Sir Wilfrid says he has her reasons in black and white. He sets his trap: "Because a way had opened before you to freedom—and in planning to take that way, the fact that an innocent man would be sent to his death meant nothing to you. You have even included that final deadly touch of how you yourself managed accidentally to wound Leonard Vole with a ham knife." Romaine, caught, cries: "I never wrote that! I wrote that he did it himself cutting the ham."

Sir Wilfrid is triumphant.

Romaine, casting aside all restraint, curses.

LEONARD (*shouting*)—Leave her alone. Don't bully her.

ROMAINE (*looking around wildly*)—Let me out of here. . . . Let me go. . . . (*About to collapse.*)

Patricia Jessel and Francis L. Sullivan in "Witness for the Prosecution"

JUDGE—Usher, give the witness a chair. (ROMAINE *sinks on chair, sobs hysterically and buries her face in hands.*)   Sir Wilfrid, will you now read the letter aloud so that the jury can hear it?

SIR WILFRID—"My beloved Max.   An extraordinary thing has happened.   I believe all our difficulties may be ended.   I can come to you without fear of endangering the valuable work you are doing in this country.   The old lady I told you about has been murdered and I think Leonard is suspected.   He was there earlier that night and his fingerprints will be all over the place.   Nine-thirty seems to be the time.   Leonard was home by then, but his alibi depends on me—on *me*.   Supposing I say he came home much later and that he had blood on his clothes—he did have blood on his sleeve, because he cut his wrist at supper, so you see it would all fit in.   I can even say he told me he killed her.   Oh, Max, beloved! tell me I can go ahead—it would be so wonderful to be free from playing the part of a loving, grateful wife.   I know the cause and the Party come first, but if Leonard were convicted of murder, I could come to you safely and we could be together for always.   Your adoring Romaine."

Asked by the Judge if she has something to say, Romaine, frozen in defeat, says: "Nothing," but to a pleading Leonard, she fairly spits that of course she wrote it.

Myers, his case and witness gone, is in no more position to continue than Romaine. The Judge sounds a warning to Romaine that this is not the end of the matter for her. . . . "In this country you cannot commit perjury without being brought to account for it . . . the sentence for perjury can be severe. . . ."

Instructed to address the jury, Sir Wilfrid completes his defense as the lights dim; when they go on again, the jury is returning with their verdict: "Not guilty." And the session is over.

Discharged and free to leave, Leonard joins Mayhew and Sir Wilfrid on the emptying courtroom floor. While they are engaged in mutual congratulations, Romaine is led into the room by a cautious policeman who doesn't want her to leave until the menacing crowd has dispersed and she can safely get by.

Sir Wilfrid prevents her approaching Leonard, who is drawn to one side by Mayhew. While Mayhew and Leonard talk of the fortune he is about to receive, and Leonard boyishly dismisses it as meaning little after all he's been through, Sir Wilfrid balefully eyes Romaine. Not unhappily, he tells her that she can expect a prison sentence for perjury: "It may interest you to know," he says, "that I took your measure the first time we met. I made up my mind then to beat you at your little game, and, by God, I've done it. I've got him off—in spite of you!"

ROMAINE—In *spite* of me!

SIR WILFRID—You don't deny, do you, that you did your best to hang him?

ROMAINE—Would they have believed me if I had said that he was at home with me that night, and did not go out? Would they?

SIR WILFRID (*slightly uncomfortable*)—Why not?

ROMAINE—Because they would have said to themselves: This woman loves this man—she would say or do anything for him. They would have had sympathy with me, yes. But they would not have *believed* me.

SIR WILFRID—If you'd been speaking the truth they would.

ROMAINE—I wonder. . . . I did not want their sympathy—I wanted them to dislike me, to mistrust me, to be convinced that I was a liar. And then, when my lies were broken down—then they believed! . . . (*Makes gesture of hands.*) So now you know the whole story, mister: like to kiss me?

SIR WILFRID (*thunderstruck*)—My God!

ROMAINE—Yes, the woman with the letters. I wrote those letters I brought to you. I was that woman. It wasn't *you* who won freedom for Leonard. It was *I*. And because of it I shall go to prison. . . . (*Her eyes close.*)   But at the end of it Leonard and I will be together again. Happy . . . loving each other.

SIR WILFRID (*moved*)—My dear . . . but couldn't you trust me? We believe, you know, that our British system of justice upholds the truth. We'd have got him off.

ROMAINE—I couldn't risk it. (*Slowly.*)   You see, you *thought* he was innocent—

SIR WILFRID (*with quick appreciation*)—And you *knew* he was innocent. I understand.

ROMAINE—But you do not understand at all. *I* knew he was *guilty.*

But the play is still not over. The author still has a trick or so up her sleeve. If you have not been fooled so far perhaps you can go on and guess it. Mrs. Christie has particularly requested that the outcome should not be published at the present time.

THE FLOWERING PEACH *

A Drama in Eight Scenes and an Epilogue

By Clifford Odets

[Clifford Odets *acted for the Theatre Guild and its young off-shoot, the Group Theatre, before having his plays produced by the latter group. He was born in Philadelphia in 1906 and began his career acting in stock companies. For the Group he wrote "Awake and Sing," "Waiting for Lefty" and "Golden Boy" among others. Other Broadway successes include "The Big Knife" and the very popular "The Country Girl." This last was made into a most successful motion picture.*]

A ROOSTER crows, and dawn is near as old man Noah stumbles into his primitive living room. Trying to escape the horror of a recent dream, he drinks deeply from a jug, then wanders heavily about the room. His wife, Esther, finds him on his knees.

Esther feels the drinking is the cause of his trouble. Once her annoyance at being waked up has passed, she quietly asks him what he dreamt. "Esther, *tuchter*," Noah solemnly says, "the whole world's gonna be destroyed!" "Our world?" says Esther. "And that was the dream? That's all? . . ." Daylight begins coming through the latticed windows, as, more in relief than anxiety and with a certain enjoyment, she questions Noah. "God appeared to me in a dream," he tells her with a heartbroken glance. With a loud laugh, Esther says: "Noah, Noah, tell the truth—when they gave out the brains, you weren't hiding behind the house?" Noah ignores this for another drink. "You had enough to drink," Esther says. "He pours and he pours, just like a pig."

Noah (*loftily*)—You should be satisfied that I drink, otherwise I'd leave you. (*The drink in him,* Noah *wipes his mouth and sets himself a little grandly, head cocked to one side.*) Esther, hear me

180

what I say, Esther. . . . God sent me a dream. Before Him the
earth is corrupt and filled with evil an' greed. You hear me? The
end of all flesh is come. Everything that's living in the earth will
be destroyed.

ESTHER (*jibingly*)—Thus spake the Lord?

NOAH (*warningly*)—You're not so smart, girlie!

ESTHER (*dryly*)—And how will all this happen? What, He'll
make a fire?

NOAH (*with inner seeing*)—A rain. He'll bring a flood—a flood
of waters—so much rain the whole damn place will be drowned off!
. . . I'm sick, I'm sick. My soul is sick! (*Watching him*, ESTHER
*speaks with some uneasiness, for she is beginning to be worried by
his condition.*)

ESTHER—Why don't you come back to bed and get some sleep?
I mean it—sleep all day—you won't be missed. (*Turns to him.*)
By the way—who are you that God sends you a dream? Why, be-
cause your grandfather was Methuselah?

NOAH (*bristling*)—A damn good man, sister!

ESTHER (*jibing*)—Just like you and our three sons—damn good
man!

Noah, unhappy at God's giving him so big an order, muses that
his son Japheth should have children, because "everybody will go
down in the flood, but we'll be saved—with our sons and their wives
together." In thorough disgust, Esther warns him to stay away from
liquor and do something useful around the house. . . . "Kill some
mice today. There's a few in the kitchen so fresh they stand there
watching me cook." And saying he's sick and that's another reason
for his not drinking, she overrides his protest: "So if you're not sick,
why should *we* be saved? And our sons with their wives, they're
such bargains? Answer me a question, a *realism*—why should *we*
be saved?" Esther warns him he'll be lucky if they don't lock him
up for spreading this crazy story. Noah's anger with her is momentarily deflected by Japheth's entrance. He orders this obedient
son to round up Ham and Shem, and have them here before the
Shabbos, before sundown.

Esther is sure Shem and his wife, Leah, won't like being sum-
moned while they're getting in the olive crop. Japheth wants to
know what he should tell them. Noah orders: "You'll tell Shem a
big building proposition came up! The Customer is very impatient,
can't wait, understand? Needs an estimate right away, hear me?"
Esther, not wishing to have Noah seem foolish to his son, waits for
Japheth to leave before lashing out: "Now you did it good! First

we had a flood—now we're building a house!" "Yes, old friend of mine, but not a house," Noah answers, "an ark! a boat, three stories high—"

Esther is derisive, but Noah proudly tells her of God's plans for the ark's door, windows, and roof, and that it will float on the face of the deep. All Esther can do is pity him when his sons hear this foolishness. "This time," she swears, "I won't take your part against the boys . . . you'll sail alone, my sailor, on the lonely deep." "Lonely times is nothing new to me . . . ," answers Noah. It's because he's such a pest, Esther says; people don't like hearing him talk as if God talks only to him and he's the only one who knows the Commandments—why doesn't he stop talking and "eat a pair of eggs." As fond of him as always, annoyed with him as usual, Esther has no time for sparring, what with all her Friday baking. But before she goes, she can't resist asking: "Tell me, fool, in your whole lifetime, you ever even *seen* a boat?"

Noah (*turns to her. With huffy dignity*)—I seen a boat, many times—twiced.

Esther (*mockingly*)—Twiced. And where, by the way, are we when it rains?

Noah—Inside, floating around, decent and dry, with all the animals.

Esther (*pricking up her ears*)—What animals . . . ?

Noah (*surprised at her reaction*)—*All* the animals—of every kind a pair, clean and unclean. Everything that creeps an' walks an' flies—

Esther (*incredulously*)—And all this God told you in one single dream . . . ?

Noah (*jaunting around*)—Told it to me in one dream, yeh! So now you know.

Soon he feels the presence of the Lord again. Frightened and deeply concerned over what she thinks a recurring illness, Esther leaves.

Noah, rocking himself for comfort, speaks out: "Lonely times again? . . ." If God would only let him off this time—he's too old to have people laugh at him; he doesn't have the gizzard for it. But as the Presence of God is heard through a certain musical rustle . . . a widening shimmer . . . and a long roll of thunder, Noah gives in, falling to his knees, his head bowed low. After a moment he tilts his head a little and his nose twitches like a rabbit's. "Lord?" he asks. "You sure you don't mean some other man? Maybe a certain matter didn't enter your mind." What does he know about boats, he slyly says. "Ast my Esther an' she'll tell you when I was near water. Bread is bread, I know it—a pickle is a pickle, a knife is a knife—but *boats?* You need a sailor for that, a sailor from way back. (NOAH's *slyness is reproved by a brief but angry thunder clap.* NOAH *nods meekly but he is heartsick nevertheless.*) Awright, whatever you tell me to do, I'll do it. . . . (*Then nodding.*) Yes, I remember everything to a 'T.' The length of the ark should be three hundred cubits, fifty cubits the breadth an' thirty cubits the height. . . . (*Nodding again.*) I'll try to convince my sons to do what You say, but with my oldest boys I'm altogether no good! You'll have to help me, 'cause they'll lock me up for a noisy old man. (*Abruptly.*) You're here yet . . . ? But wait a minute—the *main* point we didn't get to! You're talking about a total destruction of the whole world an' this is something terrible—!"

Noah timidly asks if God is still here, but the Presence has faded away; and Noah, not knowing whether he's asleep or awake, is alone with his thoughts. Roosters crow in the distance, as lights quietly dim.

SCENE II

As the sun is sinking, the family discuss Noah and his dream. Shem, the self-important oldest son, has to get all the facts straight, but after hearing the dream a good four times, is no nearer a decision than before. Shem's wife Leah, at loggerheads with Esther, speaks of the loss of business and prestige if they give in to Noah. Ham, the second son, is as disrespectful as he dare be. Only Japheth sees reason in his father's words: "It hasn't rained since early spring . . . floods are possible, I mean. If Poppa says he had the dream, he had it . . . he didn't make it up." It's not in Noah's nature, Japheth points out, to imagine anything as cruel as the end of the world.

JAPHETH—I'm saying that Poppa's been sent a real vision.

NOAH—He understands.

SHEM—But do you understand the practical consequences if we took this serious?

JAPHETH—Of course I do. All life would be destroyed. . . .

SHEM—It would mean giving up everything I own to build a boat!

LEAH—And what about reaping and planting the autumn crops?

SHEM—Yeah, who'd do all that while we build the ark? The man in the moon?

HAM—Shem, you're up in the moon yourself. If you build an ark, you believe in the flood. But, if you believe in the flood, why worry about crops?

LEAH—Exactly!

HAM (*enjoying it all*)—But if you don't believe in the flood, why build the ark?

Having triumphantly played on their confusion, Ham smirks at his praying father.

Noah, rising, says: "God told you—He's speakin' to you in my mouth—what you should do! Bring in the harvest. Plenty of things needed for the trip—for forty days an' nights alone it will rain—" "He's got us on that boat again!" cries Ham. "Lost my patience with you—" snaps back Noah, "an independent man's tellin' you!" Noah turns to Shem and says imperiously: "A flood is coming. The world will be destroyed, but we'll be saved! And I don't say it again!"

Shem wouldn't outwardly show disrespect to his father, but carefully indicates that they all think he's out of his mind. Ham pounds away: "Yeah, did you ever give a thought to a simple item like the animals . . . ? You said, didn't you, a pair of each?" Quite readily, Noah answers, "Oh, some *more* than a pair. The clean ones, what you call kosher, *seven* pairs." "How do we capture just *one pair?*" demands Ham.

Noah, sure that God wouldn't tell him a thing that couldn't be done, tries to puzzle this out. Japheth, placing a sympathetic hand on his father's shoulder, announces it's time to let the sheep in the fold. He is sympathetic but finds the dream . . . "a bitter dose to take." Shem, prickly because Japheth refuses all his offers of jobs, says he's curious of Japheth's opinion: "You would or you wouldn't build the ark?" "Maybe I wouldn't . . ." says Japheth. "I might decide to die with the others. . . ." Shem laughs. "What's funny?" says Japheth. "Someone, it seems to me, would have to protest such an avenging, destructive God!" Shem is shocked at his impiety: "I'll be honest for a change! Poppa's in his second childhood an' you're not outta your first!"

Japheth tends to the sheep, while the others prepare for the *Shabbos* supper. There is only a brief interval of peace: Leah's scream over a mouse results in more bickering—bickering over how the mouse should be caught and killed. But the animal that runs into Noah's cupped hands is no mouse. A falsetto little song is heard. "God has sent us a gitka . . . she sings for us . . . ," Noah announces to his awed family.

Japheth enters the room strangely excited. He too listens to the high little song, but when it stops he calls out: "Look out the windows, everyone! Poppa, look out the windows!" God has done more than send them a gitka.

NOAH (*peering out the windows*)—More, Esther, is coming down the road?
ESTHER—Yeh, more . . . yeh . . . (LEAH *has begun whimpering and moving away from the window. Dazed, leaning on a table,* SHEM *is muttering, "No. No. No."* HAM's *voice rises hysterically.*)
HAM—They are standing beside the sheep!
SHEM—Don't want to see it!
HAM—Nothing is moving!
SHEM—Don't want to see that!
NOAH (*shading his eyes*)—*Tuchter,* what is by the fence?
ESTHER—Never seen such an animal like that . . .

A whirring of wings announces the arrival of birds, too.
Leah starts a near panic, sure they're going to be killed, but Noah orders his family to stay where they are. Except for Japheth, they all guiltily fall on their knees. But Noah tells them: "Children, these are the creatures (and not all yet) God has sent . . . to enter the ark with us. They are sacred to us, and we are sacred to them. Yeh, this was my dream." Then he asks Esther to bring fire for the candles. Ham, burbling that he always wanted to be a good man, is ordered to prove it by fetching his neglected wife Rachel. "Through the animals?" Ham nervously cries, but amid groans and tears, prepares to go for her. Shem begs his father's forgiveness.

NOAH (*gently*)—Be quiet, Shem. To me don't bow an' pray—you dasn't. Only to God above let us lift our voice with love an' honor. (NOAH *sits behind the Sabbath candles, with the others grouped around him. Outside the daylight is fading fast, and with it the sounds of the animals.* THE MEN *have covered their heads and* NOAH *intones the traditional words as he lights the candles; he blesses and lifts his head and his eyes are awash with tears.*) . . . Oh, Lord, our God, the soul is rejoiced in Thee and Thy wonders. Here the family . . . is united to serve You as You asked. Give us strength and truth to serve Thee . . . (*Outside, a murmur of holy music is heard, mingled with the bleating of the puzzled sheep. Inside,* JAPHETH, *alone and horror-struck, stands apart from the family scene.*)

Scene III

High on the barren, broiling hillside, hammers and axes are at work. Beyond the stubby stern of the ark, the women, hour after hour in the heat, continue to sort fruits and pack the vats and jars with the harvest. Esther tends to be sharp with Leah, pleasant with Ham's wife, Rachel. Ordering them to get water and milk for the returning men, she can't resist wondering what the large bunch of keys is doing at Leah's waist. When Leah haughtily marches off without deigning an answer, Esther laughs: "Leah I never liked too much—stubborn, you know. An' nothin's good enough for her. Her mother, the old lady, the same way. . . ." To her shy daughter-in-law she says, "How long, Rachel, are you married to our Ham?" "Five years. . . . Why?" Rachel asks politely. "It's a long time to be unhappy," Esther thinks. "Maybe I could teach you a few things on the trip. Go take the milk . . ." and as Rachel nervously smiles and obeys, Esther encourages her: ". . . you're a fine person."

Noah, painfully feeling his old age, finds many things to disturb him. Primarily he's bitter because he's no longer able to do a man's work; but everything worries him . . . little things like finding a mate for the gitka, important things like finding a mate for Japheth. And Japheth's attitude causes the old man additional worry. Esther excuses this in Japheth: "He's tired. Whatta you want? Almost by himself he's building the whole ark!"

Noah—I do him credit, but we don't fit to each other if he don't give respect. Disrespect to a father is disrespect to God!

Esther (*firm but mild*)—He's your son—tell him to take a wife.

Noah (*haughtily*)—Such a boy, so strange, what could he offer a decent girl?

Esther (*promptly*)—He could offer her a nice boat ride!

Japheth, on his way to poulticing a lame tiger, finds Noah even ready to argue over the animal's name: "*Teeger*, nicht tiger!" Japheth pleasantly replies: "Fine, Poppa, you say teeger and I'll say tiger," then hesitantly he adds: "And while it's on my mind, Poppa . . . what about a rudder for the ark?" Noah says frigidly: "You mentioned it before, no? Well, don't mention it again. The good Lord steers the ark, not us. . . ." To Japheth's respectful protest: "Excuse me, Poppa . . . that doesn't seem right," Noah snaps: "You see, Esther. Everything's a damn fight with him!" Exasperated, Esther wants her difficult husband to give Japheth the praise he merits. She angrily tells Noah that as long as he's so good at hearing God, why can't he hear his son cry each night? "Every night!" Esther says, "To God. God an' God again! God should make him a good man! He should spare the world, the children. . . ."

But as the family gathers for supper, bitterness is also evident among the sons. The older brothers resent Japheth for trying to tell them how to build the ark. "No doubt about it," Shem says, "he's very skilled—but he's no boss over me!"

ESTHER (*quietly*)—Who is boss over you?

SHEM—Who? Poppa, God—

ESTHER—Who's building the ark every day, stitch by stitch, Poppa? God? (LEAH *rises*.) You sit down, Leah.

NOAH (*murmuring*)—Fair, a fair question.

SHEM (*confused*)—Be that as it may, Momma—

ESTHER—What can you build, coins one on top of another? And you (*to* HAM), what? A pile of empty bottles in a back yard?

NOAH—In this regard Mother is a shrewd an' respectable one hundred per cent right!

Japheth won't be accused of bossing anyone, particularly his father, whom he respects and reveres. Noah appreciates this, but complains that Japheth has changed lately. "Because I insist upon a rudder? I can't help it—a rudder is vital to the health of the ark. Would you want me to lie?" Japheth answers. Noah tells him: "Sonny, the Supreme Being who elected us—He made me the chairman, didn't He? He'll see I don't fall outta the chair! But I asted you, for instance, maybe five times to take a wife. . . .

JAPHETH (*pausing and squirming*)—But how can I do that, Poppa? How can I take a wife in times like these?

NOAH (*with gentle insistence*)—But God tells you to do it, don't He? The new world will need babies, bushels an' bushels of babies.

JAPHETH—And what about the bushels of babies who will die in the flood? Since you bring it up . . . is this vengeful God the very God I was taught to love?

NOAH (*recoiling*)—Sonny, you mustn't, you dasn't talk this way. . . .

JAPHETH—Forgive me, Poppa, but I must! Because I can't stay here!

NOAH (*turning cold*)—Can't stay here . . . ?

JAPHETH—No, I can't. I cannot work for this brutal God!

Slowly and with real grandeur, Noah says: "The Lord is good for anybody an' everybody, at all times! He was wonderful for the world in the old days an', blessed be His name, He will be for the new days to come! . . ." But Japheth, on the verge of tears, is determined to go.

Scene IV

With Japheth's departure, work has virtually come to a standstill, though a crude ramp now leads to the ark. In the dusty, impossible heat, Esther fans herself, Rachel sews, Leah peels potatoes; Shem is pacing up and down, while Ham is comfortably stretched out fast asleep.

Noah, tired, sweaty, pathetically old, comes slowly up the hill. Swinging some bags off his shoulder, he sits down on a rock to pull himself together. He found it impossible to buy seed from the townspeople. *"They stoned me outta town!"* the old man cries. The whole family is aghast. A moment later Japheth, feeling the ark can't be built without his aid, returns. He does this not for the sake of his God, or of his brothers (whom he still refuses to talk to), but for his parents. And he was helped to return by a smiling girl, Goldie.

Goldie, who was dying with curiosity to see the boat everyone speaks about, had saved Japheth from a drunken mob the previous night. Her obviously easygoing ways and ready laugh bother Esther, but please Ham.

Another visitor, a tax collector, arrives on their hilltop. He shows some interest in their animals but mainly in Shem. Japheth explains to his father: "This man came to collect taxes, and Shem is about to bribe him." Shem refuses to say what he sold, until the man angrily tells Esther why he is here: "Taxes! Taxes on the sales of almost thirty thousand shekels' worth of land and orchards!" Noah is horrified, and orders Shem to take all the money and turn it over to the tax collector. Leah asks quickly: "Who says there's any money to give?" "On the ark," says Noah bitterly, "nothing will be for sale, no investments, hear me? Money is unholy dirt on the ark—"

Shem, feeling he is nothing without his money, turns murderous when asked to hand over Leah's keys. Japheth has to knock him out to get them. In accepting them, the man tells Noah: "You got strong convictions. I admire the insanity of your belief! Good luck." And keys in hand, departs.

Goldie, having watched this show, announces: "I feel depressed.

You people really believe this, don't you?" But Ham, with a light
in his eye, quickly persuades her to go see his animals.

Noah wonders: "Why did God pick this family? With none of
my sons I don't fit. . . . Japheth's got a wife?

ESTHER (*warningly*)—Later.

NOAH—She's a nice girl? (JAPHETH *rises, takes bucket from
spring, exits.*)

ESTHER—Later. . . . (*He stands with his sense of grieving shame,
his eyes caught by the eagles in the trees.*)

NOAH—Nobody's so good as God can be . . . but it's up to Him
to gimme what I need to do His work. . . . (*Holding out his hands.*)
See them bones? That ain' hands no more, it's bones! (*Looking
upward.*) You say to the eagle, fly! Even to a little bitty of an
eagle like me, fly, fly higher and higher! But You have shrinked
away his wings and he couldn't do it! Why did You pick me . . . ?
Honorable Sir . . . ? For what?

Deeply touched, Esther advises her sadly tired husband to lie down.
"I miss meself a little drink now and then . . . ," Noah confesses
as he goes to the shade of some bushes to take his rest.

Esther and Rachel, letting Noah sleep, quietly compare notes on
Goldie. To Esther, "A person like her, she fits to Ham . . . the
way you fit to Japhie." Goldie, on her return from visiting the animals, shows the truth of this in her appreciation of Ham's "quick
wit." But Esther, ever just, ignores this and thanks Goldie for saving Japheth's life. As a strange, inexplicable wind comes up, she
even asks a nervous Goldie to spend the night with them.

The Presence of God has begun to shimmer broadly over the scene;
in the background behind the bushes Noah cries out in his sleep. To
Esther the cries become so frightening that she sends Rachel for the
boys. She tries to waken Noah, but when Japheth and Shem take
hold of their thrashing father, trying to find out what is wrong, they
suddenly see. Even Esther steps back when Noah gets to his feet.
He has become a young man of fifty, with eagle-bright eyes and red-
dish hair. As God's Presence once more fades away, Noah, aware
of his new body, falteringly tells Esther: "God gave me . . .
strength." Goldie is fascinated as Noah, completely in command,
moves in on his troublesome sons: "Boys," says Noah, "keep clear.
Between us there should be no more fights. . . . How long more for
the ark to be finished? For an instance . . . ?

JAPHETH—Nine to eleven weeks.
NOAH—And if I work, like on roofin'?
JAPHETH—Less.

Everyone watches, as Noah, thoughtfully picking up his staff, says: "Esther, gimme a few figs in my pockets, yeh?" Quite friendly now, he tells Japheth he'll forget all his foolish remarks, "but be careful for the future. Because Somebody Upstairs, He hears you, every word. So you'll build the ark, but maybe you won't sail on it." Once more the undisputed head of the family, he is ready to play a return engagement in the valley. Firmly gripping his staff, he sets off for town, to buy seeds.

SCENE V

More of the ark can be seen, as the women in ant-like lines file back and forth with food and household articles. The weird, terrifying light in the sky shows the time is drawing near. Looking down over the valley, Noah and Shem see clouds the like of which they've never seen.

SHEM—Any hour. If there's a wind, any hour.
NOAH—You hear, Esther? Any hour, he thinks, if a wind comes.
ESTHER—Yeh. It's lucky we took the animals on board awready. (ESTHER *looks up at the sky. There is a moment of brooding silence, fringed by the distant bird-song. Only* ESTHER *sees* JAPHETH *enter left with his "luggage" . . .*)
SHEM (*incredulously*)—The sun rising in the west and setting in the east! Why don't the people see? Where are their brains?
ESTHER (*quietly*)—So what should they do if they see . . . ?
NOAH (*still peering*)—Pray!
JAPHETH—For what? . . . (NOAH *and* SHEM *turn and look at* JAPHETH, *but he turns and without another word walks out to the left. In the background* HAM, *watering the animals, comes and goes with a pair of buckets.*)
SHEM—That attitude—it's gonna cost him dear, that attitude.
ESTHER—It's gonna cost us dear, that attitude.

Leah and Rachel continue at their back-breaking tasks, with Goldie—in a state of near-collapse—following Leah's orders.

Noah and Esther voice their distress over Japheth's defection, and are miserable when they think of their friends. Esther says: "I keep thinking of old lady Kamen, a grandmother nineteen times! What'll happen to her?" "And what'll happen, old friend, to thousands and thousands of others?" Noah asks. And he notices that in the midst of all this Esther has made woolen cloth, and wonders why. He's forgotten, Esther tells him, that old people get chilly. In his new-found youth he also doesn't realize that he's worth flirting with, which is just what Esther can't help doing. She has picked up a large wide hat decorated with fruits, berries and flowers: "I found it last week. Maybe from thirty years back." Putting it on, she gives him a look: "I'm pretty? You'll take me for a walk?" "One thing, sister—with such a hat you couldn't go hungry," Noah replies. Esther, unperturbed, decides to take it, *for the sun.*

Noah refuses to persuade Japheth to join them on the ark. But Esther makes it clear he'd better try: "Because I'll swear to you one thing, Noah—if he don't go, I won't go!"

Goldie has her troubles; she sits down miserably near Esther, who understands what the trouble is: "You're nervous, *tuchter?*" "You called *me* daughter . . . ?" Goldie gratefully says. "Doesn't this make *you* nervous?" Esther answers grimly: "The last few weeks, like everyone else, I'm in the bushes five times an hour!" Notwithstanding, she goes after Noah with the lunch he forgot to eat.

Ham now furtively sashays up to Goldie to proposition her. She won't have it; she gave in to him last time because she was frightened—she wants nothing further to do with him.

HAM (*sarcastically*)—With your background, you frighten very easy. What was it, hysterics? (*Touches her shoulder.*)

GOLDIE—It was hysterics and I'm on the verge of hysterics right now, so go away!

HAM (*moves towards her. Firmly*)—Don't raise your voice! I'll see you tonight.

GOLDIE—No, I'd rather go and tell your mother the truth—you blackmailed me! (*She moves to a basket and lifts it.*) I'm warning you, Ham. I'm not very stable. If you don't go away I'll begin to scream—!

Goldie carries the basket to the ark, and Rachel takes over Ham. Apparently everyone knows about Ham and Goldie except Noah, and Rachel warns Ham not to let Noah find out. In answer, she gets taunts and smirks before Ham goes about last-minute duties.

As Rachel pleaded with Ham, Esther now pleads with Rachel. As a last resort, would Rachel beg Japheth to join the family on the ark, to make him feel that he is needed and wanted by Noah? Rachel promises to try, then tactfully leaves mother and son together.

JAPHETH—You're mad at me, Momma?

ESTHER—I can't be glad at you, sonny. Suddenly you're a stranger—nobody knows you. What is that? (*Enter* OLD MAN.)

JAPHETH—Sometimes that happens when a boy grows up.

ESTHER—And to what did you grow up? To die in the cold, cold water? (*She looks past her son at an* OLD MAN *who has entered from lower left, two of his* COMPANIONS, *as old as he, lingering behind.*) You want to drink, Mister? Help yourself.

OLD MAN—Thank you. God is good. . . . (ESTHER *emptily replies as her eyes shift back to her son.*)

ESTHER—I'm really surprised nobody came here today, except these olden time religious. (*Dropping her voice.*) Poppa expects you'll marry that girl. He won't take her without you. . . . You like her?

JAPHETH—She's a perfect stranger to me.

ESTHER—Ham likes her very much . . . a tested recipe by now . . . and Rachel knows it.

JAPHETH (*quietly, looking at his hands.*) Momma, do me a last favor. . . . Tell Poppa the ark needs a rudder. . . .

ESTHER (*angrily, standing*)—He don't care about *that* now! He's worried about *you,* the way *I* am, the way Rachel is!

Japheth begs his mother to love him always, but she quite violently orders him to get away—"You just got rich, that's your trouble," Esther says. "You just became a man an' you're spending it as fast as you can, throwing it in everyone's face. . . . Remember what I say!" The Old Man, with his pail of water, passes by, murmuring: "God is good. . . ." Esther, with an empty gesture, repeats: "God is good . . ." and goes off beyond the ark.

Rachel is no more successful with Japheth than his mother was, but she tries to find out for what Japheth is willing to remain behind. Japheth answers: "Those roads down there! The patterns they make! They're not cobwebs, those roads, the work of a foolish spider, to be brushed away by a peevish boy! Those roads were made by men, men crazy not to be alone or apart! Men, crazy to reach each other!" After a bitter pause, he says, "Well, they won't now. . . ."

RACHEL—Japheth, this sounds wrong to me. If you think people should reach each other . . . the ark is the only place they'll do it now.

JAPHETH (*impatiently*)—Rachel, you won't make me change my mind.

RACHEL—Japheth, I beg you to think!   There is idealism now in just survival.

Something else holds Japheth back: there's the problem of the two of them. "I love you," Japheth tells Rachel, "and couldn't live and work beside you on the ark." Over her protests he insists, "And I can't remember the time I didn't!" "I don't want to hear it now—" cries Rachel. "You're not inspired by your love for your mother or me. You're inspired by your pain, and it's vile."

Now frightened flights of birds, swirls of dust, preface the rains. "Where did the wind come from suddenly?" Rachel cries. "From the bosom of God's infinite mercy," Japheth answers.

Japheth calls to his family and points out what is happening. "The grass blows," says Noah, "the wind shakes the dust . . . it's the end of the world. . . ." Then he briskly asks Shem if all the animals are on board. Shem answers: "Everything alive is on board, yes, sir." "It looks close," Noah feels, then adds: "Esther, *tuchter*, don't excite yourself. Get everything ready. The Lord waits an' watches."

During these last moments of hectic activity, with everyone giving a hand, the Old Men reappear, and one of them approaches Noah.

OLD MAN—Take us, Noah. . . . Take us with you.

NOAH (*gently but firmly*)—This an' only this is His orders, the family, brother. Please, please don't ast me again. (*Everyone is impressed by a silent flash of deep lightning.*)

OLD MAN—We know the Old Law. Take *one* of us.

NOAH (*shaking his head*)—Please don't ast me again.

OLD MAN—We know the Old Law *behind* the Old Law—it will be forgotten. (EACH OLD MAN *says of the other,* "Take him, take him," *etc.* ESTHER *steps in with assistance.*)

ESTHER—He would like to do it in the worst way, but he dasn't.

In grave disappointment the Old Men retire to one side to chant and intone Hebrew prayers.

With the lightning and thunder increasing in violence, Japheth still refuses all orders—whether from God or his father—to go on the ark. Esther in desperate anger shouts: "But then you'll die in the water!" "I'd rather die in protest, Momma," he says, "than live." "Protest?" cries Esther. "That's foolish! You think you know what's right? So have your own sons an' teach them!" An enraged Noah will have no more. Declaring the power of God is in his arm, he knocks out his son, and asking the Lord to forgive him, orders Shem to carry the unconscious figure onto the ark. . . . "The time is short," says Noah.

Goldie wishes to confess her sins to Esther before accepting an invitation on the ark. Esther won't hear her: "Excuse me," says Esther, "the truth isn't the truth right now! It's a big luxury we can't afford!" She almost shakes sense into the girl, then orders: "Now don't stand on ceremony, an' give a hand. . . ." Goldie sets to work.

The rain breaks in sheets over the valley: Noah orders all windows and doors of the ark tightly closed, and everyone on board.

NOAH—Come, old friend, I'll help you . . . to your new home.

ESTHER—What did I forget . . . ? Noah, my heart is in my mouth. . . .

NOAH (*face furrowed with pain*)—My hands is cold as ice can be. . . .

ESTHER (*finally, sighing deeply, she permits him to lead her towards the ark but abruptly she pulls away, saying:*)—The hat! My hat! (*As she goes to the right to pick up the hat,* NOAH *abruptly cries:*)

NOAH—What did I forget? The gitka! The little gitka! (*He goes to the right and at the base of the tree picks up the precious sawdust box in which the gitka lives. Then he and* ESTHER *start for the ramp together again.* THE CHILDREN *watch them with humorless faces;* GOLDIE *and* RACHEL *are weeping softly. Lightning, thunder and denser rain now.* THE OLD MEN *are chanting aloud, their unbowed heads beginning to drip like running candles.* THE BOYS *reach down to help their mother up, but* NOAH *stays on the ground and looks out again, this time looking upward.*) For the last time, oh Lord, must it be . . . ? (*As if in answer, the world seems to shake with thunder.* NOAH *sobs aloud, blinded alike by tears and rain.* SHEM *steps down and takes his arm, saying in a choked voice:*)

SHEM—Come, Poppa. . . .

SCENE VI

On board the ark, Noah sits on deck, the gitka in his lap, sadly musing over the lost world. As he looks over the waters, he thinks back to his father Methuselah, his own evangelical youth, his sixty years with Esther, his downfall from drink. . . . " But God Awmighty, blessed be His name, He found me out and give me back my good name to some extent. . . . (*With holiness.*) Yeh, here's me and there's that miserable, no-good, lonely wild world out there.

. . . You'll go downstairs, girlie," he tells the gitka. . . . "Tell them it's the forty-first day . . . the big rains is over. . . ."

The personal problems of the passengers of the ark are far from over: Japheth is still feuding with Noah over his refusal to marry Goldie and his holding out for the rudder. Noah as usual finds it difficult to control himself and barely manages it.

NOAH—Awright—we change the subject. Why is the ark so slanty?

JAPHETH (*at work*)—Some cargo must've shifted—I'll look later.

NOAH- What's this I hear we have no snails on board . . . ?

JAPHETH—We have one, the murmex snail.

NOAH—But what good is one?

JAPHETH—With snails the he is a he *and* a she.

NOAH (*astonished*)—He's a she? A he *and* a she? Lucky person! Sonny, it's an honor to you how you took care— (*He turns and is surprised to find that* JAPHETH *has drifted to the other side of the housing with his tools.*) Went away? Looks to me like a good boy, but I dunno. . . . (SHEM, *with his one-track mind, is looking ahead.*)

SHEM (*ruminating*)—Did you ever realize, Poppa, when we land— granting all goes well—that the whole world will be ours?

NOAH (*with a dour chuckle*)—Ours? Awright, whatever you'll grow with your own hands, it's yours. People you can't hire no more to work for you.

SHEM—Yeh, that's what worries me. . . .

NOAH—The whole world stinks of ruined bodies an' rotten grass. And today, Shem, on this sacred wood, your head's fulla business . . . ?

SHEM—Poppa, sir, I give emphatic prayer and thanks! But later, sir, you'll admit, it behooves us all to use our God-given brains.

NOAH (*angrily*)—No, I don't hit with this talk! You're awready workin' how to take from your brothers an' your brothers' children!

For the last week Noah has also known that Ham has been hitting the bottle. Shem has been paying Ham with liquor to do his daily chores for him. Noah is ready to cry, but roars instead: "Both of you—an' Japheth, too!—your name's gettin' worser to me by the minute! Maybe He'll tell me some day why He picked this family."

Rachel, on the other hand, has become stronger while on the ark. Ham's taunts no longer fluster her; even he can see the change in his wife. "If we don't change on the Holy Ark where will we change?" says Rachel. And she is determined never to live with Ham again.

Japheth, wanting to marry Rachel, is equally determined to have nothing to do with Goldie. Rachel is troubled: "I would marry you . . . but your father won't permit it."

JAPHETH—Ham was right—you're changing. Well, I'm changing, too—and my father—innocent and stubborn as he is—he'll have to change!

RACHEL—All my life I've been afraid—

JAPHETH—You mustn't be afraid—I'll make you strong!

RACHEL (*stirred*)—Japheth, you're right! I look around . . . what else can happen? Thank you, thank you, Japheth, that you need me—

JAPHETH (*gently*)—Let me kiss you, Rachel, here in God's clear air. . . .

There being no privacy on the ark, Esther as she comes up the stairs sees the two together, but greets them tactfully and sends Japhie down to Noah. To Rachel Esther says: "You're looking very good today, Rachel, but take a piece of advice, keep your hands busy and later we'll have a talk." Rachel joins the other girls, who are optimistically hanging out the wash. "If the sun comes out I will be a happy woman," says Esther. "I'm easy to satisfy, God."

The ark is a busy place. Downstairs there have to be fires made in an attempt to dry things out; animals have to be cared for; the odd slant of the ark must be investigated; and, of course, Leah and Shem have to conspire. Between chores, people constantly cross each other's path on deck. Goldie holds out nobly against Ham's advances, and Esther seems to be holding out against Noah. Instead of her husband sleeping beside her, she has Rachel in her bed. Noah is decidedly put out: ". . . And I'll ast you again—what's Rachel livin' in our bedroom, sleepin' in my bed with you?"

ESTHER—Oh, you, don't you get so fresh, you!

NOAH (*prancing*)—This is fresh by you? A woman I slept with her in one bed for sixty years—suddenly I'm sleepin' on the couch. Whhhy . . . ?

ESTHER—Do me a favor, Noah, an' don't bother me, hey?

Noah is shocked and hurt, but deeply concerned when he sees Esther really sobbing.

NOAH—*My* Esther is cryin' . . . ?

ESTHER (*crying*)—Whatta you want from me, Noah? I'm a tired old woman . . . you're a young man . . .

NOAH—You're my wife, Esther, for sixty years . . .

ESTHER (*sadly, shaking her head*)—No, no more . . . an old lady, like your mother . . .

NOAH (*sparking up*)—Don't ever forget, girlie, it's a big knot, a helluva, how we're tied together.

Esther, getting control of herself, knowing that this mess isn't Noah's fault, still wishes him to sleep on the couch.

Noah is ready to go into action to straighten out his family. As they all assemble on deck, he crisply tells them: "Maybe you lost the sense for it, so I'll tell you all—the ark is a temple! An' each an' everyone, we live in the service of the Lord: He's Boss over me an' I'm boss over you, yeh: The way it begins to stand there's better ones in the water than here on the deck. . . ." His first undertaking is to marry Goldie to Japheth, and he runs into a stone wall. No one backs him up except Shem, who declares pompously: "In my considered opinion, Poppa is completely right. In unstable times respect for authority must prevail." Incensed at this hypocrisy, Japheth asks the family if it knows why the ark tilts so dangerously. Shem and Leah, he goes on, are guilty of hoarding manure! They've stuffed their room with it to the ceiling, and look forward to the time when fuel will be needed and they alone can sell dried manure briquettes.

NOAH—On the Holy Ark he's makin' business! Manure! With manure you want to begin a new world? Everybody's life he put in danger!

ESTHER—Poppa's a hundred per cent right.

NOAH (*harshly*)—You'll dump it overboard right away! (ESTHER *begins to navigate a little.*)

ESTHER—If you made it to sell, Shem, you're a low dog! But if you made it for the family—

SHEM (*picking up the cue*)—But, Momma, that's what I did—I made it for the family!

ESTHER (*pretending surprise*)—You hear, Noah?

NOAH—Esther, you shouldn't take his part, hear me?

ESTHER—But if it's for the family, why throw it overboard . . . ? (NOAH *looks at her, aware that she is putting something over on him; he turns away with tight lips, hands behind his back.* ESTHER, *stolidly:*) Shem made a useful thing from nothing, yeh? Why kill the man with brains? No, make him use it for the *family!*

Noah again insists that Japheth marry Goldie, only to meet with open rebellion: Japheth wants to marry Rachel, who has been de-

serted by Ham, who in turn wants Goldie. What's more, in this
marital mixup Esther seems to be on the children's side. "Whatever
you're saying, all of you, it's a thing I hate," he cries, "as well as I
hate murder! The ark is a holy temple!" "No," says Esther doggedly, "it's a stable—around the clock a Turkish bath for animals!
People are wore out from work an' misery." Noah warns them all
that they're going too far: "Where marriage an' divorce is concerned,
it says in the rules an' regulations, from way back—"

ESTHER (*impatiently*)—But since "way back" people are changing, Noah!

NOAH (*writhing*)—No, girlie, He didn't destroy the whole world,
the Awmighty, to find all the sins on the ark! (*Exploding.*) Esther,
don't you see—you're blind? *They don't stop acting like human
beings!!*

JAPHETH—God had to pick human beings to help Him, didn't He?
Now, if He doesn't like it that human beings act like human beings,
He's out of luck!

NOAH (*enraged*)—Who's outta luck?!

ESTHER—God's outta luck. . . . And you'll hit me first.

Noah feels God will handle them, they'll be stricken down. At
first he daren't look at the impending slaughter, then can't resist a
peek at his surprisingly healthy family: "They're still alive, the hate-
able persons . . . ?" he breathes. The long-awaited sun now bursts
through the clouds.

The various couples re-sort themselves happily, and joy reigns.
Esther, however, is suddenly caught by so terrible a pain that she
is unable to move. And Leah, on top of this, tells her the news that
Noah has disappeared with a whole keg of brandy. "Brandy?" says
Esther. "I'll go see. I took your part . . . but don't make a mis-
take, children, Noah is my favorite boy. . . ."

SCENE VII

While Noah has been on a binge, and Esther has lain at death's
door, Japheth and his rudder have taken over. When after nine
whole weeks of drinking, Noah emerges soberly on deck, his prayers
for forgiveness and guidance are quickly forgotten at the sight of
Japheth steering the ark.

NOAH— . . . And God never said we should steer the ark! Tomorrow first thing you'll take it off!

JAPHETH (*temper slipping*)—And God didn't tell you to invent the hoe and the rake and yet you did!

NOAH (*flatly*)—I was a youngster then—what did I know? If you'll ast me today, I'm sorry I done it!

JAPHETH (*incredulously*)—Sorry? You said sorry?

NOAH (*fiercely*)—Yeh, yeh, yeh! It made work too easy an' people for loafers!

JAPHETH—Not so loud, please—Momma's sick downstairs.

NOAH (*haughtily*)—Last night I seen her, never mind. Who do you think I stopped drinkin' for? You? (*A few unhappy asides.*) I'm altogether in a lonely sorta way. I slept many times with the cows the last weeks—sweet persons. Maybe we were saved for the animals, not ourself. (*Then.*) I'll go down an' see Mother, but she don't want me. . . .

Noah feels nobody loves him, or respects and loves God. Japheth yells back at him: "God doesn't want the respect of a slave upon its knees—" "You think you know what God wants?" cries Noah. "Take the rudder off—!" Noah further warns Japheth to give up his brother's wife. Maybe that's why his mother is sick. . . . "God sent a judgment against us . . . He'll take her away. . . ." Noah quickly takes that back, not believing that anything can really happen to Esther on the ark.

But something seems to be happening to the ark. All during Noah's nine-week drunk, Japheth has been plugging up leaks. Now Ham excitedly reports that the ark has sprung a bad one, and begs Japheth to hurry below to repair it. Shem adds his pleas, but all Japheth does is sit calmly telling them to wait. . . . "For months I've asked myself a question: "Is Poppa a saint or a fool? Now I know he's half of each . . . but I never know which half is operating—" Shem wildly yells at him to plug up the leak, but Japheth answers: "Poppa claims the ark is in Divine Hands only? Well, I'm ready to agree. . . . We'll throw off the rudder. And I'll give up Rachel and marry Goldie." Noah blesses God, as Japheth announces there's no need to go below because he, like Noah, has faith. As Noah raises his hands in gratitude, he is almost thrown on his face by a huge lurch of the ark. This, explains Japheth, was caused by the water rushing into another hold. "Why is the water so close?" puzzles Noah. Shem shouts in fear. Ham rushes up with the bulletin that the cows are udder-high in water.

JAPHETH (*quietly*)—I'm ready, Poppa, to take the rudder off.

SHEM—Poppa, tell Japheth to go below and stopper up that hole!

JAPHETH—Poppa, I'm ready to take the rudder off right now!

NOAH (*a little sickened but hiding it*)—*Now*, you mean? You wanna do it *now?*

SHEM—There is only a broken eggshell between us and the sea: The ark is sinking by inches! Tell Japheth to go to work with me!

NOAH (*slowly turning*)—Japhie, you think you should . . . ?

SHEM—Stop this insanity!

NOAH—Japhie knows about such things . . . he'll use his own judgment. . . . (*Another lurch of the ark!* THE THREE MEN *stagger. Cow sounds, etc. Timidly:*) Sonny, why don't you use your judgment. . . . You know, to fix . . .

JAPHETH (*simply*)—To use my own judgment, Poppa, I'd have to trust myself.

NOAH (*poignantly*)—So, really . . . why don't you trust yourself?

JAPHETH—Because you don't permit that!

NOAH—But we can't do too much as God don't want it, can we?

JAPHETH (*pressing him*)—I don't know what you're talking about and I don't know what God wants, do you?

Japheth refuses to fix the leak until he has Noah's word that the rudder stays. Noah weakly gives in, but angrily draws the line at the other condition: that he marry all four of them by noon that day. Noah would prefer to drown. Japheth counters that he will fix the ark but will never speak to Noah again. With trembling voice Shem says to his father: "I'm very ashamed to say it . . . but your youngest son is a better man of God than you!"

Noah, left alone, is too hurt to move: "The oldest day of my life . . ." he says. "What did I done, God . . . ? (*Sighing.*) I'll let the boys run things. I'll be the janitor on the ark . . . it fits to me. (*Picking up gitka.*) Oh, gitka. My Esther is sick? Maybe dying? I'm ashamed to face her. God is far away, children . . . we're lonely people . . ."

SCENE VIII

The waters have so swiftly receded that there is a general feeling among the passengers that their journey will soon end. Noah has even sent out two doves to look for land.

Suddenly an old man again, but with a sweet new humility, Noah talks to the animals on equal terms, but fails to talk at all to his sons. He avoids Japheth at the helm, and seeks the company of an old, tired lion instead, and watches for his doves.

JAPHETH—What are you fighting about? You and your doves.

NOAH (*to* SHEM. *Haughtily and quietly*)—Tell a certain person Mother will feel better on the ground. That's why I'm watchin' for the doves. I'm tryin' to find her a little piece of land soon in the worst way.

JAPHETH—What do you mean? You're afraid that Momma will die?

NOAH—No! Yes, I am afraid! I cannot see any future without Mother! If she dies, I will go right with her . . . so help me, God, which is true.

SHEM (*rises*)—If you're afraid, Poppa, let's be afraid together.

NOAH (*shaking his head*)—No, Sonny, that's no medicine to me.

And he goes behind the deckhouse.

Esther, wasted and shockingly changed, reaches the deck with Goldie's help and sits down heavily in a chair. While the girls fuss over her, Noah hides. Goldie puts the gitka in Esther's lap and Esther puts on her fancy big hat. Once settled, Esther wants Noah: "Where's Poppa? Noah? . . . He hiding again? (*Calling angrily.*) Noah!"

NOAH (*timidly and innocently appears with the little broom in his hand*)—You want me, Esther? I'm sweepin' . . .

ESTHER—Go, children, I wanna be with my husband alone.

NOAH—Esther, you came up for fresh air. (ESTHER *looks at him scornfully as* THE CHILDREN *discreetly scatter,* SHEM *joining* JAPHETH *for a whispered conference at the rudder.*)

ESTHER—If you would look how you look, it's only a shame. . . .

NOAH (*falteringly*)—Maybe I'll get you something, a few crackers, a muffin?

ESTHER (*annoyed*)—Noah, I'll bite your ears off in a minute! You couldn't come down to see me? Put the broom away, you fool!

NOAH (*growing huffy*)—Now, now, my dear lady—it's not necessary, such a talk. (*Abruptly, seeing her wince.*) How are you feelin'?

Esther, with her usual spirit, snaps back at him but then asks him to come closer. When he is seated beside her, she begs him: "Marry the children . . . for the sake of happiness in the world. . . ."

NOAH—Old friend, it hurts me to refuse you, but it stands in the books for a thousand years—

ESTHER (*head nodding*)—But all the books are in the water now.
. . . Marry the children before I go. . . .

NOAH (*scoffingly*)—First place, He won't permit such marriages,
the God I know. And secondly, He won't let nothing happen to you,
the God I know.

ESTHER (*growing very tired*)—Maybe you don't know Him . . .
any more . . .

NOAH (*cheering her up*)—Don't you worry, we'll have a promised
land together. I'm your particular friend, hear me?

ESTHER (*shaking her head weakly*)—The children, their happiness . . . is my last promised land. . . .

Everyone looks for the dove's return except Esther, who simply
wants to sit in the sun. "I'll take the hat to shade my eyes," she
says. Then dizzily calls to Noah: ". . . help me . . . I'm a baby,
I'm a baby. . . . Noah, I'll tell you a mystery—" Noah stands at
a loss: ". . . We're the only living people in the world and Esther
is down and out. I'll put a great big page on the table an' I'll write
it out some day, what happened on this trip. . . . It's a lonely story,
God. What was it for?" Rachel's cry that she sees a bird brings
everyone running. The dove, bearing a green leaf from an olive tree,
swoops down into the excited knot of people. Noah shouts: "A tree!
Esther, there is open land in the world somewhere! Our trip is done,
old friend. . . ."

But Esther is gone from them.

SHEM—Her hat fell off. She's dead, Poppa.

NOAH—I'll sit. . . . No, I'll go stand by the wall. (*Shouting.*)
What? You'll go so far but don't go too far! (*Motionless.*) Shem,
tell me the truth, make or break—"

SHEM—She's dead.

NOAH (*with an abrupt howl*)—Jaaphieee! I have trouble.
Sonny, help me, I'm in trouble. (*He puts himself in* JAPHETH's *arms
and cries like a child. Recovered, he wipes his eyes and says:*)
Children, the whole night is ahead to give thanks to Heaven. Go
better now every husband should kiss each wife, as Mother wanted.
And I'll go kiss mine and close her eyes. . . .

EPILOGUE

The ark, having come to rest on high ground, looks, in the early
morning light, like part of a Japanese print. It rests gently tipped

in the pink earth, and beyond the centrally placed gangplank blooms a young peach tree.

Grouped round the gangplank—waiting for Noah to come off the ark—are the women, all big with child. Goldie and Rachel take it easy among their few belongings, Ham kids Goldie from a lolling position on deck. But Leah and Shem are still systematically amassing their possessions. Ham joshes Shem: "Let history record that one year ago you came aboard with eight bundles—you're leaving with twenty-nine! Why did Poppa give you the two extra cows?" Shem answers that it's because he's a man of responsibility, and what's more, Leah adds, Noah will probably come to live with them. Ham isn't so sure: he would guess Noah would go with Japheth; Goldie hopes that because of her cooking, Noah will choose them. Rachel peacefully looks about her: "The world looks washed. . . ."

Noah now disembarks. No longer the least bit despotic, he is humorous, gentle, somewhat wistful, and thoroughly affable. With a strange little hat on his head, and Esther's plant and the dove's cage in his arms, he wants to be sure: "All the animals went away? Nothing's at all left on board?" "No, sir," respectfully answers Japheth.

Leah comes abruptly to what they all want to know: ". . . Who'll you go with?" she asks Noah. "Children—" says Noah, "I'll stay with Shem. Why? It's more comfortable." And he makes his farewell: "Go now, children, an' be fruitful and multiply. . . . An' everywhere and in all things, replenish the earth—" Shem can't wait to get busy: "Let's start, Poppa, before the sun gets too high." "Go ahead," says Noah, "I'll catch up."

There are kidding and affectionate leave-takings, as Goldie, Ham, Leah and Shem start off down the hill. Noah adds: ". . . be careful, girls, going down the hill—" After the noisy departure, a hush falls over the scene.

NOAH—What kinda tree is so beautiful?

JAPHETH—It's a flowering peach, Poppa.

NOAH—Peach . . . (*Thinking a long thought.*) Before you look up . . . It's the first April without Mother. (JAPHETH *has broken off a small branch of the bloom and hands it to* RACHEL, *who turns and gives it to* NOAH. *This precious gift he accepts with a nuance of a smile, murmuring:*) From the new earth.

RACHEL—Now we are a story—a legend.

JAPHETH—What's ahead, Poppa?

NOAH (*holding up the bloom*)—This is ahead—a fruitful world

. . . the people need happiness. For a year we stood in a boat an'
looked ourselves in the face.

JAPHETH—We were forced to face ourselves, you mean?

NOAH—I'm listening, tell me. . . .

JAPHETH—I don't know. But we've all changed.

NOAH—An' He changed, too . . . ?

JAPHETH—Maybe God changes when men change.

With a final embrace, and loving words, Japheth and Rachel leave.
"Write sometime,' says Noah, with a forlorn wave of the hand, a
sniff and a last tear. "Right here I could sleep out my remaining
years . . . till Esther wants me," he murmurs. Then, cocking his
head, he hears the returning Presence of God. (*Dreamily*.) "You're
hanging around, Lord? That's just how I feel. (*Listening*.) No, I
won't get off the ark. Forgive me, Sir, excuse me. . . . First a little
guarantee, a covenant, and then I'll go. . . . (*Watchful and waiting*.) You know what I want, Lord. Just like you guarantee each
month, with a woman's blood, that men will be born . . . give such
a sign that you won't destroy the world again. . . . (*He waits
tensely until the musical hum relaxes into a quality of benevolence,
and, relaxing and smiling, asks:*) Where shall I look? Where? (*Anyone who would be watching sees the rainbow in the sky before* NOAH
turns and sees it with an awed clasping of his hands.) Thank you,
Lord above, thank you. . . . (*Abruptly cocking his head.*) But
what I learned on the trip, dear God, you can't take away from me.
To walk in humility, I learned. (*He crosses down the ramp.*) And
listen, even to *myself* . . . and to speak softly, with the voices of
consolation. Yes, I hear You, God— Now it's in man's hands to
make or destroy the world. . . . I'll tell you a mystery. . . ."

THE DESPERATE HOURS *

A Melodrama in Three Acts

BY JOSEPH HAYES

(Adapted from Mr. Hayes' novel of the same name)

[JOSEPH HAYES *was born in Indianapolis in 1918. While still in his teens he spent two years in a monastery, made a hitch-hiking tour of the south, pushed wheel chairs at the Dallas Fair, managed a small ice house and did farm and warehouse work. At twenty he married, and he and his wife, Marrijane, worked their way through Midwestern University editing a drama magazine. In 1941 he moved to New York and for ten years was in the editorial department of a play publishing house. During this time he wrote several TV scripts and short stories for magazines. "The Desperate Hours" is his first novel and has already been made into a motion picture scheduled for release next year. His only previous play to be produced on Broadway was "Leaf and Bough" in 1949.*]

IT'S an autumn morning in Indianapolis, when Bard, the morning relief man, arrives at the Sheriff's office. Taking off his jacket, he apologizes casually to the officer on duty for being late. Winston answers sleepily: "You've got a lovely excuse." Bard, riffling through the reports on the desk, acknowledges this: "I'll tell her you think so."

To judge from the police reports, nothing seems to have happened during the night, but something he reads suddenly makes Bard go tense. He asks Winston about it, who dismisses it between yawns as a prison break in Terre Haute—the news came through hours ago: "The three of them busted out some time before dawn . . ." Bard, asking why he wasn't called, signals on the intercom for Fredericks of the state police, then mutters: "Terre Haute's only seventy miles away. They could've walked here by now!"

FREDERICKS' VOICE (*on the intercom*)—I wondered when you'd start yipping, Bard.

BARD—Fredericks . . . anybody sitting on anything?

FREDERICKS' VOICE—I'm sitting on just what you're sitting on, Deputy. Only mine ain't sweatin'.

BARD—Griffin's woman . . . Helen Laski . . . any dope on her?

FREDERICKS' VOICE—Not a trace. Chicago . . . Cleveland . . . St. Louie. All we know is she was here in town three weeks ago.

BARD—Just don't let any cop touch her. She's the beacon'll lead us straight . . .

FREDERICKS' VOICE—Bard . . . It's an FBI case, anyway. . . . The city police've ripped whole buildings apart. We got the highway blocked. We're working through all the dives . . .

BARD—If Glenn Griffin wants to come here, no roadblock's gonna stop him. And he's too sharp to hole up any place you'd think of looking.

FREDERICKS' VOICE—Look, lad . . . get that chip off your shoulder. You want Griffin so bad, go get him. (BARD *flips off the intercom*. WINSTON *reluctantly removes his coat*.)

Winston wonders if this is Bard's Glenn Griffin; Bard affirms he is, and one of the others with him is his brother Hank; the third convict he doesn't know about. Winston tells him about Samuel Robish, a nasty lifer, then reluctantly goes back on duty to the teletype machine.

As Winston leaves the office, Bard telephones his wife. In comparatively gentle tones, he kids her into going to his mother's for the day, without telling the neighbors where she's going. His smile fades as he hangs up; and Winston comes back with Carson of the FBI, and a teletype message. "How are you?" snaps Bard. "Look," he pounds at the message, "it says they beat up the farmer south of the prison before daybreak. How come we're just getting it?" Carson explains: "They left him in his barn out cold . . . ripped out his phone. He just staggered into a general store and reported his car stolen . . ." Has this been put on the air? Bard inquires. "Deputy," says Carson, "I've been in touch with Sheriff Masters by telephone." "I hope," Bard growls, "he's enjoying his extended vacation. He sure picked a fine time to leave me in charge here." Because Bard knows Glenn Griffin better than any other officer, Carson asks him to head this section. Feeling the weight of this responsibility, Bard slowly agrees, then begins at once to fire orders, ready to follow every tip. The one thing he knows is: ". . . just as long's Glenn Griffin's running around free and safe . . . with that prison guard's .38 in his paw—well, it's not free or safe for anyone else. No decent people anywhere . . . whether they've ever . . . heard of Glenn Griffin or not."

This same morning at the Hilliard home in suburban Indianapolis finds Eleanor Hilliard placing empty milk bottles outside the front door as her son Ralphie comes from the dining room. The ten-year-old, dressed for school, is carrying a football along with a glass of milk he's reluctant to drink. When his mother comments on his leaving his bike, again, out overnight, Ralphie answers: "It didn't rain." Eleanor, in an "or else" tone, orders him to get it in the garage before going to school. Now Dan Hilliard crosses to the stairs from the dining room. "Cindy, it's eight-thirty!" he yells. "Can't a girl straighten her girdle in peace?" floats down the stairs.

DAN—Girdle? . . . Girdle! . . . Ellie, can a twenty-year-old child with a figure like Cindy's . . .
ELEANOR—It's a joke, Dan.
DAN—Oh. Thank the Lord. She has to have a solid hour for primping and then she complains all the way downtown because we don't live in the city limits.

Dan next has his troubles with the newsboy, who throws the newspaper with a hard thud against the door and then disappears before Dan can get his hands on him. Eleanor has her usual trouble with Ralphie over his milk: today it tastes sour, yesterday it tasted like chalk; and then as always Dan has to wait for his daughter. "In half a minute she'll come prancing down those stairs and start urging *me* to hurry," he says as he returns to the dining room for his second cup of coffee.

Cindy comes down those stairs and casually inquires about her father and all his shouting. "What does he shout every morning at eight-thirty?" asks Eleanor. "He shouts it's eight-thirty," Cindy answers. Then, passing Dan, she reminds him to hurry, though she in turn goes for a cup of coffee.

Ralphie's contribution to the morning is a "moron" joke; a reminder to Eleanor not to call him "Ralph*ie*"; and a joyful account of the big game that's to be played after school: "Fourth grade versus fifth grade. We'll slaughter 'em."

He kisses his mother good-by, kids his sister about her beau, Chuck, and with great formality, shakes hands with Dan. Once out the side door, he leaves his bike just where it was.

Dan is upset that he no longer rates a kiss from his too-grown-up son, and worries over Cindy's new beau: "This young lawyer Cindy works for . . . She can't be serious, can she?" Eleanor thinks she might well be. "She's only twenty years old," explodes Dan, and is reminded that Eleanor had married him when she was nineteen. "Well," adds Dan, trying to prove something, "I didn't drive a Jaguar."

Eleanor, as Cindy and Dan are about to leave, automatically cautions Dan: "Careful, now, Dan." Cindy chides her: "Mother, you say that every morning of the world. What could possibly happen to a man in the personnel office of a department store?" She goes out the door first, leaving Dan to give Eleanor *his* automatic morning kiss and a bit of advice: "If you're going to use the car today, buy some gas first. Before you have to walk a mile for it this time."

Once rid of her family, Eleanor leans against the door, gives a "whew" of relief, pushes back her hair, and prepares to start the day's chores. She passes through her tidy living room up the stairs to Ralphie's not so tidy bedroom. She snaps on his portable radio, picks up some of his clothes, and goes down the upstairs hall presumably to the bathroom hamper. By the time she returns to Ralphie's room, the newscaster has reached the end of: ". . . five-state alarm. Police authorities have requested all citizens to be on the lookout for a 1941 Dodge sedan . . . gray . . . mud-spattered . . . bearing Indiana license plates number HL 6827 . . . that is HL 6827. . . . One of the convicts is wearing a pair of faded blue farmer's overalls which were . . ." Eleanor, preferring music, flips the dial, then starts in on Ralphie's bed. The door chime interrupts this. "Wouldn't you know it . . ." says Eleanor, ". . . every time . . ." And goes to open the door.

(*The young man who stands there . . . still out of sight . . . is in his mid-twenties and wears faded blue farmer's overalls. He is tall, with—at the moment—a rather appealing boyish expression on his handsome face.*)

GLENN—Sorry to bother you, ma'am, but it looks like I lost my way. (*As he speaks,* ROBISH *and* HANK GRIFFIN *appear from left and enter the house by the side door, stealthily.*) Could you kindly direct me to the Bowden Dairy? I know it's somewhere in the neighborhood, but I must have the wrong . . .

(HANK GRIFFIN—*who is younger than* GLENN, *shorter, not so handsome, with a confused, hard but somehow rather sensitive face . . . remains in the pantry, looking out the window of the side door.*

Robish *is large, bull-like, slow, with a huge head sunk between bulky upthrust shoulders. He goes into the kitchen and at once reappears in the dining-room door. Both wear prison garb. The following action has a cold, machine-like precision about it.*)

Eleanor (*her back to the room*)—Let me see. I've seen that sign. But there are no dairies very close. You see, this is a residential . . . (Robish *now stands in the room.* Eleanor *becomes conscious of his presence. She breaks off and turns. In that moment* Glenn *whips out the gun, comes in and pushes* Eleanor *to the center of the room. He slams the door and locks it, then moves down to right of* Eleanor.)

Glenn—Take it easy, lady. (*As her mouth trembles.*) Easy, I said. You scream, the kid owns that bike out there'll come home an' find you in a pool of blood. (Glenn *only nods to* Robish, *who stumps up the stairs, looks into* Cindy's *room (which we can't see), into* Ralphie's, *to the left of the upstairs hall, then enters the master bedroom opposite, opens the closet and takes a suit of clothes off a hanger.*) You there, Hank?

Hank (*speaking as he moves into the living room and stands left at the foot of the stairs*)—All clear out back. Lincoln in garage . . . almost new. Garage lock broken. (Eleanor *looks at* Hank, *who returns her stare boldly. A shudder goes through her. Above,* Robish *is examining and discarding various of* Dan's *clothes in the bedroom . . . creating havoc.*)

Glenn comes up to Eleanor and says he'll take the keys to the Lincoln. "Keys?" chatters Eleanor. "Keys?" "Lady," Glenn orders, "when I talk, you snap. Snap fast!" And Eleanor manages to tell him where they are in the pantry.

Robish reports from the upstairs hall: "Nobody home but the missus." This is what Glenn figured. He examines the house, opens the den door, takes a look at cabinets, talking away at the same time: "Good-lookin' family you got, lady. I seen 'em leavin'. How many bedrooms up there, Robish?" Robish, coming down with his loot, answers: "Four. An' two complete johns, for Chrissake . . ."

Robish likes Dan's suit, and Glenn likes the house. He takes a cigar from its box, gives a sniff and a click of the teeth: "Class, all the way. I guess you're tumbling to the idea, ain't you, lady?" Eleanor still hopes against hope that they'll leave. Now Robish meets with disappointment: he can find no liquor. Glenn orders him to keep a lookout from the den window. Hank is acting more efficiently: he reports back to Glenn that their gray car is in the garage, and the Hilliard Lincoln is in the driveway—but low on gas.

Robish now feels the need of a gun. It's Hank who—searching the upstairs on orders—finds one and pockets it. Glenn starts riding Robish, and Hank comes down and joins in the fun. Hearing Hank laugh, Robish lunges at him, only for Glenn to flourish his gun and say: "Listen. . . . How many times I gotta tell you? Keep your mitts off the kid . . . you don't want your skull laid open." Robish retreats to the den: "Coupla brothers! Shoulda knowed better. Ain't neither one dry back-a the ears yet."

Eleanor has to watch all this in horror. She sees the gun Hank has taken from her husband's drawer, she listens to Glenn gloating over how he avoided the police, and purring over the comfort of her living-room armchair: "Foam rubber, I betcha. Foam rubber, lady?" Eleanor nods. "I seen the ads. Melts right into your tail!" Glenn crows.

Eleanor learns how long they plan to stay: "Be outta here by midnight, lady." "Midnight?" asks Hank in surprise: "I thought you said Helen was waiting . . ." "Not in town, Hank," Glenn answers. "We don't make it so easy for 'em. She left three weeks ago."

HANK (*laughs, grabs a fistful of cigarettes from the box on the coffee table, picks up the lighter, and crossing in front of* ELEANOR, *lights it several times in her face*)—I don't care if we never leave. (*He exits into the dining room and reappears in the pantry where he stands looking out through the side door.*)

GLENN (*rises and crosses above right of sofa*)—Now, lady . . . you think you can talk on the phone without bustin' into tears?

ELEANOR (*gets up with great difficulty, takes a feeble step, then gets control of herself and walks with dignity and determination to the phone table, upper left of the front door. She turns to face* GLENN—Whom do you want me to call? (GLENN *laughs and moves up to right of her.*)

GLENN—I always go for a gal with guts! That's *whom* we're gonna call . . . a gal with real guts! Person to person . . . Mr. James calling Mrs. James . . . Atlantic 6-3389 . . . in Pittsburgh. Pittsburgh, PA. (*As* GLENN *says PA, the lights in the Hilliard home black out. The left masking is flown and the right masking lowered. Then, the lights bump up in the Sheriff's office.*)

In the Sheriff's office, at 5:30, Bard is hanging up the phone. Helen Laski, he announces triumphantly, has just been located at a hotel in Pittsburgh. In a few minutes, he's sure, they'll have a record of all calls coming from and going there. Carson is curious: "Bard, stop me if I'm out of line . . . but what's this thing to you? You personally?" For Bard, it's the first law of the jungle.

The disappointments start: Winston's lead turned out to be a dud; then from over the phone comes the news: "Helen Laski checked out of the Avalon Hotel last night. No phone calls, no messages received today . . ."—which leaves them . . . "beating their tails ragged over nothing around here."

Carson, knowing Bard, suggests: "Why don't you put some more patrol cars on the streets, anyway? Just in case?" Between pacings Bard exclaims: "That damn jalopy's been reported in every state in the Union . . . sixty times in Indiana alone! The earth won't open up and swallow it!" He goes back to his desk and decides: "Okay, let's try anything . . ." As he reaches for the phone, Bard asks: *"Where is that beat-up gray car?"*

BLACKOUT

At the Hilliard house, all is in readiness for the rest of the family's return: Robish is stationed out of sight in the den; Hank, coke in hand, at the side door, listening to music on Ralphie's radio; Glenn is at his post by the living-room windows; and Eleanor, haggard but still alert, sits bolt upright on the living-room couch. An atmosphere of invasion hangs over the whole messed-up house: now, at the end of the afternoon, there are cigarette butts and scraps of food everywhere.

When the black car finally arrives, and Hank reports a woman coming around to the front door, Glenn threatens a terrified Eleanor with his gun, saying: "You don't have to do nothin' but keep your trap shut." Then he covers the front door, and Cindy, who enters, backs away, ready to go right out of the house again. Glenn simply turns the gun on Eleanor: "We still got your old lady, sis." Thus stopped, Cindy shuts the door, and Glenn remarks: "That's bein' real sensible." Cindy looks at Glenn and Robish, then asks her mother: "How long have these animals been here?" Eleanor attemps to warn Cindy, and the fading smile on Glenn's face is a warning in itself: "Spitfire, too . . ." he says smoothly. "You watch out, redhead." Hank's shouted notice that Dan has been looking into the garage and is coming round fast to the front door, makes Glenn shove Cindy into a chair with the further warning: ". . . no talking. Not a goddam word."

Dan bursts in, newspaper in his hand: "Ellie, whose car is that in . . ." and Glenn slams the door behind him. As Dan takes an impulsive step towards him, Glenn in a flat, cold tone says: "It's loaded. . . . (*Pointing to door.*) Now, lock it . . . *please.*" Eleanor quickly reassures Dan that she's all right and that Ralphie hasn't as yet come home. Cindy gets in her bit: "The house is crawling with them, Dad." Glenn, sizing her up, says: "Don't get me jumpy, redhead, this thing's liable to explode." Then Dan recognizes Glenn from the evening newspaper. Glenn's not displeased. He laughingly takes the newspaper: "Lotsa people heard-a-me, didn't they? Front page. They always gotta use the same goddam picture."

Dan says: "Griffin, you fire that thing . . . and you'll have the whole neighborhood in here in two minutes." Glenn agrees he doesn't want to take that chance any more than Dan does, and tells Robish Dan's . . . "a smart-eyed bastard . . ." But why, Dan asks, does he have to choose his house? "Your break, pop," Glenn tells him. "I like the location—those empty lots'n both sides. The bike parked on the nice lawn. I like suckers with kids. They don't take no chances."

DAN—Anyone who could think up a scheme like that is . . .

GLENN (*cutting in*)—. . . is smart, pop.

ELEANOR (*quickly*)—Dan! They've done nothing.

GLENN—Now I'm gonna explain the facts-a-life to you, Hilliard. You listen, too, redhead . . . listen good. You can get brave . . . any one of you . . . just about any time you feel up to it. Might even get away with it. *But* that ain't sayin' what'll happen to the others . . . the old lady here . . . the redhead . . . the little guy owns the bike. (*Slight pause.*) Okay . . . pop, you got it all the way now. (*Another pause. DAN moves to above right of sofa and drops his hat on the sofa. ELEANOR's hand and his meet. DAN turns to GLENN.*)

DAN—How long?

GLENN—Now, that's the kinda sensible talk a guy likes to hear. . . .

DAN (*firmly*)—How long?

GLENN—Matter of hours . . . before midnight . . . maybe sooner. Meantime, everything goes on just like normal.

DAN—Why midnight?

GLENN (*almost politely*)—None-a your goddam business.

ELEANOR—They have a friend coming . . . with money.

DAN—What if . . .

GLENN (*speaking at the same time, stops DAN*)—Lady, you speak when I tell you.

DAN—The police are looking everywhere for you. . . . What if . . .

GLENN—They ain't looking here, pop. They show here, it ain't gonna be pretty.

DAN—They could trail your friend . . .

GLENN—Let's get one thing straight, pop. (*He circles up center gesturing to the window, right.*) Any red lights show out there . . . you folks get it first. (*There is a slight pause.* DAN *crosses to the window and peeks out between the drawn drapes.* GLENN *laughs, backing toward the newel post with the gun casually covering* DAN.) Gives you a funny feelin', don't it? You don't know what's happenin' . . . or where . . . or what it adds up to . . . for you. Ever had that feelin' before, pop? Me, I get it all the time. Even kinda like it. But you and me . . . we ain't much alike, are we, pop?

"Thank God!" says Cindy.

Dan tries to get rid of them by offering the same amount of money they're expecting, and gets laughed at condescendingly by Glenn, who has had a look at Dan's checkbook. Robish, however, is attracted by a fast getaway, and infuriates Glenn by protesting: "This guy talks sense! Don't I have nothin' to say . . ." "No," snarls Glenn. "You ain't got a goddam stinkin' thing to say! You, Hilliard—I see what you been up to. Robish here, he ain't got a brain. *But* he ain't got a gun, either. Don't try to get in between, you smart-eyed sonofabitch. Clickety-clickety-click." He makes a gesture as though turning a crank at Dan's temple. . . . "I can see those wheels going around in there, pop. Don't ever try that again!" With which Glenn orders Eleanor to serve them up dinner. Dan countermands the order. Glenn comes to a fast boil: "Listen, Hilliard. . . . I had an old man like you. Always callin' the tune. Outside his house, nobody. Inside, Mister God! Little punk went to church every Sunday . . . took it from everybody . . . licked their shoes . . . tried to beat it into Hank'n me . . . be a punk, be a nobody . . . take it from you shiny-shoed, down-your-noses sonsabitches with white handkerchiefs in your pockets." Glenn grabs Dan's handkerchief, spits on it, hurls it to the floor, and tells Dan: ". . . you remember, pop. . . . I could kill you just for kicks. . . . Now," he tells Eleanor, "get out there'n cook it."

Ralphie, cheerfully late, comes through the door, tries to duck out again, and gets grabbed and viciously shaken by Robish. Once more Dan moves fast, frees Ralphie, who runs to his mother's arms, then himself goes after Robish. Glenn yowls: "It ain't gonna be

like this. . . . Not like this, see!" and crashes his gun hard on
Dan's shoulder, so that Robish is in a position to lunge at Dan.
But Glenn steps between them: *"You hear me, Robish? Nothin's
gonna screw this up!"* and orders him to get out.

His swagger regained, Glenn orders Cindy to the kitchen with her
mother. Seeing Hank block Cindy's path, Glenn gleefully encourages him. But Hank says: "I don't go for redheads," and lets her
by. By now Dan's watchful eye is trained on Hank. Noticing this,
Glenn says: "Kid's been in stir for three years, pop. Don't cost
nothin' to look." His eyes still on Hank, Dan warns: "Just don't
try changing your mind, young fellow."

With Ralphie watching from the sofa, Glenn tricks Dan into saying he doesn't have a gun in the house; then Glenn slyly adds:
"That's right. You don't. Show him, Hank." Hank pulls out
Dan's automatic—"There for a minute," says Glenn, "I thought
you was gonna lie to me, pop," and orders Dan to listen to him.
. . . "That dough's halfway here by now and nothin's gonna foul
this up, see? You pull any of that muscle-stuff again . . ." "That
won't happen again," Dan says. But when Glenn threatens to let
Robish work over him, so that afterwards Dan wouldn't know what
was happening to the rest of his family, Dan, quietly but with new
strength, tells him: "Griffin, hands off."

GLENN—I don't go for threats.

DAN—Hands off, that's all I know! If one of you touches one
of us again . . .

GLENN—Don't talk tough to me, Hilliard . . .

DAN— . . . I can't promise what'll happen. . . . I can't promise
anything . . . if one of you touches one of us again. I don't know
what I'll do. Can't you understand that, you half-baked squirt?
I'll make you use that gun, Griffin. So help me. We're done for
then, but so are you. (*Drops voice.*) It won't matter then whether
your friend gets here or not. . . . (GLENN *is impressed, struggling
to keep up the front, grinning emptily.* . . .)

BLACKOUT

SHERIFF'S OFFICE

While Winston tries to catch up on some sleep, Bard does his usual
smoking and pacing, till the intercom suddenly breaks the news that
Helen Laski has been spotted. She's approaching Columbus, Ohio,
driving slowly and carefully. She's heading west, and should be in

Indianapolis by eleven or twelve that night. Bard exults: "I told you they were homing pigeons, Tom. They do it every time . . . right back to the womb that spewed them." "Okay," says Winston, "they're pigeons. You're an owl. I'm sleepy."

BARD—They're layin' low here now . . . thinkin' how clever they been . . . gettin' Laski out of town so she could backtrack to 'em. Clever! *Not so damned!*

WINSTON—Jess, you're raving. How long since you ate solid food?

DUTCH'S VOICE (*on intercom*)—Jess . . .

BARD (*flips intercom button*)—Yeah, Dutch?

DUTCH'S VOICE—Your wife called again. She says she's still at your mother's but drowning in a sea of words . . . whatever that means.

BARD (*with a laugh*)—Tell her to stay there all night, Dutch. Tell her I said it's Be-Kind-to-Talkative-Mothers Week. (*He flips off the intercom and turns exultantly to* WINSTON.) About twenty miles out of town, we'll put a real tag on Miss Helen Laski and she'll breeze right in and lead us straight to the hole! How many hours till midnight, Tom?

WINSTON—By my watch (*The light begins to dim.*), too god-damned many.

At the Hilliard house, Glenn has cleverly stationed the family around the living room with the curtains wide open. Anyone passing would think the Hilliards were looking at television: whereas the only one with any mind to look at the silent set is Robish, seated (out of sight of the window) on the stairs.

Glenn sends Ralphie to bed, approving when Dan immediately follows him upstairs. Robish is critical, and Glenn sets him straight: "It's his house, Robish. Hilliard's on our side now. Pop don't want that kid hollerin' out a window up there any more'n we do."

In the privacy of Ralphie's room, Dan has an uphill job trying to convince his son to give up all ideas of derring-do. It's so hopeless that Dan can't control his anger: "Ralphie, didn't you hear? If you got out of here . . . even if you brought the police . . . do you know what would happen? Son, do you want them to kill your mother? your sister? Do you want to be the reason they did it?" Ralphie spots the fear in Dan's voice, even though at first Dan denies it. Dan decides to change tactics: "Yes, son . . . yes, I'm scared. But I'm not ashamed of being scared. . . . Sometimes it's better to be scared. You think about that now. You think hard about that, hear?" Ralphie's unimpressed; he refuses to be scared, and what's more, he's sure Cindy isn't, either.

A telephone rings and tension quickens throughout the house. At gun point, Cindy is made to answer, and tries to put off her date, but fails. Hank, who monitored the call over the upstairs hall extension, said it wasn't Cindy's fault that she couldn't stop Chuck from coming to take her dancing. Glenn makes a split-second decision: "Okay, you be ready, cutie. When boy friend stops out front, you duck out. . . ." He then changes the guard on Ralphie, substituting Eleanor for Dan, whom he wants downstairs immediately.

To the general amazement, Glenn is not only allowing Cindy to go out, but tells Dan to take his car out to get gas and have it checked. Robish protests: "You ain't lettin' 'em *both* out?" "The kid and missus stay," Glenn explains. "Him or the redhead pull something, they know what'll happen here. Pop here's a smart cookie. He don't want no coppers settin' up machine guns on his nice smooth lawn . . . throwin' tear gas through his windows . . ." (*He moves close to* DAN, *threateningly.*) ". . . 'cause that happens, you know who's gonna get it, don't you, Hilliard? Not you." He gestures upstairs. "Them. I'm gonna see to it personal. An' you're gonna stay alive to remember it the rest of your life." Dan asks Cindy if she hears that. "I'll do anything," says Cindy, "to get away from that voice."

Robish hopes to cash in on all this gadding about by getting some liquor. Dan flatly refuses to get him any, and Glenn backs him up. But Glenn falls for Robish's sly: "You lettin' this joker give the orders?" "Nobody gives me orders," says Glenn. "Not ever again!" He orders bourbon for Robish, and tells Cindy to bring home the late papers.

After Cindy goes off with Chuck in his Jaguar, Glenn starts to worry: "If that spitfire tries anything . . ."

DAN—Griffin . . . what if the police track you down? Sooner or later . . . through no fault of ours . . . what if . . .

GLENN—I'd never know who done it, pop. . . .

DAN—But you couldn't blame *us* if . . .

GLENN (*slowly*)—Hilliard, I got news for you. I—can—do—anything—I—want. Nice family you got here, pop. You love that woman of yours, you ain't gonna reach for no phone in that filling station. Them coppers're after me, y'know. They don't give a hoot in hell about you. *Or* your family. Clickety-clickety-click (*He gestures as before.*) . . . give you something to think about, pop.

After Glenn has ushered Dan out of the house, he joins Hank in the pantry. Hank doesn't respond to Glenn's "I told you I'd shack you up in style, didn't I?" Hank is depressed, sucks away at his coke, brooding that he never had a date in his life.

GLENN—Date? Hell, you laid enough babes to . . .

HANK—Naw, I mean a *date*. Y'know . . . ordinary things like that.

GLENN (*scornfully*)—Malted milks? Hot dogs at a drive-in?

HANK—Maybe . . .

GLENN—You got it comin', kid . . . all the babes you can handle and still walk straight up.

HANK—Babes like Helen?

GLENN (*astonished*)—Yeah. . . . What's the matter with Helen?

HANK—She's a tramp.

BLACKOUT

It's 8:56 on the Sheriff's clock, when Bard gets the bad news from Carson that "Helen Laski's not coming. She made one simple mistake. She ran a red light on the outskirts of Columbus. A patrol car gave chase." An outraged Bard cries: "Carson . . . are you telling me they arrested Helen Laski for a traffic violation? Good God, they had orders! It's been on every teletype for hours . . . *do not arrest!*" Helen wasn't arrested, Carson tells him. She gave the police the slip, abandoned her car, and disappeared. Carson is quite philosophical about such mistakes, but Bard isn't. Convinced you can't afford mistakes against a mind like Griffin's, he orders all calls, incoming and outgoing, to be checked from eight o'clock to now, and straight through the night. . . . "Any number to any number. Names, addresses, the works . . ." Meanwhile, all they can do is wait.

BLACKOUT

Robish has been waiting for a drink for eighteen years. When Dan arrives, and is expertly frisked by Glenn, all he comes up with is a pint of liquor. Robish rages: "Chrissake, a pint!" And then is further outraged: "Kee-rist . . . eighteen years an' then you can't get it open."

Dan, obviously, now has a new fear. He doesn't answer Glenn's question whether he got any ideas while out of the house. Dan calls upstairs to Eleanor, who answers: "We're all right, Dan. Cindy's not back yet." "Pop," demands Glenn, "when I ask you a question, you answer." "No," says Dan flatly, "no ideas." Then, briskly and unpleasantly, Glenn orders Dan to go upstairs to Eleanor and bed. The new horror that has Dan in its clutches now comes out: "Griffin, . . . when you do leave tonight, we're staying in this house. My family. All of us." "Yeh, yeh," absently answers Glenn, his thoughts on Hank. "You give me a fair shake. I give you a fair shake." With this, Dan heavily goes upstairs.

Hank's attitude has been increasingly puzzling to Glenn. "I did teach you everything, didn't I, Hank?" presses Glenn. "Yeah," says Hank. "Everything . . . except maybe how to live in a house like this," and he goes back to his station in the pantry. Glenn follows.

GLENN—Live here? We ain't gonna *live* here.

HANK—No. Or any place like it. Ever.

GLENN—Hank, what the hell's . . .

HANK—When Helen gets here, are we gonna give Hilliard a fair shake?

GLENN (*angrily*)—Anybody ever give *you* a fair shake?

HANK—Who the hell ever had a chance?

GLENN (*an idea*)—The redhead! She got you goin', kid? Tell you what, kid. . . . When we leave, we'll take her along. Just for you.

HANK (*after a pause*)—*Fair shake!*

GLENN (*anger again*)—What you think I'm gonna do? Nobody's gonna be suspicious if we got two women'n the car. We'll take 'em both. (*He gives* HANK *a playful punch.*) You give me the idea yourself.

Upstairs, Eleanor consoles Dan: "It won't be long now. . . ." But Dan, realizing that Griffin may go back on what he says, is beside himself with fear for his family—a fear that is communicated to Eleanor, as she asks Dan what he is thinking. "I'm thinking," says Dan, "a man could be haunted forever . . . afterwards by the thought that if he'd done just this at just the right time . . . or that at just the proper moment . . . he might have prevented it all." Eleanor's idea that when the intruders leave, Dan will be able to pick up the phone, suddenly sounds false even to her. "They won't let you do that, will they?" "Of course they will, darling," Dan tries to console her. But Eleanor is beginning to realize: "They'll have to take someone along." "No, Ellie, no." Dan tries to bluff: "The thought never occurred to me."

During this agonized conversation, Ralphie has come from his room to his parents' door; when Dan catches sight of him, he tries to cover up. But it's no use. Ralphie comes right to the point: "Are you going to let them . . . what you just said? . . ." Eleanor puts her arms around him. "Dear, your mother had a wild idea, that's all. Those men haven't even thought of that." Ralphie cries: "I don't want them to take me along with them." Dan, taking hold of Ralphie's shoulders, tells him: "I wouldn't let them do that, Ralphie. You ought to know I wouldn't let them do that." But Ralphie backs away, and as he leaves the room, says with hideous logic: "How are you going to stop them?"

Cindy's arrival home causes Eleanor to turn off their light, as they stand tensely by. At the side door Hank—his gun ready—draws back. And Cindy, coming up to the side door, has a difficult time with Chuck, who has chosen this of all nights to propose. He is confused at the way she has acted. Putting him off, Cindy says she'll tell him tomorrow at the office. "You'll tell me one thing right now," . . . Chuck persists. Cindy, turning away, tells him it doesn't concern him. Chuck turns her around toward him and takes her hands: "If it concerns you, it concerns me. There. That's all I've been trying to say all evening. You've done something to me, Cindy. I've known a lot of girls . . . but . . . but you've opened doors . . . in me . . . in the world. So I've got to know . . . now . . . have I been kidding myself? Are you closing the doors?" Suddenly, Cindy, touched and desperate, flings her arms around him, kissing him. Watching from inside, Hank turns away. Chuck decides now to come in and find out what's on Cindy's mind—even to face her family if that's what's bothering her. He takes her keys from her and opens her door; Cindy pushes past him, blocking the doorway. "All right, Cindy. I'm not coming in . . ." says Chuck, and Cindy closes the door in his face. Inside, she leans limply against it, while Chuck stares at the door for a moment, then takes the keys that are still in it, and walks away pocketing them. His car door slams, the motor starts, and the car drives away.

Because Hank orders Cindy to show herself to Glenn, she has to come up against a drunken Robish, who won't let her pass him to get up the stairs. Hank, his gun hidden from view, tells her to go up to the second floor. Robish thinks drunkenly that it would be a fine idea to search Cindy. Dan, hearing the commotion, calls down to Glenn: "Griffin, if you intend to let him get away with this . . ." Glenn barks to Dan to stay where he is, but Dan, slowly coming closer, threatens him: "Griffin, you don't want to have to use that gun of yours, do you? . . ." and he inches between Robish and Cindy, Robish having swung Glenn out of the way. At this point, Hank steps in, his automatic trained on Robish. Bewildered, Robish bawls: *"Where'd yuh get that gun?"* Told by Glenn to sleep it off, he staggers towards the back of the house muttering: ". . . Okay. Ya wait. Ya-*all* wait. . . ."

As a really grateful Cindy thanks Hank, who tries to pay no attention, Glenn is alerted by a slam of the side door. At the same time, Ralphie takes it in his head to sneak down the back steps. Glenn shouts to Hank to cover Cindy and Dan, and heads quickly for the pantry and the side door.

Hank waves his gun at Dan and Cindy, who, suddenly on cue from Dan, puts on a fainting act. Dan steps towards her to help, but Hank yells: "Don't move, mister!" "Dammit," says Dan, "this child is sick. If there's any decency in you at all . . ." At which point Ralphie goes banging out the side door. Hank calls out: "Glenn?" but there's no answer. Somewhat rattled, Hank, his eyes on Dan but his automatic in front of Cindy, bends over her. With animal swiftness, Cindy sinks her teeth into Hank's wrist; and Hank, with a cry of pain, drops the gun. Dan crashes into Hank, while Cindy picks up the gun. Then Dan shoves Hank out the front door, locks it behind him, yells to Eleanor to get on the phone, orders Cindy to go upstairs, and, too impatient to wait for Eleanor to make the call, dials the operator himself. Suddenly Eleanor screams: "Don't, Dan . . . for God's sake!" She screams again: "Dan, don't! Ralphie's not in the house!" The operator can be heard asking for Dan's call, as, almost inaudibly, he breathes: "God Almighty," and hangs up.

Ralphie didn't get away. Glenn has him at the back door, and Ralphie cries: "Dad! Dad, he's hurting my arm." Eleanor cries down: "Dan, was that Ralphie? *Was that Ralphie?*" Dan calls to Eleanor to stay where she is, to Griffin not to shout, and to Cindy: . . . "take your mother to her room. If you hear a shot . . . make the call!"

Eleanor goes to the door of her room, while Cindy stands by at the upstairs phone. Dan goes to the pantry. "We go now, Hilliard," calls Glenn, . . . "they find the brat in a ditch." Dan follows instructions to turn on the pantry light and throw out his gun. Glenn comes in pushing Ralphie before him, saying: "You're both covered, pop." Ralphie, still defiant, tells his father: "I . . . I tried." "So did I," gently says Dan, adding, "Go up to your mother now."

Hank picks up the gun that Dan threw out the door, then on orders from Glenn goes for Robish, whom Glenn has beaten up. Glenn now turns his full attention to Dan: "Couldn't wait, could you, pop? Less'n a hour an' you couldn't wait." Hank pushes a

Karl Malden, Malcolm Brodrick and Paul Newman in "The Desperate Hours"

staggering Robish into the living room to collapse on the sofa, while Glenn underlines what's ahead for Dan: "I hadda put Robish on ice for a while, pop . . . 'cause he couldn't learn who was runnin' things aroun' here. I guess I gotta learn you, too." And Glenn systematically and quietly beats Dan up with his pistol butt. When Dan crumples to the floor, Glenn strikes three more vicious blows, then rises, steps over the body, and joins Hank in the living room.

BLACKOUT

CURTAIN

ACT II

In the Sheriff's office, Carson, glancing at his watch, says calmly: "It's another day . . . in case anyone's interested." Bard continues to fret, and waits as if he were a caged animal. Carson theorizes: "It'll break, Bard. You can stretch a wire just so tight." But there is still no trace of a phone call from Helen Laski. Bard is particularly irritated to have to watch Carson play solitaire, and says: "Carson, you deal me just one of those cards and I'm gonna report you to J. Edgar Hoover. . . ."

All evidence to the contrary, Bard is sure (because he knows Griffin's twisted, snarled-up brain so well) that those brothers are right here in town. Carson wants another good reason why he's in town. "Carson," says Bard, "did you ever look into the eyes of one of those crazy kids . . . and hear him say, 'You got yours coming, copper'? Between his teeth . . . with his broken jaw wired up tight. . . . 'I'll get you.' That's why I know he's here and that's why I'm going to get to him before he gets to me." And Bard doesn't promise merely to arrest him.

BLACKOUT

At the Hilliard house, Cindy is watching over a sleeping Ralphie, while in the master bedroom Eleanor nurses and watches over Dan. In the dim light of the room, Eleanor pleads, very tenderly, with Dan to take no more risks. But, dazed as he is, he can only think of his love for Eleanor and for his family, and refuses to pass up any chance to save them: "Ellie, I can't. . . . I'm feeling along a blank wall. In the dark. If I find a hole . . . or even a crack . . . I've got to explore it." Again Eleanor pleads with him: "Dan, look at yourself. Your head. Next time . . . you don't know. You don't know. He'll kill you." But Dan grimly knows: "He won't kill me as long as he needs me." And looking at his wife's tired face, he curses Griffin. . . . "When this is over," he gently tells her, "we're going to have a maid in here. Full time." But tonight, they're still in the jungle where every noise makes Eleanor start.

Glenn's call comes through, and throughout the house everyone snaps to attention. Hank covers the upstairs phone, as Glenn instructs Helen Laski to mail the stuff she's carrying to a name and address he gives her, promising: ". . . Soon's I get it, we'll make tracks, doll. . . . See you Louisville. You know where." Dan follows Hank down the stairs, anxious to know what's happening. All Glenn tells him is . . . "Tell you in the morning, pop . . . after breakfast." Dan is so shocked by this that he starts for Glenn, and only backs upstairs when Glenn levels a gun at him.

Back in his room with Eleanor, Dan is ready to blow up . . . frustration and rage make him want to have it out with the Griffins . . . he's going to get them out of his house. Eleanor has all she can do to prevent his leaving the room. "How long," he asks, "can we go on sitting on top of a volcano?" Eleanor takes his hand and says: "Dan, you're going to lie down now! I'm telling you!" Thrusting away from her, Dan shouts: *"You're not telling me what to do!"* Appalled, both suddenly realize what Griffin is doing to them: "How can he know," Dan says, his arms around Eleanor, "that scum down there . . . how can he know how to do this? A boy who never loved anyone in his life." They turn the light out and sit together on the bed, Eleanor encircled in Dan's arms.

Downstairs, Hank, worried that the police may have traced Helen Laski's call, wants to clear out. Glenn won't budge till the money comes and isn't bothered about the call being traced, because it didn't come from Columbus, but from Circleville. . . . "Them dumb coppers might be tracin' calls outta Columbus, Hank, but not outta no jerktown like Circleville. . . ." And right here is where he has to be to have that "copper put on ice for good." Full of conflicting emotions, Hank listens to Glenn's pleas to stick with him on this. . . . "You're . . . Hank, you're all I got. You know that. It's you'n me against 'em all. . . ." Trapped, Hank says: "I know, I know . . ." "You don't know nothin'," cries Glenn. "I gotta get this outta my brain. I gotta sleep again. You didn't lay in that bed . . . pain twistin' down in your gut . . . months . . . jaw clamped in a vise . . . eatin' that slop through a tube . . . months . . . till pretty soon there ain't nothin' in your mind but the face-a the guy that done it. Me with my hands up . . . tossin' out my gun . . . and that bastard walkin' up'n cloutin' me. I can still hear the way the bone cracked . . . an' me with my hands up!"

BLACKOUT

"Yeah, he had his hands up," Bard is telling Carson. "Trying to surrender. After he'd plugged one of the best damn cops ever walked. . . ." Only after the policeman was screaming in the gutter did Griffin throw out his empty gun. Bard couldn't bear to let this grinning face get away with it, and cracked him right in the face, which "according to Glenn's warped code was double-crossing him." Carson reminds Bard quietly that it's according to the police code, too. Bard points out the weakness of their criminal system; Carson agrees but adds that's all they've got . . . and Bard had no right to break Glenn's jaw nor will he have the right to kill him, "unless it's the only way to stop him . . ."; otherwise Bard will be no better than Glenn. Carson has made his point. Bard is thoughtful as Carson next suggests breakfast.

After breakfast, Glenn is ready with orders for the seething family: Cindy and Dan are to go to their offices as usual, while Ralphie is to stay home from school.

The strain is beginning to tell: Ralphie snickers at Glenn for being scared of the thud of the morning newspaper, and Eleanor is ready to boil at the cruel, inhuman game he is playing with her family. Suddenly, she explodes and slaps Glenn full across the face. Dan grabs her protectively, waiting for Glenn's reaction. "Whole family gettin' tough this morning," Glenn says. "Nothin' personal, ma'am." "It's personal, all right," snaps Dan, and deciding not to leave his family, refuses to go to the office. Glenn doesn't like this, and as a result gets short-tempered with Hank, then changes his tone and says mildly that he and Hank won't be leaving until they have their money—and the money was sent to Dan's office.

A loving family tries to reassure Dan, Cindy even holds his coat for him. Glenn coldly warns Dan to have a story ready for his head wounds, ". . . 'cause it wouldn't take much of a slip today, pop. Just a little one and you're gonna wish you never come back through that door." Dan, with real dignity, sounds a warning of his own. If anything goes wrong at his house, Dan threatens to go after Glenn as Glenn is after the policeman. . . . "You've turned me into your kind of animal now, Griffin," says Dan. "Do you understand that?" When Glenn tries to brush it off, Dan grabs him: *"Do you understand that?"* "Sure, pop . . ." smirks Glenn, "I got you. All the way." "And if not you," Dan adds . . . "your brother." Glenn is at once aroused: "You come near Hank and . . ." "That's the deal, Griffin," announces Dan, and leaves with Cindy.

Eleanor and Ralphie, under Robish's eye, sit together on the living-room sofa. Glenn goes to Hank, who's worrying how they're crowding their chances.

And another source of danger looms in the person of old Mr. Patterson, the trashman, arriving for his monthly check. While Hank takes Ralphie upstairs, Eleanor has to face the old man, and write out a check for him, trying—while aware of Glenn and his gun—to seem completely natural. While Eleanor is off in the living room, Mr. Patterson notices cigarette butts, a newspaper and a radio in the pantry, and hears Eleanor talking to Glenn: "You . . . uh . . . got company?" he asks Eleanor, as she gives him the check. "You feelin' yourself?" he asks next, observing her strangeness. Eleanor, desperate to be rid of him, mentions a slight cold. But Mr. Patterson, fatally curious, now comments on the gray car in the garage: "Your daughter buy herself another one of them second-hand cars?" "No," says Eleanor, with Patterson looking hard at her, "No."

Patterson stops near the garage, writes down the license plate numerals, and goes, a doomed man, to his truck. Though Glenn is undecided what to do, Robish isn't. He insists that Glenn give him his gun. . . . *"Gimme the gun. . . ."* and in spite of Hank's calling down: "Glenn . . . we don't want a murder rap ridin' us!" Glenn turns over his gun to Robish, who is all set to hop on the back of the old man's truck.

Eleanor, on the sofa, is beside herself. Hank thinks Glenn crazy to plan having Hilliard bring Robish back with him that evening. Glenn says nastily: "He will when I'm done with him on the phone. Pop don't want Robish picked up any more'n we do . . . an' tippin' the cops this address . . ." Hank draws Glenn's anger: "What're you stewin' about? You're free, ain't you?" Hank pulls away and starts for the den: "I was freer in that cell!" Glenn vents his jagged emotions on the weeping woman, telling her to shut up, to go some place else to cry. Eleanor, with difficulty, gets up and starts for the stairs: "Poor man . . . that poor old man . . . he wouldn't hurt a fly."

BLACKOUT

At 7:49, Bard, at the Sheriff's office, is wondering: "Who'd want to pump three slugs into the back of an innocent old guy like that?" Bard is nagged by the fact that Patterson was killed with a .38, just like the Terre Haute prison guard. But coincidences don't bother Fredericks of the state police—he thinks Bard's obsessed.

Carson empties a manila envelope of all the stuff found on Patterson's body, all the personal things—photographs, cash, checks, plus some scraps of paper. Bard smooths these last out while Carson tells how the body was found in a wood, where Patterson must have run from his truck. "Hold it," says Bard very, very quietly. "God. Lookit this. . . . State Attorney's office examined this stuff?" Carson imagines they have—then takes a look and he too says: "Good Lord!"

WINSTON—Patterson might've got just a quick glance. In a hurry, y'know. . . .

FREDERICKS (*cynically*)—He heard it on the radio . . . jotted it down just in case . . .

WINSTON—But if you change that 3 to 8, you got it. Maybe his eyes . . . a old man like that . . .

BARD (*thoughtfully*)—Or there was mud on the plate . . .

WINSTON—Jess, if you change that 3 to 8, you got it!

BARD (*with a throb in voice*)—Just for a while . . . just for a little while now . . . we're going to change that 3 to 8. We'll just kinda pretend Mr. Patterson didn't own a radio. We're gonna pretend he saw that license. Tom . . . these checks. Start working backwards. (*As* WINSTON *rises and* CARSON *goes by a file cabinet.*) Names, addresses, telephone numbers, where they work. Everything.

FREDERICKS (*between* BARD *and* WINSTON)—Sure, let's go on a wild goose chase . . . to break the monotony.

BARD—These were the last people saw him alive. These and whatever other customers live in that neighborhood. Let's find that neighborhood and let's scour it down with a wire brush.

Winston says what's on his and Carson's mind: "He was right. . . . This is it." Bard asks if there are any bets that that beat-up gray car isn't near where Patterson worked. He has no takers, as he asks via the intercom for a city map and city directory. To Carson he voices his hope: "Now. If only we can get to 'em before some other innocent citizen stumbles across their path . . ."

BLACKOUT

Eleanor, at gun point later that evening, has to open the door for Ralphie's school teacher. Steeling herself to face Miss Swift at the door, Eleanor helplessly has to watch the aggressive lady barge into the living room. She has come on account of Ralphie's absence from school; noticing the complete disorder of the living room, she says: "I—I dare say I should have telephoned first." Out of nervousness as well as good manners, Eleanor asks Miss Swift to sit down, and she sits down—on the whiskey bottle. Eleanor's explanation of Ralphie's absence doesn't impress the lady—she has no use for colds. Moreover, she's not sure that Eleanor is a good judge of them, and gets up intending to go and examine Ralphie to her own satisfaction. Eleanor hastily forbids her, while Ralphie calls down: "I'll be down in a minute, Miss Swift."

Miss Swift's distress increases mightily when Dan, accompanied by Robish and Cindy, enters the house. One look at Miss Swift, and Dan stages an impromptu drunk scene to get Robish out of the sight and mind of the startled teacher. He hospitably propels Robish to the dining room, telling him: "You know where I keep it, Johnny. Help yourself." Out of Miss Swift's line of vision, Robish draws his .38. Dan continues a pleasant drunk, until Ralphie dashes down the stairs and shoves his composition book in the hands of his nonplused teacher. Dan immediately commands Miss Swift to give it to him before she can even glance at it. Opening the book, Dan needs only one glance to see what Ralphie's been up to. Ralphie scoots upstairs to his room, while Dan says: "So this is what they call a composition nowadays. You encourage such drivel, Miss Swift?" "Mr. Hilliard," answers Miss Swift, "in all fairness . . . I don't think you're in any condition to discuss anything tonight." "In that case," Dan answers, "I'll read it in the morning."

Miss Swift, with a sympathetic hand on Eleanor's arm, assures her that what she has seen tonight will in no way affect her belief in Ralph, and, with a last glance at Dan, she marches out the door.

Hank quickly sees to it that the door is once more locked, then listens to Robish wanting to stop Miss Swift. "Sure, Robish," says Hank, ". . . shoot up the whole town!" Glenn's approval of Dan's performance stops Robish: "Gotta hand it to you, Hilliard. You had that dame in a real stew. You'd of made a good con man." Robish thinks no more of going after Miss Swift, but the tensions around the house don't lessen.

First, Glenn discovers that Robish didn't get the piece of paper out of Patterson's pocket; next he learns that Robish won't return the gun to him. Says Robish: "I kinda like th' feel of it." He also refuses to obey Glenn's orders: "Get on the back door yourself, Griffin. Stuff it!"

Hank and Dan are the next to cause trouble. When they realize that Glenn all along hadn't expected the money until tomorrow, Dan is enraged. Glenn tells him: "Take it easy, pop . . . 'n stay healthy. . . ." and says to a shocked Hank: "Yeah . . . tomorrow. What's one more night?" "Christ!" exclaims Hank. "Griffin," says Dan, "I've played your filthy game up to now . . . but by bringing that ape back here after he killed a man . . . we're accessories now." At this point, Hank decides to hang on to his automatic, too, and takes it with him to the pantry. "How do you like that, pop?" says Glenn. "They both got the guns . . ." he loudly adds for Hank's benefit, "Only they ain't got half a brain between 'em. Without me, they're cooked . . . an' they know it."

As Cindy gives Glenn another of her flip answers, his jangling nerves make him shout threateningly: *"There're ways of shuttin' that pretty face of yours, redhead!"* At which moment Hank, almost hysterical, reports Chuck's Jaguar driving past the house. Grabbing Cindy, Glenn forces her to the window: "If you pulled a fast one, spitfire . . ."

HANK (*in panic*)—Glenn . . . listen . . .

GLENN (*turning back into the room*)—Lemme think, willya?

HANK—Glenn! They're not gonna stop comin' to the door!

GLENN (*crossing to him*)—Yellow, Hank?

HANK—*Yeah . . . okay . . . yellow! They're not gonna stop comin' to the door!*

BLACKOUT

At 8:25, Bard, while checking a map of Indianapolis, issues orders over the radio to start knocking on those "high-toned doors." They must check every one of the trashman's customers, as well as the garages. Bard switches off the current light. Carson a minute later brings in an anonymous letter that casts a different light on that suburban picture. Bard starts reading the letter—which had been delivered to the city police at noon. His tone, brisk at first, quickly changes to a hushed whisper: "To the Police. . . . Innocent people will be in the house or automobile with the three fugitives you want. If you shoot, you will be responsible for taking the lives of people who have done no harm. Any attempt to trace this letter will only endanger my family. . . ." Bard, holding the letter to the light, remarks that the handwriting is disguised and there are no watermarks.

FREDERICKS—It's a blind.

BARD (*whisper . . . touched*)—The idiot.

CARSON—That letter's no blind.

BARD—But he ought to *know!* God, doesn't he know? Carson, isn't there some way to get word to this guy, whoever he is, that you can't play ball with savages like that?

CARSON—How? Without tipping them he wrote that?

BARD—*You* take a shot in the dark, federal-man. They'll tear that poor guy to ribbons, inside and out, before they're done. You can't co-operate with scum like that!

CARSON—No? . . . What would you do, Jess? I'd say he was smart to write that. Might keep some itchy-fingered officer from shooting his wife or child.

BARD—Itchy-fingered like me, Carson?

CARSON—You got more sense. That's what's eating you, friend.

You know what a spot the man's on. . . . What would you do, Jess . . . under the circumstances?

BARD—I'd play ball.

And he plays ball now, canceling the orders, telling the police to: "Bury those prowl cars, *bury* 'em." Fredericks comments: "You can't put off a showdown, lad." "Nobody wants a showdown any more'n I do . . ." Bard says, adding: "but not if it means getting some poor slob's family massacred!" He calls over the mike: "You hear me, Tom? Keep those patrols off the streets! Stash 'em!" Winston's voice reports back that Chuck's Jaguar is cruising up and down; Bard's answer is to haul Chuck in. That's fine for Winston; he's positively elated: "It'll be a pleasure to arrest anybody!"

Fredericks can't wait to move tear gas and riot guns into that neighborhood; after that, Bard's not surprised that Hilliard wouldn't trust the police to help him. . . . But Fredericks is going ahead, just in case, . . . as Bard is left to puzzle over his new feelings.

BLACKOUT

For Hank, Chuck's cruising by the Hilliard house is the last straw. "Glenn," he confesses, "I've had it." "What're you talkin' about?" Glenn snaps. "The old man with the trash," says Hank, ". . . the teacher . . . now this guy goin' by out there . . . over'n over. I've had it." Glenn, after telling Robish to cover Dan and Cindy, follows Hank to the pantry. "I ain't going to the chair," says Hank, " 'cause that ape in there got trigger-happy." Glenn promises that after they get the dough the next day, they'll pull up stakes. *"What good's the dough gonna do you in the death house?"* cries Hank. "I gotta pay Flick to take care of Bard, don't I?" yells back Glenn.

Hank won't wait; he is determined to go right now. Even Dan advises against his leaving alone. Hank's mind is made up: "They won't catch me, Mr. Hilliard. Don't worry about that." This is too much for Glenn: "Look who's tellin' who not to worry! You're talkin' like Hilliard was our old man. . . . If Hilliard was our old man, he'd have something coming to him from way back!" As Hank unlocks the door, Glenn pleads: "Listen, Hank . . . you can't duck out on me. Christ, kid . . . it's always been *us*. You'n me. Listen. . . . Without you . . . without you . . ." Hank, automatic in hand, refuses to be stopped by anything or anyone. Momentarily Cindy crosses his mind, and Glenn, aware of what Hank is thinking, urges him to take her. Dan says very carefully: "Your brother knows it's not that simple, Griffin." Glenn answers fiercely:

"I'll make it that simple. *Hank gets what he wants!*" With a look of longing in Cindy's direction Hank chokes: "I doubt it, Glenn. I doubt if I ever will," and goes out, slamming the door.

Glenn is wild, broken up, as he stomps about throwing blame in all directions, particularly at Dan, who tells him to take hold of himself. Hearing the noise, Eleanor leaves Ralphie, while Glenn rages: "You satisfied now, you smart-eyed bastard? Clickety-clickety-click, you got at him, didn't you?" In spite of Dan's warning about letting himself go on this way, Glenn rails against the house, and against the Hilliards: "That goddam spitfire'n her fancy skirts swishin' . . . that brat an' his 'composition'!" He orders "Pop" to go upstairs and give Ralphie a good old-fashioned lacing. If Dan won't, Glenn says, he'll have Robish show him how it should be done. Eleanor cries: "I hope they get your brother. I hope they kill him."

Dan goes slowly to Ralphie's room, and very gently tries to make the boy understand he has to do anything his father tells him. Then Dan asks him to cry. Ralphie simply can't. It's only when Robish, hearing no cries, starts upstairs, that Dan slaps Ralphie. He then gathers the boy into his arms, while Ralphie cries louder and louder.

BLACKOUT

No matter how tough he is, Bard is unable to get anything out of Chuck, until he shows him the newspaper headlines, and says: "We know they're up there somewhere . . . holed up in one of those nice houses . . . so . . ." Chuck says nothing, but looks as if someone has kicked him. Eventually, he says his girl lives up there, but still refuses to tell her name, and shown Dan's letter, won't give him away, either, though he cries admiringly: "He's . . . he's quite a guy!" In fact Chuck is willing to face prison rather than endanger the family. This is not necessary, for at this point the case breaks wide open, with a call from Carson about Hank. Hank was caught trying to steal a car, and decided to shoot it out. The gun was registered in Daniel C. Hilliard's name.

Bard identifies Eleanor Hilliard's check among those given to Patterson, while Winston reads from a list: "Hilliard, Daniel. Wife Eleanor. One son age ten, Ralph. One daughter age twenty, Cynthia . . . called Cindy." "Okay," says Bard after a slight pause: "Carson, throw a cordon around the Hilliard house. Let no one in or out of that block. Only keep everything out of sight of the window. I'll be up there in ten minutes. And Carson . . . have the newsboys got this?" "Not yet. Not even the death," he answers. "Well, for God's sake, keep 'em off it." "We'll try, Jess," Carson promises.

But Chuck stubbornly insists they can't move in—remember Mr. Hilliard's letter! He has an idea that someone should be sneaked in, to act as buffer between Griffin and the family. Bard, full of orders for the coming action, brushes him off, tells him to get out. Chuck, yelling back: "What are you going to do?", leaves with an idea of his own. Winston, rifle in hand, comments: "The boy's got a good question, Jess." "A damn good question," admits Bard. "I wish I had the answer. Well, let's get on it now. Let's get up there."

BLACKOUT

ACT III

In the middle of the night, while Glenn's mood fluctuates between fear and apathy, Robish baits him about Hank's being captured or shot. The decisive telephone call announcing the arrival of the money at the store leaves Glenn sagging with despair that the night watchman at Dan's store wasn't Hank.

Upstairs, Dan is ready to go for the money immediately, feeling this is the moment to make a break: it is dangerously late to wait for one to occur. In the privacy of their bedroom, Dan tells Eleanor he is determined to get Glenn out of the way, and then if necessary, have Robish use the remaining bullets to kill Dan. There is no other way. With Griffin's cracking up, there is safety for no one. Eleanor, ready to scream or collapse, controls herself as best as she can and tries to dissuade Dan: "We're not saved if you die . . . do you imagine a man like that (Robish) has to have bullets to . . . against Ralphie? . . . or Cindy? . . . or me? Do you?" "All right," says Dan, realizing that he was succumbing to panic. "We're not saved if you die," Eleanor drums into him. "All *right*, Ellie," Dan answers. "Oh, God, darling," she says as she sinks on the bed, "Dan, you're the hub . . . it all revolves around you. If anything . . ." It's more than she can bear to think of. She places her hand in his. "Dan, we can't let them panic us now." Their moment of understanding is abruptly ended by Robish's calling Dan to hurry.

Robish and a Glenn who is now a grotesque caricature of his former self run headlong into each other on what Dan's to do with the money. Robish orders Dan to bring it straight home for the getaway—with Cindy remaining at home. Glenn jerkily gives his orders: Cindy is to go with her father to get the payoff money and deliver it to a man named Flick in the Lombardi Grill; and there will be no getaway with the rest of the money until Flick signals he's got his.

Robish is disgusted and impatient with Glenn; he wants Cindy around so there can be two dames in the car. . . . Glenn, hesitant and vague, calls Flick at his hotel, while Robish decides: "I lay my hands'n that dough, yuh can rot'n here, Griffin. . . ."

BLACKOUT

In a neighboring attic, the police have set up emergency head-quarters, equipped with radio apparatus and rifles with telescopic lenses. Looking with binoculars through the attic window, Carson sees Hilliard and Cindy leave their house. Winston calls in over the radio to ask if he's to pick them up. Bard, knowing from a phone tap that Dan is heading for the store, orders Winston to pick him up after he gets his mail, to bring him here. . . . "Come in here from the north, though . . . and careful nobody in the Hilliard windows can see you."

Fredericks, by now, finds it not only ridiculous but risky not to start moving in.

FREDERICKS—Let's get one thing straight. There's going to be blood. There's only two people in that house now.

BARD—Two human beings . . .

FREDERICKS—Okay. . . . Measure them against the just-as-inno-cent people those two can knock off if they bluff their way out of this trap.

BARD—The guy's wife and kid!

FREDERICKS—Lad, you're putting a weapon in the hands of every felon in the country, you let . . .

BARD (overriding)—I didn't invent the scheme, dammit! I'm doing all I can. We've got sixty officers in those woods now . . . the streets are blocked off . . .

FREDERICKS—Bastards like them're wily. . . .

BARD (turning to CARSON)—Those're escapees from a federal prison in there. You call it!

CARSON (turns from window slightly)—I'll string along with you, Deputy. . . . At least until we speak to Hilliard.

FREDERICKS—O-kay, lads. It's your baby. I'm just a sour old man hates to see frisky young slobs make fools of theirselves. (Harshly.) But pity's a luxury your badge don't afford.

News of Griffin's call to Flick now comes through. Bard instructs a city detective to pick up Cindy and Flick in the Lombardi Grill, aware of the signal Flick was to give Glenn. Bard wonders what all this means, as Carson—at the window—observes that something is going on behind the Hilliard house. To Bard it looks like someone stretched out on the ground.

BLACKOUT

Upstairs, at the Hilliard house, Eleanor and Ralphie are looking out the bedroom window, as Robish—more and more uncertain what to do—is sure he saw someone out back. He gets no help from Glenn, who by now is in a mental daze. Mad and bewildered, Robish snarls: "Who yuh tryin' to con? I tell yuh, I seen somethin' move out by the garage." "Goblins, Robish. . . ." Glenn laughs, feeling sure they're now snug as can be, and in another hour will be on their way to Hank and Helen in Louisville. During this conversation, Chuck, using Cindy's key, slips into the Hilliard house, and by now is in Ralphie's room.

BLACKOUT

Over in the attic, they're worried about Chuck's bringing another gun into the Hilliard house. They're worried that a reckless amateur could botch up everything. Bard hopes, however, that Chuck is lying low . . .: "waiting for someone to make a move . . . us or them . . ." Fredericks' considered opinion is: "Lads, you're up a creek." Carson is sure ". . . the boy's smart enough to know he's done for if he doesn't get them both at the same time, and fast."

Winston's voice over the radio warns them: "Jess, . . . Hilliard's on his way upstairs. Tread easy now, you guys. This gentleman's had it." Dan, on his arrival, immediately arouses sympathy. At first he denies having written the letter, then, in flat, washed-out tones, asks: "Where'd I slip up?" "You didn't," Bard tells him, "Young Griffin's dead. He had your gun."

Dan, hearing Bard's name, slowly registers. He reveals Griffin's plot to kill Bard, but turns wild and threatening when he hears that Bard had Cindy and Flick picked up: "You fool—you damned clumsy fool . . ." "Okay, Hilliard. Let off steam," Bard answers. "Take a swing. How'd I know what they'd send your girl into? I swear . . ." "Swear?" Dan cries. "What can you swear to? That when I'm not back in there in time . . . When Flick doesn't call . . . they won't jump to the conclusion that . . ." Bard can reassure him about Flick's call; they can handle the signal. But Bard doesn't want Dan to go back in his house. Showing him the envelope with the money, Dan says: "Until they get that . . . they're not coming out." "Then," says Fredericks, "we move in."

*George Mathews, Paul Newman, Karl Malden, Nancy C
and Malcolm Brodrick in "The Desperate Hours"*

Grizzard, Patricia Peardon

With this, Dan erupts: "What am *I* supposed to do . . . *sit up here and watch it happen?*"

FREDERICKS—It's plain suicide for you to go back in there now!

DAN (*a look at the window*)—That may be. There comes a time when that fact doesn't enter in. . . . You don't give a hang about a life or two . . . what's one more?

BARD (*drops envelope with money on box. He is having an inner struggle trying to decide*)—Mr. Hilliard . . . we're trying to help you.

DAN—Then clear out! Get away. Take your men . . . your rifles . . . your floodlights . . . and *get away*.

CARSON (*picks up the envelope with money and holds it out to Dan*)—We can't do that, Mr. Hilliard. I'll give you ten minutes . . . from the time you walk through that door over there. Shortly after you're inside, we'll give them the telephone signal they're waiting for. If you need us, flicker a light. You've got ten minutes. It's on your shoulders.

Bard, to give him the whole picture, tells Dan that Chuck is in the house . . . with a gun. Does Dan want a gun? Putting the envelope in his inside topcoat pocket, Dan refuses one, knowing he'll be searched. But as he leaves, to go down the attic stairs, he changes his mind, and accepts the offer. Bard, asking him if he knows how to use it, hands Dan his own revolver.

There is general surprise as Dan breaks open the revolver and empties it of all bullets.

FREDERICKS—Are you crazy?

DAN—Maybe. Only a crazy man'd go in there with an empty gun. Griffin doesn't think I'm crazy.

BARD—That's a pretty long shot, isn't it?

DAN—I don't have any short ones in sight. Do you?

As Dan leaves, Bard instructs Winston over the radio to take him back to his car, then asks: "How'd you like to be riding up to *your* door like that, Fredericks?" Fredericks admits: "Just luck I'm not . . . or you." Bard says: "Yeah. They didn't happen to pick on us. That's all."

BLACKOUT

Glenn, not giving a damn whether Cindy's with Dan or not, is primed for the trip to Louisville, needing only the money Dan's bringing. To make Glenn search him, Dan—warning his family to stay upstairs—pretends not to have it. Robish roars, while Glenn, starting to frisk Dan, says: "Who you kiddin'? Take your hands outta your pockets . . . please . . ." and finds the gun, just as Robish says *he'll* take the cash. Glenn gleefully covers Robish, who would tear Dan limb from limb for this outrage. "You bastard!" he yells at Dan. "Not pop. Not my old pal, pop?" says Glenn, pocketing the money, and, gun pointed, adds: "Any objections, Robish?"

The telephone rings three times, as Glenn stands listening to it. When he's sure there won't be a fourth ring, he laughs: "Well, that takes care of Bard. Time to break up housekeeping." As Robish says, "Let's get outta here," Eleanor, crossing to the bedroom door, switches on the lights, and sees Chuck in the hall. He signals her to silence; she closes and locks her door, and stands there with Ralphie, waiting.

Glenn, in high spirits and in a hurry to be with Hank, goes upstairs for his hostages and shields. Dan, playing for time, can't stop him. But as Glenn starts kicking in Eleanor's locked door, Chuck surprises him with a head blow from behind. Glenn collapses, and falls back into Ralphie's room.

Gun in hand, Chuck starts quietly down the stairs, but Robish spots and shoots him first. Chuck, falling, fires into the floor. Robish lunges to the floodlit front door, opens it and steps out bawling: "I got one of yuh . . . who wants it next? Yuh hear me?" Dan rushes from his spot by the dining room, gives Robish a terrific shove, and shuts and locks the door on him. At which point, Eleanor dashes recklessly down the stairs calling: "Dan . . . Dan . . . Dan . . ." Left alone, Ralphie sees Glenn rousing himself, and backs into the bedroom. Glenn, the floodlights full on him, comes at the child with his gun.

In the attic, Bard pleads with Carson to hold fire and give Dan five more minutes: . . . *"Somebody shoved that big guy out the door."* Carson is willing, and calls into the mike: "Fredericks, . . . Robish is in the Hilliard car. He's armed. Stop him." Bard then picks up the P.A. mike, and his voice booms out in the distance: "Hilliard! Do you need us? Hilliard!"

(BLACKOUT, *during which* BARD's *voice, in full volume, repeats its message over the P.A.*)

Eleanor, instructed by Dan to get Chuck out of the house, is helping him, when Ralphie starts yelling for his father. With Eleanor and a limping Chuck on their way to safety, and Chuck's pistol in his pocket, Dan goes to Ralphie's rescue.

Glenn, with Ralphie as his shield, is sure he can still make a getaway. Dan tells him to let go of his son. In answer, Glenn puts his gun behind Ralphie's neck. "You move, kid," Glenn tells him, "I'll blow your head off." Ralphie is assured by Dan that Glenn can't possibly hurt him. "Try budgin', kid, you'll find out," answers Glenn. "Now," Dan instructs Ralphie, "I want you to do exactly as I tell you. Because that gun is not loaded. . . ." "Stop bluffin', Hilliard," says Glenn, "and let's get . . ." "It has no bullets in it, Ralph," continues Dan. "Do you understand that?" Ralphie nods. "You're lyin'! . . ." cries Glenn. "You wouldn't've brung it in here if . . ." *"Run!"* orders Dan, stepping out of Ralphie's way. Out of the bedroom, down the stairs, and through the front door Ralphie runs, as Glenn clicks and clicks the revolver. Desperately, his revolver upraised, he starts for Dan, only to meet the barrel of Dan's pistol.

Dan turns Glenn from a wild man into a stunned, listless figure by telling him that Hank is dead, riddled with police bullets. He rubs this in. Glenn now wishes to die himself and get it over with quickly. He tries to goad Dan into killing him, saying: "Go ahead. . . . You ain't got it in you." Bard changes Dan from a bloodthirsty to normal man with a P.A. message: "Hilliard, can you hear me? . . . your wife and son are here with us. They're both safe!" Thanking God he's not a killer, Dan steps forward, slaps Glenn hard in the face, and orders him to "Get out of my house!"

Staggering, whining with self-pity, his mind gone to pieces, Glenn starts down the stairs. Instead of leaving the house with his hands up, Glenn brandishes the empty gun and goes out the door to his death.

Over in the attic, Bard slowly lowers his rifle, and in spite of Carson's saying that Griffin asked for it, feels "just . . . a little disgusted with the human race." "Including Hilliard?" asks Carson. With a wan smile, Bard looks at him and says: "Thanks, Harry. . . . No, not including Hilliard." "World's full of Hilliards . . ." Carson adds, as he turns to go.

THE DARK IS LIGHT ENOUGH *

A "Winter Comedy" in Three Acts

BY CHRISTOPHER FRY

[CHRISTOPHER FRY *was born in Bristol, England, in 1908, the son of an architect, Charles Harris, who wanted him to become a clergyman. Upon his father's death he took his mother's maiden name. He wrote his first play at eleven and his first verse-play at fourteen. As a young man he acted and taught. Success came after World War II with "The Lady's Not for Burning," which was followed by "Venus Observed," "A Sleep of Prisoners" and such adaptations as Anouilh's "Ring Round the Moon."*]

IT is a snowy Thursday evening during the winter of 1848. In an Austrian country house, near the Austro-Hungary border, a small group of intellectuals wait for the Countess.

Standing near the great staircase, her three guests are amazed at the Countess' absence, and at the odd fact that she had left her house, alone, that morning, to drive out into a snowstorm, and disappear in the direction of the advancing Hungarian army.

JAKOB
Isn't it true that in more than twenty years
She has only once before failed her Thursday,
When her son Stefan was born?

KASSEL
                    Not even once.
"Good God," she said, "I think the monkey
Means to be born on Thursday evening."
But she received us all at seven o'clock,
And at nine, when Gyorki was saying, as usual,

That there is no clear truth except the present
Which alters as we grasp it,
She bowed to us in the doorway, and said
"We must freely admit the future," and withdrew
To give birth to Stefan.

JAKOB
                    But what future
Can make her withdraw today and abandon her Thursday?
A message of two lines would have put our minds
At rest.

KASSEL
                    Do you think so? I have always found
Her handwriting to be her way, not
Of giving but of withholding information. . . .

Her son Stefan enters and produces a letter from the Countess,
but as Kassel had said, it tells them nothing.

The little group of men are concerned about her:

STEFAN
                    But will you tell me
What I should have done, or do now, if my mother's lost?

BELMANN
Ah, there we have the difficulty.
This Thursday world of ours is now
More like the world than ever.
The goddess of it, in her Godlike way,
Is God knows where. We can only hope
She will condescend to appear in her own time.

JAKOB
No, no, we must be anxious. I should have
No peace for a moment if I thought I lacked anxiety.
You might pray for her safety, Belmann,
Instead of inventing crackpot blasphemies.

BELMANN
Blasphemies? Why do you think I blaspheme?
You know the Countess has the qualities of true divinity.
For instance: how apparently undemandingly
She moves among us; and yet

Lives make and unmake themselves in her neighborhood
As nowhere else. There are many names I could name
Who would have been remarkably otherwise
Except for her divine non-interference.

KASSEL
Good heavens, she would rather be dead
Than be responsible for any change
In any soul in the world.

BELMANN
She can't escape it.
If she should die, her gravestone would play havoc
With the life of the mason who carved it.
She has a touching way
Of backing a man up against eternity
Until he hardly has the nerve to remain mortal.

Stefan's first thought had been to seek help of his sister and her
husband Peter in Vienna. This country house is directly in the
path of the Hungarian revolutionists. Although Peter is a Hungarian, he finds he can best serve Hungary by serving the Austrian
government. But these marching Hungarians, says Stefan, think
it's they who stand "for truth and light, and kill accordingly."

Having said all this to his mother's guests, Stefan tells them to
make themselves at home and ring for wine. He himself then goes
upstairs.

Belmann, not one to let something pass, corrects Kassel's remark
that the Countess never interfered with a soul. What about her
conscripting her daughter, when only seventeen . . .

"Into a marriage with that rag of hell
Richard Gettner: that invertebrate,
That self-drunk, drunken, shiftless, heartless,
Lying malingerer, Richard Gettner,
Than whom of all the tribe of men
There was no man more likely to make her wretched."

Jakob calls Belmann a liar, but has to admit he never knew Gettner—only read his first book in school. His first and last book,
sneers Belmann, as he continues his attack on the man. Jakob
won't stand for any more of this and says with flamboyant gallantry:

"The Countess can be sure, wherever she may be,
Her name is safe in this house, even though
It means the end of one of us, either you or me.
Discuss this with pistols, as soon as you like:
Tomorrow or Saturday."

BELMANN
                    Don't be troublesome,
Jakob.

KASSEL
Preposterous. Ring the bell again.

JAKOB
No, no, I mean it. At last I can show myself
What these evenings have meant to me. I shall fight you.

BELMANN
We shall miss you, Jakob.
Let us, by all means, shoot at one another
If you think it will improve human nature.
And what is to happen after that?

JAKOB
                    I'm only
Concerned with this moment of loyalty.

BELMANN
                         I respect it:
But don't question my integrity.

JAKOB
Very well; I call you a liar.

BELMANN
                    Well, so I sometimes am.
But don't question my integrity.
It was an act of dark night
To marry her daughter to him. And, thank God,
He was mad, or no man, or had some faint
Kick of conscience, enough to make him have mercy
And never touch her. And so for a time
She walked in his house looking in the mirrors

And after a few months came away,
And the Church dissolved all, as though
Mortal mistakes were snow; and she was married
To Count Peter the sturdy. By so small
A margin was misery missed and her mother undamned.

The servants—Bella and Willi—finally arrive with refreshments, and the welcome announcement that the Countess has come home. Willi lets slip that she hasn't come home alone, that there's a gentleman with her, but Bella hushes him up, and then refuses to answer Belmann's prying questions.

Belmann thereupon answers them himself. He is sure that Gettner is behind the Countess' mysterious day. Jakob had heard that Gettner was off with the Hungarian army. That pleases Belmann, who almost sings:

"With the Hungarian army: off he went
Roaring into their arms, the great lover
Of his country's enemies. Indeed, loving
The enemy is almost the only commandment
He's never broken. Whoever hates his race,
His Emperor, his culture, or his mother
Wins—well, not his heart, which is apparently
Only locomotor,
But all the enthusiasm of his spleen."

Bella, coming down the stairs with Stefan, hurries to the door, worried that this next caller may be Stefan's sister Gelda. Gelda it is, full of concern for her mother as she hurries into the room. Then, seeing the man who, unnoticed, has come down the stairs, she stops dead.

BELMANN
Gettner, by God!

GETTNER
By God, no other.
I remember you, too, but without astonishment.
It's Thursday night. The intellectual soul
Of Europe comes down to the stream to drink. What's this
Floating belly-upwards? A dead fish?
Gettner, by God!

Amid the men's reactions of unpleasant surprise, Gelda begs Gettner for some sign of recognition. "Why?" says he. "You must know I recognize you. . . .

But then you also know, I suppose, the ten
Years have improved you to a kind of beauty,
And you'd like to see that I see that.
Well, if it gives you pleasure to be commended
By what remains of a bad husband,
Be pleased: I've noticed and admired.
Where's your *good* husband this vile night?"

Told that Peter is following Gelda, Gettner cries what a fool to send his wife on a country visit in such weather—and such danger. Belmann quickly calls him on this, reminds Gettner that he himself drew the Countess out under such conditions. And, Belmann adds, is Gettner dining with . . . his enemies tonight?

Gelda and Kassel ask Belmann to stop his questions—in good time they may find out. But Belmann wants to know exactly where Gettner stands, in order to know how he himself should behave. Gettner doesn't seem to mind: he casually admits going over to the Hungarians, and fondly recalls his moment of conversion to their cause—a wet, windy Sunday, when his self-esteem needed the boost that only liberty, justice and revolution could provide. Belmann never manages to ask his next question, for the Countess enters.

Asking their forgiveness, knowing she has it, Countess Rosmarin lightly remarks:

"How few you are. Can so many
Of my friends have died in a week? I was anxious
You should all be astonished to hear
That this morning, by the confusing light
Of one lantern I harnessed the horses, poor angels,
With my own insufficient hands. Will you believe me?"

A devoted chorus believes her. Gelda shows concern over the kind of day her mother has been through; the Countess shows concern over her daughter's presence so far from safe Vienna. But she marvels, too, at her day: the perilous ride through the snow, the ability to find poor hunted Richard. Some of the others want to know why Richard is hunted.

GETTNER

I'm a deserter, simply, I expect
You understand that.

STEFAN

A deserter, simply!

KASSEL

Good God!

COUNTESS

Why are you shocked?
He has left them with a whole army but one.
Can they not be perfectly troublesome with that?

BELMANN

In my stupidity I seem to be
One conversion behind. To what dear cause
Are you devoted tonight? What hearts
Do you cherish at present?

At the moment, Gettner is frank to admit, none attract him. Tonight causes, faiths, and truths seem all too dreary and boring.
Belmann needs a drink. The doctor, fascinated, wants to know if
the Countess realized what she was getting into this morning, or if
she realizes even now. He knows very well, she tells him, that she
knows the true world. She heard it on the march today. To her
ears and Richard's it sounded like a pack of howling dogs.
Stefan is furious that Gettner drew her into this, but the Countess
dismisses everything about it except the weather. Gelda takes her
part, as does Kassel, who argues that Gettner wasn't responsible for
the weather, and may not even have realized that the Countess
would go any distance. . . . Gettner quickly interrupts:

"Doctor,
Don't let's give me any imaginary virtues.
I'd have prayed and begged and bullied her to fetch me
If the roads had been under fire and water,
If the distance and the danger had been trebled
And death not unlikely.
There was no one else I could believe would come;
Except the firing squad, which I was not
In the mood to welcome."

Kassel is bothered by what effect Richard's presence here, probably with valuable information, will have on the Hungarians. Gettner calmly tells the doctor he is right: he is infectious. Until the armies pass onward to Vienna he's bound to bring this house great uneasiness.

JAKOB

It's true what he says; Countess, did you think of it?
Suppose they come this way, and suppose by some chance
They know where Gettner's hiding, may it not
Be very unpleasant, most of all for you
Who in your innocence of heart brought him among us?

COUNTESS

Innocent?
I am always perfectly guilty of what I do,
Thank God.

BELMANN

Countess, you see we're here in a trap
With you and this gentleman of uncertain future.
May we presume to doubt your wisdom and care for us?

Again Jakob takes offense that anyone, mainly Belmann, could doubt the Countess.

But the Countess, aware of the thrusts and parries of her friends, seems for the moment apart from the fight. And Gettner, no matter what they all say, won't die to oblige anybody;

"Nor for the sake of keeping up
Decent appearances. Before I do
I'll get down on all fours, foot-kissing,
Dust-licking, belly-crawling,
And any worm can have me for an equal,
Rather than I should have no life at all."

BELMANN

Well, that, I think, is clear.
You have a remarkably short distance to go.

Exhausted, bemused, the Countess feels almost unconcerned: It is as if she were looking on all this uncertainty from a great distance. But she realizes that, for the others, time is pressing and the Hun-

Katharine Cornell and Tyrone Power in "The Dark Is Light Enough"

garians are not far away. Indeed, snatches of a soldiers' song can now be heard. Jakob, throwing open the window, makes audible the shouting of military orders.

Gettner, realizing that the army has stopped at the gates, imperiously inquires where the Countess chooses to hide him—bidding her be good enough to remember that this is life and death to him.

Not at all irritated by his manner, the Countess tells him mildly that if he wishes, he can hide in the little bell-turret. This decided on, the next problem is what to do about the knocking at the door.

Bella, coming to the Countess for instructions, is told serenely that if she wants a door in the morning, she'd better open it to the soldiers. At which point, Gettner, aware that not a man in the room cares a fig for him, cravenly implores them to

"Have a respect for my life,
For the sake of your sleep to come, don't betray me.
Go to your imaginations, gentlemen:
Think of death by shooting."

BELMANN
I should more likely weep for stags or partridges.

COUNTESS
Do, then. Weep for what you can.
It's grateful to our brevity
To weep for what is briefer,
For nothing else will.

GETTNER
(*Leaning from the landing of the stairs*)
Lie, lie! O Christ, lie for me!

Bella is pleased to announce that the Hungarian officer in charge is an old visitor to this house, Colonel Janik, and behind him in the mob of soldiers, there's someone else—but she has no chance to say who.

Asking Countess Rosmarin to put aside thoughts and manners of other days, Janik briefly duels with her over today's trip and the point of his visit.

JANIK
What does the name Captain Gettner
Mean to you, Countess?

COUNTESS
A fantasy, Colonel.

JANIK
I trusted you to be serious, but I see,
Madam, you mean to play.

COUNTESS
I was astonished
For a moment, you must let me be astonished,
Though I should know the world has many surprises
And Richard with a commission might possibly
Be one of them.

JANIK
I wish I might convey
The pressure of tonight and dawn tomorrow
Which is on my heart,
And ask you, therefore, to respect it.

COUNTESS
Colonel,
You can be certain I do; but you mustn't expect
All men to leave their gentler world for yours.

JANIK
It has been reported that you were seen
With Captain Gettner in your sleigh;
That you apparently brought him to this house.

COUNTESS
It is a house to which I bring my friends.

JANIK
You may not have understood that Captain Gettner
Is a deserter.

COUNTESS
What else could he possibly be?
Suppose our friend has found himself
No longer bound in understanding to you,
Either in the pursuit of meaning or in any
Wholehearted belief, what except a deserter
Can he possibly be?   He might not have supposed

You would let him resign and send him off
With your blessing on his way.

JANIK
                    This is a night
For simplicities, madam. I have two thousand men
Standing in the snow, their lives my trust.
Peace may go in search of the one soul
But we are not at peace.

COUNTESS
                    You are not
At peace, Colonel.

The Countess has no weapons to prevent Janik's searching the
house, she only wonders that he should use violent means when she
could be won over by any of God's truths he might put before her.
She even promises him

                    ". . . I shall never make
Myself, or my friends, my way of life
Or private contentment, or any
Preference of my nature, an obstacle
To the needs of a more true and living world
Than so far I have understood. Only
Tell me what is in this war you fight
Worth all your dead and suffering men.
Your faith is, your country has been refused
Its good rights, for many years too long.
So be certain, whatever the temptation,
No man is made a slave by you.
To you Austria is a tyranny.
Then, to the number of those men who die,
And far beyond that number infinitely,
Surely you will show
One man over another has no kingdom. . . .

"Otherwise," she says, "how shall I understand your war?"
The Countess wonders at the quaint freedom that lets us make
up our minds and not be free to change them, she who changes her
mind for pure relaxation two or three times a day. To save his
cause for him, she firmly tells Janik that he may not search her
house.

Not wishing further dangerous delays for his men, Janik simply produces his trump card: his prisoner, Count Peter Zichy. The Countess now has the free choice of keeping Gettner—by giving up her son-in-law Peter.

Stefan loudly berates himself for causing Peter's plight; but Peter very pleasantly absolves him from blame: "Time and place have conspired against us," he tells Stefan.

Janik, suggesting that the Countess brought Gettner here that he might give valuable information to Peter and the Austrian government, says again to the Countess: Give up Gettner, or Peter must remain the Hungarians' prisoner.

COUNTESS
Colonel, no man is mine to give you.

PETER
Bargaining with family affection, Colonel,
Isn't war. As I know this house, you have my word
There's been no conspiracy.

JANIK
So on your word
My men can pride themselves, as they go into battle,
That I failed to lead them even to the arrest
Of one deserter from the hands of a woman
Because of the word of the Emperor's Government.
Sir, for many centuries we have been able
To judge the word of the Emperor's Government.

PETER
You should know I love Hungary.

JANIK
I know that you're Hungarian. I know
Your voice in the Austrian Council must of course
Be moderate. I do not know
You love Hungary.

PETER
How shall I tell you
I love Hungary? Your love goes to war,
Mine stays at home, and there's no comparison:
You march with Buda-Pesth, and I reason with Vienna.

You have the benefit of passion, Colonel:
The world can see you with your life held high
Ready to hurl it out of your living hand
For the sake of Hungary, even perhaps
To lose the life of Hungary, too; and Hungary loves you.
Whereas, whatever I wish, in fact I see
Hungary's best future in Austria's friendship,
And I remain, if you like, the fool
Of my own faith and fallibility,
And Hungary scorns me; there's no comparison.
I see you love Hungary, I think it may be
To Hungary's sorrow. For me, there's nothing to show;
But indeed there can be love without evidence.

Janik knows him for a sincere man, but in the wrong kind of world. And back he goes to the matter at hand: the Countess' choice. Over Stefan's impassioned protests, the Countess says there is no choice. Stefan appeals to the doctor for help and is told by Peter to be quiet. "Deep water," says Peter, "is for those who can swim." Kassel waits to have his opinion asked; Belmann and Jakob do not. For Belmann there is no choice between a man and a rat; for Jakob there is no such thing as spiritual democracy. For once they agree on something, but the Countess now is giving her full attention to Peter.

Using his own words: "there can be love without evidence," Countess Rosmarin decides against him. Believing in his love for Hungary, though he works for the Emperor, she asks him to believe in her love for him though she leaves him in Janik's hands.

Janik courteously bids Peter accompany him, while Stefan entreats Gelda to make Gettner surrender himself. Gelda refuses.

Richard was her husband once, she says, hard though it was. On the other hand, her life with Peter has been so loving and smooth and full of understanding that she can ask him not to ask Richard to die. "There's no fear of that," Peter answers; "no one need ever die for us. . . ." And to Janik, Peter says: "Coming."

As he calmly takes his leave, a torn Gelda cries: "What am I doing, Peter?" Stefan flaunts his guilt, Belmann makes clear his indignation, and even the doctor wonders: ". . . Whether the drive you took so far in the snow, Rosmarin, is finished even yet." "No good can come of it," growls Belmann, to which Jakob adds, "No good will ever come of Gettner." The Countess concedes: "That may be true."

ACT II

The Hungarians had marched off the Countess' estate, but were surprised by Austrian troops, and promptly returned to lick their wounds.

Gettner, hiding out restlessly in the stables, receives Stefan and his news of the Hungarians. Trying to assume his mother's reasonable tones, Stefan probes away at what makes Gettner tick, how much he cares for his mother.

GETTNER
There's no one on earth
I would put to more trouble.

STEFAN
You're succeeding.   Already
Her house and her quiet have gone.   You set
Great store by your life.   What secret value has it
Which makes you claim so much for keeping it?

GETTNER
Unless I live, how do you think I can know?

STEFAN
Suppose its value should be the chance to die
At the right moment?

GETTNER
That's an assumption
Very difficult afterwards to verify.

Stefan, wanting Gettner to accept his challenge to a duel, tries to make the invitation more palatable, says what a bad shot he is. Gettner dismisses him and it: "How shall I add to the pleasures of your family by waving a pistol at you? . . . My boy, you think too poorly of me. I would never trouble a soul beyond my own small needs." And then adds: "I possess enough honor to remain dishonored without indignation—"

Next to visit the stables is Gelda. She too comes with news of the Hungarians. They are now in full possession of the house, into which they have moved their wounded, and from which they are moving the Countess.

Not too concerned over the Countess, Gettner is worried where it will now be safe for *him*. Gelda consoles him by saying he will have to hide out only a day or two. Gettner decides the one way to get through these long hours is to drink himself insensible. He freely admits that he expects more from other people than he has any intention of giving himself. He asks Gelda how she feels about sacrificing her *good* husband for his sake. "I think neither of deep regrets nor of no regrets," answers Gelda. "You are the only one who gained, Richard, so be grateful." But he refuses to be till he knows why she acted as she did.

GELDA

Very well, I'll tell you.

I was a failure to you once. I know
No more about that than I did. But now
In the simpler matter of guarding you
I shall try not to fail.

GETTNER

Is there another

Word in the language so unnecessary
As "fail" or "failure"?
No one has ever failed to fail in the end:
And for the very evident reason
That we're made in no fit proportion
To the universal occasion; which, as all
Children, poets, and myth-makers know,
Was made to be inhabited
By giants, fiends, and angels of such size
The whole volume of human generations
Could be cupped in their hands;
And very ludicrous it is to see us,
With no more than enough spirit to pray with,
If as much, swarming under gigantic
Stars and spaces. In this insecure
Situation, I found from the first,
Your mother managed to find a stability
Beside which any despair was compelled to hesitate:
And I was half caught in an expectation of life
Which she was good enough to show no sign
Of expecting from me.
But then—in the way a good hostess
Brings to your notice a fine possession
Without precisely pointing to it—

She made me aware of you;
And to root myself in her radiance
I married you. What did she mean by it? . . .

Gelda's innocence so threw him off that there was no other course
for him but to remain apart from her. It wasn't a question of
failure.

But, listening to Gelda now, he is tempted to be less than perfect
in his dealings with her. She, by unintentionally turning back to
old memories, has awakened feeling in both of them.

GETTNER

Now which of us has the fear?
You may have withdrawn the words, but they implied
A kindness which you can't help leaving with me,
Which has to be confirmed. My curiosity
Is great; I begin to wonder who you are.
                    (*He kisses her.*)
How dead are the husband and the wife? No words, **now.**
And yet I also wonder how it must feel
To be so close to a living body
Which in a question of hours may well
Be dead, gone, and promising to be rotten?

GELDA

Why won't you be fair? You cheat and cheat.
Be good to me.
            (*They kiss again, and stand apart.*)

GETTNER

            You were quite right to remember
I married you. It was time I should be reminded.

GELDA

Was it?

GETTNER

            The human arms can seem
A great security, for the time they hold.
Pathetically, since they secure nothing.
Nevertheless, it was what you meant.

GELDA

Nevertheless, it could perhaps have been what I meant.

GETTNER

I'm extremely grateful.

Warning him that the Hungarians are on their way to the stable, Stefan tells Gettner if he wants to save himself for better things, he'd better hide. Admonishing them to not let him starve, Gettner disappears up the ladder to the loft.

Bella and Willi, loaded with supplies, now lead in the Hungarian soldiers carrying the Countess' furniture. The soldiers seem not half so bothered by Bella's bossiness as by their Colonel's. But the Countess, entering with Janik, seems not bothered at all: "You shall see," she tells the Colonel, "it is only a little hardship. You may put me out of your mind, as you put me out of my house. . . ."

Bella sniffs at her mistress' concern for the soldiers: "Who started it, madam?" is her age-old cry. The Countess has no idea, and because it would take too long to get to the root of it, she won't answer. She feels, however, that by exiling her to the stables the Colonel has at least united her with his men "who are so willing to die for what death will take away from them."

Under her spell, Janik asks to kiss her hand. Over Gelda's protests, the Countess thanks him: "To one as poorly circumstanced as I am, it is most considerate and friendly." Her hand duly kissed, she adds, "Now go back to your mischief." Janik, though apologizing, refuses to repent. He is sure that he has put new heart into his unhappy soldiers by permitting them the vandalism of taking the house. . . . "You gave a thousand bodies unexpected comfort," he tells the Countess, "when you put yourself at odds with us yesterday." If that is so, she says, then Richard Gettner's desertion has turned into a benefit. "You will want to give Richard Gettner his liberty to do more good with," she finishes. That's only woman's logic, says Janik, who can't understand why she should champion such a man. In the end it can only mean disturbing her peace.

The Countess rebuts:

"Life has a hope of him
Or he would never have lived. Colonel,
Can you prophesy the outcome of your war?
Yet you still go about it. Richard lives
In his own right, Colonel, not in yours
Or mine."

As long as Gettner's kept out of his way, Janik won't search for him; and will even allow her the company of her son-in-law Peter, along with Peter's guards. The Countess gratefully thanks him as he leaves.

Alone with her daughter, Rosmarin's thoughts go back to Gelda's marriage to Richard that she did nothing to prevent, and the silence between mother and daughter on this subject. To this day, Gelda would rather not discuss it, but the Countess does the talking: she allowed her to marry Richard, though she knew that at best Gelda would find in loving this difficult man a very special form of happiness. She knew Richard was no brute, no pursuer of evil. . . . Gettner laughs, and for his benefit the Countess raises her voice so he won't miss her description of him as a man by a January sea, stripped to swim, but powerless either to go into the water or get back into his clothes. She wishes that some day he would take the plunge or dress.

Belmann and Jakob together carry a painting into the stable but differ in their reasons for doing so. And in arguing they bring up yesterday's controversy over the Countess' behavior.

BELMANN
I said in your absence,
There were things you had done which were arguably
Reprehensible.
COUNTESS
You showed yourself
A master of the obvious. And Jakob
Rightly challenged you for describing me
With such little wit. If his rapier has
No better point, Jakob, you can receive it
On a wide front, and come back to play patience with me.

But now it seems that Jakob is more immediately concerned with the outcome of the duel and Belmann's life in the hereafter than with what caused the duel. Belmann accuses him, not of thinking of his soul, but of wanting to get out of the whole affair. "It's not so!" cries Jakob. "I deny that, absolutely." "I can see," says the Countess, "nothing will ever happen to either of you."

Peter, arriving under guard, and with unexpected wounds, tells his sympathetic family what happened. Yesterday he found himself the very soul of the revolution, grabbing a sword and fighting with his captors against the Austrians. But it wasn't that he was won over to their ideas; his personal experience in the battle only strengthened the beliefs he had always held. He was never more certain that the Hungarians were doing a greater wrong to themselves than to the Austrians. What's more, he was grateful to his mother-in-law for bringing Gettner here, thus providing him with the knowledge he lacked . . . "which in a way has altered nothing and altered it thoroughly."

Belmann ventures to point out to Jakob: "the truth of what he was saying yesterday: . . . how apparently

"Undemandingly the Countess moves among us:
And yet lives make and unmake themselves
In her neighborhood as nowhere else."

COUNTESS
If, as well as turning a fine phrase,
You also spoke the truth, how proud of you
We all should be.

BELMANN
Thank you, my dear Countess.
Yet I'll wager you, Jakob:
One man the Countess will never change
By her divine non-interference:
Ten kronen against Gettner's chances.

JAKOB
Your stable behavior, I imagine.

Even the Hungarian soldiers come under her spell, as she lends a sympathetic ear to their homesick talk of wives. And when Gettner, drunk and annoyed at being ignored, comes down the ladder looking for company, specifically Gelda's, the Countess smoothly prevents the soldiers from going into action.

Gettner makes a maudlin claim to Gelda. Peter, trying hard to be sensible, says if he can drink himself to safety, let him. Gettner makes it difficult for everyone, including the guards, by his brazen behavior.

SECOND GUARD
I don't know why you have to choose
To walk into us, and in front of witnesses.

COUNTESS
None of us can be called a witness. There are times
When our very so-so vision can rescue itself
Only by failing altogether. I am sure

Neither of you wish to arrest him, and I
Have given my word to the Colonel that Captain Gettner
Shall not be allowed to cross his path. You had better
Undo your collars and sit down again.

Gettner is annoyed that, just when he thinks he has taken a
courageous plunge, he should be considered a fool:

"God's a woman. That surprises you,
But it's perfectly evident in every aspect
Of the arrangement. Create you to think
You're the beloved of God, the blest
Pair of you in a confederation of longing,
With the whispers hot in your ear: Immortal man,
Immortal man achieve me.—And then
You're made another generation of:
The frank daylight's turned full on you,
And her finger withers you with scorn."

He makes for Gelda with the obvious intention of embracing her.
He entreats her: "Let me kiss you, or else they'll laugh at me."
Since Gelda, despite everyone's warning, makes no move, Gettner
kisses her. Peter tries hard to control himself; Stefan not so hard.
But when Gettner starts taunting Peter, saying that Gelda has a
mind to love him—which Gelda doesn't deny having told Gettner—
everyone but Peter and the Countess explodes. When Peter won't
rise to Gettner's bait, Gettner suddenly feels: "Can't keep things
how they should be. Well, I know I'm drunk."

Knowing this is not the time for words, the Countess quietly
whips up a performance of village dances by her now devoted slaves,
the Hungarian guards. As the mouth organ plays, and the soldiers
perform, Stefan removes the pistols from the holsters the guards
had taken off in order to dance. Under cover of the rhythmical
clapping for the dance, Stefan slaps Gettner across the face. As it
was meant to, the slap so angers the man that he forgets his peaceful feelings and steps outside with Stefan.

The Countess next requests a bawdy song she heard the soldiers
singing during her snowy sleigh ride. While the embarrassed soldiers are improvising a bowdlerized version, two shots ring out.
Belatedly the soldiers discover that their pistols, Gettner and Stefan
have all disappeared.

Just as suddenly, with drunken dramatics, Gettner returns. Before his wild announcement that he has killed Stefan can do much

harm, Dr. Kassel quiets things down. He reports that Stefan's death has been exaggerated.

KASSEL

Stefan is alive, Rosmarin.

COUNTESS

You've come to say so, little physician.
I hadn't let him go so easily.

KASSEL

The orderlies will bring him here, Rosmarin,
You must know he is hurt, but, the blessing of being so young,
New life will graft on a thread. By a stroke of luck
I was near when it happened. This precious idiot
Saw Stefan fall and went nowhere near him,
Belted off like a madman, and brought
His hideous farrago of nonsense to you.

The guards agree that the sooner they can get Gettner to the Colonel the better off everyone will be. Belmann completely agrees; but the Countess begs the guards not to injure her son by placing Richard's death at his door; not to turn his challenge into a judgment. Instead they are to pray for Stefan and Richard, because they are the life they pray for. . . . "And because there is nothing on the earth which doesn't happen in your own hearts." She then addresses Richard, asking for his arm to lean on: "My body sometimes tells me I'm not here for ever—Richard." But Gettner makes no move to help her. The Countess almost falls, but thrusting aside Jakob's and Kassel's helping hands, she says:

"No, no, that is over now. Perhaps for a moment
He drew in a draft of my strength. And now
He comes on again with life, as I do. I can stand,
I can welcome him. I need no help."

ACT III

Stefan and the Countess, re-established in the house, have both been at the point of dying (Stefan is slightly on the mend now); Richard has vanished, and the revolution seems to have spluttered out.

Suddenly Peter reappears. Finding Gelda overjoyed that he's

safely out of it, Peter answers: "No one is safely out of it ever."
He has come only to tell her that he's racing to Vienna.

PETER

The Hungarians are broken completely.

GELDA

It was what you were afraid of.

PETER
                                    I was afraid
They'd lose the liberties they were beginning to gain
Lately; not that we should lose the humanity
We took of God two thousands years ago.

GELDA

Peter, what is it?

PETER

The government is shooting and hanging
Every Hungarian of note who fought in the war.
They're holding contemptuous, contemptible
Courts-martial on the field, and executing
Men, one after the other—men
Whose families have given generations
Of service to the Emperor.

   What torments him most is the thought that if he had never left
Vienna, some of these lives might have been saved, . . . "Whether
Stefan's message of alarm for Rosmarin wasn't one cause of these
deaths and the endless consequences . . ."
   What torments Gelda most is her need to talk to Peter and make
her explanations.

GELDA

In the still of my mind
I know I've never done anything to hurt us;
Only in the wandering, so easily cheatable
Part of me, where a right thought—
Or at least an excusable thought—suddenly
Finds it has taken pity on a horde
Of domineering wrong ones. It may have been right,
That first instinct, to put out with a lifeboat
For Richard, but on to it scrambled

Such a crew of pirates, my curiosity,
My pride, my ambition to succeed
Where I failed before, my longing to discover
What conversions could be made by love,
We all began to sink. And it was Stefan
Who rescued me, when he nearly died for the truth;
You and I are the truth.

PETER
If that contents you
It will always content me.

GELDA
I don't know whether
You're hurt or angry.

PETER
Neither; I love you,
But I'm impatient.

Other worlds are coming to an end tonight, he tells her, more irreparably than theirs. He must go.

Jakob and Belmann are delighted to see Peter, and to learn that the Hungarians have come to grief. Gelda asks them not to hold him. "Why off so soon?" wonders Jakob. Peter tells them:

"We're celebrating victory
By executing every considerable officer
We can lay our hands on. I think someone
Should go and ask them why."
(*Exit* PETER.)

BELMANN
So he should. Though the degrees of distinction
Between admirable, permissible, and outrageous slaughter
Haven't yet been made perfectly clear to me.
I understand we should lament an earthquake
And prepare to contrive an earthquake
With equal zest.

Jakob feels much better now the revolution is over and he can return to a normal life; Belmann concedes that with Gettner gone, things look slightly more encouraging.

Dr. Kassel, back from delivering a baby into this puzzling world, lets them know that their immediate world is to suffer a blow: The Countess will not hold them here much longer. Gelda thinks that her mother knows this and is willing to die.

But just now the Countess is bending her will to descending the staircase, to joining her friends for a final Thursday. She starts her slow, tortuous trip down the steps, talking all the while to the worried, admiring group below. She refuses all help, she refuses to conserve her strength in any way.

As she manages a step, she asks for news of the world—the world she is leaving. She particularly would like to know of Richard Gettner. She regrets that when he disappeared, her favorite horse disappeared with him, but since she can do nothing about this, she is determined to have everyone concentrate on this last Thursday discussion, since there may be no other.

BELMANN
If it entertains you, if you insist,
We'll make believe this is to be a farewell.

COUNTESS
You're very grudging.

JAKOB
It's impossible!
How can you bear to think of it?

COUNTESS
But you've always thought of it, Jakob,
In the pleasure and conversation of these evenings.
The argument, philosophy, wit, and eloquence
Were all in the light of this end we come to.
Without it there would have been very little
To mention except the weather. Protect me
From a body without death. Such indignity
Would be outcast, like a rock in the sea.
But with death, it can hold
More than time gives it, or the earth shows it.
I can bear to think of this:
I can bear to be this, Jakob,
So long as it bears me.

On this last Thursday, another hunted man comes to the Countess' house. This time it is Colonel Janik, demanding nothing for himself, apologizing for his intrusion, hoping to find Peter and some help for Hungary.

The Countess asks the anguished man for the song she has been trying to remember, the soldiers' song. He impatiently sings a few bars. The Countess then tells him it is not safe to leave her house.

Jakob and Belmann burst out with objections to the Countess' harboring a new fugitive. But it is Janik who says proudly: "I neither want protection, nor would I ask to be given it here. I've troubled this house enough." Notwithstanding, he is soon on his way to the bell-turret, protesting:

"What am I letting you do? You'll find
These men are more determined. There's little chance
It will turn out well."

The only thing the Countess seems to fear is her new absent-mindedness, and that she may plead with the military for the wrong man.

And the other man appears. Gettner returns to see if all the rumors he has been hearing of the Countess' death are true. It was extraordinary how, as he was going away from her at a full gallop, this rumor outran him and met him at each stop. . . .

"In the end I was so sick of the information,
And sick of seeing faces
Plastered with tears and rain, the road became
A nightmare and impassable.
So I turned round, which I now see
Was unnecessary. I should have stuck
To my first incredulity, and ridden
Straight on over the faces."

The Countess is proud of those tears; and though she apologizes for spoiling his journey, he has brought her great happiness.

GETTNER
Great hypocrite! You know I had no intention
Of giving you pleasure. And I wonder
You like to let your thirst for admiration
Lap up these tears.
COUNTESS
                    As they were wept for me
It's just as well I am here to appreciate them.

BELMANN

Will someone give me the word to get rid of this man?

Jakob finds it hard to control himself, but Kassel warns them both against violence for the sake of their Countess.

Belmann, not in his usual form, tells Gettner of Janik's presence in the bell-turret, and asks him to persuade the Countess against further disasters.

Gettner merely shows his annoyance at someone else taking his place. The Countess soothes him, and riles her friends by asking to be left alone with Gettner for a half-hour.

Their talk starts out with a sickroom gambit from Gettner that is promptly squashed by the Countess.

But Gettner finds her illness so terrible a blow that he even goes so far as to suggest that he is the cause of it. The Countess has never been able to understand the arithmetic of cause and effect; but it is the world's arithmetic, Gettner supposes, that if he's to be set loose, she is to be caught. . . . Since there can be no living without her, Gettner asks the Countess to marry him.

Charmed by his proposal of beginning life when she is dying, the Countess still refuses him. She doesn't love him. This Gettner won't believe:

"I've nothing to say.
If you say so I can't contradict you.
I imagine it's more than ever satisfactory
To have done so much for a mere liking."

COUNTESS

Don't praise me; I never in my life
Was so unfit for praise. It would have been
Easier to love you than to like you, Richard.

Asked then what he means to her, the Countess says: "Simply what any life may mean." Gettner resorts to self-pity, and the Countess tells him that neither of them need despair . . . she won't leave him until she can love him. He doesn't care for that idea of anxious waiting. . . . The Countess then adds: "I don't mean necessarily here."

Gettner is not prepared to wait, and means to leave on a fresher horse than the one he stole the last time. He says good night and goes out. (*The* COUNTESS *sings again.*)

COUNTESS

There was more to come, so I imagine,
But then they were interrupted.
I wish I could go on singing.
I am very much in love with something; . . .

But what it is she can't remember—
More hammering at the door brings back Gettner, who understandably wants to avoid the Austrians come for Janik, and is detouring by way of the house to the stables.

". . . You can't sleep now," he tells the Countess; "you've given your word to receive them. . . ." As he opens the window to make his escape, the hammering increases. He turns to the Countess' chair.

GETTNER

You're dead, Rosmarin. Understand that.
What is there to stay for? You never showed
Any expectations of me when you were alive,
Why should you now?
This isn't how I meant that you should love me!
(*He closes the window and comes back to her and speaks curtly.*)
Very well, very well.

Be with me.
(*Hammering on the door. Enter* BELLA.)

BELLA

They must be quiet! How can I send them away
If they will come in?

GETTNER

You can't send them away,
Bella, if they will come in.

BELLA

But Madam—

GETTNER

She knows
They're here. She says yes, we're to let them in.
Go to the door, Bella, and let them in.
(*The hammering at the door increases as* BELLA *goes out.*)

BUS STOP *

A Play in Three Acts

BY WILLIAM INGE

[WILLIAM INGE *was born in Independence, Kansas, in 1913, and educated at the University of Kansas and Peabody College. With Maude Adams he taught at Stephens College, Columbia, Missouri, and once conducted a playwriting class at Washington University in St. Louis. He was drama, film and music editor for the St. Louis "Times-Star." In 1950 the production in New York of his "Come Back, Little Sheba" immediately placed him in the category of the "most promising" playwrights. "Picnic," produced in 1953, proved his right to this title, winning for him both the Drama Critics Circle Award and the Pulitzer Prize. Now with "Bus Stop" his position as one of our top dramatists is assured.*]

IN the dingy street-corner restaurant of a small Kansas town (which buses driving through use as a rest stop), two uniformed women are getting coffee and food ready for the next busload of passengers.

It is one A.M., and everything is rather lackadaisical inside the restaurant, while outside a March blizzard is in progress. Elma, the high school girl waitress, stands at the window watching the snow sweep by: "March is coming in like a lion," she says. Grace, the restaurant owner, stands at the wall telephone, jiggling for the operator. Elma bets her the bus will be late. Grace disagrees: "The roads are okay as far as here. It's ahead they're havin' trouble. I can't even get the operator. She must have more calls than she can handle."

Grace, going to work at the counter, hopes Elma's folks won't worry about her being out in this weather. Reassuring her, Elma leaves the window to help with the dishes, glad that she has a home to go to. Grace in her amiable hard-boiled fashion answers: "Well, I got a home to go to, but there ain't anyone in it . . . ," then adds:

". . . if I didn't have this restaurant to keep me busy, I'd prob'ly go nuts. Sometimes, at night, after I empty the garbage and lock the doors and turn out the lights, I get kind of a sick feelin', 'cause I sure don't look forward to walkin' up those stairs and lettin' myself into an empty apartment." "Gee," says Elma, "if you get that lonesome, why don't you write your husband, tell him to come back?" Grace thinks this over for a moment, and decides it's because she was just as lonesome when he was here . . . he was no company . . . they would come down to breakfast strangers.

Elma finds it pleasant working for Grace; Grace admires Elma for being such a good student and "a kid with good sense." ". . . I wish someone coulda reasoned with *me* when I was your age. But I was a headstrong brat, had to have my own way. I had my own way all right, and here I am now, a grass widow runnin' a restaurant, and I'll prob'ly die in this little town and they'll bury me out by the backhouse."

Will, the big black-bearded sheriff, comes in out of the snow to announce that Grace will have to hold the bus from Topeka. The highways probably won't be cleared until morning. Warmed by coffee, Will still gets angry at the storm. "Maybe," he figures, "it's just 'cause I'm a sheriff, but I like to see things in order."

As Grace gives Elma last-minute instructions, the sound of the bus motor can be heard over the howling wind: "Better fill some water glasses, Elma. Remember the doughnuts are left over from yesterday but it'll be all right to serve 'em. We got everything for sandwiches but *cheese*. We got no cheese." Will prods her: "You *never* got cheese, Grace." "I guess I'm kinda self-centered, Will," she drawls. "I don't care for cheese m'self, so I never think t'order it for someone else." It occurs to Grace that the bus driver is going to be Carl, so she tells Elma: "Remember, honey, *I* always serve Carl."

Suddenly the door swings open and the wind seems to blow in a pretty, frantic, little, made-up blonde. Cherie, dressed in net and sequins, a tarnished gold fur-trimmed jacket, and open-toed sandals, would be considered skimpily dressed in any climate. As she runs towards the counter, dragging an old straw suitcase, she anxiously cries: "Is there some place I kin hide?" Her southern accent is straight out of the Ozarks.

GRACE (*taken aback*)—What?
CHERIE—There's a *man* on that bus. . . . I wanta *hide*.
GRACE (*stumped*)—Well, gee . . . I dunno.
CHERIE (*seeing the sign above the rear door, starting for it*)—I'll

hide in the powder room. Listen! If a tall, lanky cowboy comes in here, you kin jest tell him I disappeared.

GRACE (*her voice stopping* CHERIE *at the door*)—Hey, you can't hide out there. It's cold. You'll freeze your . . .

CHERIE (*having opened the door, seeing it is an outside toilet*)—Oh! It's outside.

GRACE—This is just a country town.

CHERIE (*starting again*)—I kin stand anything fer twenty minutes.

GRACE (*stopping her again*)—I got news for ya. The bus may be here all night.

CHERIE—What?

GRACE—The highway's blocked. You're gonna have to stay here till it's cleared.

CHERIE (*shutting the door, coming to counter, lugging her suitcase. She is about to cry*)—Criminey! What am I gonna do?

Grace goes out to Carl, leaving Cherie to a sympathetic Elma—and a professionally curious Will. Elma introduces him to Cherie as the sheriff, quickly adding: "But everyone likes him. Really." Cherie doesn't want anyone arrested: "I need protection." Under Will's questioning she races on about the man, a cowboy who's after her, that she met in Kansas City: ". . . I work at the Blue Dragon night club there, down by the stockyards. *He* come there with the annual rodeo, and him and the resta the cowboys was at the night club ev'ry night. Ev'ry night there was a big fight. The boss says he ain't gonna let the cowboys in when they come back next year."

WILL—Then he followed ya on the bus?

CHERIE—He *put* me on the bus. I'm bein' abducted.

And he's planning to take her to his Montana ranch and marry her. "Yor against it?" asks Will. Cherie doesn't want to go to any "God-forsaken ranch." "Well," says Will, "if this cowboy's really takin' ya against yor will, I s'pose I'll have to stop him from it." Elma is sure he can—to her, Will is "invincible." Will won't hear of that: ". . . A man's gotta learn that, the sooner the better. A good fighter has gotta know what it is to *get* licked. Thass what makes the diff'rence 'tween a fighter and a *bully*." Even so, Cherie shudders: "There's gonna be trouble. I kin feel it in my bones."

The next passenger seems to be very cheerful. Dr. Lyman, a

ruddy, gray-haired, boyish-looking man of fifty, dressed in an old Burberry, happily surveys the room over his wool muffler. He's full of liquor and quotations. While Elma hides Cherie's bag for her behind the counter, Cherie takes a side look at Will and remarks: "Looks kinda like Moses, don't he?" Elma tells her that Will's a deacon in the Congregational Church. "My folks," says Cherie, "was Holy Rollers. Will ya gimme a cup a coffee, please? Lotsa cream."

When Carl, the bus driver, appears, Will gives him the news of how long it will take to have the roads cleared. Dr. Lyman, wanting something cleared up for himself, barges in on their conversation. He is hopeful, but not completely sure, that he has crossed the state line. Not too pleasantly, Carl sets him straight that he's in Kansas. Then Grace takes Carl's coat, preparing to make him comfortable; and Dr. Lyman, with a glint in his eye and poetry on his lips, makes a beeline for Elma.

Elma, increasingly pleased—but increasingly puzzled—by Dr. Lyman's elaborate gallantries, doesn't know what to make of him. Dr. Lyman tells of his plans that he's only too willing to change: "I have a ticket in my pocket to Denver, but I don't have to get there. I never have to get anywhere. I travel around from one town to another just to prove to myself that I'm *free*." Elma, in her young literal way, tells him of the next bus stop, Topeka. This Dr. Lyman immediately associates with the Menninger Clinic, while to Elma Topeka means all the cultural advantages of a capital. Their discussion is curtailed by Dr. Lyman's wanting a drink. Seeing he can't get one in the restaurant, he wryly refuses the coffee and food offered him: "No, my girl," he says, "you're not going to sober me up with your dainties. I am prepared for such emergencies." And he whips a pint bottle of whiskey from his overcoat pocket and calls for a bottle of lemon soda. Benignly smiling at Elma, he heavily spikes the soda, and promises to be *most* cautious about Will's seeing him drink.

Will is hearing from Carl all about Cherie's cowboy Nemesis and his cowboy companion. Carl would just as leave let them stay asleep and freeze in the bus. . . . "One of 'em's a real troublemaker. You know the kind, first time off a ranch and wild as a bronco. He's been on the make fer this li'l blonde down here. . . ." "She's been tellin me," Will says. "I've had a good mind to put him off the bus, the way he's been actin'. I say," continues Carl, "there's a time and place fer ev'rything." For Carl, this seems the time for him and Grace. And Will, sizing up the situation, goes over to the fire to read a paper.

CARL—Ya know what, Grace? This is the first time you and I ever had more'n twenty minutes t'gether.

GRACE (*coyly*)—So what?

CARL—Oh, I dunno. I'll prob'ly be here mosta the night. It'd sure be nice to have a nice li'l apartment to go to, some place to sit and listen to the radio, with a good-lookin' woman . . . somethin' like you . . . to talk with . . . maybe have a few beers.

GRACE—That wouldn't be a hint or anything, would it?

CARL (*faking innocence*)—Why? Do you have an apartment like that, Grace?

GRACE—Yes, I do, but I never told you about it. Did that ornery Dobson fella tell you that I had an apartment over the restaurant?

CARL (*in a query*)—Dobson? Dobson? I can't seem to remember anyone named Dobson.

GRACE—You know him better'n *I* do. He comes through here twice a week with the Southwest Bus. He told me you and him meet in Topeka sometimes and paint the town.

CARL—Dobson? Oh yah, I know Dobson. Vern Dobson. A prince of a fella.

GRACE—Well, if he's been gabbin' to you about my apartment, I can tell ya he's oney been up there *once,* when he come in here with his hand cut, and I took him up there to bandage it. Now, that's the oney time he was ever up there. On my word of honor.

CARL—Oh, Vern Dobson speaks very highly of you, Grace. Very highly.

GRACE—Well . . . he better. Now what ya gonna have?

Carl wants ham and cheese on rye. Grace is sorry but there's no cheese. What's more, there's no rye. Dr. Lyman chimes in here, causing Carl to exclaim: "That's all I ever get on my bus, drunks and hoodlums." Unabashed, Dr. Lyman reels off to Elma the saga of his wives and divorces, and winds up spouting poetry. Cherie— shivering with cold—attracts Elma's attention by asking for the doughnuts.

ELMA—Do you honestly work in a night club?

CHERIE—Sure! I'm a chanteuse. I call m'self *Cherie.*

ELMA—That's French, isn't it?

CHERIE—I dunno. I jest seen the name once and it kinda appealed t'me.

ELMA—It's French. It means "dear one." Is that all the name you use?

CHERIE—Sure. Thass all the name ya need. Like Hildegarde. She's a chanteuse, too.

ELMA—*Chanteuse* means singer.

CHERIE—How come *you* know so much?

ELMA—I'm taking French in high school.

Cherie reflects about this: she never got as far as high school. Elma, listening to how Cherie got her start in show business, is a most sympathetic audience. It all started with winning a second prize in an amateur contest in Joplin, Mo. This got Cherie to Kansas City and another contest got her to the Blue Dragon. "Is that where you're from, Joplin?" asks Elma. "No," Cherie answers, "Joplin's a *big* town. I lived 'bout a hundred miles from there, in River Gulch, a li'l town in the Ozarks. I lived there till the floods came, three years ago this spring, and washed us all away."

Carl, leaving Grace for a moment, approaches Will: "You gonna be here a while, Will?" Carl wants to wake the cowboys and leave them in Will's charge. He also has a whispered word for Will that seems to be about Dr. Lyman. Will is very much surprised. Carl concludes: "So ya better keep an eye on *him,* too." This accomplished, Carl gives Grace a meaningful look and wink, and starts off. "Ain't you comin' back, Carl?" Stretching elaborately, Carl excuses himself: "To tell the truth, Will, I git so darn *stiff,* sittin' at the wheel all day, I thought I'd go out fer a long walk." "In this blizzard?" says Will. "You gone crazy?" "No," says Carl. "That's just the kinda fella I am, Will. I like to go fer long walks in the rain and snow. Freshens a fella up. Sometimes I walk fer hours." And he nonchalantly goes out, leaving a most skeptical sheriff behind

Dr. Lyman suddenly feels in the mood for poetry, and exuberantly starts reciting sonnets that it pleases Elma to recognize as Shakespearean. Elma studied Shakespeare at school; she memorized the Balcony Scene from *Romeo and Juliet.* Dr. Lyman says: "Ah! I wish I had been there to see." Cherie, wishing to set forth her own position with regard to Shakespeare, says: "Where I went to school we din read no Shakespeare till the ninth grade. In the ninth grade everyone read *Julius Caesar.* I oney got as far as the eighth. I seen Marlon Brando in the movie, though. I sure do like Marlon Brando."

Dr. Lyman, with "spoofing seriousness," talks to Cherie until Bo Decker, her picturesque twenty-one-year-old cowboy, bursts in. Accompanied by his older companion, Virgil Blessing, he stands at the door, leaving it wide open to the wintry blasts. Bo makes quite an appearance in his tight jeans, horsehide jacket and Stetson; Virgil who is fortyish, tidier—and much quieter—than Bo, carries a guitar case.

Bo (*calling across the room*)—Cherry! How come you get off the bus, 'thout lettin' me know? That any way to treat the man you're gonna marry?

WILL (*lifting his eyes from the paper*)—Shut the door, Cowboy!

Bo—Thass no way to treat a fella, Cherry, to slip off the bus like ya wanted to get rid of him, maybe. And come in here and eat by yourself. I thought we'd have a li'l snack t'*gether*. Sometimes I don't understand you, Cherry.

CHERIE—Fer the hunderth time, my name ain't *Cherry*.

Bo—I cain't say it the way you do. What's wrong with *Cherry*?

CHERIE—It's kinda embarrassin'.

Will once more asks firmly to have the door shut. Virgil quickly closes it, but Bo becomes insolent, not caring whether Will is a sheriff or not. He doesn't care to have any man tell him what to do. Virgil warns him that there always comes a time. . . . Ignoring Virgil, Bo holds forth for the benefit of all: "My name's Bo Decker. I'm twenty-one years old and own me m'own ranch up in Timber Hill, Montana, where I got a herd a fine Hereford cattle and a dozen horses, and the finest sheep and hogs and chickens anywhere in the country. And I jest come back from a rodeo where I won 'bout ev'ry prize there *was*, din I, Virge? (*Joshing, he elbows* VIRGIL *in the ribs.*) Yap, I'm the prize broncobuster, 'n steer-roper, 'n bulldogger, anywhere 'round. I won 'em all. And what's more, had my picture taken by *Life* Magazine. So," says Bo, confronting Will, "I'd appreciate your talkin' to me with a little respect in yor voice, Mister, and not go hollerin' orders to me from across the room like I was some no-'count servant."

Having made a considerable impression on the company, Bo doesn't let them down with an ordinary man's appetite: he places an order with Elma that will keep her busy for hours, one so large that it makes Cherie wince. "Wait till I get ya up to Susie-Q," bellows Bo at Cherie. "I'll fatten ya up. I bet in two weeks' time, ya won't recognize yorself." Putting a bear-like arm around her, and kissing her, Bo exclaims: "But doggone, I *love* ya, Cherry, jest the way ya are. Yor about the cutest li'l piece I ever did see. And man! When I walked into that night club place and hear you singin' my favorite song, standin' before that orkester lookin' like a angel, I told myself then and there, she's fer *me*. I ain't gonna leave this place without her. And now I got ya, ain't I, Cherry?" She tries to push him away, finally crying: "Bo! fer cryin' out loud, lemme *be!*" Cherie can't stand this constant mauling. Thus insulted, Bo announces in stentorian tones that he never had to coax any woman to make love to him. Virgil is saved from having to corroborate this by the arrival of a platter of hamburgers for Bo.

Grace, complaining of a headache, puts Elma in charge: " 'Cause the only thing for me to do is go upstairs and lie down a while. That's the only thing gonna do me any good at all." From his chair by the stove, Will asks with quiet amusement: "What's the matter, Grace?" Grace, who has already reached the rear door, says: "I got a headache, Will, that's just drivin' me *wild.*" "That so?" says Will.

Dr. Lyman now takes up Elma's time. The girl is delighted by his attentions, but Bo, still ravenous, now calls for the next part of his order. Too impatient to wait for Elma to bring it, Bo hurdles the counter to get the food himself. There are fireworks when he catches sight of Cherie's hidden suitcase.

He asks angrily why Cherie brought the bag out of the bus. She won't answer, and becomes frightened when he starts trying to shake it out of her. Will intercedes: "Leave the little lady alone, Cowboy."

Bo—Mister, ya got no right interferin' 'tween me and my feeancy.

Will—Mebbe she's yor feeancy and mebbe she ain't. Anyway, ya ain't gonna abuse her while I'm here. Unnerstand?

Bo—*Abuse* her?

Will (*to* Cherie)—I think you better tell him now, Miss, jest how you feel about things.

Cherie is scared to death to tell him. She finally blurts out that she's not going with Bo to his ranch; that with Will's help she will stay here, and take the next bus back to Kansas City.

Bo (*grabbing her by the shoulders to reassure himself of her*)—Ya ain't gonna do nothin' of the kind.

Cherie—Yes, I am, Bo. Ya gotta listen to me and b'lieve me. I ain't goin' with ya. That's final.

Bo (*in a most personal voice, baffled*)—But, Cherry . . . we was *familiar* with each other.

Cherie—That don't mean ya gotta *marry* me.

Bo (*shocked at her*)—Why . . . I oughtta take you across my knee and blister yer li'l bottom.

The more Cherie protests, the more she tells him not to come near her, the more ferocious Bo becomes, pulling her forcibly to him. Will breaks it up, saying that it becomes his business when the little lady asks him for protection. This in itself is a blow to Bo, but what reduces him to silence is Will's saying: "Yor overlookin' the simple but important fack that the little lady don't love *you*." This is the fact Bo hasn't cared to face. Virgil steps in to pacify him, but Bo yanks himself away and paces up and down. Will repeats: "Ask the li'l lady, if ya don't b'lieve *me*. Ask her if she loves ya." Bo stubbornly refuses: "I won't ask her nothin' of the kind." "All right, then," Will says, "take my word for it." "I wouldn't take yor word for a cloudy day. I'm tellin' ya, she loves me. And I *oughtta* know," snarls Bo. By now he is obviously so unsure of himself that Will feels it's safe to leave. He tells Cherie: "I don't think you'll be bothered any more, Miss. If y'are, my station's right across the road. You kin holler." Cherie dabs her eyes and thanks him. Before leaving, Will sees that Elma is all right, too, and gives Dr. Lyman such a penetrating look that the professor squirms.

After Will goes, Bo dashes to Virgil for the help he needs. Virgil busies himself with his guitar as Bo hesitantly admits: "Well, I . . . I just never realized . . . a gal might not . . . love me."

ACT II

It is a few minutes later, with everyone doing his best to pass the time. Virgil is playing softly on his guitar, Bo is brooding in a corner, Cherie has found a movie magazine, and Dr. Lyman—drink in hand—is courting Elma.

Dr. Lyman's theories on modern education and his dramatic account of how he lost his last college teaching job greatly entertain the easily impressed young girl. All this is a preamble to his arranging a date with her when she visits her sister in Topeka. He has it all worked out to arrive in Topeka first, then meet her bus. . . .

Virgil's ballad ends to Cherie's applause, just as Will comes back in with a thermos to be filled with coffee for the highway workers. Waiting for Elma to fill it, he makes a quick check: "Everyone behavin'?" he asks. "Of course," Elma answers. Will looks puzzled: "Grace not down yet?" "No," answers Elma. "I didn't see Carl any place outside," Will adds. "Suppose somethin' coulda happened to him?" Elma tells him not to worry. "I s'pose he can take care of himself," Will concedes. Paying for the coffee that Elma hands over, he says loudly, for Dr. Lyman and Bo to hear: "If anyone should be wantin' me, I won't be gone very long."

Seething because of Will, Bo says to Virgil: "That dang sheriff! If it wasn't fer him, I'd git Cherry now and . . . I . . ."

VIRGIL—Where would ya take her, Bo?

Bo—There's a Justice a the Peace down the street. You can see his sign from the window.

VIRGIL—Bo, ya cain't force a gal to marry ya. Ya jest cain't do it. That sheriff's a stern man and he'd shoot ya in a minute if he saw it was his duty. Now, why don't ya go over to the counter and have yourself a drink . . . like the perfessor?

Bo—I never did drink and I ain't gonna let no woman drive me to it.

VIRGIL—Ya don't drink. Ya don't smoke or chew. Ya oughtta have *some* bad habits to rely on when things with women go wrong.

Bo, plunking himself down next to Virgil, says hesitantly—because he doesn't want to sound like "some pitiable weaklin' of a man"— how lonesome he's been these last few months. Virgil quickly tells him that it's no disgrace to feel that way: ". . . a long time ago, I gave up romancin' and decided I was just gonna take bein' lonesome for granted."

Cherie, having found a confidante in Elma, spills out her troubles with Bo; but it does occur to her that by marrying him and going to Montana she might be better off than she is now. Her great complaint is that Bo doesn't know what love is. Elma can't understand why she had decided to marry him. Cherie, worldly-wise, says: "I never did decide to marry him. Everything was goin' fine till he brought up *that* subjeck. Bo come in one night when I was singin' 'That Old Black Magic.' It's one a my best numbers. And he liked it so much, he jumped up on a chair and yelled like a Indian, and put his fingers in his mouth and whistled like a steam engine. Natur'ly, it made me feel good. Mosta the customers at the Blue Dragon was too drunk to pay attention to my songs." Under Elma's questioning, Cherie confesses to having thought Bo looked like Burt Lancaster. "But," says Cherie, "it was only what ya might call a *sexual* attraction." "Oh," says Elma. "The very next mornin'," Cherie goes on, "he wakes up and hollers: 'Yippee! We're gittin' married.' I honestly thought he was crazy. But when I tried to reason with him, he wouldn't listen to a word. . . ."

Cherie tells Elma she never agreed to marry him. The night the rodeo closed, Cherie even felt the time had come to leave Bo, so she had gone to the bus station to catch the midnight bus. Unfortunately, when she quit at the Blue Dragon, she had said which bus she was taking. Before she could get her ticket, Bo and Virgil were there, and Bo had bought three tickets for Montana. . . . Says Cherie: ". . . I din know what to say. Then he dragged me onto the bus and I been on it ever since. And somewhere deep down inside me, I gotta funny feelin' I'm gonna end up in Montana."

Bo suddenly is conscience-stricken that, from being left as a child in Virgil's care, he may have prevented Virgil's marrying the one girl he loved. But that wasn't why Virgil didn't ask the girl to marry him.

VIRGIL—Well . . . there comes a time in every fella's life, Bo, when he's gotta give up his own ways . . .

Bo—How ya mean?

VIRGIL—Well, I was allus kinda uncomfortable around this gal, 'cause she was sweet and kinda refined. I was allus scared I'd say or do somethin' wrong.

Bo—I know how ya mean.

VIRGIL—It was cowardly of me, I s'pose, but ev'ry time I'd get back from courtin' her, and come back to the bunkhouse where my buddies was sittin' around talkin', or playin' cards, or listenin' to music, I'd jest relax and feel m'self so much at home, I din wanta give it up.

Bo—Yah! Gals can scare a fella.

VIRGIL—Now I'm kinda ashamed.

Bo—Y'are?

VIRGIL—Yes, I am, Bo. A fella can't live his whole life dependin' on buddies.

Virgil gives Bo some more advice: he must try to be more gallant, not so rough. Bo blusters: "But a gal oughtta like me. I kin read and write, I'm kinda tidy, and I got good manners, don't I?" Virgil tactfully replies: "I'm no judge, Bo. I'm used to ya." Bo lists his virtues: he's tall, strong, when spruced up he's as good-looking a fellow as a girl might hope to see. The injustice of Cherie's attitude causes him to yell: "Then, hellfire and damnation! Why don't she go back to the ranch with me?"

Cherie and Elma have got round to discussing love. Cherie is worried whether there really *is* the kind of love she has in mind. She's been going with guys, she tells a surprised Elma, ever since she was fourteen. "Down in the Ozarks we don't waste much time. . . ." "But you've never been in love?" queries Elma. "Mebbe I have and din know it. Thass what I mean. Mebbe I don't know what love is. Mebbe I'm expectin' it t'be somethin' it ain't. I jest feel that, regardless how crazy ya are 'bout some guy, ya gotta feel . . . and it's hard to put into words, but . . . ya gotta feel he *respects* ya." The man she marries has to have some regard for her beyond the loving and sex. If she goes back to Kansas City, she'll have nothing much to look forward to, so after a while she'll probably marry some guy whether she thinks she loves him or not. ". . . Who'm I to keep insistin' I should fall in love? You hear all about love when yor a kid, and jest take it for granted that such a thing really exists; mebbe ya have to find out fer yorself it don't. Mebbe everyone's afraid to tell ya." This depresses Elma: "Maybe you're right . . . but I hope not."

With a squirm, Cherie decides it's time to take a chance on the cold powder room, and leaves Elma to Dr. Lyman's ideas on "love." His feeling is: "Maybe we have lost the ability. Maybe man has passed the stage in his evolution wherein love is possible. Maybe life will continue to become so terrifyingly complex that man's anxiety about his mere survival will render him too miserly to give of himself in any true relation." Dr. Lyman, like Virgil, feels: ". . . two people, really in love, must give up something of *themselves.*" "Yes," says Elma, trying to follow. "That is the gift that men are afraid to make. Sometimes they keep it in their bosoms forever, where it withers and dies," Dr. Lyman continues: "Then they never know love, only its facsimiles, which they seek over and over again in meaningless repetition." Having made Elma thoroughly gloomy, Dr. Lyman cheerfully changes the subject to their projected Topeka date, even—in his effusiveness—taking hold of her hand.

Cherie, shivering with cold from the great outdoors, comes in and asks Virgil for another song. This prompts Elma to suggest that they all put on a floor show. "A brilliant idea," seconds Dr. Lyman, "straight from Chaucer."

Everyone but Bo prepares to do something; Bo refuses to make a fool of himself. Cherie will render her "That Old Black Magic," to an accompaniment by Virgil. Dr. Lyman looks forward to playing Romeo opposite Elma's Juliet. Immediately everyone starts making preparations. Dr. Lyman discovers a paperbacked Shakespeare among the books on sale up front by the window, and he and Elma go over their lines together. Virgil and Cherie get together about Cherie's song, and, seeing them, Bo flies into a temper and breaks it up: "Thass my seat," he snarls at Cherie. Cherie jumps to her feet: "You kin have it," she hurls back. Her dressing room is to be behind the counter, so she retires to get into her costume.

Virgil tries to set the jealous Bo straight. He points out to him

that Cherie . . . "was bein' nice to me 'cause I was playin' my
guitar, Bo. Guitar music's kinda tender and girls seem to like it."

Bo—Tender?
VIRGIL—Yah, Bo! Girls like things t'be *tender*.
Bo—They do?
VIRGIL—Sure they do, Bo.
Bo—A fella gets "tender," then someone comes along and makes
a sap outta him.
VIRGIL—Sometimes, Bo, but not always. You just gotta take a
chance.
Bo—Well . . . I allus tried t'be a decent sorta fella, but I don't
know if I'm *tender*.
VIRGIL—I think ya are, Bo. You know how ya feel about deer-
huntin'. Ya never could do it. Ya couldn't any more shoot one a
them sweet li'l deers, with the sad eyes, than ya could jump into
boilin' oil.
Bo—Are you makin' fun of me?
VIRGIL (*impatient with him*)—No, I'm not makin' fun of ya, Bo.
I'm just tryin' to show ya that *you* got a tender side to your nature,
same as anyone else.

Virgil finishes: "Ya got a tender side, Bo, but ya don't know how
to show it."
Unfortunately, wanting to show his tender side to Cherie, Bo tries
to demonstrate it while Virgil is giving the opening performance of
the floor show. Cherie, dressing behind and under the counter,
hushes him: "Be quiet, the show's started." But Bo, in stentorian
tones, insists on saying his piece.

Bo—Cherry, I'm really a very tender person. You jest don't
know. I'm so tenderhearted I don't go deer-huntin'. 'Cause I jest
couldn't kill them "sweet li'l deers with the sad eyes." Ask Virge.
CHERIE—I ain't interested.
Bo—Ya ain't?
CHERIE—No. And furthermore I think you're a louse fer comin'
over here and talkin' while yor friend is tryin' to play the guitar.
Bo—Ya talk like ya thought more a Virge than ya do of me.
CHERIE—Would you go away and lemme alone?
Bo—Cherry, did I tell ya 'bout my color-television set with the
twenty-four-inch screen?
CHERIE—Yes. One million times! Now go 'way.

Having ruined Virgil's performance, Bo doesn't even think to join in the general praise and applause; he just fumes over the reception he got from Cherie.

Elma, as master of ceremonies, announces the next number. She is to play Juliet to Dr. Lyman's Romeo in the Balcony Scene. "The counter," she explains, "is supposed to be a balcony."

Dr. Lyman, with a last swig from his bottle, starts in as if all his speeches were soliloquies, and Juliet just a prop. Elma pluckily says her lines in face of this opposition. But it is Dr. Lyman, riding roughshod over Juliet, who suddenly seems to find a personal meaning in her line:

> ". . . O! be some other name:
> What's . . ."

He breaks in, but falters badly over:

> "I take thee at thy word.
> Call me but love, and—I'll be new baptiz'd;
> Henceforth—I never—will be Romeo."

By the time he reaches: "My name, dear saint, is—*hateful* to myself," he stops cold. Virgil, on a signal from Elma, prompts from the paperback:

> "Because it is an enemy to thee."

Dr. Lyman, oblivious of everything around him, dumbly repeats this as he stumbles back to his counter stool. Elma, uncertain what to do, hovers over him, while from the sidelines Bo loudly gives his opinion of Shakespeare: "Virge, if thass the way to make love . . . I gonna give up."

Once more the M.C. says: "Ladies and gentlemen, our next number is Mademoiselle Cherie, the international chanteuse, direct from the Blue Dragon night club in Kansas City. *Cherie!*" To much applause, Cherie comes forth, gaily throwing her robe to Virgil, and telling Elma: "Remember, I don't allow no table service during my number." To Virgil's accompaniment, and Bo's whistling between his fingers, Cherie hops on a table and begins her Ozark singing of "That Old Black Magic." Bo, in ecstasy, is unable to control himself. At the top of his lungs he makes up his mind to "get that gal": "Anything I ever wanted in this life, I went out and got and I ain't gonna stop now. I'm gonna git her." He gets his face slapped, as an enraged Cherie cries: "You ain't got the manners God gave a monkey." Bo is stunned as Cherie continues in a rage: ". . . and if I was a man, I'd beat the livin' daylights out of ya, and thass what some man's gonna do some day, and when it happens, I hope I'm there to *see*." Leaving behind a numb Bo, she flounces off to her dressing room.

By this time, Dr. Lyman has almost drunk himself into insensibility. Virgil and Elma go to his assistance, leaving the way wide open for Bo. Making a fast glide across the room, he scales the counter in one leap, grabs Cherie in his arms, and carries the screaming, kicking girl to the door on his way to the Justice of the Peace and marriage. Cherie screams: "Help! Sheriff! Help me, someone! Help me!" And suddenly, the door opens, and Will, hand on holster, blocks Bo's progress: "Put her down, Cowboy!" Bo, past taking advice or orders, starts swinging. Will just steps aside, and Bo goes swinging right out the door.

While Will is taking Bo on outside in the snow, Grace comes and joins the girls at the window. She's the only one who enjoys the fight: Elma can't bear to look; Cherie begins to sob. When it's all over, and Will has finished dealing with Bo, Grace retires again. Dr. Lyman chooses this moment to come to life; getting unsteadily to his feet, he announces that ". . . it takes strong men and women to love . . . ," ending with a sigh: "I . . . I never had the generosity to love, to give my own private self to another. . . . I thought the gift would somehow lessen *me*. ME!" He starts for the rear door with a wild laugh: "Romeo! Romeo! I am disgusting." Elma tries to help him, but he stops her: "Don't bother, dear girl. Don't ever bother with a foolish old man like me." He makes a rush for the outdoor rest room, as Grace, who has heard the last of his ramblings, takes Elma aside, to give her a little quiet advice.

Virgil comes in to beg Cherie not to prefer charges against Bo. He promises her that Bo will stay on his good behavior, but she's not easy to convince. Virgil finally has to tell her: "Miss . . . if he was to know I told ya this, he'd never forgive me, but . . . yor the first woman he ever made love to at all." "Hah!" explodes Cherie. "I sure don't believe that." "It's true," says Virgil. "He's allus been as shy as a rabbit." Simply amazed, Cherie cries: "My God!"

Elma has given her promise to Grace that she won't make any dates with Dr. Lyman, who now comes in and heads for the bench to sleep it off. Carl, entering a moment later, yells in disgust: "Grace, fer Christ sake! Who puked all over the backhouse?" "Damn!" Grace answers.

CHERIE (*jumps up suddenly*)—Come on, Virge. Let's go.
VIRGIL—I'm awfully glad you're gonna help him, Miss.

CHERIE—But if you're tellin' me a fib just to get him out of jail, I'll never forgive ya.

VIRGIL—It's no fib, Miss. You're the first gal he ever made love to at all.

CHERIE—Well, I sure ain't never had that honor before. (*She puts on* VIRGIL's *jacket over her "costume" and goes out with him.*)

ACT III

It's five o'clock in the morning, and through the restaurant window a peaceful dawn can be seen creeping over the white hills. The storm has subsided, outdoors and in. Bo, whipped and dejected, broods by himself; Cherie has discovered another movie magazine; the professor hasn't moved an inch. More active are Carl, vainly jiggling the telephone hook, and Virgil, watching over Bo. Elma languidly sweeps up, while Grace, slowly working behind the counter, wishes the bus would leave and they could get to bed. She's tired.

CARL (*returning to counter, he sounds a trifle insinuating*)—Had enough a me, Baby? (GRACE *gives him a look, warning him not to let* ELMA *hear.*) I'm kinda glad the highway was blocked tonight.

GRACE (*coquettishly*)—Y'are?

CARL—Gave us a chance to become kinda acquainted, din it?

GRACE—Kinda!

CARL—Just pullin' in here three times a week, then pullin' out again in twenty minutes, I . . . I allus left . . . just wonderin' what you were like, Grace.

GRACE—I always wondered about *you,* too, Carl!

CARL—Ya did?

GRACE—Yah. But ya needn't go blabbing anything to the other drivers.

Carl's honor is offended. But Grace emphasizes she doesn't want other drivers on this route, ". . . some of 'em especially, gettin' the idea I'm gonna serve 'em any more'n what they order over the counter."

Right now, Carl feels Grace has just about everything; and obviously the feeling is mutual. It takes Will, with his all-seeing eye, to make life matter-of-fact again. He has come not only to report that the highway is once again clear, but to try to straighten things out with Bo. "Cowboy," says Will, "if yor holdin' any grudges against *me,* I think ya oughtta ask yourself what you'd a done in my *place.* I couldn't let ya carry off the li'l lady when she din wanta go, could I?" Bo refuses a reply and has to be reminded that Cherie could have had Will enforce the Mann Act. Virgil adds: "That'd be a serious charge, Bo."

Bo (*stands facing* WILL)—I loved her.
WILL—That don't make any diff'rence.
Bo—A man's gotta right to the things he loves.
WILL—Not unless he deserves 'em, Cowboy.
Bo—I'm a hard-workin' man, I own me my own ranch, I got fifteen thousand dollars in the bank.
WILL—A man don't deserve the things he loves, unless he kin be a little humble about gettin' 'em.
Bo—I ain't gonna get down on my knees and *beg*.
WILL—Bein' humble ain't the same thing as bein' *wretched*.

He has to explain this to Bo by citing his own lesson. Once Will had to learn the same thing, and it wasn't any easier for Will than it now is for Bo.

Bo is very reluctant to carry out his promise to apologize to everyone, and has to be forcibly prodded. He first approaches Grace, then Elma, and doesn't find it too bad. Both women accept his apologies pleasantly. Will waives making him apologize to the prone figure of the professor. But Cherie is another matter. Bo balks badly. Warned by Will that unless he goes through with it, he won't be allowed on the bus, Bo sweats his way to Cherie. Even to say: "Cherry" is a strain for him. "Yah?" she replies. "Cherry," Bo perseveres, "it wasn't right a me to treat ya the way I did, draggin' ya onto the bus, tryin' to make ya marry me whether ya wanted to or not. Ya think ya could ever forgive me?" "I guess I been treated worse in my life," says Cherie graciously. Bo now goes beyond the letter of his promise; he gives Cherie money to get her back to Kansas City, wishing her all good luck. Touched, she wishes him the same, and they part.

Will, in a jovial mood because Bo has acted so handsomely, strolls over to the counter.

WILL—How's your headache, Grace?
GRACE—Huh?
WILL—A while back, you said you had a headache.
GRACE—Oh, I feel fine now, Will.
WILL (*looking at* CARL)—You have a nice walk, Carl?
CARL—Yah. Sure.

WILL—Well, I think ya better go upstairs, 'cause someone took your overshoes and left 'em outside the door to Grace's apartment.

Will, roaring with delight, orders coffee and rolls.

Virgil can't seem to persuade Bo to cheer up, have breakfast, and be happy about going back to the ranch. Bo finds the ranch ". . . the lonesomest damn place I ever did see." He still wants Cherie.

The sudden ring of the phone causes everyone to jump. Grace, answering, tells Carl: "Road's cleared now but you're gonna have to put on your chains 'cause the road's awful slick." "God damn!" Carl exclaims, hustling into his overcoat. "The road's clear, folks!" he calls out. "Be ready to leave as soon as I get the chains on. "That'll take about twenty minutes . . . unless someone wants to help me." Will is agreeable and joins Carl at the door.

Cherie has a confession for Bo; it's something personal and embarrassing. It all boils down to telling him about the numerous men in her life. "Virge'd told me that," admits Bo, "but I wouldn't b'lieve him." "Well, it's true," says Cherie. "So ya see . . . I ain't the kinda gal ya want at all." And she slips back to her table, leaving a silent Bo.

While Dr. Lyman, now revived and cheerful, accepts breakfast— a thing he never *eats*—from Elma, Virgil joins the chain gang outside. Bo takes this opportunity to go over to Cherie with a confession of his own. Since she brought up the subject, he has to tell her she's the *first* girl he ever had anything to do with. This embarrasses him as fully as Cherie's confession did her.

CHERIE—I never woulda guessed it, Bo.

Bo—Ya see . . . I'd lived all my life on a ranch . . . and I guess I din know much about women . . . 'cause they're *diff'rent* from men.

CHERIE—Well, natur'ly.

Bo—Every time I got around one . . . I began to feel kinda scared . . . and I din know how t'act. It was aggravatin'.

CHERIE—Ya wasn't scared with *me*, Bo.

Bo—When I come into that night club place, you was singin' . . . and you smiled at me while you was singin', and winked at me a coupla times. Remember?

He thought this was just for him, and he loved her. Cherie's: "Bo—ya think ya really did love me?" makes him thoroughly indignant. "Why, Cherry! I couldn't be *familiar* . . . with a gal I din love." Cherie, almost in tears, drifts back to her chair.

Carl, announcing: "Bus headed west! All aboard! Next stop Topeka!", heads for Grace and a relaxed farewell. Will gets a hand-shake from Bo, with an admission of no hard feelings, and heads for the door. He accepts Carl's thanks for helping with the chains, then in passing tells Cherie: "Montana's not a bad place, Miss."

A new idea occurs to Bo: he decides to give Cherie a good-by kiss. This she allows if it's different from the kisses in the past. Bo takes gingerly hold of her, and kisses her long and tenderly. Grace, not missing a trick, remarks: "It don't look like he was molestin' her now." At the end of the kiss, Bo rushes wildly to Virgil for a confab.

Helped by breakfast and a sense of doing the "right thing," Dr. Lyman asks Elma to forget the Topeka date. Then, having made this noble gesture, he even considers dropping in at the Menninger Clinic as long as he's in the neighborhood.

DR. LYMAN (*to himself*)—Friends have been hinting for quite a while that I should get psychoanalyzed. (*He chuckles*.) I don't know if they had my best interests at heart or their own.

ELMA—Golly. I don't see anything the matter with you.

DR. LYMAN—Young people never do. Good-by, my dear! You were the loveliest Juliet since Miss Jane Cowl. (*He kisses her hand and goes to get his coat*.)

ELMA—Thank you, Dr. Lyman. I feel it's been an honor to know you. You're the smartest man I've ever met.

DR. LYMAN—The smartest?

ELMA—Really you are.

DR. LYMAN—Oh, yes. I'm terribly smart. Wouldn't it have been nice . . . to be intelligent?

And he makes a chuckling, kiss-throwing exit.

Carl suddenly passes on to Grace what he heard about Dr. Lyman from Kansas City detectives: he had been picked up for loitering around schools. Grace is appalled, and even more so when Carl goes on: ". . . then they checked his record and found he'd been in trouble several times, fer gettin' involved with young girls." "My God!" Grace cries. "Did you tell Will?" Will knew, but since there was nothing on the professor at the moment, he could do noth-ing. Carl changes the subject to take his official farewell. Re-minded by Grace that they'll see each other day after tomorrow, he slaps her on the buttocks, saying: "You might get surprised . . .

what can happen in twenty minutes." Then with an "All aboard,"
he hurries out.

Bo now rushes over to Cherie: "I've been talkin' with my buddy,"
he tells her, "and he thinks I'm virgin enough fer the two of us."
Cherie snickers: "Honest? Did Virgil say that?" "Yah," Bo says,
"and I like ya like ya are, Cherry. So I don't care how ya got that
way." Cherie is deeply touched: "Oh, God, thass the sweetest,
tenderest thing that was ever said to me." And it's a foregone conclusion that Cherie will go anywhere in the world with him now.
This calls for a loud "Yahoo!" and an embrace from Bo. Grace
knew for a fact this would happen. Elma, an equally interested
spectator, didn't.

In the great excitement of getting their things and spreading the
good news, Bo won't at first believe that Virgil isn't coming, too.
"Jest one blame catastrophe after another," says Bo. But Virgil has
made up his mind to let the two be on their own, and holds out
against their joint invitations and coaxing. In desperation, Bo
starts his old game of trying to drag Virgil along with them. Cherie
stops this with the reminder: "Bo . . . ya can't do it that way . . .
ya jest can't . . . if he don't wanta go. Ya can't make him. . . ."
People, she reminds him, have their own reasons. Bo gives in when
Virgil promises to come to the ranch in the summer, and after a final
embrace with his old friend, grabs Cherie and yells: "C'mon, Cherry.
Let's make it fast." Putting his jacket over Cherie's shoulders, he
takes her suitcase and opens the door. "Bye-bye-bye, everyone!
Bye!" calls Cherie. And Virgil, wiping away a furtive tear, is left
behind.

Cleaning up the place, anxious to get some sleep, Grace tells Virgil
the next bus through will be at eight forty-five, to Albuquerque. To
a homeless Virgil, that's as good a place as any. Grace busies herself
with final chores, and with motherly advice to Elma: "Next time any
guy comes in here and starts gettin' fresh," Grace says, "you come
tell your Aunt Grace." Elma guesses she was kind of stupid.
"Everyone has gotta learn, honey," Grace tells her. Then, thinking to order some cheese on Monday, Grace is sorry about Will
Master's kidding in front of Elma: "I didn't want you to know."

ELMA—I don't see why I shouldn't know, Grace. I don't wanta
be a baby forever.

GRACE—Of course you don't. But still, you're a kid, and I don't
wanta set no examples or anything. Do you think you can overlook
it and not think bad of me?

ELMA—Sure, Grace.

GRACE—'Cause I'm a restless sort of woman, and every once in a while I gotta have me a man, just to quiet my nerves.

Elma, able to brush this aside in a grown-up way, remains pleased with her own strange conquest, glad that someone felt that way about her. "You're not gonna have any trouble," Grace tells her. "Just wait till you get to college and start meeting all those cute boys."

Now that the night's work is over, Elma takes a charming farewell of Virgil and goes home. But Grace, wanting to close up, isn't much help to him.

VIRGIL—Any place warm I could stay till eight o'clock?

GRACE—Now that the p'lice station's closed, I don't know where you could go, unless ya wanted to take a chance of wakin' up the man that runs the hotel.

VIRGIL—No—I wouldn't wanta be any trouble.

GRACE—There'll be a bus to Kanz' City in a few minutes. I'll put the sign out and they'll stop.

VIRGIL—No, thanks. No point a goin' back there.

GRACE—Then I'm sorry, Mister, but you're just left out in the cold. (*She carries a can of garbage out the rear door, leaving* VIRGIL *for the moment alone.*)

VIRGIL (*as though to himself*)—Well . . . that's what happens to some people. (*Quietly, he picks up his guitar and goes out.* GRACE *comes back in, locks back door, snaps wall switch, then yawns, stretches, sees to it that the front door is locked. The sun outside is just high enough now to bring a dim light into the restaurant:* GRACE *goes out the rear door and the curtain comes down on an empty stage.*)

CAT ON A HOT TIN ROOF *

A Drama in Three Acts

By Tennessee Williams

[Tennessee Williams *was born 41 years ago in Columbus, Mississippi, as Thomas Lanier Williams. He disliked the name and took Tennessee instead. He graduated from the State University of Iowa and has been a clerk in a shoe company, an elevator operator, a bellhop, a movie usher, a waiter and a teletyper. "Battle of Angels" was his first long play to reach production but did not see Broadway. "The Glass Menagerie" accomplished this as well as winning the Drama Critics Circle Award. In the season of 1947-1948 his "Streetcar Named Desire" won this award and the Pulitzer Prize as well. From his pen we have also had "You Touched Me" (with Donald Windham), "Summer and Smoke," the very successful "The Rose Tattoo" and the very controversial "Camino Real."*]

IN the heat of a summer's evening, Big Daddy Pollitt's family is gathered at his Mississippi Delta plantation to celebrate his birthday.

Off the pillared gallery of the plantation house, up a step, is a bed-sitting room—an airy gallery room with an ornate painted ceiling—whose crowning feature is a modernistic bar. Among the room's other furnishings are a double bed with a wicker headboard, a wicker night table, and a plain flat couch. Near the bar is a louvered door to the bathroom, and through an imaginary door there is an entrance to the hall.

While the Negro handyman and maid rush reinforcements of wine to the dining room, Margaret is heard leaving the dining room in loud disgust. She comes into the bedroom furious with the children who have spotted her pretty white dress with their dropped food. She calls to her husband, who can't hear her through the noise of his shower; so she says over again that the brats have so messed up her dress she has to change it. Brick Pollitt's terry-clothed arm reaches out of the bathroom door and pours a drink, while Brick listens to

* Copyright 1955 by Tennessee Williams. Reprinted by permission of the publisher, New Directions.

why his brother Gooper's children are "no-neck monsters": "Their fat little heads," Margaret explains, "are set on their fat little bodies without a bit of connection."

MARGARET—Hear them? Hear them screaming? I don't know where their voice boxes are located, since they've got no necks. I tell you, I got so nervous at that table tonight, I thought I'd throw back my head and utter a howl you could hear across the Arkansas border. (MARGARET *in her slip flops across the bed on her back. . . . She toys with a palmetto fan that has been lying on the bed.*) I said to your charming sister-in-law, Mae—honey, couldn't you feed those precious little things at a separate table with an oilcloth cover? They make such a mess an' the lace cloth looks so pretty. (*She sits up.*) She made enormous eyes at me and said, "Ohhhh, noooo! On Big Daddy's birthday? Why, he would never forgive me!" (*Flops onto her stomach.*) Well, I want you to know, Big Daddy hasn't been at the table two minutes with those five no-neck monsters slobbering and drooling over their food, before he threw down his fork an' shouted, "Fo' God's sake, Gooper, why don't you put them pigs at a trough in the kitchen?" Well, I swear, I simply could have di-iedd! . . .

Brick, glass in hand, a crutch under his arm, his foot in a plaster cast with steel built-in foot plate, says nothing as he hobbles to the bar for a refill. On and on Margaret goes, ticking off her sister-in-law, describing the children's acting performance in Big Daddy's honor, remarking on her sister-in-law's remarks about Brick and Margaret's childlessness. Margaret says: "Of course it's comical, but it's also disgusting; since it's so obvious what they're up to!" Against the general laughter coming from the dining room, Brick remarks: "What are they up to, Maggie?" "Why, you know what they're up to!" she exclaims, then sitting bolt upright: "I'll tell you what they're up to, boy of mine!—they're up to cutting you out of your father's estate, now that we know Big Daddy's—dyin' of— *cancer.*" Brick wasn't aware they knew. Margaret says she was sure even before today's report confirmed it, and Brick's brother and his wife must also have been sure, otherwise they wouldn't have disrupted their summer plans to bring their whole tribe down here. Margaret says this is the reason they've been making so many references to Silver Hill, the place for treating alcoholics and dope fiends: ". . . and you don't take dope. Otherwise, you're a perfect candidate for Silver Hill, Baby, and that's where they aim to ship you."

Brick silently hobbles to the gallery step, while Margaret continues without a let-up: "Then Brother Man could get a-hold of the purse strings and dole out remittances to us, maybe get power of attorney and sign checks for us and cut off our credit wherever, whenever he wanted! How'd you like that, Baby?" Brick doesn't say, but Margaret piles it on how Brick has done everything to aid and abet this Silver Hill scheme of his brother's: he gave up his job for drink; he careened down the athletic field jumping hurdles at three in the morning; he provided a nice little item for the newspapers: ". . . a human interest story about a well-known former athlete stagin' a one-man track meet on the high school athletic field last night—but was slightly out of condition and didn't clear the first hurdle! Brother Man Gooper claims he exercised his influence t'keep it from goin' out over AP and UP an' every other damn P!" Brick slips onto the gallery as Margaret's words pursue him: he still has one big advantage, she tells him, Big Daddy dotes on him and loathes Brother Man and Brother Man's wife, and tolerates Margaret. . . . "In fact—I sometimes suspect that Big Daddy harbors a little unconscious 'lech' for me."

BRICK—What makes you think Big Daddy has a lech for you, Maggie?

MARGARET (*sliding an ice cube between her breasts as she speaks*) —Why, he always drops his eyes down my body when I'm talkin' to him, drops his eyes to my boobs an' licks his old chops!

BRICK—That kind of talk is disgusting.

MARGARET (*drops ice cube on bar, leans against bar, facing front*) —Did anyone ever tell you that you're an ass-aching Puritan, Brick? I think it's mighty fine that that ole fellow, on the doorstep of death, still takes in my shape with what I think is deserved appreciation!

Margaret next takes in Brother Gooper and wife Mae's purposeful talk about their five children; Brick goes back to the bar. Leaning his crutch against it, never interrupting, only giving Margaret an odd look now and then, Brick rubs dry his hair. Margaret now launches an attack against Gooper's social pretensions, and his thinking he made a fine match in marrying Mae Flynn, when all he got was another social climber like himself. Margaret says: "Of course, Mae Flynn came out in Memphis eight years before I made my debut in Nashville, but I had friends at Ward-Belmont who came from Memphis, and they used to come to see me and I used to go to see them for Christmas an' spring vacations, so I know who rates an'

Tennessee Williams

who doesn't rate in Memphis society. . . ." Brick stands by casually sipping his drink as Margaret does a job on Papa Flynn: he barely escaped the Federal Pen, for his shady manipulations.

Margaret doesn't find envy in her heart for Mae Flynn's being that unforgettable thing, a cotton queen; she has some pretty funny stories about cotton queens. Catching sight of Brick in the mirror, Margaret gasps slightly. He starts to whistle "By the Light of the Silvery Moon." She wheels on him: "Why are you looking at me like that?" "Like what, Maggie?" says Brick, whistling some more.

MARGARET—The way y'were lookin' at me just now befo' I caught
your eye in the mirror and you started t'whistle! I don't know how
to describe it, but it froze my blood! . . . I've caught you lookin'
at me like that so often lately. What are you thinkin' of when you
look at me like that?

BRICK—I wasn't conscious of lookin' at you, Maggie.

MARGARET—Well, I was conscious of it! What were you thinkin'?

BRICK—I don't remember thinkin' of anything, Maggie.

MARGARET—Don't you think I know that—? Don't you think
I—know that—?

BRICK—Know *what*, Maggie?

MARGARET—That I've gone through this—*hideous—transforma-
tion*—become—*hard! Frantic! Cruel!* That's what you've been
observing in me lately. How could y'help but observe it? That's all
right. I'm not thin-skinned any more, can't afford to be thin-
skinned any more. But, Brick—Brick—

BRICK—Did you say something?

MARGARET—I was *goin'* t'say something: that I get lonely. Very!

BRICK—Ev'rybody gets that.

MARGARET—Living alone with someone you love can be lonelier—
than living *entirely* alone!—if the one that y'love doesn't love you.

BRICK (*turns to face her*)—Would you like to live alone, Maggie?

MARGARET (*turning to him*)—*No. God! I wouldn't.*

As Brick lies down on the couch with his drink balanced at his side,
Margaret looks appraisingly at him: to her eyes he's the only drinking man she's ever known who's kept his looks and hasn't run to fat.
Brick, turning away from her, says: "I'm gettin' softer, Maggie."
"Well," answers Margaret, "sooner or later it's bound to soften you
up. It was just beginning to soften up Skipper when—" She stops
short, as Brick sits up and looks at her. "I'm sorry," Margaret
amends. "I never could keep my fingers off a sore. I wish you
would lose your looks. If you did, it would make the martyrdom of
St. Maggie a little more bearable. But no such goddam luck." Sitting on the side of the bed, she marvels at how wonderfully detached
he's always appeared. And, as the voices of men on the croquet
ground drift into the room, Margaret remembers what a wonderful
lover Brick was ". . . and I think mostly because you were really
indifferent to it. Isn't that right? Never had any anxiety about it,
did it naturally, easily, slowly, with absolute confidence and perfect
calm, more like opening a door for a lady, or seating her at a table,
than giving expression to any longing for her. Your indifference
made you wonderful at lovemaking. *Strange*. But . . ." Over the

click of croquet mallets and the voices of the players, Margaret says: "You know, if I thought you would never, never, *never* make love to me again—I would go downstairs to the kitchen and pick out the longest and sharpest knife I could find and stick it straight into my heart. I swear that I would!"

Margaret can't bear Brick's silence, nor will she remain silent about Skipper. ". . . silence about a thing just magnifies it. It grows and festers in silence, becomes malignant. . . ." Nor will Margaret give Brick his crutch; she begs him to lean on her, instead of which he throws off her encircling arms. "I don't want to lean on your shoulder!" he shouts, hurling her away from him. Margaret slides the crutch back along the floor, commenting: "That's the first time I've heard you raise your voice in a long time, Brick. A crack in the wall of composure?" "It just hasn't happened yet, Maggie," says Brick—that "click" he gets after the right amount of liquor.

Margaret begs him not to take another drink until after Big Daddy's birthday party. Brick has forgotten that it is his father's birthday, and having forgotten it, he now won't write a card for a present Margaret bought. He doesn't want to fool Big Daddy. "Just write 'Love, Brick,' for God's sake!" cries Margaret.

As Brick refuses point-blank, Mae Flynn Pollitt, with an archery bow in her hand, stops outside the door to listen. "You've *got* to!" Margaret cries.

BRICK—I don't have to do anything I don't want to do. You keep forgetting the conditions on which I agreed to stay on living with you.

MARGARET—I'm not living with you. We occupy the same cage.

BRICK—You've got to remember the conditions agreed on. (SONNY, *one of* MAE's *children, runs up behind* MAE, *tries to grab the bow from her and says: "Mommy, give it to me, I had it first!"*)

MARGARET—They're impossible conditions.

BRICK—Then why don't you—? (MAE *shoos* SONNY *out, and turns toward the door to the room.* MARGARET *becomes aware of something going on in the hall.*)

MARGARET (*to* BRICK)—*Hush!* (*Turns to the door.*) Who is out there? Is somebody at the door? (MAE *pushes open the imaginary hall door, and sweeps past* MARGARET, *crossing to* BRICK. SONNY *sneaks back into the hall, and drops to his hands and knees behind the bar.*)

MAE (*holding the bow aloft*)—Brick, is this thing yours?

MARGARET—Why, Sister Woman—that's my Diana Trophy. Won it at an intercollegiate archery contest on the Ole Miss campus.

MAE—It's a mighty dangerous thing to leave exposed round a house full of nawmal rid-blooded children attracted t'weapons.

MARGARET—"Nawmal rid-blooded children attracted t'weapons" ought t'be taught to keep their hands off things that don't belong to them.

Taking the bow with her into the bathroom, Margaret hears Mae gushing about the show the children put on for Big Daddy. Coming back into the bedroom, she says: "It breaks my heart that we missed it! But, Mae? Why did you give dawgs' names to all your kiddies?" "Dawgs' names?" shrills Mae. "Dixie an' Trixie an' Buster an' Sonny an' Polly," says Margaret. "Sounds t'me like an animal act in a circus, four dogs and a parrot!" "Maggie, honey," says Mae, facing her squarely, "why are you so catty?"

Brother Gooper, coming for Mae with a drink in his hand, cracks to Brick: "How's your liquor supply holdin' up, buddy?" and takes his wife back to the show. Once more alone, Margaret continues: "I wonder what Dixie's real name is." "Maggie," says Brick, "why are you so catty?" Because, she decides, "I'm consumed with envy and eaten up with longing."

Margaret hopefully lays out Brick's clothes, but he refuses to dress. He finally agrees to pajamas, for which Margaret thanks him.

BRICK—Don't mention it. (*Distantly, the hawk cries twice.* BRICK *looks up, searching for the hawk.*)

MARGARET (*rising, runs to* BRICK, *kneels above him*)—Oh, Brick —Brick, how long does it have t'go on? This punishment? Haven't I done time enough? Haven't I served my term? Can't I apply for a pardon?

BRICK (*holding his crutch behind* MARGARET *in his left hand*)— Maggie, lately your voice always sounds like you'd been running upstairs to warn somebody that the house is on fire!

MARGARET—Well, no wonder, no wonder. Y'know what I feel like, Brick? *I feel all the time like a cat on a hot tin roof!*

BRICK (*rising*)—Then jump off the roof, jump off it. Cats can jump off roofs and land on their four feet uninjured.

MARGARET—Oh, yes!

BRICK—Do it—fo' God's sake, do it!

MARGARET—Do what?

BRICK—Take a lover.

MARGARET—I can't see a man but you! Even with my eyes closed, I just see you! Why don't you get ugly, Brick, why don't you please get fat or ugly or something so I could stand it? (*She embraces his legs.*)

Hearing the children's singing continue, Margaret gets up and locks the door. When Brick asks her why she did that, Margaret says for privacy; and is promptly told not to make a fool of herself.

Big Mama's rasping, loud voice comes through the locked door: she has the most wonderful news about Big Daddy. Not able to tolerate a locked door in her house, Big Mama disappears and pops through the gallery door to the room. Brick has conveniently gone back to the bathroom, so while waiting for him Big Mama carries on a conversation with Margaret at the top of her voice. She all too briefly commiserates with Margaret over the stain on her dress; she very quickly passes over the children's getting it dirty. "So what?" says Big Mama, hanging the dress on a hook behind the door.

MARGARET—You know, Big Mama—that you just don't dare to suggest there's any room for improvement in their—
BIG MAMA (*calls toward bathroom*)—Brick, hurry out!—Shoot, Maggie, you just don't like children.
MARGARET—I do *so* like children! Adore them!—well brought up . . .
BIG MAMA (*gently, loving*)—Well, why don't you have some and bring them up well, then, instead of all the time pickin' on Gooper's an' Mae's?

Hearing Gooper yell for her to come say good-by to some guests, Big Mama brays her good news into the bathroom: they have just received a completely negative report from the Ochsner Clinic, there's nothing wrong with Big Daddy but something called a spastic colon. "Can you hear me, son?" she calls in deafening tones. "He can hear you, Big Mama," Margaret answers for him. "Then why don't he say somethin'? God A'mighty, a piece of news like that should make him shout. It made me shout, I can tell you. I shouted an' sobbed an' fell right down on my knees! Look!" demands Big Mama, hoisting her skirt to display her knees. "See the bruises where I hit my knee caps? Took both doctors to haul me back on my feet!" She laughs, embraces Margaret and rubs Margaret's back briskly. "Big Daddy was furious with me! But ain't that wonderful news? After all the anxiety we been through, to get a report like that on Big Daddy's birthday? Big Daddy tried to hide how much of a load that news took off his mind, but he didn't fool *me*. He was mighty close to cryin' about it *himself!*"

The hullabaloo increases with Sookey, the maid, yowling for Miss Ida to come to the phone, while Gooper yells again for Big Mama, who is loath to leave until she sees how Brick is. The noise continues as Big Mamma yells the good news on the hall phone to deaf kin in Memphis.

Brick, returning for a booster shot, tosses the empty bottle on the bed and retires to the bathroom. Big Mama, having Margaret spell her on the telephone call to Memphis, stays behind looking unhappily around the room and noticing a bottle on the bed where she thinks a second pillow should be. As Margaret returns, Big Mama is tenderly putting back on the bed the pillow Brick had taken to the couch.

BIG MAMA (*pointing at the bottle*)—Don't laugh about it! Some single men stop drinkin' when they git married and others start! Brick never touched liquor until—

MARGARET—*THAT'S NOT FAIR!*

BIG MAMA—Fair or not fair, I want to ask you a question, one question: d'you make Brick happy in bed?

MARGARET—Why don't you ask if he makes *me* happy in bed?

BIG MAMA—Because I know that—

MARGARET—*It works both ways!*

GOOPER (*offstage*)—Come on, Big Mama.

BIG MAMA (*before leaving*)—Something's not right. You're childless, and my son drinks. (*Points to bed.*) When a marriage goes on the rocks, the rocks are *here*, right *here!*

MARGARET—That's—not fair . . . (*Rises, crosses to mirror area, stares at herself.*) Who are you? (*Answering herself, in a small voice.*) I am Maggie the Cat!

BRICK (*from bathroom*)—Has Big Mama gone?

MARGARET—She's gone. (BRICK *reappears, crosses to bar, refills glass.*)

MARGARET (*still at mirror*)—You know, our sex life didn't just peter out in the usual way, it was cut off short, long before the natural time for it to, and it's going to revive again, just as sudden as that. I'm confident of it. . . .

And she is determined to stay attractive until the moment when he sees her as other men see her now. As Brick crosses to the gallery, Margaret calls to him: "Look, Brick! How high my body stays on me!—nothing has fallen on me!—not a fraction! My face looks strained sometimes, but I've kept my figure as well as you've kept yours, and men admire it. I still turn heads on the street. Why, last week in Memphis everywhere I went, men's eyes burned holes in my clothes, at the country club and in restaurants and department stores, there wasn't a man I met or walked by that didn't just eat me up with his eyes and turn around when I passed him and look back at me. Why, at Alice's party for her New York cousins, the best-lookin' man in the crowd followed me upstairs and tried to force his way in!" All she gets from Brick is: she should have let him in the powder room. But Margaret doesn't intend giving Brick any grounds for divorce, even though Brick says he would be mighty relieved if she took a lover. She just intends staying on that hot tin roof as long as she has to.

As Big Daddy, puffing away on a big black cigar, strolls across the lawn, while Big Mama tags along singing to him, Margaret reveals to Brick that the true clinical report showed Big Daddy dying from a hopelessly malignant cancer. Big Mama, who got the false report meant for Big Daddy, will be told by her family after Big Daddy has gone to bed.

This, Big Daddy's last birthday, is being celebrated with everybody jockeying for position in the race for his money. Since there is no will, Gooper and Mae are scheming to cut off the drunken, childless side of the family. And Margaret, sure she can't face old age without money, is already facing an empty present. As Brick pours another drink, she starts in about Skipper, feeling it was a fatal error ever to have told Brick about that thing with Skipper. Brick turns on her, warning her to shut up, that she's fooling with something that nobody should fool with!

As Margaret cries she won't stop no matter what, that the truth has to come out, Brick calls to a child outside the room: "Little girl! Hey, little girl! Tell the folks to come up! Bring everybody upstairs!" Margaret threatens to go on telling the truth in front of everybody, "Because it's got to be told and you, you—you never let me! (*Pause.*) You had one of those beautiful ideal things they tell about in the Greek legends, it couldn't be anything else, you being you, and that's what made it so sad, that's what's so awful, because it was love that never could be carried through to anything satisfying or even talked about plainly."

BRICK—Maggie, you got to stop this!

MARGARET—Brick, I tell you, you got to believe me, Brick. I *do* understand all about it! I—I think it was—*noble!* Can't you tell I'm sincere when I say I respect it? My only point, the only point that I'm makin', is life has got to be allowed to continue even after the *dream* of life is—all over. (BRICK *puts his drink in the wicker seat, rests his crutch across the back of the seat.*)

BRICK—Maggie, you want me to hit you with this crutch? Don't you know that I could kill you with this crutch?

MARGARET—Good Lord, man, d'you think I'd care if you did?

BRICK—One man has one great good true thing in his life. One great good thing which is true! I had friendship with Skipper. You are namin' it dirty!

MARGARET—I'm not namin' it dirty! I'm namin' it clean!

BRICK—Not love with you, Maggie, but friendship with Skipper, and you are namin' it dirty!

MARGARET—Then you haven't been listenin', not understood what I'm sayin'! I'm namin' it so damn clean that it killed poor Skipper! You two had somethin' that had to be kept on ice, yes, incorruptible, yes! and death was the only icebox where you could keep it!

BRICK—I married you, Maggie. Why would I marry you, Maggie—(*Lifts crutch warningly.*) if I was—?

MARGARET—Brick, don't. Let me finish! I know, believe me, I know that it was only Skipper that harbored even any *unconscious* desire for anything not perfectly pure between you two! (BRICK *turns . . . rests crutch on bed, his hands clenched around the shaft of the crutch.*)

Margaret remembers the blissful beginning of their marriage, when both Brick and Skipper turned down wonderful jobs so that they might continue to be football heroes together. Pro-football heroes. But things weren't right: Margaret was between them. Skipper took to drink; Brick landed in the hospital with a spinal injury. At this point Margaret—after a drinking bout with Skipper—said flatly that he should either stop loving her husband or confess it to Brick.

Brick starts ominously striking the bed, as Margaret tells of Skipper's frightened slap across her mouth, then of his pathetic attempt that night to prove he was a man. After Margaret tells of Skipper's failure with her, Brick murderously lunges at her with the blunt end of his crutch. As Margaret runs from him, she admits that her action led to Skipper's dying of drink and drugs, she doesn't even want to whitewash her behavior, but she cries: ". . . *Skipper is dead! I'm alive! Maggie the Cat is alive! I'm alive, alive!*" Brick swings wildly at her, and in swinging crashes to the floor. At the same time Buster, Sonny, Trixie and Dixie rush into the room firing cap pistols. "What's Uncle Brick doin' on the floor?" asks Buster. "I tried to kill your Aunt Maggie, but I failed, and I fell," Brick answers. Handing Brick back his crutch, the children charge

Margaret with a barrage of cap-shooting. Margaret covers her face
with her hands and screams: "Stop! You stop that—you monsters!"
Dixie stays behind the other children to pass along something she's
picked up: "You're jealous," she says to Margaret, "you're just
jealous because you can't have babies!" Then with a simpering look
over her shoulder, she goes away. Brick hobbles to the couch, while
Margaret laughs wildly.

MARGARET—You see? They gloat over us bein' childless, even in
front of their no-neck monsters! Brick, I've been to a doctor in
Memphis. I've been examined, an' there's no reason why we can't
have a child whenever we want one. Are you listenin' to me? Are
you? Are you *LISTENIN' TO ME?*
BRICK (*he has picked up his glass from the wicker seat*)—Yes, I
hear you, Maggie, but how in hell on earth do you imagine that
you're going to have a child by a man that can't stand you?
MARGARET—That's a problem that I will have to work out.

And Margaret wheels toward the hall, to face the approaching
birthday procession.

ACT II

Everyone is assembled in Brick's room for the party. Mae is talking the ear off the local doctor about the various shots her children
receive; Gooper is having a businesslike conversation with the local
minister about church memorials; Big Daddy, full of dislike for
everyone near him, makes it impossible to celebrate his birthday.
When congratulated, he answers: "Crap!" Seeing his wife acting
gay, he yells: *"Big Mama, will you quit horsin'?"* And to the children's rendition of "Happy Birthday" and their unsought encore of
"Skinamarink-a-doo" Big Daddy cries: "Jee-sus!"
The only one Big Daddy wants to see is Brick, who's avoiding
him. Addressing him from the door of the gallery, Big Daddy calls
down what was he doing on the athletic field last night? ". . . Was
it jumpin' or bumpin' that you were doin' out there?" Ignoring Big
Mama's genteel protest, Big Daddy bellows a brutal: *"Quiet!"* Getting back to his original question, he continues: "I ast you, Brick,
if you was cuttin' yourself a piece o' poon-tang last night on that
cinder track." Ignoring Gooper's laugh, he repeats: "I thought
maybe you were chasin' some wild poon-tang—" Mae, so proper,
quickly removes the minister from Big Daddy's line of fire. "B'by,
Preacher," says Big Daddy, turning once more to the subject at hand.
The women, obviously trying to change the subject with talk of

blowing out candles and drinking Big Daddy's health, anger him further: *"I told you to stop it, now stop it, quit this bull!"* he shouts. When Big Mama persists, Big Daddy aims his remarks squarely at her. "I just know you don't mean it," protests Big Mama.

BIG DADDY—Oh, yes, I do, oh, yes, I do mean it! I put up with a whole lot of crap around here because I thought I was dyin'— An' you thought I was dyin' an' you started takin' over; well, you can stop takin' over now, Ida, because I'm not goin' to die, you can just stop this business of takin' over because I'm not dyin'. I went through that laboratory and the exploratory operation and there's nothin' wrong with me but a spastic colon. An' I'm not dyin' of cancer which you thought I was dyin' of. (DR. BAUGH *takes his glass and goes out through the hall door.*) Ain't that so? Didn't you think that I was dyin' of cancer? Ain't that so, Ida? Didn't you have an idea I was dyin' of cancer an' now you could take control of this place an' everything on it? I got that impression, I seemed to get that impression. Your loud voice everywhere, your damn busy ole body buttin' in here an' there! (MAE *and* REVEREND TOOKER *have started in along right gallery toward upper right doors.*)

BIG MAMA—Hush! The Preacher!

BIG DADDY—Rut the Preacher! Did you hear what I said? Rut the cotton-pickin', chicken-eatin', memorial-stained-glass Preacher! (MAE *skillfully turns the* PREACHER *at the doors. . . .*)

BIG MAMA—I never seen you act like this before an' I can't think what's got into you!

BIG DADDY—I went through all that laboratory an' operation an' all just so I would know if you or me was boss here! Well, now it turns out that I am an' you ain't—and that's my birthday present— an' my cake an' champagne—because for three years now you been gradually takin' over. Bossin', talkin', sashayin' your ole butt aroun' this place I made! I made this place! (*Crosses downstage, speaks directly to audience.*) I was overseer on it! I was the overseer on th' old Straw an' Ochello plantation. I quit school at ten! I quit school at ten years old an' went to work like a nigger in th' fields. An' I rose to be overseer of th' Straw an' Ochello plantation. An' ole Straw died an' I was Ochello's partner an' the place got bigger an bigger an' bigger an' bigger! I did all that myself with no goddam help from you, an' now you think that you're just about to take over. Well, I'm just about to tell you that you are not just about to take over, you are not just about to take over a goddam thing. Is that clear to you, Ida? Is that very plain to you now? Is that understood completely? I been through the laboratory from A to Z.

. . . I've had the goddam exploratory operation, an' nothin' is wrong with me but a spastic colon—made spastic, I guess, by all the goddam lies an' liars that I have had to put up with, an' all th' hypocrisy that I have lived with all these forty years that I been livin' with you! Now, blow out the candles on th' birthday cake! Take a deep breath an' blow out th' goddam candles on th' cake!

BIG MAMA—Oh, Big Daddy, in all these years you never believed that I loved you—

BIG DADDY—Huh!

BIG MAMA—And I did, I did so much. I did love you. I even loved your hate an' your hardness, Big Daddy!

Fighting her tears, Big Mama takes the cake out along the gallery, as the field hands now start singing. "Wouldn't it be funny," says Big Daddy to himself, "if that was true?" And dismissing Margaret, he calls Brick to him.

Tonight Big Daddy, out of sheer relief, is on a talking jag. Ordinarily it's hard enough for him to talk directly to Brick; tonight he gets on every subject except the one he primarily wants to talk about. He and Brick agree that in spite of Margaret's having a better shape than Mae, basically the two women are alike. "We married into society, Big Daddy," explains Brick. "Why do both of 'em have that same anxious look?" asks Big Daddy. "Well," says Brick, "they're sittin' in th' middle of a big piece of land, Big Daddy, twenty-eight thousand acres is a big piece of land an' so they're squarin' off on it, each determined to knock off a bigger piece of it than th' other whenever you let go." "I got a surprise for those women," growls Big Daddy. "I'm not goin' to let it go for a long time yet, if that's what they're waitin' for." Mae, eavesdropping on the gallery, hears this and Brick's: "That's right, Big Daddy. You just sit tight an' let 'em scratch each other's eyes out."

Big Daddy, knowing that Mae's been eavesdropping, tears into her the minute she comes into the room. He can't stand spying and sneaking, and her sniffs and tears affect him not one bit as he backs her right out of the room again. "Shut up, shut up, shut up!" Big Daddy yells. "I'm goin' to move you an' Gooper out of that room next to this!! It's none of your goddam business what goes on here at night between Brick an' Maggie. You listen at night like a couple of ruttin' peekhole spies, an' go an' give a report on what you hear to Big Mama an' she comes to me an' says they say such an' such an' so an' so about what they heard goin' on between Brick an' Maggie, an', Jesus, it makes me sick! I'm goin' to move you an' Gooper out of that room. I can't stand sneakin' an' spyin', it makes me *pewk*. . . ."

Alone with Brick, Big Daddy starts in on Brick's drinking. But, not getting Brick's attention, he's off again on what he learned from his European splurge with Big Mama. "You know how much I'm worth?" he asks. "Guess how much I'm worth! Close on ten million in cash an' blue-chip stocks—outside, mind you, of twenty-eight thousand acres of the richest land this side of the Valley Nile! But a man can't buy his life with it, he can't buy back his life when his life has been spent, that's one thing not offered in th' Europe fire sale or in th' American markets or any markets on earth, a man can't buy his life with it, he can't buy back his life with it when his life is finished. . . . That's a sobering thought, a very sobering thought, and that's a thought that I was turning over in my head, over an' over an' over, until today—I'm wiser an' sadder, Brick, for this experience which I just gone through. . . ."

Another thing Big Daddy thinks he learned: "The human animal is a beast that dies, but the fact that he's dyin' don't give him pity for others, no, sir, it—" Brick interrupts his father by going to the bar. Big Daddy, says Brick, can shoot the breeze all he wants because tonight the load is off him, but his son would like to be quiet while he drinks. Communication between people is always difficult, but tonight it's impossible between his father and himself.

But Big Daddy continues to talk about his feelings on mortality, and after a while begins to think of the pleasures of life: a drink, for a starter, then the sky's the limit. "You feel better, Big Daddy?" asks Brick. "Better? Hell! I can breathe! All my life I been like a doubled-up fist—poundin', smashin', drivin'! Now I'm goin' to loosen these doubled-up hands an' touch things *easy* with 'em." What Big Daddy says he's looking forward to now is pleasure with women. At sixty-five he still has desires, and it took death to show him that scruples and conventions about it are a lot of crap. Now he's going to have a ball. That's right, a ball, a ball!" he tells Brick. "Hell, I slept with Big Mama till, let's see, five years ago, till I was sixty an' she was fifty-eight, an' never even liked her, never did!"

This conversation is constantly interrupted by trespassers from gallery to hall, by noisy telephone conversations, by Big Mama's exuberant affections whenever she comes near. Big Daddy's roars as she minces about merely make her gurgle. "All that I asks of that woman," says Big Daddy to the air in front of him, "is that she leave me alone. But she can't admit to herself that she makes me sick. That comes of having slept with her too many years. Should have quit much sooner, but that ole woman, she never got enough of it. An' I was good in bed. I never should have wasted so much of it on her. They say you got just so many an' each one is numbered. Well, I got a few left in me, a few, an' I'm goin' to pick me a good one to spend 'em on. I'm goin' to pick me a choice one. I don't care how much she costs. I'll smother her in minks! I'll strip her naked an' smother her in minks an' choke her with diamonds! I'll strip her naked an' choke her with diamonds an' smother her with minks an' run her from Jackson to Memphis— *non-stop!* Yes, son," he tells Brick, "I'm *happy.* I'm happy, son, I'm happy!"

But death had made Big Daddy blind to his son's plight . . . he had no idea a son of his was turning into an alcoholic right under his nose. He prepares now to do something about it; he's going to straighten Brick out. Brick proves indifferent. Furious, Big Daddy gets tough. As Brick hobbles away from him to the gallery, Big Daddy yanks the crutch from under him, spilling him face down on the gallery catwalk. What's more, Big Daddy won't let him have either crutch or drink till they get this drink business settled. Playing on his father's sympathies, Brick says *"mendacity"* is the cause of his drinking—not one single lie or liar, but a whole tangle of them. He gets his drink as Big Daddy orates: ". . . I could write a book on it an' still not cover the subject! Well, I could, I could write a goddam book on it an' still not cover the subject anywhere near enough! Think of all th' lies I got to put up with! Pretenses! Ain't that mendacity? Havin' to pretend stuff you don't think or feel or have any idea of? Havin', for instance, to act like I care for Big Mama! I haven't been able to stand the sight, sound or smell of that woman for forty years! Church! It bores the bejesus out of me, but I go! I go an' sit there an' listen to that dam'fool preacher! Clubs! Elks! Masons! Rotary! *You* I do like for some reason, did always have some kind of real feelin' for—affection —respect— Yes, always," Big Daddy says with bows in Brick's direction. "I don't know why, but it is! *I've* lived with mendacity! Why can't *you* live with it? Hell, you got to live with it, there's nothin' *else* to live with except mendacity, is there?"

Brick thinks drink does the trick. Listening to this, Big Daddy tells Brick he's been thinking about him: "Should I or should I not, if the jig was up, give you this place when I go? I hate Gooper an' those five screamin' monkeys like parrots in a jungle an' that bitch Mae! Why should I turn over twenty-eight thousand acres of the richest land this side of the Valley Nile to not my kind? But why in hell, on the other hand, Brick, should I subsidize a dam'fool on the bottle? Liked or not liked, well, maybe even—loved! Why should

I do that? Subsidize worthless behavior? Rot? Corruption? An'
this I will tell you frankly. I didn't make up my mind at all on
that question an' still to this day I ain't made out no will! Well,
now I don't *have* to! The pressure is gone. . . . I can just wait
an' see if you pull yourself together or if you don't."

BRICK—That's right, Big Daddy.
BIG DADDY—You sound like you thought I was kiddin'.
BRICK—No, sir, I know you're not kiddin'.
BIG DADDY—But you don't care—?
BRICK—No, sir, I don't care—   (*Crosses to gallery.*)
BIG DADDY—*Wait! Wait, Brick!* Don't let's leave it like this,
like them other talks we've had, we've always—talked around things,
we've—just talked around things like some rotten reason, I don't
know what, it's always like somethin' was left not spoken, somethin'
avoided because neither of us was honest enough with the other—
BRICK—I never lied to you, Big Daddy.
BIG DADDY—Did I ever to *you?*
BRICK—No, sir.
BIG DADDY (*his arm on* BRICK'S *arm*)—Then there is at least two
people that never lied to each other.
BRICK—Yes, sir, but we've never *talked* to each other.
BIG DADDY—We can *now.*

So he gets back to Brick's reason for drinking, and as Brick vaguely
rambles on, Big Daddy bluntly says Brick is passing the buck.

BIG DADDY—Yep, you're passin' the buck, you're passin' the buck
to things like time and disgust with mendacity, an'—crap! If you
got to use that kind of language about a thing it's ninety-proof bull
an' I'm not buyin' any.
BRICK—I had to give you a reason to get a drink.
BIG DADDY—What did you say?
BRICK—I said: I had to give you a reason to get a drink.
BIG DADDY—You started drinkin' when your friend Skipper died!
(*Pause.*)
BRICK—What are you suggestin'?
BIG DADDY—I'm suggestin' nothin'— But Gooper an' Mae sug-
gested that there was somethin' not right, exactly, in your—
BRICK—"Not right"—?
BIG DADDY—Not, well, exactly normal in your—friendship with—
BRICK (*turning back to* BIG DADDY)—They suggested that, too?

I thought that was Maggie's suggestion. Who else's suggestion is it, is it *yours?* How many others thought that Skipper and I were—?

The preacher Tooker—looking for the men's room—barges in on them, and is told to use Big Daddy's bathroom at the end of the gallery.

Big Daddy wants Brick to realize that he's bummed around so much in his day that he can understand anything: "Look, Brick, I can understand anything. Christ! The year I came here, in 1910, I wore my shoes through, hocked my gear, hopped off a yellow dog freight car half a mile down th' road, slep' in a wagon of cotton outside th' gin. Jack Straw an' Peter Ochello took me in, hired me to manage this place, which grew into this one— When Jack Straw died, why, old Peter Ochello quit eatin' like a dog does when its master's dead, an' died, too." "Skipper is dead," cries 'Brick. "I have not quit eatin'!" "No," says Big Daddy, "but you started drinkin'." Brick at last shows emotion: *"You think so, too!* You think so, too? You think me an' Skipper did—did—did—*sodomy*— together?"

As Brick cries that his father is accusing Skipper and him of being a pair of dirty old men, and then of being like Straw and Ochello, he strikes out at Big Daddy, loses his balance, refuses Big Daddy's support and throws himself face down on the bed. Gradually he raises himself, and faces his father: "Big Daddy, you shock me, Big Daddy, you—you—*shock* me! Talkin' so—casually—about a thing —like that. Don't you know how people *feel* about things like that? How, how *disgusted* they are by things like that? Why, at Ole Miss, when it was discovered that a pledge in our fraternity, Skipper's and mine, did a, attempted to do a—unnatural things with—we not only dropped him like a hot rock, we told him to git off the campus, an' he did, he got!—all the way to—"

BIG DADDY—Where?

BRICK—North Africa, last I heard!

BIG DADDY—Well, I have come back from further away than that, I just now returned from the other side of the moon, death's country, son, an' I'm not easy to shock by anything here. Always, anyhow, lived with too much space around me to be infected by th' ideas of other people. One thing you can grow on a big place more important than cotton—is *tolerance!* I grown it.

BRICK (*sitting up, recovering crutch*)—Why can't exceptional friendship, *real, real, deep, deep friendship* between two men be re-

spected as somethin' clean an' decent without bein' thought of as—
fairies!

BIG DADDY—It can, it is, for God's sake. I told Mae an' Gooper—

BRICK—To hell with Mae an' Gooper! (*Rises and crosses down-stage.*) To hell with all dirty lies an' liars! Skipper an' me had a clean, true thing between us, had a clean friendship practically all our lives, till Maggie got the idea you're talkin' about. Normal? No. It was too rare to be normal, any true thing between two people is too rare to be normal. Oh, once in a while he put his hand on my shoulder or I'd put mine on his, oh, maybe even when we were tourin' the country in pro football an' sharin' hotel rooms, we'd reach across the space between th' two beds an' shake hands to say good-night, yeah, one or two times we—

BIG DADDY—Brick, nobody thinks that's not normal!

Birthday fireworks burst over the lawn as Big Daddy prevents Brick from further sidestepping the issue of Skipper's and his own crack-up.

Brick, pinned down, announces they're really going to have that true talk Big Daddy's been wanting, but as he talks against the background of fireworks, his words are like fireworks, too. It's Maggie's tale all over again that Brick tells, only she carries the blame throughout. Maggie forced him into marriage; she made a show of being the world's best sport during the football season, although it was she who poisoned Skipper's mind. It was she who convinced Skipper of . . . "the dirty, false idea that what we were, him an' me, was a frustrated case of that old pair of sisters that lived in this room, Jack Straw an' Peter Ochello! He, poor Skipper, went to bed with Maggie to prove it wasn't true, an' when it didn't work out, he thought it *was* true! Skipper broke in two like a rotten stick—nobody ever turned so fast into a lush—or died of it so quick. Now are you satisfied?" Calmly, judiciously, Big Daddy asks him if *he* is satisfied. Something is left out.

Talking against Gooper's voice on the phone in the hall, Brick admits he has left out a long-distance call from Skipper. Skipper called to make a drunken confession on which Brick hung up. ". . . the last time we spoke to each other in our lives." Big Daddy, outraged that his son had hung up without a word to his friend, bears down.

BIG DADDY—Anyhow, now we have tracked down the lie with which you're disgusted an' which you are drinkin' to kill your disgust with. It wasn't Maggie. Maggie, nothin'! It was you! You been

passin' the buck. This disgust with mendacity is disgust with yourself! You dug the grave of your friend an' kicked him in it!—before you'd face truth with him!

BRICK—*His* truth, not *mine!*

BIG DADDY—His truth, okay, but you wouldn't face it with him!

BRICK—Who can face truth? Can *you?*

BIG DADDY—Now don't start passin' th' rotten buck again, boy!

BRICK—How about these birthday congratulations, these many,
many happy returns of th' day, when ev'rybody but you knows
there won't be any!

Having turned the knife in his father, Brick wants to halt; but
the enormous man, stunned though he is, shouts to his son to finish
what he was saying. Brick tells him to leave all the twenty-eight
thousand acres to Gooper and Mae. Big Daddy blusters he'll out-
live all of them; then asks: "Brick, have they been lyin'? About
the report from th' clinic? Did they—did they find—somethin'?
Cancer—maybe?"

BRICK—Mendacity is a system that we live in. (*The field hands
start to sing.* MAE *and* GOOPER *hurry into lawn area, up right.*)

MAE—Oh, Big Daddy, th' field hands are singin' fo' you!

GOOPER—Field hands singin' fo' you, sir. (*They hurry out.* BIG
DADDY *stands transfixed.* BRICK *hobbles to him.*)

BRICK—I'm sorry, Big Daddy. My head don't work any more.
Maybe it's bein' alive that makes people lie, an' bein' almost *not*
alive makes me sort of accidentally truthful. I don't know, but,
anyway, we've been friends—an' bein' friends is tellin' each other
th' truth. You told *me!* I told *you!* (*He drops his head against
his father's shoulder.*)

BIG DADDY (*shouting, suddenly*)—CHRIST—DAMN—

GOOPER (*managing fireworks display*)—Let—'er—go—! (*Fireworks blaze furiously.*)

BIG DADDY (*as he crosses out to the hall door and down the gal-
lery*)—DAMN ALL—LYIN' SONS OF—LYIN' BITCHES! YES
—ALL LIARS, ALL LIARS, ALL LYIN', DYIN' LIARS! LYIN'
—DYIN'—LIARS! LIARS! LIARS!

ACT III

The moment that Gooper and Mae have been waiting for arrives.
Big Daddy has retired for the night, and Big Mama has been sum-
moned to Brick's room.

Flanked by the family props—Dr. Baugh and the Reverend

Tooker—Gooper and Mae ghoulishly close in on Big Mama. From her wicker chair, Big Mama first begs for Brick, then for some air. "Why are you all surroundin' me," cries Big Mama, "like this?" Brick, alone, remains on the gallery outside this claustrophobic circle.

Mae tells Big Mama to calm herself. "Calm yo'self yo'self, Sister Woman!" Big Mama shouts. "How could I calm myself with everyone starin' at me as if big drops of blood had broken out on m'face? What's this all about?" "Doc Baugh," says Gooper as if addressing a meeting, "Big Mamma wants to know the complete truth about th' report we got from the Ochsner Clinic." Big Mama is close to shrieking, as Dr. Baugh, in flat, clinical tones, tells the results of Big Daddy's tests. As Mae keeps mingily interrupting, Brick, on the gallery, covers his ears and sings "By the light, by the light, of the silvery moon!" He is told to shut up, with the Reverend Tooker adding *"Shh! Shh! Shh!"* to all these interruptions.

DR. BAUGH— . . . But we had this bit of tissue run through the laboratory an' I'm sorry t'say the test was positive on it. It's malignant. (*Pause.*)

BIG MAMA—*Cancer! Cancer!*

MAE—Now, now, Mommy—

GOOPER (*at the same time*)—You had to know, Big Mama.

BIG MAMA—*Why didn't they cut it out of him? Hanh? Hanh?*

DR. BAUGH—Involved too much, Big Mama, too many organs affected.

MAE—Big Mama, the liver's affected, an' so's the kidneys, both. It's gone way past what they call a—

GOOPER— —a surgical risk. (BIG MAMA *gasps.*)

REV. TOOKER—Tch, tch, tch.

DR. BAUGH—Yes, it's gone past the knife.

"That's," says Mae, "why he's turned yellow!"

Pushing Mae away from her, Big Mama cries for Brick, for her "only son." Gooper and Mae don't like being read out of the family like this, and protest. Big Mama shouts: "Gooper never liked Daddy!" Mae shouts back: "That's not true!" Reverend Tooker feels this is the time to go and does.

Big Mama is utterly exhausted, but the Gooper troupe are not yet through. With Dr. Baugh's help, they are ready to start Big Daddy on morphine at the earliest minute. Big Mama's cries of protest are all but ignored.

Dr. Baugh, having done his duty, starts to leave. His parting words are: ". . . keep your chin up, Big Mama." Gooper accompanies the doctor to the hall: "She's goin' to keep her ole chin up, aren't you, Big Mama?" he says, then: "Well, Doc, we sure do appreciate all you've done. I'm tellin' you, we're obligated."

Free for a second from Gooper, Big Mama calls Margaret to her: "Margaret, you've got to co-operate with me an' Big Daddy to straighten Brick out now . . . because it'll break Big Daddy's heart if Brick don't pull himself together an' take hold of things here."

MAE (*overhearing*)—Take hold of what things, Big Mama?

BIG MAMA (*sits in wicker chair,* MARGARET *standing behind chair*) —The place.

GOOPER—Big Mama, you've had a shock.

MAE—Yais, we've all had a shock, but—

GOOPER—Let's be realistic—

MAE—Big Daddy would not, would *never,* be foolish enough to—

GOOPER— —put this place in irresponsible hands!

BIG MAMA—Big Daddy ain't goin' t'put th' place in anybody's hands, Big Daddy is *not* goin' t'die! I want you to git that into your haids, all of you!

MAE—Mommy, Mommy, Big Mama, we're just as hopeful an' aptimistic as you are about Big Daddy's prospects, we have faith in prayer—but nevertheless there are certain matters that have to be discussed an' dealt with because otherwise—

Gooper is now prepared to marshal his forces. The doctor's report was only the opening gun. Libelous and acrimonious family cracks ensue, with the women squaring off, and Margaret protecting Brick and herself from this "deliberate campaign of vilification for the most disgusting and sordid reason on earth, and I know what it is! *It's avarice, avarice, greed, greed!*"

BIG MAMA—Oh, I'll scream, I will scream in a moment unless this stops! Margaret, child, come here, sit next to Big Mama.

MARGARET—Precious Mommy.

MAE—How beautiful, how touchin' this display of devotion! Do you know why she's childless? She's childless because that big, beautiful athlete husband of hers won't go to bed with her, that's why!

GOOPER—You jest won't let me do this the nice way, will yuh? Aw right—I don't give a goddam if Big Daddy likes me or don't like me or did or never did or will or will never! I'm just appealin' to a sense of common decency an' fair play! I'm tellin' you th' truth— I've resented Big Daddy's partiality to Brick ever since the goddam day you were born, son, an' th' way I've been treated, like I was

barely good enough to spit on, an' sometimes not even good enough
for that. Big Daddy is dyin' of cancer an' it's spread all through
him an' it's attacked all his vital organs, includin' the kidneys, an'
right now he is sinkin' into uremia, an' you all know what uremia is,
it's poisonin' of the whole system due to th' failure of th' body to
eliminate its poisons.

MARGARET—Poisons, poisons, venomous thoughts and words!   In
hearts and minds! That's poisons!

GOOPER—I'm askin' for a square deal an', by God, I expect to
get one. But if I don't get one, if there's any peculiar shenanigans
goin' on around here behind my back, well, I'm not a corporation
lawyer for nothin'! I know how to protect my interests.

Hearing the rumble of distant thunder, Brick finally comes in to
avoid the storm, and runs into nasty talk from Gooper and Mae.
As they imitate his limp, and snort that he must have been injured
playing football, thunder rumbles and the winds come up. Mae triumphantly pretends to remember the very game: "The punch bowl,
honey, it was the punch bowl, the cut-glass punch bowl!" "That's
right!" exclaims Gooper. "I'm always gettin' the boy's *bowls* mixed
up!" As—to make his point—he pats Brick on the butt, Margaret
rushes at him, shouting and striking him. Mae goes for Margaret,
and Gooper now has both hands full keeping the women apart.

When things are quieter inside—though outside the storm is roaring—Gooper presents his documents. The minute he got the news
from the clinic, he had the best bankers and lawyers start drawing
him up a plan. He modestly calls this work a preliminary outline,
"But it does provide a basis—a design—a possible, feasible *plan!*"
"It's a plan," Mae adds, "to protect the biggest estate on the Delta
from irresponsibility." Big Mama, using the language she learned
from Big Daddy, tells Gooper to put that thing away before she
gets hold of it and tears it up. Over Gooper's protests, she yells
at him to stow it, she doesn't care what it is called—"Basis! Plan!
Preliminary! Design! I say—what is it that Big Daddy always
says when he's disgusted?" Brick supplies the word. "That's right,"
says Big Mama, "CRAPPP! I say CRAP too, like Big Daddy!"
"Coarse language don't seem called for in this—" says Mae. "Somethin' in me," says Gooper, "is deeply outraged by this. *Nobody's
goin' to nothin'* till Big Daddy lets go of it, and maybe just possibly
not—not even then! No, not even then!"

The children's frightened cries because of the storm make Mae
leave the room, and Gooper has to go look after his car. This leaves
Big Mama alone with Brick and Margaret, to remind her son of Big

Daddy's love for him, and Big Daddy's fondest dream: Brick's child . . . ," a grandson as much like his son as his son is like Big Daddy . . ."

Along the gallery, a seemingly undisturbed Big Daddy now makes his way, joking with the help about the storm. As he approaches, Big Mama hurries from the room so that he won't see her distraught face.

Big Daddy enters the room and effectively blocks Mae's re-entering it. Gooper squeezes past him, in order to get his documents off the bed and out of sight.

BIG DADDY—I heard some mighty loud talk. Sounded like somethin' important was bein' discussed. What was the powwow about?

MAE (*flustered*)—Why—nothin', Big Daddy . . .

BIG DADDY (*taking* MAE *with him*)—What is that pregnant-lookin' envelope you're puttin' back in your brief case, Gooper?

GOOPER (*at foot of bed, caught, as he stuffs papers into envelope*) —That? Nothin, suh—nothin' much of anythin' at all . . .

BIG DADDY—Nothin', huh? Looks like a whole lot of nothin', don't it? Well, I just got one more question to ask. (*Sniffs.*) What is the smell in this room? Don't you notice it, Brick? Don't you notice a powerful and obnoxious odor of mendacity in this room?

Brick plays along, in total agreement, as Mae and Gooper try to hide the brief case. To Big Daddy it smells like *Death.*

Big Daddy next takes notice of his wife's sobbing: "What's wrong with that long, thin woman over there, loaded with diamonds? Hey, what's-your-name, what's the matter with you?" Margaret speaks of Big Mama's dizzy spells, to which Big Daddy says: "You better watch that, Big Mama. A stroke is a bad way to go."

Margaret comes close to Big Daddy and exclaims that he's wearing Brick's cashmere birthday robe . . . "the softest material I have ever felt." "Yeah," says Big Daddy, "this is my soft birthday, Maggie. . . . Not my gold or my silver birthday, but my soft birthday, everything's got to be soft for Big Daddy on this soft birthday." Margaret falls on her knees at Big Daddy's feet, and seeing he's wearing the Chinese slippers that were her birthday present, she now announces her *big* present to him. She announces that she has Brick's child in her body.

Big Daddy lifts Margaret to her feet, then taking a fresh cigar from his bathrobe pocket, bites off the end, looks Margaret over, and makes his own announcement: *"Uh huh, this girl has life in her body, that's no lie!"* His next words are just as decisive: "Gooper, I want my lawyer in the mornin'."

To Brick, Big Daddy says he's off to the belvedere on the roof to survey his kingdom before he gives it up—his twenty-eight thousand acres of the richest land this side of the Valley Nile. Then, with Big Mama cooing endearments at his side, Big Daddy leaves the room and moves majestically down the gallery.

Gooper and Mae have no intention of taking Margaret's birthday present lying down, they promise to fight above or below the belt every inch of the way. As Gooper goes out, he tells Margaret and Brick: "We're jest goin' to wait an' see. Time will tell— Yes, sir, little brother, we're jest goin' to wait an' see."

The clock strikes twelve as Brick feels "the click." Finally, at peace, Brick picks up his pillow and starts for the couch. Maggie seizes the pillow and, as Brick watches her "with growing admiration," throws it back on the bed. Her next move is to sweep the bar free of bottles, hurling them one by one on the lawn; there is to be no more liquor. . . . "I told a lie to Big Daddy," Margaret says, "but we can make that lie come true. And then I'll bring you liquor, and we'll get drunk together, here, tonight, in this place that death has come into! What do you say? What do you say, Baby?" Brick crosses to the bed, and tells her: "I admire you, Maggie." He sits down, looks up at the overhead light, then at Margaret. She reaches for the light, and turns it off, then kneels quickly at Brick's side: "Oh, you weak, beautiful people," she says, "who give up with such grace. What you need is someone to take hold of you—gently, with love, and hand your life back to you, like something gold you let go of—and I can! I'm determined to do it—and nothing's more determined than a cat on a tin roof—is there? Is there, Baby?" And she gently touches his cheek.

INHERIT THE WIND *

A Play in Three Acts

By Jerome Lawrence and Robert E. Lee

[*Though still in their early thirties* Jerome Lawrence *and* Robert E. Lee *form one of America's most prolific and versatile writing teams, having collaborated for Broadway, Hollywood, radio, TV, books, magazines, record albums and Helen Traubel's night-club act. Their musical "Look, Ma, I'm Dancin'" was produced by George Abbott on Broadway in 1948. In radio they have won every major award, including two Peabody Awards and the Variety Showmanship Award. Lee was born in Elyria, Ohio, and attended Ohio Wesleyan where he was an astronomy major. Lawrence was born in Cleveland and is a Phi Beta Kappa graduate of Ohio State.*]

IT is the dawn of a hot July day in the sleepy, obscure town of Hillsboro. The part of Hillsboro visible in the foreground of the stage is the courtroom, beyond and above whose nonexistent walls lie small-town streets converging on the courthouse square.

The square lies in dimness, as Rachel Brown, carrying a suitcase, hurries into the courtroom. Her suitcase contains fresh clothing for Bert Cates, the prisoner of Mr. Meeker the bailiff.

Mr. Meeker, feeling that a prison is hardly a suitable place for a minister's daughter, thoughtfully brings Cates to the courtroom and tactfully leaves the two young people alone.

Almost before she has given Cates his clothing, Rachel bursts out: "Bert, why don't you tell 'em it was all a joke? Tell 'em you didn't mean to break a law, and you won't do it again!"

CATES—I suppose everybody's all steamed up about Brady coming . . .

RACHEL—He's coming in on a special train out of Chattanooga. Pa's going to the station to meet him. Everybody is!

313

CATES—Strike up the band.

RACHEL—Bert, it's still not too late. Why can't you admit you're wrong? If the biggest man in the country—next to the President, maybe—if Matthew Harrison Brady comes here to tell the whole world how wrong you are—

CATES—You still think I did wrong?

RACHEL—Why did you do it?

CATES—You know why I did it. I had the book in my hand, Hunter's Civic Biology. I opened it up, and read my sophomore science class Chapter Seventeen, Darwin's "Origin of Species." (RACHEL *starts to protest*.) All it says is that man wasn't just stuck here like a geranium in a flowerpot; that living comes from a long miracle, it didn't just happen in seven days.

Not only is there a law against such talk, answers Rachel, but everybody says what Bert did was bad. Cates, however, doesn't find things so clear-cut or easy. Rachel, torn between the town's righteous ways and Cates' puzzling ones, embraces him and leaves.

Mr. Meeker returns to lean on his broom and muse: "Imagine Matthew Harrison Brady comin' here. I voted for him for President. Twice. In nineteen hundred, and again in oh-eight. Wasn't old enough to vote for him the first time he ran. But my pa did. I seen him—" he continues, "at a Chautauqua meeting in Chattanooga. The tent poles shook!"

Cates, hardly comforted by this, doesn't know whom the Baltimore paper is sending to represent him. Meeker has only one comment to make about Cates' lawyer: "He better be loud."

After Cates returns to his cell, the courtroom lights fade; in the square the townspeople begin the hot day.

The storekeeper unlocks his store. The Reverend Brown, all scowls, barely manages "good morning" as he checks the banners to welcome Brady and the picnic lunch to feed him. Agog at Brady's imminent arrival, the townspeople look forward to the boom times his presence will bring to Hillsboro. According to one, "Looks like the biggest day for this town since we put up Coxe's army."

The children start selling lemonade, the band is assembled at the decorated station, one hawker is selling hot dogs, another Bibles, when Hornbeck enters the square.

MRS. KREBS—You're a stranger, aren't you, mister? Want a nice clean place to stay?

HORNBECK—I *had* a nice clean place to stay, madam, and I left it to come here.

MRS. KREBS—You're gonna need a room.

HORNBECK—I have a reservation at the Mansion House.

MRS. KREBS—Oh? That's all right, I suppose, for them as *likes* havin' a privy practically in the bedroom.

HORNBECK—The unplumbed and plumbing-less depths! Ahhh, Hillsboro—Heavenly Hillsboro. The Buckle on the Bible Belt. Hallelujah.

HAWKER—Hot dog?

BIBLE MAN—Bible?

HORNBECK—Now, that poses a pretty problem. Which is hungrier? My stomach or my soul? My stomach! (*Buys a hot dog.*)

BIBLE MAN—Are you an evolutionist? An infidel? A sinner?

HORNBECK—Why, of course I am. Isn't everybody? (HORNBECK *sees the organ-grinder's monkey.*) Grandpa! Welcome to Hillsboro, sir. Tell me. Have you come to testify for the defense or for the prosecution? No comment? That's fairly safe. But I warn you, sir—you can't compete with all these monkeyshines!

Thus fortified by a hot dog, Hornbeck is a loud observer of the passing show.

The crowd at the station starts singing "Old-Time Religion" and between shouts of welcome, a bass drum can be heard beating the march, as a lone trumpet carries the melody.

A militant parade bearing banners comes up the street from the station. Surrounded by the banners' slogans: ARE YOU A MAN OR A MONKEY?, DOWN WITH DARWIN, BE A SWEET ANGEL . . . Matthew Harrison Brady makes his appearance. A sixty-five-year-old giant of a man, his balding head under pith sun helmet, his paunch covered by an alpaca jacket, Brady seems equipped with a built-in spotlight that always leaves pretty, proper Mrs. Brady in his shadow. But the nation's perennial "Second Lady" seems not only resigned, but contented.

First removing his helmet, next his coat, Brady thanks the crowd in ringing, humorous tones for this warm welcome. He blesses the fan lady for the gift of a fan, and while vigorously using it says: "My friends of Hillsboro, you know why I have come here. I have not come merely to prosecute a lawbreaker, an arrogant youth who has spoken out against the Revealed Word. I have come because what has happened in a schoolroom of your town has unloosed a wicked attack from the big cities of the North!—an attack upon the law which you have so wisely placed among the statutes of this state. I am here to defend that which is most precious in the hearts of all of us: the Living Truth of the Scriptures!"

Amid much emotional cheering and applause, Brady graciously stands for a photograph, first with the Mayor at his side, then for propriety's sake, with his coat on and with the Reverend Brown on his other side. Through the Governor of the state, the Mayor bestows upon the grateful Brady an honorary colonel's commission. The reception's finishing touch Brady enjoys even more: the Ladies' Aid buffet lunch. "Ahhh," says Brady, surveying the food, "what a handsome repast!" As the ladies beam at his praise, Brady piles mountains of food on his plate.

BRADY—What a challenge it is, to fit on the old armor again! To test the steel of our Truth against the blasphemies of Science! To stand—

MRS. BRADY—Matthew, it's a warm day. Remember, the doctor told you not to overeat.

BRADY—Don't worry, Mother. Just a bite or two. (*He hoists a huge drumstick on his plate, then assails a mountain of potato salad.*) Who among you knows the defendant?—Cates, is that his name?

DAVENPORT—Well, we *all* know him, sir.

MAYOR—Just about everybody in Hillsboro knows everybody else.

BRADY—Can someone tell me—is this fellow Cates a criminal by nature?

RACHEL (*almost involuntarily*)—Bert isn't a criminal. He's good, really. He's just—

Her father steps in to force her to answer any question Brady might want to ask, and Brady, taking Rachel aside, inquires—between enormous mouthfuls of food—all about Cates.

Around the picnic table a discussion arises concerning the identity of the defense attorney. The Mayor, turning to Mrs. Brady, remarks cockily: "Whoever it is, he won't have much of a chance against your husband, Mrs. Brady!" More cocky than any of them, Hornbeck interrupts: "I disagree." He introduces himself as E. K. Hornbeck of the Baltimore *Herald:* "I am a newspaperman bearing news," he broadsides. "When this sovereign state determined to indict the sovereign mind of a less-than-sovereign schoolteacher, my editors decided there was more than a headline here. The Baltimore *Herald*, therefore, is happy to announce that it is sending two representatives to "Heavenly Hillsboro": the most brilliant journalist in America today—myself. And the most agile mind of the Twentieth Century—Henry Drummond." That does it: the name is like a whiplash. All Hillsboro has heard of this man who has successfully defended brutal murderers.

The Reverend Brown remembers Drummond from a courtroom in Ohio, and can still see the "slouching hulk of a man, whose head juts out like an animal's. You look into his face, and you wonder why God made such a man. And then you know that God didn't make him, that he is a creature of the Devil, perhaps even the Devil himself." Thus the Reverend Brown manages to have children crying in their mothers' skirts.

Even Brady, returning with an empty plate, and full of information garnered from a confused and guilty Rachel, pales at his opponent's name. But quickly pulling himself together, he says: "I believe we should welcome Henry Drummond." "Welcome him!" cries the astonished Mayor.

BRADY—If the enemy sends its Goliath into battle, it magnifies our cause. Henry Drummond has stalked the courtrooms of this land for forty years. Where he fights, headlines follow. (*With growing fervor.*) The whole world will be watching our victory over Drummond. (*Dramatically.*) If St. George had slain a dragon-fly, who would remember him? (*Cheers and pleased reaction from the people.*)

MRS. BLAIR—Would you care to finish off the pickled apricots, Mr. Brady? (BRADY *takes them.*)

BRADY—It would be a pity to see them go to waste.

MRS. BRADY—Matt, do you think—?

BRADY—Have to build up my strength, Mother, for the battle ahead. (*Munching thoughtfully.*) Now, what will Drummond do? He'll try to make us forget the lawbreaker and put the law on trial. (*He turns to* RACHEL.) But we'll have the *answer* for Mr. Drummond. Right here, in some of the things this sweet young lady has told me.

After a toast, in "good American lemonade," to the success of their cause, and after he has offered flowery thanks to everyone, particularly the Ladies' Aid for their nice little picnic repast . . . "And if I seemed to pick at my food," he tells them, "I don't want you to think I didn't enjoy it—but, you see, we had a box lunch on the train" . . . accompanied by the singing crowd, the Bradys cross the square to Hillsboro's one hotel.

That night in the courtroom Hornbeck, munching on an apple, is inspecting tomorrow's scene of battle. When Rachel rushes in to see Cates, Hornbeck, with reporter's license and his own form of brass, asks what her relationship is to Cates. At first the over-wrought girl ignores him, but then when he hauls out and hands her a tear sheet of an article he has written, she is surprised to find someone friendly to Cates.

Puzzled, Rachel says to Hornbeck: "You don't seem like the kind of person who'd write an article like this— You seem too—"

HORNBECK—Cynical? That's my fascination. I do hateful things for which people love me, and lovable things for which they hate me. I am a friend of enemies, the enemy of friends. I am admired for my detestability. I am both Poles and Equator, with no Temperate Zones between.

RACHEL (*looking up from the copy*)—You make it sound as if Bert is a hero. I'd like to think that, but I can't. A schoolteacher is a public servant: I think he should do what the law and the school board want him to. If the superintendent says, "Miss Brown, you're to teach from Whitley's Second Reader," why, I don't feel I have to give him an argument.

HORNBECK—Ever give your pupils a snap-quiz on existence?

RACHEL—What?

HORNBECK—Where we came from, where we are, where we're going?

RACHEL—All the answers to those questions are in the Bible.

HORNBECK (*with genuine incredulity*)—*All?!* You feed the youth of Hillsboro from the little truck garden of your mind?

RACHEL—I think there must be something wrong in what Bert believes, if a great man like Mr. Brady comes here to speak out against him.

HORNBECK—Matthew Harrison Brady came here to find himself a stump to shout from. That's all.

RACHEL—You couldn't understand. Mr. Brady is the champion of the ordinary people, like us.

HORNBECK—Wake up, Sleeping Beauty. The ordinary people played a dirty trick on Colonel Brady. They ceased to exist. (RACHEL *looks puzzled.*) Time was when Colonel Brady was the hero of the hinterlands. Water boy for the great unwashed. But they've got inside plumbing in their heads these days. There's a highway through the backwoods now; and the trees of the forest have reluctantly made room for their leafless cousins, the telephone poles. Henry's Lizzie rattles into town, and leaves behind the Yesterday-Messiah—standing in the road alone, in a cloud of flivver dust. (*He laughs a little, at the picture he has drawn.*) The boob has been de-boobed! Colonel Brady's virginal small-towner has been *had*—by Marconi and Montgomery Ward. . . .

The courtroom fades into darkness as Hornbeck, finishing his apple, strolls up to the courthouse square. There in the hot redness of the sunset, the storekeeper is closing his store for the night; the organ-grinder and his monkey are making their last tour of the square, and a child is giving the monkey its last penny. Silent and motionless, Hornbeck stands by watching. As the faces of the buildings become intensely red in the last blaze of the sun, a long, ominous shadow falls across them—a shadow cast by Drummond's approaching figure. Hunched over, head jutting forward, valise in hand, Drummond trudges up the road. His shadowed face so scares the child that she runs off shrieking: "It's the Devil!"

Hornbeck crosses slowly to Drummond's side. "Hello, Devil," he says, shaking hands. "Welcome to Hell."

Scene II

It is a few days later, and jurors for Cates' trial are being chosen. The man currently being questioned is perfectly acceptable to Drummond: he hasn't heard of Darwin, he doesn't read the Bible; in fact, he doesn't know how to read. After the juror's triumphant dash for his seat in the box, Brady has a suggestion. Since it is ninety-seven degrees in the courtroom and bound to get hotter, Brady feels they should remove their "superfluous outer garments." Drummond tells the Judge: "I don't know if the dignity of the court can be upheld with these galluses I've got on." When he takes off his coat, the crowd's reaction to his bright-red suspenders shows what he means. Ever so affably Brady asks: "Is the counsel for the defense showing the latest fashion in the great metropolitan city of Chicago?" Ever so pleased, Drummond answers: "Glad you asked me that. I brought these along special." Cocking his thumbs in the suspenders, he finishes: "Just so happens I bought these galluses at Peabody's general store in your home town, Mr. Brady. Weeping Water, Nebraska." As he gets his laugh, he jauntily snaps the suspenders. Mr. Brady is no longer affable.

The next prospective juror not only believes in the Holy Word of God, but in Matthew Harrison Brady. Drummond, without asking him a question, turns thumbs down.

BRADY (*annoyed*)—Does Mr. Drummond refuse this man a place on the jury simply because he believes in the Bible?

DRUMMOND—If you find an evolutionist in this town, you can refuse him!

BRADY—I object to the defense attorney rejecting a worthy citizen without so much as asking him a question!

DRUMMOND (*agreeably*)—All right. I'll ask him a question. (*Saunters over to* DUNLAP.) How are you?

DUNLAP (*surprised*)—Kinda hot.

DRUMMOND—So am I. Excused.

Brady now objects to Drummond's levity. Drummond objects to the bench's addressing Brady as "Colonel"; he's not aware, he says, that Mr. Brady has a military record. He further advises the bench to break Brady—make him a private.

Deeply disturbed at this turn of events, the Mayor feels it necessary to appoint Drummond a "temporary honorary colonel." Drummond orates: "Gentlemen, what can I say? It is not often in a man's life that he attains the exalted rank of 'Temporary Honorary Colonel.' "

The two colonels then get back to picking the jury. Mr. Sillers, their next candidate, is not so easy to place as the first two were. Brady finds him suitable, and accepts him. When Drummond proves that Sillers lets his wife handle all religion for the two of them, while Sillers works at his feed store, Brady changes his mind. Drummond says: "This man is all right. Take a box seat, Mr. Sillers." Now Brady won't have Sillers, and Drummond claims that he's out of order. . . . "The prosecution has already accepted this man." With that, wrangling among all the attorneys becomes hot and heavy. Brady wants the jurors to conform "to the laws and patterns of society." Conformity is just what Drummond objects to.

DRUMMOND—All I want is to prevent the clock-stoppers from dumping a load of medieval nonsense into the United States Constitution.

JUDGE—This is not a federal court.

DRUMMOND (*slapping his hand on the table*)—Well, dammit, you've got to stop 'em somewhere.

Pounding his gavel, the Judge rules both Brady and Drummond out of order. Then, because of the heat and the lateness of the hour, he orders the court recessed. But, adds the Judge: "The Reverend Brown has asked me to make this announcement. There will be a prayer meeting tonight on the courthouse lawn . . . to pray for justice and guidance. All are invited." Drummond now objects louder than ever. He objects to this plug for Reverend Brown's product and to Reverend Brown's courtroom banner: "Read Your Bible." He demands equal billing for evolution and Darwin. The Judge finds this preposterous, finds Drummond out of order, and adjourns the court.

Brady and his crowd of admirers make their slow, confident way from the room, leaving an ostracized group consisting of Drummond and the frightened young couple, Rachel and Cates. As Drummond puts papers in his brief case, he hears Rachel suddenly begging him to call the whole thing off, to have Cates admit that he's wrong and apologize.

Drummond, kindness itself, listens to the distraught girl. He listens to bewildered Cates, who never imagined it was going to be like this, worse than if he had committed murder.

CATES—People I thought were my friends look at me now as if I had horns growing out of my head.

DRUMMOND—You murder a wife, it isn't nearly as bad as murdering an old wives' tale. Kill one of their fairy-tale notions, and they call down the wrath of God, Brady, and the state legislature.

RACHEL—You make a joke out of everything. You seem to think it's so funny!

DRUMMOND—Lady, when you lose your power to laugh, you lose your power to think straight.

CATES—Mr. Drummond, I can't laugh. I'm scared.

DRUMMOND—Good. You'd be a damned fool if you weren't.

Rachel points out bitterly that every time Drummond swears he hurts Cates' cause, that he only seems to want to make speeches against the Bible, that he doesn't care about Cates. "Well, I care about what the people in this town think of *him*," she says. "Can you buy back his respectability by making him a coward?" asks Drummond. He understands what Cates is going through. . . . "It's the loneliest feeling in the world—to find yourself standing up when everybody else is sitting down. To have everybody look at you and say, 'What's the matter with him?' I know what it feels like. Walking down an empty street, listening to the sound of your own footsteps. Shutters closed, blinds drawn, doors locked against you. And you aren't sure whether you're walking toward something—or if you're just walking away. . . . Cates, I'll change your plea and we'll call off the whole business—on one condition. If you honestly believe that you're wrong and the law's right. Then the hell with it. I'll pack my grip and go back to Chicago, where it's a cool hundred in the shade."

Cates asks Drummond what he himself thinks. His presence in Hillsboro is Drummond's answer. Cates then quietly determines not to quit. It is now that Rachel confesses between her tears what terrifies her: Brady is using her testimony to convict Cates.

Cates becomes panicky; before he goes back to the jail he begs Rachel not to tell what he had told her in privacy. "Don't you understand? The words I've said to you—softly, in the dark— just trying to figure out what the stars are for—or what might be on the back side of the moon—" Over the bailiff's interruption he cries: "They were questions, Rachel. I was just asking questions! If you repeat those things on the witness stand, Brady'll make 'em sound like answers. And they'll crucify me!"

Cates goes back to his cell with Meeker, as Rachel numbly stands by. Drummond takes her gently in hand—first finding out her name, then telling her not to be afraid of Brady. . . . "He only *seems* to be bigger than the law." He discovers that it's not Brady Rachel is afraid of; it's her father. The motherless girl has been always frightened to death of the Reverend Brown. "Is it true?" she asks. "Is Bert wicked?"

DRUMMOND (*looking* RACHEL *directly in the face*)—Bert Cates is a good man. Maybe even a great one. And it takes strength for a woman to love such a man. Especially when he's a pariah in the community.

RACHEL—I'm only confusing Bert. And he's confused enough as it is.

DRUMMOND—The man who has everything figured out is probably a fool. College examinations notwithstanding, it takes a very smart fella to say, "I don't know the answer!" (DRUMMOND *puts on his hat, touches the brim of it as a gesture of good-by, and goes slowly off.*)

ACT II

SCENE I

In the courthouse square that night, surrounded by reporters from all over the world, Brady upbraids Hornbeck for his "biased reporting." "I'm no reporter, Colonel," snaps Hornbeck, "I'm a critic." Brady hopes for Hornbeck's attendance at tonight's prayer meeting; it may prove a source of enlightenment. Hornbeck wouldn't miss it for anything. While the crowd assembles beneath the platform that workmen have constructed, the Reverend Brown leads Brady up the steps. Both men are more than comfortable on these planks: this is their second home.

With all the tricks of an old-school movie actor, Reverend Brown clutches the rail, peers down into the upturned faces and starts the show: "Brothers and sisters, I come to you on the Wings of the Word—The Wings of the Word are beating loud in the treetops! The Lord's Word is howling in the wind, and flashing in the belly of the cloud!

WOMAN—I hear it!
MAN—I see it, Reverend!
BROWN—And we *believe* the Word!
ALL—We believe!
BROWN—We believe the Glory of the Word!
ALL—Glory, Glory! Amen, amen!

The Reverend Brown leads his whipped-up audience through the first five days of the Creation, to the troubles of the Lord on the sixth day, the morning of the sixth day . . .

BROWN (*dropping his voice almost to a whisper*)—He looked about Him, did the Lord; at all His handiwork, bowed down before Him. And He said, "It is not good, it is not enough, it is not finished. I . . . shall . . . make . . . Me . . . a . . . *man!*" (*The crowd bursts into an orgy of hosannahs and waving arms.*)
ALL—Glory! Hosannah! Bless the Lord who created us!
WOMAN (*shouting out*)—Bow down! Bow down before the Lord!
MAN—Are we good, Lord? Tell us? Are we good?
BROWN (*answering*)—The Lord said, "Yea, thou art good! For I have created ye in My Image, after My Likeness! Be fruitful, and multiply, and replenish the earth, and subdue it!"

He whips them further into shouting that they believe the Word, the Truth of the Word, and curse the man who denies the Word. "Do we cast out this sinner in our midst?" Brown shouts. "Yes!" they cry. Rachel is battered and shaken by the sounds of the crowd's responses. Her father asks: "Do we call down hell-fire on the man who has sinned against the Word?" "Yes!" roars his crowd. Now deliberately breaking the rhythm, Brown prays to the heavens for a sign to strike down this sinner as in the days of old. . . . "Let him feel the terror of Thy sword! For all eternity, let his soul writhe in anguish and damnation—" "No!" screams

Rachel, rushing to the platform. "No, father! Don't pray to destroy Bert!" Brown answers with: "Lord, we call down the same curse on those who ask grace for this sinner—though they be blood of my blood, and flesh of my flesh!" This is too much, even for Brady, who comes forward: "Reverend Brown, I know it is the great zeal of your faith which makes you utter this prayer! But it is possible to be overzealous, to destroy that which you hope to save—so that nothing is left but emptiness." Brown turns. "Remember," Brady says, "the wisdom of Solomon in the Book of Proverbs—(*Softly.*) He that troubleth his own house . . . shall inherit the wind." He leads Brown to a chair, reminding the crowd: "The Bible also tells us that God forgives His children. And we, the children of God, should forgive each other." With his blessing, he dismisses the townspeople.

The singing crowds having departed, Brady crosses the square to Drummond, the lonely, ever-watchful spectator. "We were good friends once," Brady says to him. "I was always glad of your support. What happened between us? There used to be a mutuality of understanding and admiration. Why is it, my old friend, that you have moved so far away from me?" They study each other. "All motion is relative," Drummond says slowly. "Perhaps it is *you* who have moved away—by standing still."

SCENE II

Two days later, Brady has Howard, an uncomfortable thirteen-year-old pupil of Cates', on the stand. Establishing the fact that Cates made no reference to Genesis in his teaching the world's beginnings, "Ladies and gentlemen," says Brady with an oversized gesture . . .

DRUMMOND—Objection! I ask that the court remind the learned counsel that this is not a Chautauqua tent. He is supposed to be submitting evidence to a jury. There are no ladies on the jury.

BRADY—Your Honor, I have no intention of making a speech. There is no need. I am sure that everyone on the jury, everyone within the sound of this boy's voice, is moved by his tragic confusion. He has been taught that he wriggled up like an animal from the filth and the muck below! (*Continuing fervently, the spirit is upon him.*) I say that these Bible-haters, these "*E*vil-utionists," are brewers of poison. And the legislature of this sovereign state has had the wisdom to demand that the peddlers of poison—in bottles or in books—clearly label the products they attempt to sell!

(*There is applause.* HOWARD *gulps.* BRADY *points at the boy.*) I
tell you, if this law is not upheld, this boy will become one of a
generation shorn of its faith by the teachings of Godless science!
But if the full penalty of the law is meted out to Bertram Cates, the
faithful the whole world over, who are watching us here and listening to our every word, will call this courtroom blessed! (*Applause.*
Dramatically, BRADY *moves to his chair. Condescendingly, he mut-*
ters:) Your witness, sir.

DRUMMOND (*rises, slouches toward the witness stand*)—Well, I
sure am glad Colonel Brady didn't make a speech!

Drummond's humor falls flat. But he continues in a relaxed and
amiable fashion to talk to Howard, wishing to establish over the
objections of Prosecutor Davenport that Howard has a right to
think, that the teachings of Cates didn't hurt Howard in any way,
physically or morally. Brady cries: "Ask him if his Holy Faith in
the scriptures has been shattered." "When I need your valuable
help, Colonel," replies Drummond, "you may rest assured I shall
humbly ask for it." Then he asks Howard: "Do you believe everything Mr. Cates told you?" Howard isn't sure. "I gotta think it
over," he says. "Good for you," says Drummond.

Noting that Howard's father is a farmer with a new tractor,
Drummond now asks Howard if he figures the tractor's "sinful"
because it's not mentioned in the Bible; or if the telephone's an
instrument of the Devil? "I never thought of it that way," replies the boy. "Neither did anybody else," booms Brady. "Your
Honor, the defense makes the same old error of all Godless men!
They confuse material things with the great spiritual realities of
the Revealed Word! Why do you bewilder this child?" he asks
Drummond. "Does right have no meaning for you, sir?" Slowly,
after a long, thoughtful pause, Drummond answers in a low voice:
"Realizing that I may prejudice the case of my client, I must say
that 'right' has no meaning to me whatsoever!" Over the buzz of
the courtroom, Drummond says: "Truth has meaning—as a direction. But one of the peculiar imbecilities of our time is the
grid of morality we have placed on human behavior: so that every
act of man must be measured against an arbitrary latitude of right
and longitude of wrong—in exact minutes, seconds, and degrees!
Do you have any idea what I'm talking about, Howard?" "No,
sir," says Howard, and is benevolently excused by Drummond.

Davenport calls the next witness for the prosecution, Rachel
Brown. Looking to neither right nor left, wanting to get it over
with as quickly as possible, Rachel hurries to the stand. Brady,

now with exaggerated gentleness, takes her on. First, he wishes to know if Bert Cates and Rachel still attend the same church, and if Cates dropped out, why? Rachel tells Cates' reason for no longer attending: One of his favorite pupils drowned. At the child's funeral, Reverend Brown said that this fine eleven-year-old, being unbaptized, had not died in a state of grace. Cates leaps to his feet, shouting: "Tell 'em what your father really said! That Tommy's soul was damned, writhing in hell-fire!" A juror yells: "Cates, you sinner!" Cates cries out: "Religion's supposed to comfort people, isn't it? Not frighten them to death!" Drummond pushes Cates back into his seat, requesting that his remarks be stricken from the record. "But how," says Brady, "can we strike this young man's bigoted opinions from the memory of this community?" Then turning, all set to play his trump card, Brady says: "Now, my dear. Will you tell the jury some more of Mr. Cates' opinions on the subject of religion?"

Over Drummond's objections to this hearsay testimony, Rachel is told to continue. This she finds nearly impossible to do. The Judge reminds her she is testifying under oath. Brady prompts her to describe her innermost feelings when Bert Cates said to her: "God did not create man! Man created God!" Hemmed in by the crowd's loud reactions and by Drummond's loud objections, Rachel blurts out: "Bert didn't say that. He was just joking. What he said was: 'God created man in his own image—and man, being a gentleman, returned the compliment.'" Laughing uproariously, Hornbeck ostentatiously writes this down.

Brady, too, is pleased; and goes on to question Rachel about Bert's comments on the holy state of matrimony, and whether he had compared it with the breeding of animals. Close to collapse, Rachel is unable to say another word. Brady excuses her from the stand over the loud objections of Drummond, who wants to cross-examine her. Cates, distressed at Rachel's condition, tells Drummond to let her go, which he reluctantly does. After Rachel steps down, the prosecution intends calling no further witnesses; the Judge instructs the defense to proceed with its case.

But the defense has nowhere to go. Drummond calls one after another of the experts he has brought to testify in Bert Cates' behalf, but Brady objects to each and every one of them. He turns down the head of the Department of Zoology at the University of Chicago; he won't let agnostic scientists use this courtroom for their heresies. But he also turns down a deacon of the Congregationalist Church, who happens to be professor of geology and archaeology at Oberlin. Drummond next calls one of the most brilliant minds in the world, a famous anthropologist and author. Brady smugly objects.

Drummond tells the bench that these noted scientists' testimony is basic to the prisoner's defense—that, far from being a crime, what Bert Cates quietly told his class is accepted in enlightened communities everywhere. "In this community," states the Judge, "the opposite is true. Therefore, no experts are needed to question the validity of a law already on the books." "In other words," scowls Drummond, "the court rules out any expert testimony on Charles Darwin's 'Origin of Species' or 'Descent of Man'?" The court so rules.

Flabbergasted, Drummond for a single moment is helpless; but the next minute he has a gleam in his eye—and the possibility of an acceptable witness who can give expert testimony on the Holy Bible. This time Brady handsomely makes no objection to such a man. "Good," says Drummond, and with relish announces, "I call to the stand one of the world's foremost experts on the Bible and its teachings—Matthew Harrison Brady."

The spectators break loose; the prosecutor objects; the Judge is confused. Over the prosecutor's worried protests, Brady grandly says he will take the stand. Whereupon the Judge, rapping for order, says: "The court will support you if you wish to decline to testify—as a witness against your own case. . . ." Brady, with magnificent conviction, retorts: "Your Honor, I shall not testify *against* anything. I shall speak out, as I have all my life—on behalf of the Living Truth of the Holy Scriptures!"

The giant of a man is sworn in, and on preliminary questioning modestly admits to being an expert on the Bible. When, however, Drummond assumes that Brady has memorized nothing from Darwin, Brady answers that since he is wholly uninterested in the pagan hypothesis of the *Origin of Species*, he has never read and never will read the book. Drummond loudly demands how Brady can wage a Holy War against something he knows nothing about. Davenport, scenting a ruse to admit Darwin into the testimony, objects. The Judge, in full agreement, orders Drummond to confine his questions to the Bible.

With an air of finality, Drummond snaps shut his volume of Darwin, and gets a Bible from the bailiff. Now playing in Brady's "ball park," he thumbs through the Bible while play-acting and lightly wisecracking. He feels his way from Jonah to Joshua—from "the big fish" of the Bible to the sun's standing still. Brady lets "faith" and God take care of his answers on the solar system and all questions of natural law: "Natural law," answers Brady calmly and patiently, "was born in the mind of the Heavenly Father. He can change it, cancel it, use it as He pleases. It constantly amazes me that you apostles of science, for all your supposed wisdom, fail to grasp this simple fact."

Still thumbing through the Bible, Drummond stops to inquire about Cain's wife—where in the world did she come from?

DRUMMOND—Mrs. Cain. Cain's wife. If, "In the beginning" there was only Adam and Eve, and Cain and Abel, where'd this extra woman spring from? Ever figure that out?

BRADY (*cool*)—No, sir. I will leave the agnostics to hunt for her. (*Laughter.*)

DRUMMOND—Never bothered you?

BRADY—Never bothered me.

The Bible satisfies Mr. Brady. "It frightens me to imagine the state of learning in this world if everyone had your driving curiosity," says Drummond, passing on to all the "begats" at the beginning of the Bible. ". . . and Arphaxad begat Salah; and Salah begat Eber—" These, says Brady, are the generations of holy men and women of the Bible. How, wonders Drummond, did they go about all this begatting? About the same way as today? Brady gets a fine laugh with: "The process is about the same. I don't think your scientists have improved it any." Drummond then calls begatting the biological function known as *sex*, and asks Brady what he, not as a father, or as a husband, or as a Presidential candidate thinks of it, but as a Biblical expert. Brady names it "Original Sin"; Drummond narrowly asks him if this made the holy men and women then less holy, and for answer gets a scowl from Brady; an interruption from the prosecutor, who would like to know how this bears on the case; and a request from the court to justify this line of questioning. Drummond gives a fiery answer: "You've ruled out all my witnesses. I must be allowed to examine the one witness you've left me in my own way!" With great dignity, Brady tells the court that he is willing to endure Mr. Drummond's contempt for all that is holy, because he is simultaneously pleading the case of the prosecution. Drummond shouts his objections: something *is* holy to Drummond. The individual human mind is what he holds most sacred. And he passionately sings the praise of reason, and the advance of man's knowledge. He also acknowledges the lovely things one loses with every step of progress: when Darwin moved us forward to a hilltop, from

Paul Muni in "Inherit the Wind"

where we could see the way we had come, we had to abandon our faith in the pleasant poetry of Genesis. Brady shouts: "We must *not* abandon faith. Faith is the important thing!"

But then why did God plague us with the power to think? Drummond asks Brady. "Why do you deny the *one* faculty which lifts man above all other creatures on the earth: the power of his brain to reason? What other merit have we? The elephant is larger, the horse is stronger and swifter, the butterfly more beautiful, the mosquito more prolific, even the simple sponge is more durable! (*Wheeling on* BRADY.) Or does a *sponge* think?

BRADY—I don't know. I'm a man, not a sponge. (*There are a few snickers at this; but the crowd seems to be slipping away from* BRADY *and aligning itself more and more with* DRUMMOND.)

DRUMMOND—Do you think a sponge thinks?

BRADY—If the Lord wishes a sponge to think, it thinks.

DRUMMOND—Does a man have the same privileges that a sponge does?

BRADY—Of course.

DRUMMOND (*roaring for the first time: stretching his arm toward* CATES)—This man wishes to be accorded the same privilege as a sponge! *He wishes to think!*

The applause that greets this is as a slap to Brady, who cries out that Cates is a deluded man, he's wrong. Drummond says: "It's sad that we aren't all gifted with your positive knowledge of right and wrong, Mr. Brady."

Introducing a rock covered with fossils of prehistoric marine creatures, Drummond says that his uncalled witness, Dr. Page of Oberlin, believes this rock is at least ten million years old, that these creatures were in this county when the mountains were submerged in water. Brady regains his confidence, and immediately feels very much at home when the "Flood" is brought into the picture. Only, he corrects Drummond's professor's date: the rock cannot be more than six thousand years old. He has his own authority, a Biblical scholar, a Bishop, who has determined the exact time of the Creation: the twenty-third of October, 4004 B.C., at nine A.M. Drummond lightly takes hold of this hour of Creation, and mildly wonders whether it was *Eastern Standard* or *Rocky Mountain* Time. He draws laughter from the spectators: "It wasn't Daylight Saving Time, was it? Because the Lord didn't make the sun until the fourth day!"

BRADY (*fidgeting*)—That is correct.

DRUMMOND (*sharply*)—That first day. Was it a twenty-four-hour day?

BRADY—The Bible says it was a day.

DRUMMOND—There wasn't any sun. How do you know how long it was?

BRADY (*determined*)—The Bible says it was a day.

DRUMMOND—A normal day, a literal day, a twenty-four-hour day? (*Pause.* BRADY *is unsure.*)

BRADY—I do not know.

DRUMMOND—What do you think?

BRADY (*floundering*)—I do not think about things that . . . I do not think about!

DRUMMOND—Do you ever think about things that you *do* think about? (*There is some laughter. But it is damped by the knowledge and awareness throughout the courtroom that the trap is about to be sprung.*) Isn't it possible that first day was twenty-five hours long? There was no way to measure it, no way to tell! Could it have been twenty-five hours? (*Pause. The entire courtroom seems to lean forward.*)

BRADY (*hesitates—then:*)—It is possible. . . . (DRUMMOND'S *got him. And he knows it! This is the turning point. From here on,* DRUMMOND *is fully in the driver's seat. He pounds his questions faster and faster.*)

DRUMMOND—Oh. You interpret that the first day recorded in the Book of Genesis could be of indeterminate length.

BRADY (*wriggling*)—I mean to state that the day referred to is not necessarily a twenty-four-hour day.

DRUMMOND—It could have been thirty hours! Or a month! Or a year! Or a hundred years! (*He brandishes the rock underneath* BRADY'S *nose.*) Or *ten million years!*

The prosecutor leaps up in protest. By this time there is so much tension, so much excited reaction in the court, that the Judge pounds for order. Davenport demands to know what Drummond is trying to do; Brady knows what he's trying to do: he's trying to destroy universal belief in the Bible. Drummond now shouts that he's trying to stop these bigots and ignoramuses from controlling education in the United States. No one can hear Davenport's plea as the Judge hammers for order.

Drummond answers Brady's blast by saying that the Bible is a good book but not the only book.

BRADY—It is the Revealed Word of the Almighty. God spake to the men who wrote the Bible.

DRUMMOND—And how do you know that God didn't "spake" to Charles Darwin?

BRADY—I know because God tells me to oppose the evil teachings of that man.

DRUMMOND—Oh. God speaks to you.

BRADY—Yes.

DRUMMOND—He tells you exactly what's right and what's wrong?

BRADY (*doggedly*)—Yes.

DRUMMOND—And you act accordingly?

BRADY—Yes.

DRUMMOND—So you, Matthew Harrison Brady, through oratory, legislation, or whatever, pass along God's orders to the rest of the world! (*Laughter begins.*) Gentlemen, meet the "Prophet from Nebraska"!

From now on, Brady painfully and ineffectually tries to stop the flow of hostile laughter while Drummond pours on more confusion. Drummond climaxes his ridicule of Brady: "Must men go to prison because they are at odds with the self-appointed prophet?"

Trembling and incapable of speech, Brady rises, towering over his tormentor. Drummond continues: "Extend the Testaments! Let us have a Book of Brady! We shall hex the Pentateuch, and slip you in neatly between Numbers and Deuteronomy."

The laughter that greets this has Brady in a frenzy. He tries to retain the audience that is no longer his—he begs them to listen. Drummond curtly says: "The witness is excused." But Brady's voice cannot stop—it tells the people what he stands for, what he believes in.

BRADY—I believe in the truth of the Book of Genesis! (*Beginning to chant.*) Exodus, Leviticus, Numbers, Deuteronomy, Joshua, Judges, Ruth, First Samuel, Second Samuel, First Kings, Second Kings—

DRUMMOND—Your Honor, this completes the testimony. The witness is excused!

BRADY—Isaiah, Jeremiah, Lamentations, Ezekiel, Daniel, Hosea, Joel, Amos, Obadiah—(*There is confusion in the court. The* JUDGE *raps.*)

JUDGE—You are excused, Colonel Brady.

BRADY—Jonah, Micah, Nahum, Habakkuk, Zephaniah—

Brady beats his clenched fists in the air with every name. . . .
Over the confusion, the Judge raps for order and adjourns the court
until ten o'clock the following morning.

The court clears—spectators, reporters, curiosity-seekers all now
cluster around Drummond, all now leave with him. Ignored, alone,
still erect on the witness stand, Brady chants: "Haggai, Zechariah,
Malachi . . ." His voice trails off, and he sinks down into his
chair. Crushed, crying to Mrs. Brady, "Mother. . . . They're
laughing at me, Mother!", he needs her arms to comfort and baby
him.

ACT III

The following day, in the dimly lit courtroom Cates and Drummond sit at the defense table nervously awaiting the jury's verdict.
Brady, in a corner of the room, finds solace in wolfing a box lunch.
In this atmosphere even Hornbeck hasn't much to say to or about
anyone, and retires to the shadows to read a newspaper.

Drummond, with his years of experience in trial law, has a fair
idea how things are, but can't be sure. One thing he knows: "A
lot of people's shoes are getting hot. . . ." Brady, in spite of his
haughty attitude and disdainful glances in their direction, can't
be sure of the outcome, either.

That new intruder in public events, the radio announcer, arranges with the irritated Judge where to place his microphone.
The Judge has more important things to worry about than this:
the Mayor now tells him that the boys over at the state capitol
want him to go easy—it's too near election time to have the voters
steamed up.

The radio takes Drummond's mind off what's to come. He aim-
lessly approaches the announcer to inspect his new-fangled instrument. "Radio," says Drummond. "God, this is going to break
down a lot of walls." Hastily the radio man tells him: "You're
not supposed to say 'God' on the radio!" "Why the hell not?"
asks Drummond. With a protective look at his radio the man
says: "You're not supposed to say 'hell,' either." "This is going
to be a barren source of amusement," says Drummond, as he
saunters away.

The radio's only fascination for Brady is that he wants to be
sure his thunderous voice will project properly.

The hour has arrived. The scurrying crowd settles in its seats,
and Meeker calls them to order. The jury is led in, as the radio
announcer says in a low but dramatic voice: "This is Harry Ester-
brook, speaking to you from the courthouse in Hillsboro, where

the jury is returning to the courtroom to render its verdict in the famous Hillsboro Monkey Trial case—the Judge has taken the bench. And in the next few minutes we shall know whether Bertram Cates will be found innocent or guilty." Gingerly, he places the microphone before the annoyed Judge.

The unanimous decision is "guilty." The audience responds wildly but not unanimously: there are some boos along with the cheers. Brady is pleased, but his victory is a bitter one.

Drummond just waits. When the Judge raps for order and tells the prisoner to rise for his sentence, Drummond sharply reminds him: "Is it not customary in this state to allow the defendant to make a statement before the sentence is passed?" The red-faced Judge, reminded, so allows. Tentatively, as a "simple school-teacher," Cates starts to speak. "Not any more you ain't!" comes from a lady in the audience. "I *was* a schoolteacher," quietly amends Cates. "I feel I am . . . I have been convicted of violating an unjust law. I will continue in the future as I have in the past, to oppose this law in any way I can. . . ."

On Cates' finishing, there is a crack of applause, distinctly disturbing to Brady, but not nearly as disturbing as the Judge's sentence proves to be. Bertram Cates is merely fined one hundred dollars. Thus the Evolution Law explodes like a wet firecracker. Brady leaps to his feet, loudly taking exception to such puny punishment, where the issue is so titanic. . . .

DRUMMOND (*biting in*)—I object!

BRADY—To make an example of this transgressor! to show the world.

DRUMMOND—Just a minute. Just a minute. The amount of the fine is of no concern to me. Bertram Cates has no intention whatsoever of paying this or any other fine. He would not pay it if it were one single dollar. We will appeal this decision to the Supreme Court of this state. Will the court grant thirty days to prepare our appeal?

JUDGE—Granted. The court fixes bond at . . . five hundred dollars. I believe this concludes the business of this trial. Therefore, I declare this court is adjour—

BRADY (*hastily*)—Your Honor! (*He reaches for a thick manuscript.*) Your Honor, with the court's permission, I should like to read into the record a few short remarks which I have prepared—

DRUMMOND—I object to that. Mr. Brady may make any remarks he likes . . . long, short or otherwise. In a Chautauqua tent or in a political campaign. Our business in Hillsboro is completed. The defense holds that the court shall be adjourned.

BRADY (*frustrated*)—But I have a few remarks—

JUDGE—And we are all anxious to hear them, sir. But Colonel Drummond's point of procedure is well taken. I am sure that everyone here will wish to remain after the court is adjourned to hear your address. (BRADY *lowers his head slightly, in gracious deference to procedure.*) I hereby declare this court is adjourned, sine die.

"Which side won?" cries a child amid the rising courtroom babble. Howard yowls back: "I ain't sure. But the whole thing's over."

But it isn't. During the courtroom mob's seventh-inning stretch the Judge asks quiet so that everyone can listen to Colonel Brady. Only a few of the faithful quiet down. Hornbeck is arranging to pay for Cates' bail; Eskimo Pies and lemonade are hawked to the parched spectators; and kids chase each other, as the lemonade slops about the room.

All the while, Brady, first with his famous attention-getting gesture, then with his even more famous bugle-like tones, tries to catch the courtroom's ear. The few people who listen seem almost resentful. The announcer then pushes Brady towards the mike, which makes him lose the few listeners he had. Vain, cussed, knowing the whole thing to be an anticlimax, Brady is determined to make these people hear him. He becomes red-faced and strident in his futile attempt. Some people even leave the room. The final indignity is the announcer—the program's time being up—removing the mike. Brandishing his speech as though it were Excalibur, with his eyes almost popping from his head, Brady emits a frantic rasp, then becomes speechless.

His silence paradoxically produces silence. Watching in terror, Mrs. Brady sees her husband slowly keel and topple over. Meeker and Davenport break his fall. Now the curious pay attention, so much so that Meeker has to clear the way that Brady can be carried across the street to the doctor's. As the men move with their heavy burden, a strange, hollow voice, as if from some great distance, comes from Brady.

BRADY (*as he is carried out*)—Mr. Chief Justice, citizens of these United States. During my term in the White House I pledge to carry out my program for the betterment of the common people of this country. As your new President, I say what I have said all my life . . . (*Only* DRUMMOND, CATES *and* HORNBECK *remain, their eyes fixed on* BRADY'S *exit.*)

DRUMMOND—How quickly they can turn. And how painful it can be when you don't expect it. (*He turns.*) I wonder how it feels to be Almost President three times—with a skull-ful of un-delivered inauguration speeches.

HORNBECK—Something happens to an also-ran. Something happens to the feet of a man who always comes in second in a foot race. He becomes a national unloved-child, a balding orphan, an aging adolescent who never got the biggest piece of candy. Unloved children, of all ages, insinuate themselves into spotlights and rotogravures. Split pulpits with their pounding. Show me a shouter, and I'll show you an also-ran. A might-have-been. An almost-was.

CATES—Did you see his face?

Meeker, entering, doesn't know how Brady is, though he's surprised more folks haven't passed out in this heat. Hornbeck says carelessly that he's all right. . . . "Give him an hour or so to sweat away the pickles and the pumpernickel, to let his tongue forget the acid taste of the vinegar victory. Mount Brady will erupt again by nightfall."

At this point Cates asks: has he won or lost? The jury was only twelve men, Drummond tells him, millions will say he's won. He's smashed and made a joke of a bad law. . . . It's going to be tough for this jobless schoolteacher, but "tomorrow, it'll be something else . . . and another fella will have to stand up. And you've helped give him the guts to do it!"

Cates, with his new-found pride, is free on bail. Rachel, armed once again with a suitcase, her own this time, joins him. She will be permanently at his side now that she has decided to leave her father. She has a puzzling new concept about allowing ideas to percolate whether she likes or understands them, or not.

Then the Judge enters with the news of Brady's death. Drummond can't imagine a world without Matthew Harrison Brady. When Hornbeck goes into a typical speech saying why weep for that "Barnum-bunkum, Bible-beating bastard," Drummond blows up.

DRUMMOND (*rising*)—You smart-aleck! You have no more right to spit on his religion than to spit on *my* religion. Or my lack of it.

HORNBECK—Well, what do you know!   Henry Drummond for the defense—even of his enemies!

DRUMMOND—There was much greatness in this man.

HORNBECK—Shall I put that in the obituary?

DRUMMOND—Write anything you damn please.

HORNBECK—But how do you write an obituary for a man who's been dead thirty years?   "In Memoriam: M.H.B."   Then what? Hail to the apostle whose Letters to the Corinthians were lost in the mail?   Two years . . . ten years . . . and tourists will ask the guide, "Who died here?   Matthew Harrison Who?"   (*A sudden thought*.)   What did he say to the minister?   It fits.   He delivered his own obituary.   (*Finds the Bible*.)   Here it is.   His book.   (*Thumbing hastily*.)   Proverbs, wasn't it?

DRUMMOND (*quietly*)—"He that troubleth his own house shall inherit the wind: and the fool shall be servant to the wise of heart."

HORNBECK—Mr. Drummond.   We're growing an odd crop of agnostics this year!

DRUMMOND—I'm getting damned tired of you, Hornbeck.

HORNBECK—Why?

DRUMMOND—You never pushed a noun against a verb except to blow up something.

HORNBECK—That's a typical lawyer's trick.   Accusing the accuser.

DRUMMOND—What am *I* accused of?

HORNBECK—I charge you with contempt of conscience, self-perjury.   Kindness aforethought.   Sentimentality in the first degree.

DRUMMOND—Why?   Because I refuse to erase a man's lifetime? I tell you—Brady had the same right as Cates: the right to be wrong!

HORNBECK—"Be-Kind-to-Bigots" Week.   Since Brady's dead, we must be kind.   God, how the world is rotten with kindness.

DRUMMOND—A giant once lived in that body!   (*Then quietly*.) But Matt Brady got lost.   Because he was looking for God too high up and too far away.

HORNBECK—You hypocrite!   You fraud!   You're more religious than *he* was!   (*He starts to go out*.)   Excuse me.   I must get me to a typewriter and hammer out the story of an atheist who believes in God!

Cates tells Drummond he doesn't know how he'll pay him for an appeal; Drummond says he doesn't want his money.   He begins to pack his brief case, preparing to catch the train.   Rachel, intending to accompany Cates, says they'll all leave together on that train. The young couple go off to get ready. Drummond notices the copy of Darwin that Cates forgot to take with him. "Say—you forgot—!" he calls after him.

Drummond takes the volume. Then he notices the Bible. He weighs them thoughtfully, slaps them together, side by side, and puts them in his brief case. Slowly he climbs up to street level and crosses the empty square.

A GRAPHIC GLANCE
By Hirschfeld

William Tabbert, Walter Slezak, Florence Henderson and Ezio
Pinza in "Fanny"

PHILADELPHIA

342

Dorothy Stickney and Howard Lindsay in "Life with Father"

Jennifer Jones and Robert Flemyng in "Portrait of a Lady"

Donald Cook, John Dall and Polly Bergen in "Champagne Complex"

Jessica Tandy, Dorothy Stickney and Hume Cronyn in "The Honeys"

Myron McCormick, Gloria Vanderbilt, Franchot Tone and Harold Lang in "The Time of Your Life"

Bobby Van and Vera Zorina in "On Your Toes"

HIRSCHFELD NEW HAVEN

Libby Holman and Gerald Cook in "Blues, Ballads and Sin-Songs"

Luba Malina, Abbott Lee Ruskin, George Voskovec, Betty Field and Paul Henreid in "Festival"

David Opatoshu, Henry Lascoe, Leon Belasco, Hildegarde Neff,
Don Ameche and Philip Sterling in "Silk Stockings"

When the New York Times *in accordance with its traditional policy refused to print the figure on the left as an advertisement for "Reclining Figure," the lady was garbed, altered (and accepted) as on the right.*

The Aquazanies and June Earing in "Aquashow"

Larry Jackson, Bernie Lyman, Helen Davidson, Bobby Specht,
Donna Atwood and Willie Kall in "Ice Capades of 1955"

Vincent Price in "Black-Eyed Susan"

PLAYS PRODUCED IN NEW YORK

PLAYS PRODUCED IN NEW YORK

June 1, 1954—May 31, 1955

(Plays marked "Continued" were still running on June 1, 1955)

CAROUSEL

(79 performances)

Musical in two acts, based on Ferenc Molnar's *Liliom,* as adapted by Benjamin F. Glazer, with book and lyrics by Oscar Hammerstein 2nd, music by Richard Rodgers. Revived by the New York City Center Light Opera Company (William Hammerstein, Director) at the New York City Center of Music and Drama, June 2, 1954.

Cast of characters—

Carrie Pipperidge	Barbara Cook
Julie Jordan	Jo Sullivan
Mrs. Mullin	Winifred Heidt
Billy Bigelow	Chris Robinson
First Policeman	Russell Goodwin
David Bascombe	Stanley Carlson
Nettie Fowler	Jean Handzlik
June Girl	Mavis Ray
Enoch Snow	Don Blackey
Jigger Craigin	John Conte
Hannah	Dusty Worrall
Boatswain	Robert Pagent
Arminy	Marilyn Bladd
Second Policeman	William W. Reynolds
Captain	Boris Aplon
Heavenly Friend (Joshua)	Jay Velie
Starkeeper	Daniel Reed
Louise	Bambi Linn
Carnival Boy	Robert Pagent
Enoch Snow Jr.	James Martindale
Principal	Russell Goodwin

Townspeople: Marilyn Bladd, Lila Caputo, Rina Falcone, Barbara Ford, Ellen Gleason, Sheila Mathews, Dorothy Mirr, Gloria Sacks, Greta Thormsen; Benjamin Bajorek, Dawin Emanuel, Russell Goodwin, Charles Kuestner, James Martindale, Roland Miles, Benjamin Plotkin, William W. Reynolds, Joseph Tanner.

Dancers: Ann Barry, Ann Dunbar, Ruby Herndon, Anne Meislik, Meri Miller, Eloise Milton, Mavis Ray, Nadine Revene, Francine Savery, Gini Turner; Rudy Jenkins, Don Little, Don Martin, Dick Rogers, Philip Salem, Mark Ward, Mark West.

Children of the Prelude: Claudia Crawford, Adele Newton, Chris Snell.

Staged by William Hammerstein; conductor, Julius Rudel; dances by Agnes De Mille, restaged by Robert Pagent; settings by Oliver Smith; costumes by John Boyt; lighting by Jean Rosenthal; assistant to William Hammerstein, Michael Shurtleff; production stage manager, Lucia Victor; stage manager, Hans Sondheimer.

Carousel was first produced April 19, 1945, by The Theatre Guild at the Majestic Theatre for 890 performances.

(Closed August 8, 1954)

HAYRIDE

(24 performances)

Hillbilly, folk musical in two acts. Produced by Barron Howard and Jack Stone at the Forty-Eighth Street Theatre, September 13, 1954.

Cast of characters—

Sunshine Sue
Cousin Joe Maphis and Rose
Lester Flatt and Earl Scruggs
   and the Foggy Mountain Boys,
   Paul Warren, Jake Tulloch, Curly Sechler
The Coon Creek Girls,
   Lilly May, Rosie, Black Eyed Susan
The Trail Blazers,
   Ray Smith, Roy Horton, Johnny Newton
Eddy (Texas) Smith
Quincy Snodgrass
Mary Klick
Zeb Robinson
Sonny Day
Fiddlin' Irving
Zag the Ozark Mountain Boy
Gene Jenkins
Jody Carver

Setting by Art Guild, Jack Woodson, Jack Derrenberger; stage manager, Daniel Pennell.

(Closed October 2, 1954)

DEAR CHARLES

(155 performances)

Comedy in three acts by Marc-Gilbert Sauvajon and Frederick Jackson, adapted by Alan Melville. Produced by Richard Aldrich and Richard Myers, in association with Julius Fleischmann, at the Morosco Theatre, September 15, 1954.

Cast of characters—

Martha .... Norah Howard
Walter .... Larry Robinson
Bruno .... Tom Raynor
Edward .... Fred Keating
Dolores .... Tallulah Bankhead

Martine	Grace Raynor
Sir Michael Anstruther	Robert Coote
Jan Letzaresco	Werner Klemperer
Jeffrey	Hugh Reilly
Madame Bouchemin	Alice Pearce
Lucienne	Mary Webster
Jean-Pierre	Peter Pell

The entire action takes place in the living room of the Darvel house in Paris. Act I.—A spring morning. Act II.—Cocktail time, a week later. Act III.—Dinner time, another week later.

Staged by Edmund Baylies; setting and lighting by Donald Oenslager; Miss Bankhead's gowns by Gene Coffin; production stage manager, Edmund Baylies.

Over-aggressive sex comedy about a Parisian lady writer who has had three children by as many lovers. Now that her children are grown and wish to make respectable marriages, she decides that she had better get married herself; and invites the three fathers to a Twenty-Years-After house party. In time, the best man among them becomes the groom.

(Closed January 29, 1955)

A MIDSUMMER NIGHT'S DREAM

(29 performances)

Comedy in three parts by William Shakespeare, with music by Mendelssohn, arranged by Gordon Jacob. Produced by S. Hurok, by arrangement with Old Vic Trust Ltd. and the Arts Council of Great Britain, at the Metropolitan Opera House, September 21, 1954.

Cast of characters—

MORTALS

Theseus, Duke of Athens	Anthony Nicholls
Hippolyta, Queen of the Amazons, betrothed to Theseus	Margaret Courtenay
Philostrate, master of the revels to Theseus	Peter Johnson
Egeus, father to Hermia	John Dearth
Hermia, daughter to Egeus, in love with Lysander	Ann Walford
Demetrius, in love with Hermia	Patrick MacNee
Lysander, in love with Hermia	Terence Longdon
Helena, in love with Demetrius	Joan Benham
Quince, a carpenter	Eliot Makeham
Bottom, a weaver	Stanley Holloway
Flute, a bellows mender	Philip Locke
Starveling, a tailor	Daniel Thorndike
Snout, a tinker	Norman Rossington
Snug, a joiner	Michael Redington

IMMORTALS

Puck, or Robin Goodfellow	Philip Guard
A Fairy	Jocelyn Britton
Oberon	Robert Helpmann
Titania	Moira Shearer
Peaseblossom	Jocelyn Britton
Cobweb	Tania d'Avray
Moth	Sheila Wright

Mustardseed ....Joan King
Indian Boy ....Rudolfo Cornejo
    Court Attendants, Pages, Musicians, Wedding Guests, etc.: Phyllis
Harcourt, Vivienne Hetzel, Barbara Leigh-Hunt, Rosemary Moore,
Gillian Neason, Jane Shore, Suzanne Steele, Betty Shale, Elisabeth
Wade, Anne Wilson; Ivan Baptie, Jeremy Geidt, David Hurst,
David Harding, Michael Hayes, William Martin, Kenneth Melville,
David Reynolds, David Rose, David Stevens, Sven van Zyl.
    Corps de Ballet: Valerie Adams, Jocelyn Britton, Mary Brookes,
Louise Carley, Tania d'Avray, Nadia de Lichtenberg, Juliet Ellice,
Mary Fenwick, Phyllis Harcourt, Vivienne Hetzel, Joan King, Mar-
garet Knoesen, Lana Kassinova, Rosemary Moore, Joanne Nisbet,
Jane Shore, Josephine Spaull, Sheila Wright; Ivan Baptie, David
Harding, David Hurst, William Martin, Kenneth Melville, Henry
Naughton, David Reynolds, Sven van Zyl.
    Singers: Gillian Neason, Suzanne Steele, Elisabeth Wade, Anne
Wilson.
    Part I.—The Prologue: The terrace of Theseus' palace, Athens;
Quince's shop, Athens.   The Overture.   The Dream: A wood near
Athens.   Part II.—The Dream: Other parts of the wood.   Part III.—
The Wedding: The palace of Theseus.
    Staged by Michael Benthall; costumes by Robin and Christopher
Ironside; choreography by Robert Helpmann, with "Nocturne" ar-
ranged by Frederick Ashton; stage manager for "A Midsummer
Night's Dream" company, David Turnbull; production manager for
The Old Vic, London, J. A. Titcombe.

(Closed October 17, 1954)

HOME IS THE HERO

(30 performances)

Play in three acts by Walter Macken. Produced by The Theatre
Guild and Worthington Miner at the Booth Theatre, September 22
1954.

Cast of characters—

Willie O'Reilly ....Donald Harron
Daylia ....Glenda Farrell
Bid ....Ann Thomas
Dovetail ....J. Pat O'Malley
Josie ....Peggy Ann Garner
Lily Green ....Loretta Leversee
Trapper ....Art Smith
Paddo O'Reilly ....Walter Macken
Mrs. Green ....Frances Fuller
Manchester Monagham ....Christopher Plummer
    The action of the play takes place in the general downstairs room
in a house in a long avenue of houses in a town in Ireland.   The
time is the present.
    Staged by Worthington Miner; entire production designed by
Marvin Reiss; stage manager, Elliott Martin.

Paddo O'Reilly, the father of an Irish family, comes home after
spending five years in prison for killing a man in a brawl. He comes
home an even worse bully than he went away: his old will to domi-
nate makes him interfere in everyone's life and his added sense of
guilt makes him flagellate others instead of himself. After going
a long way toward spoiling the happiness of everyone in the family

Paddo—in a most ignominious victory of plot over character—suddenly decides to clear out.

(Closed October 16, 1954)

ALL SUMMER LONG

(60 performances)

Play in two acts by Robert Anderson, adapted from a novel by Donald Wetzel. Produced by The Playwrights' Company at the Coronet Theatre, September 23, 1954.

Cast of characters—

```
Willie ..............................................Clay Hall
Don .................................................John Kerr
Mother ............................................June Walker
Dad ................................................Ed Begley
Ruth .............................................Carroll Baker
Harry ..........................................John Randolph
Theresa ..........................................Daniela Boni
```
　　The scene of the play is a house by a river outside a small midwestern town. The time is summer.
　　Staged by Alan Schneider; setting and lighting by Jo Mielziner; clothes designed by Anna Hill Johnstone; incidental music composed by Albert Hague; stage manager, Peter Zeisler.

A summer in the life of a midwestern household. The angle of vision is largely that of the disturbed twelve-year-old son Willie. He sees the house they live in threatened by erosion from the river that flows by it—which none of the family bothers to do anything about. He sees a father who blusters from knowing no smarter way of handling people; a married sister too self-centered to want even a family of her own; a sweet, bumbling mother who wears rose-colored blinkers. Only Willy's crippled older brother has feeling enough for the kid to help him build a crude retaining wall against the river; but it crumbles with the first storm, and the family, at the end, have to flee the house.

(Closed November 13, 1954)

THE BOY FRIEND

(279 performances)
(Continued)

New musical comedy of the 1920s. Book, music and lyrics by Sandy Wilson. Produced by Feuer and Martin at the Royale Theatre, September 30, 1954.

Cast of characters—

Hortense ....Paulette Girard
Nancy ....Millicent Martin
Maisie ....Ann Wakefield
Fay ....Stella Claire
Dulcie ....Dilys Lay
Polly ....Julie Andrews
Marcel ....Joe Milan
Alphonse ....Buddy Schwab
Pierre ....Jerry Newby
Madame Dubonnet ....Ruth Altman
Bobby Van Husen ....Bob Scheerer
Percival Browne ....Eric Berry
Tony ....John Hewer
Phillipe ....Jimmy Alex
Monica ....Berkley Marsh
Lord Brockhurst ....Geoffrey Hibbert
Lady Brockhurst ....Moyna MacGill
Susanne ....Lyn Connorty
Guests .... { Phoebe Mackay
                                              Marge Ellis
                                              Mickey Calin
Gendarme ....Douglas Deane
Waiter ....Lyn Robert
Pepe ....Joe Milan
Lolita ....Stella Claire

Act I.—The drawing room of the Villa Caprice, Madame Dubonnet's finishing school on the outskirts of Nice, 1926. Act II.—The Plage, that afternoon. Act III.—The terrace of the Café Pataplon, that night.

Staged by Vida Hope; choreography by John Heawood; settings and costumes by Reginald Woolley; New York production supervising designers: scenery and lighting by Feder, costumes by Robert Mackintosh; orchestrations by Ted Royal and Charles L. Cooke; stage manager, Charles Pratt, Jr.

Musical numbers—

ACT I

"Perfect Young Ladies" ....Hortense, Nancy, Maisie,
                                              Fay, Dulcie
"The Boy Friend" ....Polly, Maisie, Dulcie, Fay, Nancy,
                                              Marcel, Pierre, Alphonse
"Won't You Charleston with Me?" ....Maisie and Bobby
"Fancy Forgetting" ....Madame Dubonnet and
                                              Percival Browne
"I Could Be Happy with You" ....Polly and Tony
Finale Reprise: "The Boy Friend"

ACT II

"Sur La Plage" ....Maisie, Bobby, Fay, Marcel,
                                              Dulcie, Alphonse, Nancy,
                                              Pierre, Monica, Phillipe
"A Room in Bloomsbury" ....Polly and Tony
"You Don't Want to Play with Me Blues" ....Madame Dubonnet,
                                              Percival Browne, Fay,
                                              Dulcie, Nancy, Monica
"Safety in Numbers" ....Maisie, Bobby, Marcel,
                                              Pierre, Alphonse
Finale ....Entire Company

ACT III

"Riviera" ....Maisie, Bobby, Fay, Marcel,
                                              Dulcie, Alphonse, Nancy,
                                              Pierre, Monica, Phillipe
"It's Never Too Late to Fall in Love" ...Lord Brockhurst and Dulcie
"Carnival Tango" ....Danced by Pepe and Lolita
"Poor Little Pierrette" ....Madame Dubonnet and Polly
Finale ....Entire Company

See page 71.

LIBBY HOLMAN'S
"BLUES, BALLADS AND SIN-SONGS"

(12 performances)

Songs by Libby Holman, accompanied by Gerald Cook. Presented at the Bijou Theatre, October 4, 1954.

Musical settings by Gerald Cook; Miss Holman's gown for Part I by Mainbocher; for Part II by Frank Stanley; production manager, Walter Williams.

Musical numbers—

PART I
"Good Morning Blues"
"Smokey"
"Go 'Way from My Window"
"In the Evening"
"Barbara Allen"
"Rolly Trudum"

"Yandro"
"Cindy"
"Baby, Baby"
"Fare Thee Well"

PART II
"Careless Love"
"Riddle Song"
"Four Marys"
"The Loathly Bride"
"Johnny Has Gone"

"The Blues" .....Duke Ellington
"You Can't Go to Heaven"
"Number 12 Train"
"Evil Hearted Me"
"House of the Rising Sun"

(Closed October 16, 1954)

RECLINING FIGURE

(116 performances)

Comedy in three acts by Harry Kurnitz. Produced by Martin Gabel and Henry M. Margolis, in association with Peter Cusick, at the Lyceum Theatre, October 7, 1954.

Cast of characters—

William	Foster Davis
Samuel Ellis	Mike Wallace
Cass Edgerton	Georgiann Johnson
Lucas Edgerton	Percy Waram
Agramonte	Ralph Bunker
Paul Weldon	Berry Kroeger
Jonas Astorg	Martin Gabel
Denesco	David Opatoshu

Dr. Hickey ....Nehemiah Persoff
Professor Jumelle ....Alfred Hesse
    All the action of the play takes place in the library of Lucas Edger-
ton's home in Pasadena, California.   Act I.—Morning.   Act II.—
Evening, the same day.   Act III.—The following morning.
    Staged by Abe Burrows; production designed and lighted by Fred-
erick Fox; stage manager, John Cornell.

Lucas Edgerton is an eccentric and very difficult art collector.
Offered a fake Renoir, he for the first time feels aesthetic enthusiasm
for a picture rather than just acquisitive excitement; and his cowed
staff, seeing the boss so happy, haven't the courage to say the picture
is a fake.   The plot is thickened with art-world highjinks, 57th-Street
highjackers and competitiveness that seems more like conspiracy.

(Closed January 15, 1955)

ON YOUR TOES

(64 performances)

Musical comedy in two acts, with music by Richard Rodgers,
lyrics by Lorenz Hart and book by Messrs. Rodgers and Hart and
George Abbott.   Revived by George Abbott at the Forty-Sixth Street
Theatre, October 11, 1954.

Cast of characters—

Phil Dolan II ....Jack Williams
Lil Dolan ....Eleanor Williams
Phil Dolan III ....David Winters
Stage Manager ....George Church
Lola ....Dorene Kilmer
Junior ....Bobby Van
Frankie Frayne ....Kay Coulter
Sidney Cohn ....Joshua Shelley
Vera Barnova ....Vera Zorina
Anushka ....Patricia Wilkes
Peggy Porterfield ....Elaine Stritch
Sergei Alexandrovitch ....Ben Astar
Konstantine Morrosine ....Nicolas Orloff
Snoopy ....John Robb
Thug ....Nathaniel Frey
Mishka ....Patrick Welch
Ivan ....John Nola
Vassilli ....Edward Pfeiffer
Dmitri ....Ted Adkins
Leo ....Robert Lindgren
Ballet Stage Manager ....Bertram Wood
Cop ....Arthur Grahl
    Chorus—Girls: Phyllis Campbell, Lillian D'Honau, Patricia Drylie,
Katia Geneznova, Carolyn George, Marilyn Hale, Dorene Kilmer,
Helen Kramer, Sonja Lindgren, Paula Lloyd, Sigyn, Barbara Mi-
chaels, Lois Platt, Nina Popova, Ruth Sobotka, Mary Stanton, Carol
Stevens, Wendy Winn; Boys: Ted Adkins, Marvin Arnold, Johnny
Bowen, Timmy Everett, Arthur Grahl, Edward Kerrigan, Jack Leigh,
Robert Lindgren, John Nola, Edward Pfeiffer.
    The first two scenes take place fifteen years ago and thereafter the
action is contemporary.
    Production staged by George Abbott; dances staged by George Bal-

anchine; settings by Oliver Smith; costumes by Irene Sharaff; lighting by Peggy Clark; musical direction by Salvatore Dell'Isola; orchestrations by Don Walker; production stage manager, Robert Griffith.

Musical numbers—

ACT I

"Two a Day for Keith" ....Jack Williams, Eleanor Williams, David Winters
"The 3 B's" ....Bobby Van and Chorus
"It's Got to Be Love" ....Bobby Van and Kay Coulter
"Too Good for the Average Man" .....Elaine Stritch and Ben Astar
"There's a Small Hotel" ....Bobby Van and Kay Coulter
"The Heart Is Quicker Than the Eye" ....Elaine Stritch and Bobby Van
Princess Zenobia Ballet ....Danced by Vera Zorina, Bobby Van, Nicolas Orloff, George Church and Chorus

ACT II

"Quiet Night" ....Joshua Shelley and Chorus
"Glad to Be Unhappy" ....Kay Coulter and Joshua Shelley
"On Your Toes" ....Kay Coulter, Bobby Van, Joshua Shelley and Chorus
Jitterbug Couple ....Dorene Kilmer and Timmy Everett
Adagio Couple ....Paula Lloyd and Robert Lindgren
"You Took Advantage of Me" ....Elaine Stritch
"Slaughter on Tenth Avenue" ....Danced by Vera Zorina, Bobby Van, George Church and Chorus
"On Your Toes" Finale ....Entire Company

On Your Toes was first produced in New York April 11, 1936.

(Closed December 4, 1954)

FRAGILE FOX

(55 performances)

Drama in three acts by Norman A. Brooks. Produced by Paul Vroom, in association with Bernard Straus, at the Belasco Theatre, October 12, 1954.

Cast of characters—

Captain Erskine Cooney ....Andrew Duggan
Corporal Jackson ....Lionel Wilson
First Lieut. Joseph Costa ....Dane Clark
First Lieut. Harry Woodruff ....Don Taylor
Lieut. Col. Clyde Bartlett ....James Gregory
Pfc. Bernstein ....Clem Fowler
Pfc. Snowden ....Jason Wingreen
Tech. Sgt. Tolliver ....Crahan Denton
Captain Gerstad ....Addison Powell
Pfc. Herman Ricks ....Richard Carlyle
Pvt. Jacob Abramowitz ....William Hellinger
Tall German ....Eugene Smith
Short German ....Leonard Bell
Pvt. Sneider ....Robert McQueeney

The action of the play takes place in Belgium during the last winter of World War II. Act I.—Scene 1—A town hall; early evening. Scene 2—A cellar; a week later, afternoon. Act II.—Scene 1

—A country house; same afternoon. Scene 2—The cellar; five minutes later. Act III.—The cellar; a few hours later.
Staged by Herbert Swope, Jr.; scenery and lighting by Ralph Alswang; production stage manager, Herman Shapiro.

A passable thriller about World War II. Using the italics of melodrama, it tells of an outfit—commanded by a swaggering, drunken, cowardly captain—that is suddenly precipitated into the Battle of the Bulge. Detested by the men under him, the captain gets by with his violently ambitious colonel from having a political big shot for a father. Under fire, the craven captain wobbles, doublecrosses his men, schemes to run out on the job, and is finally shot by the calmest of his subordinates.

(Closed November 27, 1954)

THE TENDER TRAP

(102 performances)

Comedy in three acts by Max Shulman and Robert Paul Smith. Produced by Clinton Wilder at the Longacre Theatre, October 13, 1954.

Cast of characters—

Charlie Reader	Ronny Graham
Poppy Matson	Parker McCormick
Joe McCall	Robert Preston
Jessica Collins	Julia Meade
Sylvia Crewes	Kim Hunter
Julie Gillis	Janet Riley
Earl Lindquist	Jack Manning
Sol Schwartz	Joey Faye

The time is the present; the place, the New York apartment of Charlie Reader. Act I.—Scene 1—Six P.M. Saturday. Scene 2—Noon, the following day. Act II.—Six P.M. Saturday, three weeks later. Act III.—The next morning.
Staged by Michael Gordon; setting and lighting by Paul Morrison; costumes by Anna Hill Johnstone; stage manager, Robert Downing.

Thirty-five years old and unmarried, Charlie Reader belongs to a special New York breed—bachelors besieged in their own apartments by a stream of attractive, obliging, gift-bearing ladies who are also more than happy to cook or clean house for monsieur. In the face of such good fortune, Charlie hasn't the least desire to marry—until his much-married old school pal arrives in New York on business, enviously condemns Charlie's way of life, and soon gets Charlie engaged to two girls at once. He loses them both for a time, then regains and marries one of them.

(Closed January 8, 1955)

SING ME NO LULLABY

(30 performances)

Drama in three acts by Robert Ardrey. Produced by the Phoenix Theatre (T. Edward Hambleton and Norris Houghton) at the Phoenix Theatre, October 14, 1954.

Cast of characters—

Christine Collinger ....Beatrice Straight
Ben Collinger ....Richard Kiley
Mike Hertzog ....Jack Warden
Clay Dixon ....Larry Gates
Abe Levene ....Michael Lipton
Maddy Hertzog ....Marian Winters
Fanny Collinger ....Jessie Royce Landis
Johnny Colton Smith ....John Fiedler
Parrish ....John Marley
    The entire action occurs in a summer cottage on the Sangamon River, near Springfield, Illinois. The time is the present. Within the first two acts, however, there are scenes taking place in 1938, 1939 and 1946.
    Staged by Paul Stewart; setting by Ben Edwards; costumes supervised by Alvin Colt; lighting by Klaus Holm; production stage manager, Robert Woods; stage manager, Richard Blofson.

(Closed November 7, 1954)

PETER PAN

(152 performances)

New musical version of the play by James M. Barrie. Music by Mark Charlap; lyrics by Carolyn Leigh; additional music by Jule Styne and additional lyrics by Betty Comden and Adolph Green; incidental music by Trude Rittman and Elmer Bernstein. Edwin Lester's production presented by Richard Halliday at the Winter Garden, October 20, 1954.

Cast of characters—

Wendy ....Kathy Nolan
John ....Robert Harrington
Liza ....Heller Halliday
Michael ....Joseph Stafford
Nana ....Norman Shelly
Mrs. Darling ....Margalo Gillmore
Mr. Darling ....Cyril Ritchard
Peter Pan ....Mary Martin
Lion...Richard Wyatt
Kangaroo ....Don Lurio
Ostrich ....Joan Tewkesbury
Slightly ....David Bean
Tootles ....Ian Tucker
Curly ....Stanley Stenner
Nibs ....Paris Theodore

Crocodile ....Norman Shelly
First Twin ....Alan Sutherland
Second Twin ....Darryl Duran
Captain Hook ....Cyril Ritchard
Smee ....Joe E. Marks
Tiger Lily .... Sondra Lee
Cecco ....Robert Tucker
Noodler ....Frank Lindsay
Jukes ....William Burke
Starkey ....Robert Vanselow
Mullins ....James White
Wendy Grown-Up ....Sallie Brophy
Jane ....Kathy Nolan
Voice of Tinker Bell ....Jaye Rubanoff
    Pirates: Robert Tucker, Frank Lindsay, Frank Marasco, James White, William Burke, Chester Fisher, John Newton, Arthur Tookoian, Robert Vanselow, Richard Winter.
    Indians: Robert Banas, Don Lurio, Robert Piper, William Sumner, Richard Wyatt, Linda Dangcil, Lisa Lang, Suzanne Luckey, Joan Tewkesbury.
    Act I.—Scene 1—The nursery of the Darling residence. Scene 2—Flight to Neverland. Act II.—Scene 1—Neverland. Scene 2—Path through the woods. Scene 3—Neverland home underground. Act III.—Scene 1—The pirate ship. Scene 2—Path through the woods. Scene 3—The nursery of the Darling residence. Scene 4—The nursery many years later.
    Staged by Jerome Robbins; scenery by Peter Larkin; costumes by Motley; lighting by Peggy Clark; technical direction of Richard Rodda; orchestral arrangements by Albert Sendrey; production manager, Michael Jeffrey; executive stage manager, Robert Linden.

Musical numbers—

ACT I
Scene 1

"Tender Shepherd" ....Mrs. Darling, Wendy, John and Michael
"I've Got to Crow" ....Peter
"Neverland" * ....Peter
"I'm Flying" ....Peter, Wendy, John and Michael

ACT II
Scene 1

"Pirate Song" ....Hook and Pirates
"A Princely Scheme" ....Hook and Pirates
"Indians!" ....Tiger Lily and Indians
"Wendy" * ....Peter and Boys
"Another Princely Scheme" ....Hook and Pirates
"Neverland Waltz" * ....Liza

Scene 2

"I Won't Grow Up" ....Peter and Boys
"Mysterious Lady" * ....Peter and Hook

Scene 3

"Ugg-a-Wugg" *
"The Pow-Wow Polka" * } ..Peter, Tiger Lily, Children and Indians
"Distant Melody" * ....Peter

ACT III
Scene 1

"To the Ship" ....Peter and Company
"Hook's Waltz" * ....Hook and Pirates
"The Battle" ....Peter, Hook and Company

Scene 2

Reprise: "I've Got to Crow" ....Peter, Liza and Company

Scene 3
Reprise: "Tender Shepherd" ....Wendy, John and Michael
Reprise "I Won't Grow Up" .....The Darling Family and Lost Boys

Scene 4
Reprise: "Neverland" * ....Peter
  * Styne, Comden and Green.

(Closed February 26, 1955)

THE TRAVELING LADY

(30 performances)

Play in three acts by Horton Foote. Produced by The Playwrights' Company at The Playhouse, October 27, 1954.

Cast of characters—

Mrs. Mavis ....Mary Perry
Slim Murray ....Jack Lord
Judge Robedaux ....Calvin Thomas
Georgette Thomas ....Kim Stanley
Margaret Rose ....Brook Seawell
Clara Breedlove ....Helen Carew
Sitter Mavis ....Katherine Squire
Mrs. Tillman ....Kathleen Comegys
Henry Thomas ....Lonny Chapman
Sheriff ....Tony Sexton
    The scene is the sun parlor, side porch and yard of Clara Breedlove's house in a small Texas town. Act I.—An early spring day; eleven o'clock. Act II.—Scene 1—Five hours later. Scene 2—Two hours later. Act III.—Two days later; ten-thirty in the morning.
    Staged by Vincent J. Donehue; scenery, lighting and costumes by Ben Edwards; production stage manager, James Gelb; stage manager, Tony Kraber.

The story of a hard-beset young mother, not very bright but full of courage, married to a no-good weakling just out of jail. She comes hopefully with her child to meet him in a Texas town, but he is as weak and given to getting in trouble as ever, and at the end of the play he is heading for jail again.

(Closed November 20, 1954)

THE RAINMAKER

(125 performances)

Romantic play in three acts by N. Richard Nash. Produced by Ethel Linder Reiner, in association with Hope Abelson, at the Cort Theatre, October 28, 1954.

Cast of characters—

H. C. Curry ....Cameron Prud'homme
Noah Curry ....Joseph Sullivan
Jim Curry ....Albert Salmi
Lizzie Curry ....Geraldine Page
File ....Richard Coogan
Sheriff Thomas ....Tom Flatley Reynolds
Bill Starbuck ....Darren McGavin
    The play takes place in a western state on a summer day in a time of drought. Act I.—Day. Act II.—That evening. Act III.—Later the same night.
    Staged by Joseph Anthony; setting and lighting by Ralph Alswang; costumes by Bolasni; stage manager, William Watts.

During a drought in the '20s, the farmer father and brothers of a very plain young girl are trying to marry her off. The girl, who is blunt, uncoy and intelligent, consistently mismanages herself; failure unnerves her; and she is bleakly facing spinsterhood when a flamboyant young con man swaggers in swearing that for $100 he can bring rain. With the $100 in his pocket, he woos the girl, gives her self-confidence, and when he rides off at the end, she is about to be hitched to a proper beau.

(Closed February 12, 1955)

QUADRILLE

(150 performances)

Romantic comedy in three acts by Noel Coward. Produced by John C. Wilson and H. M. Tennent, Ltd., at the Coronet Theatre, November 3, 1954.

Cast of characters—

First French Woman ....Madeline Clive
First French Man ....Byron Mitchell
Buffet Manageress ....Patricia Quinn O'Hara
The Rev. Edgar Spevin ....Jerome Kilty
Sarah (His Wife) ....Phyllis Connard
Gwendolyn (His Daughter) ....Nina Reader
Waiter ....Bruce Webster
Courier ....Richard Longman
The Marquis of Heronden (Hubert) ....Brian Aherne
Mrs. Axel Diensen (Charlotte) ....Edna Best
Catchpole ....Harold Crane
The Marchioness of Heronden (Serena) ....Lynn Fontanne
Lady Harriet Ripley ....Brenda Forbes
Foster ....Mildred Clinton
Footman ....Rhoderick Walker
Axel Diensen ....Alfred Lunt
Octavia, Countess of Bonnington ....Dorothy Sands
Second French Woman ....Mildred Clinton
Second French Man ....Michael Lewis
    Act I.—Scene 1—The Buffet de la Gare, Boulogne; early morning, May, 1873. Scene 2—Serena's sitting room in Herondon House, Belgrave Square; some hours later. Act II.—Scene 1—The Villa

Zodiaque, St. Guillaume des Fleurs, France; two days later. Scene 2—The same; the next morning. Scene 3—The same; some hours later. Act III.—Scene 1—Serena's sitting room in Heronden House, Belgrave Square; June, 1874, afternoon. Scene 2—The Buffet de la Gare, Boulogne; early the next morning.

Staged by Alfred Lunt; settings and costumes by Cecil Beaton; setting supervised by Charles Elson; costumes supervised by Stanley Simmons; lighting by Jean Rosenthal; stage manager, William Chambers.

The story, laid in Victorian times, can be set down in a sentence: A marchioness and an American rail baron pursue their eloping spouses across the Channel, fall in love while separating the lovers, then themselves elope in turn.

(Closed March 12, 1955)

FANNY

(239 performances)
(Continued)

Musical play in two acts by S. N. Behrman and Joshua Logan, based on the trilogy ("Marius," "Fanny" and "Cesar") by Marcel Pagnol, with music and lyrics by Harold Rome. Produced by David Merrick and Joshua Logan at the Majestic Theatre, November 4, 1954.

Cast of characters—

Arab Rug Seller	Mohammed el Bakkar
Marius, son of Cesar	William Tabbert
Fanny, daughter of Honorine	Florence Henderson
Maori Vendor	Katherine Graves
Lace Vendor	Betty Carr
Customers	Toni Wheelis, Lindsay Kirkpatrick, Dolores Smith, Margaret Baxter
Claudine | Claudette } twin sisters, friends of Fanny	Tani Seitz | Dran Seitz
Charles	Wally Strauss
His Friends	Bill Pope, Dean Crane, Roland Cecill, Michael de Marco
Nanette | Mimi | Marie | Michellette } friends of Fanny	Norma Doggett | Carolyn Maye | Ellen Matthews | Jane House
Panisse, wealthy sailmaker	Walter Slezak
Sailor	Herb Banke
The Admiral, an eccentric waterfront character	Gerald Price
Moroccan Drummer	Charles Blackwell
Second Mate	Henry Michel
Fisherman	Steve Wiland
Sailmaker	Jack Washburn
Fish-stall Woman	Florence Dunlap
An Arab	Michael Scrittorale
Cesar, proprietor of cafe on waterfront	Ezio Pinza
Honorine, Fanny's mother, a fish-stall keeper	Edna Preston
Escartifique, a ferryboat captain	Alan Carney
M. Brun, customs inspector recently returned from Paris	Don McHenry

Arab Dancing Girl .... Nejla Ates
Nun .... Ruth Schumacher
Cesario .... Lloyd Reese
Butler .... Mike Mason
Maid .... Pat Finch
Garage Owner .... Tom Gleason
Priest .... Ray Dorian
Acolytes .... Gary Wright, Daniel Labeille
    The entire action takes place in and around the Old Port of Mar-
seilles over a period of years. The time: Not so long ago.
    Staged by Joshua Logan; scenery and lighting by Jo Mielziner;
costumes by Alvin Colt; dances by Helen Tamiris; musical direction
and vocal arrangements by Lehman Engel; orchestral arrangements by
Philip J. Lang; musical continuity by Trude Rittman; production
manager, Jean Barrere; stage manager, Kermit Kegley.

Musical numbers—

ACT I

"Never Too Late for Love" .... Panisse and Ensemble
"Cold Cream Jar Song" .... Panisse
"Octopus Song" .... The Admiral
"Restless Heart" .... Marius and Male Ensemble
"Why Be Afraid to Dance?" .... Cesar
                    Danced by Cesar, Marius, Fanny, Ensemble
"Never Too Late for Love"
    (Reprise) .... Cesar, Panisse and Honorine
"Shika, Shika" .... Arab Dancing Girl, Rug Seller, Ensemble
"Welcome Home" .... Cesar
"I Like You" .... Marius, Cesar
"I Have to Tell You" .... Fanny
"Fanny" .... Marius
Montage .... Fanny, Marius, Cesar, Ensemble
    "The Lovers"
    "The Sailing"
"Oysters, Cockles and Mussels" .... Ensemble
"Panisse and Son" .... Panisse
Wedding Dance .... Danced by Charles Blackwell and Ensemble
First Act Finale .... Ensemble

ACT II

"Birthday Song" .... Fanny, Honorine, Ensemble
"To My Wife" .... Panisse
"The Thought of You" .... Marius and Fanny
"Love Is a Very Light Thing" .... Cesar
"Other Hands, Other Hearts" .... Fanny, Cesar, Marius
"Fanny" (Reprise) .... Cesar, Fanny, Marius
Montage .... Ensemble
"Be Kind to Your Parents" .... Fanny, Cesario
Cesario's Party (*Cirque français*)
    Acrobats—Charles Blackwell, Michael de Marco, Ray Dorian, Bill
                                         Pope, Toni Wheelis
    Pony and Trainer—Wally Strauss, Steve Wiland
    Trained Seals—Dran and Tani Seitz
    Living Statues—Betty Carr, Ronald Cecill, Norma Doggett, Ray
                        Dorian, Ellen Matthews, Dolores Smith
    Clowns—Herb Banke, Mike Mason, Henry Michel, Jack Washburn
    Finale—Aerialist, Dean Crane and Ensemble
"Welcome Home" (Reprise) .... Cesar, Panisse

THE LIVING ROOM

(22 performances)

Drama in two acts by Graham Greene. Produced by Gilbert Miller
and Donald Albery at Henry Miller's Theatre, November 17, 1954.

Cast of characters—

Mary, the daily woman ....Hazel Jones
Rose Pemberton ....Barbara Bel Geddes
Michael Dennis ....Michael Goodliffe
Miss Teresa Browne ....Nora Nicholson
Miss Helen Browne ....Ann Shoemaker
Father James Browne ....Walter Fitzgerald
Mrs. Dennis ....Carol Goodner
   Act I.—Scene 1—The living room; late afternoon in March.   Scene
2—The same; the next morning.   Act II.—Scene 1—The living room;
three weeks later, late afternoon.   Scene 2—The same; next morning.
   Staged by Hugh Hunt; production designed by Raymond Sovey;
costumes supervised by Kathryn Miller; production stage manager,
Richard Bender; stage manager, Daniel S. Broun.

See page 92.

(Closed December 4, 1954)

ABIE'S IRISH ROSE

(20 performances)

New stage version of the comedy in three acts by Anne Nichols.
Produced by Michael Rose at the Holiday Theatre, November 18,
1954.

Cast of characters—

Mrs. Cohen ....Anna Appel
Mr. Cohen ....Lou Gilbert
Rabbi Samuels ....Roger De Koven
Solomon Levy ....Ludwig Donath
Abie Levy ....Val Dufour
Rosemary Murphy ....Judith Paige
Patrick Murphy ....Neil Fitzgerald
Father Whalen ....Douglas Rutherford
Nathaniel Jones, Baptist Minister ....Woody Parker
Bridesmaids ....Jean Lamont, Marianne Marshall,
              Maggi McDonnell, Virginia McMahon
Matron of Honor ....Marion Myser
   Act I.—The action takes place in the living room of Solomon Levy's
home in New York.   The time is spring, after World War II; eve-
ning.   Act II.—The same; a week later.   Act III.—The New York
apartment of Abie and Rosemary; Christmas time, seven months later.
   Staged by Anne Nichols, assisted by Joseph Leon; settings, lighting and costumes by Paul Morrison; production stage manager, Joseph Leon.

Abie's Irish Rose was first produced in New York May 23, 1922,
at the Fulton Theatre; first revival May 12, 1937, at the Little
Theatre.

(Closed December 4, 1954)

WEDDING BREAKFAST

(113 performances)

Play in three acts by Theodore Reeves. Produced by Kermit Bloomgarden at the Forty-Eighth Street Theatre, November 20, 1954.

Cast of characters—

Ruth ....Virginia Vincent
Norman ....Harvey Lembeck
Stella ....Lee Grant
Ralph ....Anthony Franciosa
The time is the present; the place, New York. Act I.—May and June. Act II.—July. Act III.—The same.
Staged by Herman Shumlin; settings and lighting by William and Jean Eckart, assisted by Klaus Holm; costumes by Edith Lutyens; production supervisor, Del Hughes; stage manager, Leonard Patrick.

A New York story of the romances of two young Jewish sisters who share an apartment. Ruth is a salesgirl engaged to a book-keeper: they are patiently saving up to get married, and they have a fine, limited, petty-bourgeois approach to life. The other sister, Stella, has risen somewhat snootily above her background; has gone to college, found a job on a magazine, been engaged to a doctor who jilted her for someone else. She meets a hardware salesman who is a cousin of Ruth's beau; he falls for her, rushes her, proposes to her; but though she loves him, the intellectual snob in Stella makes her resist the life he has to offer. When she begs him to become a professional man, he angrily walks out on her. When she confesses she was wrong, he walks out on her again; but at the end he is walking briskly back.

(Closed February 26, 1955)

SANDHOG

(48 performances)

Ballad in three acts by Earl Robinson and Waldo Salt, based on the short story "St. Columba and the River" by Theodore Dreiser. Produced by Phoenix Theatre (T. Edward Hambleton and Norris Houghton) by special arrangement with Rachel Productions (Howard Da Silva and Arnold Perl) at the Phoenix Theatre, November 23, 1954.

Cast of characters—

Kids—
Sandy ....David Winters
Small Fry ....Eliot Feld
Girl with a Ball ....Betty Ageloff

Ring Leader ....Yuriko
Red ....**Muriel** Manings
Air Lock Foreman ....John Carter
Night Shift Foreman ....David Hooks
Sam on the Stick ....Leon Bibb
Henderson ....Mordecai Bauman
Policeman ....Robert De Cormier
Bill Cayton ....Douglas Collins
Johnny O'Sullivan ....Jack Cassidy
Fred Burger ....Paul Ukena
Joe Novak ....Michael Kermoyan
Andy Cayton ....Rodester Timmons
Tim Cavanaugh ....David Brooks
Katie O'Sullivan ....Betty Oakes
Sharkey ....Gordon Dilworth
Sheela Cavanaugh ....Alice Ghostley
Mary Novak ....Mary Kane
Ginny Cayton ....Mareda Gaither
Sandhogs, Sandhogs' Wives ......Stephanie Scourby, Mitzi Wilson,
            Doree Simmons, Peter Maravell, Elliot Freeman
      The entire action takes place at the North River Tunnel Works and
the surrounding neighborhood in downtown New York.

ACT I

Scene 1: The Tunnel Works—A day in the late 1880's.
Scene 2: The Tunnel Works—Later the same afternoon.
Scene 3: A park bench—Dusk of the same afternoon.
Scene 4: Sharkey's Saloon—Evening of the same day.
Scene 5: The Cavanaugh flat—Early the next morning.
Scene 6: The Tunnel—Morning shift.

ACT II

Scene 1: The Tunnel Works—Afternoon; one year later.
Scene 2: The Cavanaugh flat—The same evening.
Scene 3: Sharkey's Saloon and the Cavanaugh flat—Evening; a few
         weeks later.
Scene 4: The Tunnel—Night shift.
Scene 5: The Tunnel Works—Later the same night.

ACT III

Scene 1: The New Tunnel Works—Afternoon; many months later.
Scene 2: The Cavanaugh flat—The same evening.
Scene 3: The New Tunnel—Afternoon shift; many months later.
Scene 4: The Cavanaugh flat—A few months later.
Scene 5: The New Tunnel Works—Later the same day.

      Staged by Howard Da Silva; production and lighting designed by
Howard Bay; choreography by Sophie Maslow; musical direction by
Ben Steinberg; orchestrations by Hershey Kay; costumes by Toni
Ward; production stage manager, Bernard Gersten; stage manager,
Richard Blofson.

Musical numbers—

ACT I
Scene 1
"Come Down" ....Chorus
"Some Said They Were Crazy" ....Chorus
"Stand Back" ....Robert De Cormier

Scene 2
"Hey Joe" ....Kids
"Johnny's Cursing Song" ....Jack Cassidy

Scene 3
"Come and Be Married" ....Betty Ageloff
"Johnny O' " ....Jack Cassidy and Betty Oakes
"Good Old Days" ....Gordon Dilworth and Kids

Scene 4
"Song of the Bends" ....David Brooks, Paul Ukena, Michael
Kermoyan and Rodester Timmons

Scene 5
"By the Glenside" ....Alice Ghostley

Scene 6
"High Air" ....Chorus
"Work Song" ....David Brooks, Paul Ukena and Leon Bibb
"28 Men" ....Chorus

ACT II
Scene 1
"Sandhog Song" ....Mordecai Bauman, Chorus and Kids

Scene 2
"Sweat Song" ....David Brooks
"Fugue on a Hot Afternoon in a Small Flat" ....David Brooks, Jack
Cassidy, Alice Ghostley and Betty Oakes

Scene 3
"T-w-i-n-s" ....Quartet: David Brooks, Paul Ukena,
Rodester Timmons and Michael Kermoyan
"Katie O'Sullivan" ....Quartet, Gordon Dilworth
and Kids
"Johnny O' "—Reprise and Counter Melody ....Jack Cassidy
and Betty Oakes

Interlude
"28 Men" ....Chorus

Scene 4
"High Air" ....Chorus
"Some Said They Were Crazy" ....Chorus

Scene 5
"Sing Sorrow" ....Chorus
"You Want to Mourn" ....Alice Ghostley, Stephanie Scourby,
Mitzi Wilson, Doree Simmons

ACT III
Scene 1
"Ma, Ma, Where's My Dad?" ....Kids' song and dance
"Greathead Shield" ....Douglas Collins and Kids

Scene 2
"Waiting for the Men" ....Alice Ghostley, Mary Kane
and Mareda Gaither

Interlude
"28 Men" ....Chorus
"Greathead Shield" ....Leon Bibb

Scene 3
"Ring Iron" ....Chorus
"Johnny's Cursing Song"—Reprise ....Jack Cassidy

Interlude
"Stand Back" ....Chorus and Robert De Cormier

Scene 4
"Johnny O' "—Reprise and Counter Melody ....Jack Cassidy
and Betty Oakes
"Oh, Oh, Oh, O'Sullivan" ....Paul Ukena, Rodester Timmons,
Michael Kermoyan and Douglas Collins

Scene 5
"Sandhog Song"—Finale ....Chorus

(Closed January 2, 1955)

ONE EYE CLOSED

(3 performances)

Farce in three acts by Justin Sturm. Produced by Haila Stoddard at the Bijou Theatre, November 24, 1954.

Cast of characters—

Gordon Cameron	Tom Helmore
Denia Cameron	Haila Stoddard
Easter Sunday	Moe
Mary Benson	Marjorie Eaton
Frenchy Mulligan	Harry Ellerbe
Trixie Tyson	Moultrie Patten
Cy Milton	John Fiedler
Sheriff Meyers	Iggie Wolfington
Elsa Kinney	Parker McCormick
Lowell Markey	John Baragrey
Cokey Mulqueen II	George Mathews
Sergeant (State Police)	Charles Bellin
State Policeman	Richard Everhart
An American Indian	Hal Thompson

Act I.—Scene 1—The Camerons' home in Wilton, Connecticut. Scene 2—The same; three days later. Act II.—The same; one second later. Act III.—Scene 1—On the road from New Haven to Wilton; early next morning. Scene 2—The Camerons' home; a half hour later.

Staged by Romney Brent; settings and lighting by Eldon Elder; costumes by Virginia Volland; stage manager, William Weaver.

Tale of a hard-up playboy who lives in a stable with his wife. While hubby goes off, in convict costume, to a Yale reunion, the wife's old Harvard beau turns up, in convict costume, on the lam from Sing Sing. Thereafter complications, of an increasingly forced and frantic nature, abound.

(Closed November 26, 1954)

MRS. PATTERSON

(101 performances)

Play in three acts by Charles Sebree and Greer Johnson. Songs and incidental music by James Shelton, and lyrics by the authors. Produced by Leonard Sillman at the National Theatre, December 1, 1954.

Cast of characters—

Anna Hicks	Ruth Attaway
Selma Mae	Vinie Burrows
Theodora (Teddy) Hicks	Eartha Kitt
Willie B. Brayboy	Terry Carter
Aunt Matt Crossy	Estelle Hemsley
Mr. D.	Avon Long
Bessie Bolt	Helen Dowdy
Sylvanus	Emory Richardson
Mrs. Patterson	Enid Markey
June Embree	Mary Ann Hoxworth

Rose Embree ....Mary Harmon
Fern Embree ....Joan Morgan
   The time is 1920; late summer. The action takes place at the edge
of a small town in Kentucky. Act I.—Early evening. Act II.—The
following day. Act III.—The next evening.
   Staged by Guthrie McClintic; setting and costumes by Raoul Pène
duBois; orchestrations by George Siravo; musical director, Abba
Bogin; production stage manager, Morty Halpern; stage manager,
Leonard Auerbach.

Musical numbers—

Sung by Eartha Kitt
"Mrs. Patterson"
"Tea in Chicago"
"If I Was a Boy"
"My Daddy Is a Dandy"
"Be Good, Be Good, Be Good"

Sung by Helen Dowdy
"I Wish I Was a Bumble Bee"

A play chronicling the tangled real life and aromatic dream life
of a young Negro girl whose father had deserted her mother. Teddy
Hicks lives in ramshackle poverty; mischievous, sharp-tongued, sensitive, she yearns to be "a rich white woman" on the order of her
mother's employer, Mrs. Patterson. But together with Teddy's fantasies of genteel tea-drinking in the Patterson set go episodes in-
volving raffish high-steppers and a certain "Mr. D." from Hell.
Eventually the dreams are crushed out and Teddy sets about facing
the realities she has run away from.

(Closed February 26, 1955)

HIT THE TRAIL

(4 performances)

Musical comedy in two acts, with book by Frank O'Neill, music
by Frederico Valerio, and lyrics by Elizabeth Miele. Produced by
Elizabeth Miele at the Mark Hellinger Theatre, December 2, 1954.

Cast of characters—

Jerry ....Donn Driver
Joan ....Diana Drake
Willie ....Fred Lightner
Clayton Harrison ....Paul Valentine
Lucy Vernay ....Irra Petina
Murph ....Robert Wright
Aggie July ....Toby Deane
Miller ....Charles G. Martin
Waiters ....Jack Purcell, Rene Miville
   Dancers: Jeanna Belkin, Lois Bewley, Sandy Bozoki, Diane Con-
soer, Patty Fitzimmons, Nancy Hackenberg, Robert Bakanic, Paul
Gannon, Jack Purcell, Alton Ruff, Buff Shurr and Fred Zoeter.
   Singers: Josephine Annunciata, Irene Carroll, Peggy Kinard, Dolores
Micheline, Michelle Reiner, Martha Rich, Iris Sinding, Flavine Val-

entine, Lois Van Pelt, Paul Brown, Michael King, Rene Miville, Robert Price and James Schlader.

The action takes place in Virginia City, Nevada, during the late 19th Century.

Staged by Charles W. Christenberry Jr. and Byrle Cass; dances and musical numbers staged by Gene Bayliss; settings and lighting by Leo Kerz; costumes by Michi; orchestrations by Don Walker; musical director and vocal arranger, Arthur Norris; production stage manager, Neil Hartley; stage managers, Phillip E. Schrager and John Moorehead.

Musical numbers—

ACT I

Scene 1: Outside Virginia City
"On with the Show" .... Jerry, Joan and troupers
Scene 2: Lucy Vernay's Dressing Room
"Mr. Right" .... Lucy
"Dynamic" .... Lucy and Murph
Scene 3: The Blue Sierra Casino
"Blue Sierras" .... Aggie and patrons
"No! No! No!" .... Clay
"The Wide Open Spaces" .... Clay, Aggie, Joan and Jerry
Scene 4: A Street in Virginia City
"Gold Cannot Buy" .... Townspeople
"Remember the Night" .... Clay and Lucy
"Tell Me How" .... Murph
Scene 5: Stage of Piper's Opera House
"It Was Destiny" .... Aggie and Girls
Scene 6: A Park in Virginia City
"Just a Wonderful Time" .... Jerry and Joan
Scene 7: The Blue Sierra Casino
"Nevada Hoe Down" .... Aggie and patrons

ACT II

Scene 1: Emporium (staged by Donn Driver)
"New Look Feeling" .... Lucy, Jerry, Joan and patrons
"Set Me Free" .... Lucy
"Somehow I've Always Known" .... Murph
Scene 2: Gambling Room
Reprise: "Remember the Night" .... Clay
Scene 3: A Street in Virginia City
"My Fatal Charm" .... Clay
"Men Are a Pain in the Neck" .... Aggie
Scene 4: The Blue Sierra Casino
"Wherever I May Go" .... Lucy
Scene 5: A Street in Virginia City
"Take Your Time" .... Jerry and Joan
Scene 6: Garden Behind Murph's House
"Happy Birthday" .... Company
Reprise: "Mr. Right" .... Lucy and Murph

(Closed December 4, 1954)

BAD SEED

(200 performances)
(Continued)

Play in two acts by Maxwell Anderson, adapted from the novel by William March. Produced by The Playwrights' Company at the Forty-Sixth Street Theatre, December 8, 1954.

Cast of characters—

Rhoda Penmark .... Patty McCormack
Col. Kenneth Penmark .... John O'Hare
Christine Penmark .... Nancy Kelly
Monica Breedlove .... Evelyn Varden
Emory Wages .... Joseph Holland
Leroy .... Henry Jones
Miss Fern .... Joan Croydon
Reginald Tasker .... Lloyd Gough
Mrs. Daigle .... Eileen Heckart
Mr. Daigle .... Wells Richardson
Messenger .... George Gino
Richard Bravo .... Thomas Chalmers

The action takes place in the apartment of Col. and Mrs. Penmark, in the suburb of a Southern city. Act I.—Scene 1—Early morning; a day in early June. Scene 2—Two-thirty P.M., the same day. Scene 3—Evening, the same day. Scene 4—Mid-morning, a few days later. Act II.—Scene 1—Late afternoon, the next day. Scene 2—After breakfast, the next morning. Scene 3—After dinner, the same day. Scene 4—A few days later.

Staged by Reginald Denham; setting and lighting by George Jenkins; costumes by Sal Anthony; Miss Kelly's clothes supervised by Virginia Volland; production stage manager, Porter Van Zandt.

See page 120.

LUNATICS AND LOVERS

(203 performances)
(Continued)

Farce in two acts by Sidney Kingsley. Produced by M. Kirshner at the Broadhurst Theatre, December 13, 1954.

Cast of characters—

Dan Cupid .... Buddy Hackett
Joe Gonz .... Nat Cantor
Sable Wellington .... Sheila Bond
Waiter .... Maurice Brenner
Judge Sullivan .... Dennis King
Desiree .... Vicki Cummings
Will Harrison .... Arthur O'Connell
Marian Harrison .... Mary Anderson
Policeman .... James Nolan
House Detective .... George Tyne
Hotel Manager .... Fairfax Burgher
Bellboy .... Maurice Brenner
Bride .... Lynn Merrill
Groom .... Rex Partington
Bridesmaid .... Donna Pearson

The action takes place in a suite in a hotel on West 48th Street, New York City; the time is the present. Act I.—Scene 1—Nine o'clock. Scene 2—Immediately following. Act II.—Scene 1—Four A.M., the same night. Scene 2—Immediately following.

Staged by Sidney Kingsley; production designed and lighted by Frederick Fox; production stage manager, Samuel Liff; stage manager, Jerry Adler.

See "The Season on Broadway."

WITNESS FOR THE PROSECUTION

(191 performances)
(Continued)

A murder mystery in three acts by Agatha Christie. Produced by Gilbert Miller and Peter Saunders at Henry Miller's Theatre, December 16, 1954.

Cast of characters—

Carter	Gordon Nelson
Greta	Mary Barclay
Sir Wilfrid Robarts, Q.C.	Francis L. Sullivan
Mr. Mayhew	Robin Craven
Leonard Vole	Gene Lyons
Inspector Hearne	Claude Horton
Plain Clothes Detective	Ralph Leonard
Romaine	Patricia Jessel
Third Juror	Dolores Rashid
Second Juror	Andrew George
Foreman of the Jury	Jack Bittner
Court Usher	Arthur Oshlag
Clerk of the Court	Ronald Dawson
Mr. Myers, Q.C.	Ernest Clark
Mr. Justice Wainwright	Horace Braham
Alderman	R. Cobden-Smith
Judge's Clerk	Harold Webster
Court Stenographer	W. H. Thomas
Warder	Ralph Roberts
Barrister	Henry Craig Neslo
Barrister	Brace Conning
Barrister	Ruth Greene
Barrister	Albert Richards
Barrister	Franklyn Monroe
Barrister	Sam Kramer
Policeman	Bryan Herbert
Dr. Wyatt	Guy Spaull
Janet Mackenzie	Una O'Connor
Mr. Clegg	Michael McAloney
The Other Woman	Dawn Steinkamp

The time is the present. Act I.—The chambers of Sir Wilfrid Robarts, Q.C., in London; late afternoon. Act II.—The Central Criminal Court (The Old Bailey) in London; morning, six weeks later. Act III.—Scene 1—The chambers of Sir Wilfrid Robarts, Q.C., in London; the same evening. Scene 2—The Old Bailey; the next morning.

Staged by Robert Lewis; production designed by Raymond Sovey; costumes supervised by Kathryn Miller; production stage manager, John Effrat.

See page 149.

PORTRAIT OF A LADY

(7 performances)

Play in three acts by William Archibald, based on the novel by Henry James. Produced by Lyn Austin, Thomas Noyes and The Producers Theatre at the ANTA Theatre, December 21, 1954.

Cast of characters—

Lord Warburton ....Peter Pagan
Mr. Touchett ....Halliwell Hobbes
Caspar Goodwood ....Eric Fleming
Ralph Touchett ....Douglas Watson
Isabel Archer ....Jennifer Jones
Mrs. Touchett ....Kathleen Comegys
Henrietta Stackpole ....Jan Farrand
Serena Merle ....Barbara O'Neil
Gilbert Osmond ....Robert Flemyng
Pansy ....Marcia Morris
Countess Gemini ....Cathleen Nesbitt

Act I.—Gardencourt, the English home of Mr. Touchett; the rear garden on a summer afternoon in the late Eighteen Seventies. Act II.—Scene 1—The terrace of Gilbert Osmond's villa in Florence, Italy; three months later. Scene 2—The terrace; two days later. Scene 3— The terrace; a month later. Act III.—Scene 1—The terrace; eighteen months later. Scene 2—The terrace; early afternoon the following day. Scene 3—Gardencourt; a week later, late afternoon.

Staged by José Quintero; settings and lighting by William and Jean Eckart, assisted by Klaus Holm; costumes by Cecil Beaton; piano accompaniment, Baldwin Bergersen; production stage manager, Elliot Martin.

An adaptation of Henry James' famous novel—the nineteenth-century story of a high-mettled, independent-minded young American girl, Isabel Archer, who goes abroad wanting ardently to live but knowing little about life. She rejects the safe and familiar; she refuses an unexceptionable English lord; through an intrigante's wiles she meets a corrupt, over-cultivated American expatriate who wants her solely for her money. Admiring him for his accomplishments, she marries him and has a hideous awakening. But having made her bed of spikes, Isabel sentences herself to lie in it.

Sliced paper-thin for the stage, Isabel seemed less James' heroine than somebody pushed about by the demands of the plot. Though a respectful adaptation, the play came off as Henry James glimpsed through a drizzle from a train window, with only here and there something recognizable or real.

(Closed December 25, 1954)

WHAT EVERY WOMAN KNOWS

(15 performances)

Comedy in four acts by James M. Barrie. Revived by the New York City Center Theatre Company at the New York City Center of Music and Drama, December 22, 1954.

Cast of characters—

James Wylie ....William Lanteau
Alick Wylie ....Farrell Pelly
David Wylie ....Philip Bourneuf
Maggie Wylie ....Helen Hayes

John Shand	Kent Smith
Comtesse de la Briere	Viola Roache
Lady Sybil Tenterden	Betsy von Furstenberg
Feikie	Sid Cassel
Maid	Virginia Low
Mr. Venables	John Cromwell
Manservant	George Cathrey
Bagpiper	James Roche

Electors and Townspeople: Linda Berlin, Jarmila Daubek, Anne Edwards, Mary Hara, Alison Landor, Lily Lodge, Jill McAnney, Rosemary Shein, Mearl Allen, James Bernard, Marshall Breeden, Richard Buck, Wescott Carpenter, Russell Chase, Vincent Dowling, Mark Fleischman, David Friedman, Bernard Gilmore, Sam Gordon, Erle Hall, Austin Hay, Ben Jenne, Mark Halp, Howard Lanser, Richard Marr, Paul Marin, Nelson Miller, Philip Morini, Hale Matthews, Tom Brannum, Cecil Rutherford, Kenneth Sleeper, Ted Theoharous, Matthew Tobin, David Eliot, Jay Sweeney, Don Wadley, Charles Williamson.

Act I.—The parlor of the Wylie house in a small town in Scotland; evening, about the year 1900. Act II.—John Shand's committee rooms—formerly a barber shop—Glasgow; six years later. Act III.—Scene 1—John Shand's house in London; two years later. Scene 2—The same; an afternoon some days later. Act IV.—The Comtesse's summer country cottage, in Surrey; three weeks later.

Staged by John Stix; production designed by John Koenig; music selected and arranged by Max Marlin; costume director, Grace Houston; lighting by Feder; production stage manager, Buford Armitage; stage manager, Herman Shapiro.

(Closed January 2, 1955)

BLACK-EYED SUSAN

(4 performances)

Comedy in three acts by A. B. Shiffrin. Produced by Gordon W. Pollock, in association with Hart and Goodman, at the Playhouse, December 23, 1954.

Cast of characters—

Dr. Nicholas Marsh	Vincent Price
Dr. Zelda Barry	Kay Medford
Dr. Louis Beaumont	Everett Sloane
Susan Gillespie	Dana Wynter
Peter Gillespie	Charles Boaz

Act I.—Dr. Marsh's office; an afternoon in September. Act II.—Scene 1—The following day, about midnight. Scene 2—Six weeks later; afternoon. Act III.—The office of Doctors Marsh and Barry; three years later, late afternoon.

Staged by Gregory Ratoff; sets and costumes by William Molyneux; stage manager, Richard B. Shull.

A young wife who hasn't been able to become a mother decides to seduce a neurologist as a way of having a child. A work of definitive vulgarity, *Black-Eyed Susan* pawed and lipsmacked its way through a host of double-entendres.

(Closed December 25, 1954)

RUTH DRAPER

(Her Company of Characters)

AND

PAUL DRAPER

(24 performances)

Monologues by Ruth Draper; dances by Paul Draper. Produced by Charles Bowden and Richard Barr at the Bijou Theatre, December 26, 1954.

Varied programs during three-week engagement, with selections from the following:

Monologues by Ruth Draper—

    Opening a Bazaar
    At an Art Exhibition in Boston
    The Actress
    "Vive La France," 1940
    A Children's Party in Philadelphia
    A German Teacher with a Class of Children
    A Class in Greek Poise
    A Debutante at a Dance
    A Scottish Immigrant at Ellis Island
    Three Women and Mr. Clifford
    Doctors and Diets
    A Dalmatian Peasant in the Hall of a New York Hospital
    Showing the Garden
    The Italian Lesson
    In a Church in Italy
    Three Breakfasts
    Three Generations in the Court of Domestic Relations
    An English Houseparty
    On the Porch in a Maine Coast Village

Dances by Paul Draper—

    Gigue ....Bach
    Alcina Suite ....Handel
        1. Menuet
        2. Sarabande
        3. Musette
        4. Tambourino
    Assassin ....Debussy
    Dance without Music
    "Tea for Two" ....Youmans
    Two approaches to the same subject
        1. A Sharp Character ....Lecuona
        2. In a Dance Hall ....Porter
    Satire on a Political Speech
    Folk Medley ....Traditional
    Improvisation
    Gavotte ....Thomas
    Blue Danube Waltz ....Strauss
    Irish Jig
    On the Beat ....Couperin
    Classical Blues ....Beethoven
    Menuet and Gigue ....Mozart
        Mr. Draper's accompanist, John Coleman; additional musical accompaniment by Edward Wilcox, at the piano; Aaron Bell, bass; James Crawford, drums; stage manager, Barnett Owen.

(Closed January 15, 1955)

THE SAINT OF BLEECKER STREET

(92 performances)

Music drama in three acts, with music and libretto by Gian-Carlo Menotti. Produced by Chandler Cowles at the Broadway Theatre, December 27, 1954.

Cast of characters—

Assunta	Catherine Akos
Carmela	Maria Di Gerlando
Maria Corona	Maria Marlo
Her Dumb Son	Ernesto Gonzales
Don Marco	Leon Lishner
Annina	Virginia Copeland *
	Gabrielle Ruggiero
Michele	David Poleri *
	Davis Cunningham
Desideria	Gloria Lane
Salvatore	David Aiken
Concettina	Lucy Becque
A Young Man	Richard Cassilly
An Old Woman	Elizabeth Carron
Bartender	Russell Goodwin
First Guest	Keith Kaldenberg
Second Guest	John Reardon
A Nun	Dorothy Krebill
A Young Priest	Robert Barry

Neighbors, Friends, Policemen, etc.: Theodora Brandon, Betsy Bridge, Lorraine Bridges, Elizabeth Carron, Doris Davis, Mignon Dunn, Elizabeth Dunning, Joyce Duskin, Elaine Galante, Jeanne Grant, Mary Hensley, Carroll Jones, Dorothy Krebill, Leslie MacLennan, Bessie Mijanovich, Doris Okerson, Francesco Roberto, Donna Sanders; Robert Barry, Michael Bulzomi, Richard Cassilly, Rico Froelich, Russell Goodwin, Gary Gordon, Don Grobe, Fred Jones, Keith Kaldenberg, Chester Ludgin, William McCully, Michael MacLennan, Dan Merriman, John Reardon, Reid Shelton, Alan Smith, Robert Watts.

The time is the present. Act I.—Scene 1—A cold-water flat on Bleecker Street; Good Friday afternoon. Scene 2—A vacant lot on Mulberry Street; San Gennaro Day. Act II.—An Italian restaurant; the following May. Act III.—Scene 1—A subway station; a few months later. Scene 2—The cold-water flat; several days later.

Staged by Gian-Carlo Menotti; conductor, Thomas Schippers; associate musical director, Samuel Krachmalnick; scenery and costumes by Robert Randolph; lighting by Jean Rosenthal; assistant director, Bill Butler; production supervisor, Lincoln Kirstein; production stage manager, James Vincent Russo.

* Opening-night singer, thereafter alternating with principal listed immediately following.

(Closed April 2, 1955)

THE FLOWERING PEACH

(135 performances)

Drama in eight scenes and an epilogue by Clifford Odets. Produced by Robert Whitehead for The Producers Theatre at the Belasco Theatre, December 28, 1954.

Cast of characters—

Noah	Menasha Skulnik
Esther	Berta Gersten
Japheth	Mario Alcalde
Shem	Martin Ritt
Ham	Leon Janney
Leah	Osna Palmer
Rachel	Janice Rule
Goldie	Barbara Baxley
A Strange Man } Lion	Sidney Armus
Fawns	Marjorie Barrett, Patricia Fay
Goat	Barbara Kay
First Old Man	Ludwig Roth
Second Old Man	Sidney Kay

The time is then, not now. Scene 1—Noah's home. Scene 2—The same; later. Scene 3—A high hillside. Scene 4—The same; later. Scene 5—The same; still later. Scene 6—The deck of the ark; the forty-first day. Scene 7—The ark; many weeks later. Scene 8—The ark; months later. Epilogue—The ark at rest.

Staged by Clifford Odets; settings by Mordecai Gorelik; lighting by Feder; costumes by Ballou; music by Alan Hovhaness; production stage manager, Frederic de Wilde.

See page 180.

(Closed April 23, 1955)

ANASTASIA

(176 performances)
(Continued)

Play in three acts by Marcelle Maurette, adapted from the French by Guy Bolton. Produced by Elaine Perry at the Lyceum Theatre, December 29, 1954.

Cast of characters—

Chernov	Boris Tumarin
Varya	Sefton Darr
Petrovin	David J. Stewart
Prince Bounine	Joseph Anthony
Sergei	William Callan
Anna	Viveca Lindfors
Counsellor Drivinitz	Carl Low
Sleigh Driver	Stuart Germain
Charwoman	Vivian Nathan
Dr. Sirensky	Michael Strong
Dowager Empress	Eugenie Leontovich
Baroness Livenbaum	Dorothy Patten
Prince Paul	Hurd Hatfield

The action of the play takes place in Prince Bounine's house on the outskirts of Berlin. Act I.—January, 1926. Act II.—One month later. Act III.—Two weeks later.

Staged by Alan Schneider; production designed by Ben Edwards; stage manager, John Drew Devereaux.

The scene is Berlin in 1926. Some rascals, knowing that a huge fortune of the Czar's was banked in Sweden after the Russian revolution, plot to rig up an imperial claimant for it. They find one in a waif-like sick girl who had insisted—while a patient in a Bucharest hospital—that she was the Czar's daughter, Princess Anastasia. Real or not, after being coached she passes muster with people who had once known Anastasia. But the prime test is with Anastasia's grandmother, the Dowager Empress, who, after sniffing at the girl's claims and subjecting her to a merciless grilling, is convinced she is the true princess. Everything is thereupon arranged for her to marry a prince she does not love; but at the end, on the very eve of the wedding, Anastasia vanishes.

HOUSE OF FLOWERS

(165 performances)

Musical in two acts, with book by Truman Capote; music by Harold Arlen; lyrics by Messrs. Capote and Arlen. Produced by Saint Subber at the Alvin Theatre, December 30, 1954.

Cast of characters—

Tulip	Dolores Harper
Gladiola	Ada Moore
Pansy	Enid Mosier
Do	Winston George Henriques
Don't	Solomon Earl Green
Mother	Miriam Burton
Ottilie alias Violet	Diahann Carroll
Madame Fleur	Pearl Bailey
Captain Jonas	Ray Walston
Madame Tango	Juanita Hall
Mamselle Ibo-Lele	Pearl Reynolds
The Sisters Meringue	Leu Comacho, Margot Small
Mamselle Honolulu	Mary Mon Toy
Mamselle Cigarette	Glory Van Scott
Royal	Rawn Spearman
The Champion	Geoffrey Holder
Chief of Police	Don Redman
Carmen	Carmen de Lavallade
Alvin	Alvin Ailey
Monsieur Jamison	Dino DiLuca
The Houngan	Frederick O'Neal
Duchess of the Sea	Miriam Burton
Steel Band	Michel Alexander, Roderick Clavery, Alphonso Marshall

Townspeople: Joseph Comadore, Hubert Dilworth, Phillip Hepburn, Louis Johnson, Mary Louise, Audrey Mason, Arthur Mitchell, Walter Nicks, Albert Popwell, Sabu, Herbert Stubbs.

The setting is on an island somewhere in the West Indies. The action takes place during Mardi Gras Weekend. Act I.—Scene 1— Maison des Fleurs. Scene 2—On the way to the cockfight. Scene 3—At the cockfight. Scene 4—Maison des Fleurs. Scene 5—The Houngan's hut. Scene 6—The harbor of the town. Act II.—Scene 1—Maison des Fleurs. Scene 2—Madame Fleur's salon. Scene 3— The Houngan's hut. Scene 4—Madame Tango's salon. Scene 5— Madame Fleur's salon. Scene 6—Maison des Fleurs.

Staged by Peter Brook; sets and costumes by Oliver Messel; dances and musical numbers by Herbert Ross; lighting by Jean Rosenthal;

musical director, Jerry Arlen; orchestrations by Ted Royal; production
stage manager, Lucia Victor; stage managers, John Barry Ryan, John
Scott.

Musical numbers—

ACT I
Scene 1
"Waitin' " ....Pansy, Tulip, Gladiola
"One Man Ain't Quite Enough" ....Madame Fleur
"Madame Tango's Tango" ....Madame Tango, Tango Belles
"A Sleepin' Bee" ....Ottilie, Pansy, Tulip, Gladiola

Scene 2
"Bamboo Cage" ....The Champion, The Steel Band, Do, Don't,
Pansy, Tulip, Gladiola, Madame Tango,
Chief of Police, and The Ensemble

Scene 3
"House of Flowers" ....Royal, Ottilie

Scene 4
"Two Ladies in de Shade of de Banana Tree"
Sung by ....Pansy, Gladiola
Danced by ....Carmen, Tulip and Ensemble
"What Is a Friend For?" ....Madame Fleur

Scene 5
"A Sleepin' Bee" (Reprise) ....Ottilie, Royal

Scene 6
"Mardi Gras"
Sung by ....Mother
Danced by ....Carmen, Alvin and The Ensemble
"I Never Has Seen Snow" ....Ottilie

ACT II
Scene 1
"Husband Cage" ....Pansy, Tulip, Gladiola and Ensemble

Scene 2
"Has I Let You Down?" ......Madame Fleur, Pansy, Tulip, Gladiola

Scene 3
"Voudou" ....The Houngan and The Ensemble
The Drummers ....Sabu, Joseph Comadore, Michael
Alexander, Alphonso Marshall
Duchess of the Sea ....Miriam Burton
Octopus ....Albert Popwell
Shark ....Walter Nicks, Arthur Mitchell, Alphonso Marshall
Turtle ....Joseph Comadore and Ensemble
Baron of the Cemetery ....Geoffrey Holder
(Banda dance choreographed by Mr. Holder)

Scene 4
"Slide, Boy, Slide"
Sung by ....Madame Tango and The Ensemble
Danced by ....Alvin and The Ensemble

Scene 5
"Don't Like Goodbyes" ....Madame Fleur

Scene 6
"Turtle Song" ....Royal, Ottilie and The Ensemble
Finale: "Bamboo Cage" (Reprise) ....The Entire Company
and The Ensemble
"Banana Tree" (Reprise) ....The Entire Company

(Closed May 21, 1955)

THE FOURPOSTER

(15 performances)

Comedy in three acts by Jan de Hartog. Revived by the New York City Center Theatre Company at the New York City Center of Music and Drama, January 5, 1955.

Cast of characters—

Agnes ....Jessica Tandy
Michael ....Hume Cronyn
      Staged by José Ferrer; scenery by Syrjala; costumes by Lucinda Ballard; general costume director, Grace Houston; production stage manager, Buford Armitage; stage manager, Herman Shapiro.

The Fourposter was first produced October 24, 1951, by The Playwrights' Company at the Ethel Barrymore Theatre for 632 performances.

(Closed January 16, 1955)

THE DOCTOR'S DILEMMA

(48 performances)

Play in five acts by Bernard Shaw. Revived by the Phoenix Theatre (T. Edward Hambleton and Norris Houghton) at the Phoenix Theatre, January 11, 1955.

Cast of characters—

Redpenny ....Frederic Warriner
Emmy ....Betty Sinclair
Sir Colenso Ridgeon ....Shepperd Strudwick
Dr. Schutzmacher ....Vaughn Taylor
Sir Patrick Cullen ....Philip Bourneuf
Cutler Walpole ....Will Kuluva
Sir Ralph Bloomfield Bonington ....Frederic Worlock
Dr. Blenkinsop ....Milton Selzer
Jennifer Dubedat ....Geraldine Fitzgerald
Louis Dubedat ....Roddy McDowall
Minnie Tinwell ....Peggy Pope
Waiter ....David Hooks
Newspaper Man ....Arthur Anderson
Secretary ....Fritz Weaver
      The action takes place in London at the turn of the century. Act I.—Sir Colenso Ridgeon's consulting room. Act II.—Terrace at the Star and Garter, Richmond. Act III.—Dubedat's studio. Act IV.—The same. Act V.—A Bond Street picture gallery.
      Staged by Sidney Lumet; scenery and lighting by Klaus Holm; costumes by Alvin Colt; production stage manager, Robert Woods; stage manager, Richard Blofson.

(Closed February 20, 1955)

FESTIVAL

(23 performances)

Comedy in three acts by Sam and Bella Spewack. Produced by Walter Fried, in association with Felix Brentano, at the Longacre Theatre, January 18, 1955.

Cast of characters—

```
Wong ...........................................Harry Shaw Lowe
Max Granada ....................................Paul Henried
Ruby ..........................................Patricia Englund
Sasha Rostov ..................................George Voskovec
Sally Ann Peters ...................................Betty Field
Joey Foster ................................Abbott Lee Ruskin
Martova .........................................Luba Malina
Joe Foster .........................................Pat Hingle
Emily Foster .......................................Ann Barlow
Dr. Algernon Burton ..............................James Reese
A Boy .......................................Leslie Alan Blatt
```
The action takes place in the sun room of Max Granada's Beverly Hills home.   Act I.—Morning.   Act II.—Evening, the same day. Act III.—The following morning.

Staged by Albert Marre; scenery and lights by Robert O'Hearn; costumes by Noel Taylor; production stage manager, James Gelb; stage manager, Richard Baldridge.

The scene is the Hollywood mansion of an important music impresario. Into a world of blaring phones, exploding tempers and snarling rival artists, there bursts—to make things really hum—a lady music teacher with a child prodigy. Soon she is rumored a famous pianist's mistress, and the prodigy their illegitimate son. With, in addition, the child's real father suspecting his wife, and a lady cellist buzzing with sex, this play suggested a game of musical sofas.

(Closed February 5, 1955)

THE TIME OF YOUR LIFE

(15 performances)

Play by William Saroyan. Revived by the New York City Center Theatre Company at the New York City Center of Music and Drama, January 19, 1955.

Cast of characters—

```
The Newsboy ........................................Art Ostrin
Joe, a young loafer with money and a good heart .....Franchot Tone
Arab, an Eastern philosopher and harmonica player ....Wolfe Barzell
The Drunkard ...................................Billy M. Greene
Nick, owner of Nick's Pacific Street Saloon,
    Restaurant and Entertainment Palace .........Myron McCormick
Willie, a marble game maniac .....................Fred Kareman
```

Tom, Joe's admirer, disciple, errand boy,
  stooge and friend ....Lonny Chapman
Kitty Duval, a young woman with memories ....Lenka Peterson
Harry, a natural-born hoofer who wants
  to make people laugh ....Harold Lang
Dudley, a young man in love ....Biff McGuire
Wesley, a boy who plays the piano ....Samuel Benskin
Lorene, an unattractive woman ....Justine Johnson
Blick, a heel ....Arthur Jarrett
Mary L., an unhappy woman of quality and
  great beauty ....Carol Grace
Krupp, a waterfront cop ....Mike Kellin
McCarthy, an intelligent and well-read longshoreman ...John Randolph
Nick's Ma ....Rosana San Marco
Kit Carson, an old Indian-fighter ....John Carradine
Sailor ....Tom Brannum
Anna, Nick's daughter ....Linda Berlin
Elsie, a nurse, the girl Dudley loves ....Gloria Vanderbilt
A Streetwalker ....Betty Bartley
Her Side-Kick ....Doris Roberts
A Society Lady ....Paula Laurence
A Society Gentleman ....Albert Whitley
First Cop ....Clifton James
Second Cop ....John Pelletti
Others ....David Martin, Nina Wilcox
  The action takes place in Nick's Pacific Street Saloon, Restaurant
and Entertainment Palace, at the foot of Pacific Street on the Em-
barcadero in San Francisco; and a suggestion of Room 21 at the New
York Hotel, upstairs, around the corner. The time is the afternoon
and the night of a day in October, 1939.
  Staged by Sanford Meisner; setting by Watson Barratt; lighting by
Jean Rosenthal; costume director, Grace Houston; music composed,
selected and arranged by Max Marlin and Eddie Barefield; production stage manager, Buford Armitage; stage managers, Herman Shapiro, Edwin Gifford.

The Time of Your Life was first produced by The Theatre Guild,
in association with Eddie Dowling, at the Booth Theatre, October 25,
1939, for 185 performances.

(Closed January 30, 1955)

THE GRAND PRIZE

(21 performances)

Comedy in three acts by Ronald Alexander. Produced by Shepard Traube at the Plymouth Theatre, January 26, 1955.

Cast of characters—

George ....Ken Harvey
Lucille Cotton ....June Lockhart
John Condon Mitchell ....William Windom
Brenda Johnson ....Nancy Wickwire
Mack ....Perry Bruskin
Kate Wilson ....Betsy Palmer
Robert Meredith ....John Newland
Edward Martin ....Tom Poston
Green ....Donald McKee
  The entire action takes place in the living room of Lucille Cotton's
New York apartment; the time is the present. Act I.—A week-day,
about six P.M. Act II.—Scene 1—The same night, a few hours

later.   Scene 2—The following night, at about midnight.   Act III.—
The next morning.
    Staged by Shepard Traube; setting and lighting by Pat Campbell;
costumes supervised by Virginia Volland; stage managers, Bill Ross,
Perry Bruskin.

Light, modern-style romantic comedy in which, by way of a TV
program, an attractive young secretary becomes her boss's boss for
a day.   Once she has had him mix drinks and clean her apartment,
her problem is to remain his boss by night as well.   The rest of the
play portrays hero and heroine keeping sex at fingernail's length in
the process of arriving at marriage.

The work of a man with a gift for an amusing line but no gift whatever for hewing to it, *The Grand Prize* had a cheerful air; but suffered from too much that was either second-rate or second-hand.   It
needed to trade its rubber stamp for a pruning knife.

(Closed February 12, 1955)

PLAIN AND FANCY

(143 performances)
(Continued)

Musical comedy in two acts; book by Joseph Stein and Will Glick-
man; lyrics by Arnold B. Horwitt; music by Albert Hague.   Produced by Richard Kollmar and James W. Gardiner, in association
with Yvette Schumer, at the Mark Hellinger Theatre, January 27,
1955.

Cast of characters—

Ruth Winters	Shirl Conway
Dan King	Richard Derr
A Man	John Dennis
Another Man	Chris Robinson
Katie Yoder	Gloria Marlowe
Papa Yoder	Stefan Schnabel
Isaac Miller	Sammy Smith
Emma Miller	Nancy Andrews
Ezra Reber	Douglas Fletcher Rodgers
Hilda Miller	Barbara Cook
A Young Miller	Scotty Engel
Another Young Miller	Elaine Lynn
Peter Reber	David Daniels
Rachel	Ethel May Cody
Samuel Zook	Daniel Nagrin
Levi Stolzfuss	William Weslow
Jacob Yoder	Will Able
Samuel Lapp	Chris Robinson
Abner Zook	Edgar Thompson
Ike Pilersheim	James S. Moore
Moses Zook	John Dennis
Abner Zook	Tim Worthington

An Amishman ....Herbert Surface
Another Amishman ....Robert Lindgren
Bessie ....Faith Daltry
Sarah ....Renee Orin
Esther ....Sybil Lamb
Rebecca ....Betty McGuire
Mary ....Muriel Shaw
State Trooper ....Ray Hyson
   Dancers: Sara Aman, Imelda DeMartin, Ina Hahn, Marcia How-
ard, Lucia Lambert, Joan Darby, Ann Needham, Tao Strong, Beryl
Towbin; Saint Amant, Crandall Diehl, Ronnie Lee, Robert Lindgren,
James S. Moore, Philip Nasta, Robert St. Clair, William Weslow,
David Wood.
   Singers: Marilyn Bradley, Faith Daltry, Janet Hayes, Sybil Lamb,
Renee Orin, Betty McGuire, Muriel Shaw, Betty Zollinger; Ray
Hyson, Jack Irwin, Robert Kole, Chris Robinson, John Dennis, Her-
bert Surface, Edgar F. Thompson, Tim Worthington, Paul Brown,
Jim Schlader.
   The action takes place in and around Bird-in-Hand, a town in the
Amish country of Pennsylvania. The time is the present. Act I.—
Scene 1—A section of road, outside Lancaster. Scene 2—Another
part of the road. Scene 3—The Yoder barnyard. Scene 4—The
Yoder parlor. Scene 5—Side porch of the Yoder house. Scene 6—
Barnyard on the River Farm. Scene 7—A bedroom in the Yoder
home. Scene 8—The Yoder barnyard. Scene 9—In the Yoder barn.
Act II.—Scene 1—The River Farm. Scene 2—Kitchen of the Yoder
home. Scene 3—Back porch of the Yoder home. Scene 4—Bedroom
of the Yoder home. Scene 5—A section of road. Scene 6—A Carni-
val Grounds. Scene 7—Side porch of the Yoder house. Scene 8—
The Yoder barnyard.
   Staged by Morton Da Costa; dances and musical numbers by Helen
Tamiris; sets and costumes by Raoul Pène duBois; lighting by Peggy
Clark; orchestrations by Philip J. Lang; vocal arrangements by Crane
Calder; orchestra and chorus directed by Franz Allers; production
stage manager, John Cornell; stage manager, Edward Strum.

Musical numbers—

ACT I

"You Can't Miss It" ....Richard Derr, Shirl Conway
                                               and Ensemble
"It Wonders Me" ....Gloria Marlowe
"Plenty of Pennsylvania" ....Nancy Andrews, Douglas Fletcher
                                 Rodgers, Elaine Lynn and Ensemble
"Young and Foolish" ....David Daniels
"Why Not Katie?" ....Douglas Fletcher Rodgers and the Men
"Young and Foolish" (Reprise) ......Gloria Marlowe, David Daniels
"By Lantern Light" ....Danced by Daniel Nagrin and Ann
                      Needham, with Sara Aman, Lucia Lambert, Tao
                      Strong, Saint Amant, Crandall Diehl and Bob St. Clair
"It's a Helluva Way to Run a Love Affair"...........Shirl Conway
"This Is All Very New to Me" ....Sung and danced by Barbara
                      Cook, Robert Lindgren, William Weslow
                                               and Ensemble
"Plain We Live" ....Stefan Schnabel and Ensemble
"The Shunning" ....The Company

ACT II

"How Do You Raise a Barn?" ....Stefan Schnabel, Douglas Fletcher
                      Rodgers, Nancy Andrews, Daniel
                      Nagrin and Ensemble
"Follow Your Heart" ....David Daniels, Gloria Marlowe
                                          and Barbara Cook
"City Mouse, Country Mouse" ....Nancy Andrews with Renee
                      Orin, Sybil Lamb, Muriel Shaw,
                      Ethel May Cody, Betty McGuire
"I'll Show Him!" ....Barbara Cook
"Carnival Ballet" ....Barbara Cook, Douglas Fletcher Rodgers
                                          and Company

"On the Midway"
```
Mambo Joe ..................................Daniel Nagrin
Scranton Sal ................................Sara Aman
Swami .....................................Robert Lindgren
Sailor .....................................Will Able
Barkers ......Philip Nasta, Chris Robinson, Edgar F. Thompson
Dance Hall ..................................The Company
```
"Take Your Time and Take Your Pick" ....Barbara Cook, Richard
Derr, Shirl Conway
Finale: "Plenty of Pennsylvania" ....The Entire Company

THE WISTERIA TREES

(15 performances)

Play in three acts by Joshua Logan, based on *The Cherry Orchard* by Anton Chekhov, with music, selected and arranged by Max Marlin. Revived by the New York City Center Theatre Company at the New York City Center of Music and Drama, February 2, 1955.

Cast of characters—
```
Dolly May ......................................Frances Foster
Martha .......................................Ella Raines
Henry Arthur Henry ...........................Maurice Ellis
Yancy .......................................Walter Matthau
Scott .......................................Alonzo Bosan
Lucy Andree Ransdell ..........................Helen Hayes
Antoinette ...................................Lois Smith
Cassie .......................................Evelyn Davis
Gavin Leon Andree ...........................Bramwell Fletcher
Bowman Witherspoon ..........................Will Geer
Jacques ......................................Ossie Davis
Peter Whitfield ..............................Cliff Robertson
Little Miss Lucy ..............................Jonelle Allen
Gracie .......................................Brook Seawell
Frankie ......................................Christopher Snell
Child ........................................Patty Burke
```
Guests at party: Linda Berlin, Jarmila Daubek, David Eliot, Keith Kirby, Alison Landor, Lily Lodge, Warren Oates and Jackson Young. Other servants: Philip Dean, Hilda Haynes.

The action takes place in the children's parlor, with windows opening on part of the outside gallery of Wisteria Plantation, Louisiana; the time is the end of the last century. Act I.—Spring, dawn. Act II.—Scene 1—Summer, afternoon. Scene 2—Autumn, evening. Act III.—Winter, morning.

Staged by John Stix; setting by Herbert Gahagan; costumes by Lucinda Ballard; general costume director, Grace Houston; lighting by Feder; production stage manager, Buford Armitage; stage manager, Herman Shapiro.

The Wisteria Trees was first produced March 29, 1950, by Leland Hayward and Joshua Logan at the Martin Beck Theatre for 165 performances.

(Closed February 13, 1955)

THE SOUTHWEST CORNER

(36 performances)

Play in three acts by John Cecil Holm, based on the novel by Mildred Walker. Produced by John Huntington at the Holiday Theatre, February 3, 1955.

Cast of characters—

    Orville Greenstead .... Parker Fennelly
    Marcia Elder .... Eva LeGallienne
    David Keating .... Ray Boyle
    Bea Cannon .... Enid Markey
    Edith Summers .... Jean Gillespie
    Sam Wilson .... Frank Tweddell
    Hattie Carew .... Frieda Altman
        The action takes place in a kitchen in an old Vermont farmhouse.
    Act I.—Scene 1—Late afternoon of a day in winter. Scene 2—Shortly
    before noon; one week later. Act II.—Scene 1—Late afternoon; a
    month later. Scene 2—A day in May; some weeks later. Scene 3—
    An evening; several weeks later. Act III.—A day in summer; morn-
    ing, a few weeks later.
        Staged by George Schaefer; setting designed and lighted by Ralph
    Alswang; costumes by Paul McGuire; production stage manager, John
    Edward Friend; stage manager, Bette Simone.

A fine-grained, 83-year-old lady lives alone on an isolated hilltop in Vermont. She advertises for a companion to look after her in exchange for receiving the house after she dies. The middle-aged widow she hires seems at the outset just a henbrained chatterbox, but gradually emerges as the kind of grating, grasping vulgarian who can be worse than an outright villainess. Having married the hired man and made everything in the house seem equipped with a loud-speaker, the companion next decides to move the old lady to Massachusetts. But while moving furniture at the ensuing auction sale, she dies of a heart attack, leaving the old lady safe—with friends— on her hilltop.

(Closed March 5, 1955)

THE DESPERATE HOURS

(127 performances)
(Continued)

Melodrama in three acts by Joseph Hayes, based on Mr. Hayes' novel of the same title. Produced by Howard Erskine and Joseph Hayes at the Ethel Barrymore Theatre, February 10, 1955.

Cast of characters—

    Tom Winston .... Judson Pratt
    Jesse Bard .... James Gregory
    Harry Carson .... Kendall Clark

```
Eleanor Hilliard ................................Nancy Coleman
Ralphie Hilliard ...............................Malcolm Brodrick
Dan Hilliard ....................................Karl Malden
Cindy Hilliard .................................Patricia Peardon
Glenn Griffin ....................................Paul Newman
Hank Griffin ...................................George Grizzard
Robish ........................................George Mathews
Chuck Wright ...................................Fred Eisley
Mr. Patterson ..................................Wyrley Birch
Lt. Carl Fredericks ...............................Rusty Lane
Miss Swift ......................................Mary Orr
```
The action takes place in the city of Indianapolis; the time is the present. Act I.—A day in autumn. Act II.—Later. Act III.—Later.

Staged by Robert Montgomery; setting and lighting by Howard Bay; costumes by Robert Randolph; production stage manager, Howard Whitfield; stage manager, William Weaver.

See page 205.

TONIGHT IN SAMARKAND

(29 performances)

Symbolic melodrama in three acts by Jacques Deval and Lorenzo Semple, Jr., with music composed and arranged by Sol Kaplan. Produced by Bruce Becker and Robert Ellis Miller at the Morosco Theatre, February 16, 1955.

Cast of characters—

```
Pandore ........................................Rosemary Prinz
Mario .........................................Sheppard Kerman
Angelo Farinacci ...............................Pernell Roberts
Guri ..........................................Marian Reardon
Inspector Massoubre ............................Theodore Bikel
Nericia .........................................Jan Farrand
Sourab Kayam ..................................Louis Jourdan
Poliakoff ......................................Michael Gorrin
Therese ........................................Joyce Lear
Paul Tabourier ...............................Alexander Scourby
Leontine Tabourier ...............................Rita Vale
Perignolles ...................................Halliwell Hobbes
```
Act I.—Sourab Kayam's tent, on the grounds of a traveling circus in the south of France; an autumn evening. Act II.—The same; three nights later. Act III.—Le Havre; the following April.

Staged by Alan Schneider; settings and lighting by Ben Edwards; costumes by Frank Spencer; production stage manager, David Gray, Jr.

The title comes from the Oriental legend—cf. the title of John O'Hara's *Appointment in Samarra*—concerning the inevitability of fate. Fearing the future, a much-sought-after lady tamer of tigers in a French circus gazes into an admirer's crystal ball. In the first flash-forward, she marries a juggler and dies, on her birthday, in a steamship disaster. In the second flash-forward, she marries a millionaire and dies on her birthday in the same disaster. Then, because his own future is the one thing the crystal ball cannot foretell, she marries the magician. But despite all their precautions to avoid the ship she is fated to die on, the prophecy is once again borne out.

(Closed March 12, 1955)

THE WAYWARD SAINT

(21 performances)

Comedy-fantasy in three acts by Paul Vincent Carroll, with incidental music by Sylvan Levin and dramatic pantomime by Betty Luster. Produced by Courtney Burr and John Byram, with Elliott Nugent, at the Cort Theatre, February 17, 1955.

Cast of characters—

```
Canon Daniel McCooey ...........................Liam Redmond
His Lordship, the Bishop of Oriel ...............William Harrigan
Miss Killicat ...................................Eleanor Wilson
Maura ...............................................Pat Breslin
Paedar the Puck ...............................Dennis Patrick
Baron Nicholas de Balbus ..........................Paul Lukas
Sabena ...........................................Betty Luster
Serena .......................................Marsha Reynolds
Salambo ......................................Frederic Warriner
Martyn McDara ...............................Cullen Desmond
Joe ...............................................Albert Corbin
```
    The entire action takes place in the sitting-dining room of Canon Daniel McCooey's presbytery in the little village of Kilkevin, near the Northern Irish border. Act I.—The time is the present. Act II.—Some days later. Act III.—Late afternoon, a few days later.
    Staged by John Gerstad; production supervised by Elliott Nugent; designed and lighted by Frederick Fox; costumes by Audre; general stage manager, Charles Durand; stage manager, Murray Queen.

A St. Francis-like Irish canon who is able to talk to birds, heal children and make plums grow on cherry trees acquires the reputation of being a saint. He likes this reputation no better than does the bishop who banishes him to a remote country parish. There, in the form of a worldly baron, appears an emissary of the Devil eager for such a trophy as the soul of a saint. Prodded by the baron, the canon begins to think he really is a saint, starts meddling in lives and dabbling in miracles, and soon commits some serious clerical errors. Only at the last minute is he saved from Hell and restored to his former humility.

(Closed March 6, 1955)

THE DARK IS LIGHT ENOUGH

(69 performances)

"A winter comedy" in three acts by Christopher Fry. Produced by Katharine Cornell and Roger L. Stevens, by arrangement with H. M. Tennent, Ltd., at the ANTA Theatre, February 23, 1955.

Cast of characters—

Kassel, a doctor	William Podmore
Jakob Belmann } Members of the Countess' salon	Donald Harron John Williams
Stefan, son of the Countess	Paul Roebling
Bella, a housekeeper	Eva Condon
Willi, a houseboy	Charles Macaulay
Gelda, daughter of the Countess	Marian Winters
Richard Gettner, an Austrian in the Hungarian rebel army	Tyrone Power
Countess Rosmarin Ostenburg	Katharine Cornell
Colonel Janik, a Hungarian rebel officer	Arnold Moss
Count Peter Zichy, a Hungarian in the Austrian government	Christopher Plummer
Beppy, a Hungarian corporal	Ted Gunther
Rusti, a Hungarian corporal	Sydney Pollack
Third Soldier	Jerome Gardino
Fourth Soldier	Dario Barri

The action takes place in a country house in the Austro-Hungarian Empire during the Hungarian revolution of 1848-9. Act I.—A room in the house; Thursday night. Act II.—The stables; evening, the next day. Act III.—A room in the house; the following Thursday. Staged by Guthrie McClintic; scenery and costumes by Oliver Messel; costumes executed by Helene Pons; production stage manager, Keene Curtis; stage manager, Ross Hertz.

See page 239.

(Closed April 23, 1955)

SILK STOCKINGS

(111 performances)
(Continued)

Musical comedy in two acts, suggested by Melchior Lengyel's *Ninotchka*. Music and lyrics by Cole Porter; book by George S. Kaufman, Leueen MacGrath and Abe Burrows. Produced by Feuer and Martin at the Imperial Theatre, February 24, 1955.

Cast of characters—

Peter Ilyitch Boroff	Philip Sterling
Hotel Doorman	Walter Kelvin
Hotel Manager	Stanley Simmonds
Flower Girl	Geraldine Delaney
Ivanov	Henry Lascoe
Brankov	Leon Belasco
Bibinski	David Opatoshu
Steve Canfield	Don Ameche

First Commissar ....Edward Becker
Guards ....Lee Barry, Dick Humphrey
Vera ....Julie Newmar
Commissar Markovitch ....George Tobias
Choreographer ....Kenneth Chertok
Ninotchka ....Hildegarde Neff
Reporters ....Edward Becker, Tony Gardell, Arthur Rubin
Janice Dayton ....Gretchen Wyler
Pierre Bouchard ....Marcel Hillaire
Chief Commissar ....Forrest Green
Minister ....Tony Gardell
President of Politburo ....Walter Kelvin
Saleslady ....Ludie Claire
M. Fabour ....Paul Best
Bookstall Man ....Louis Polacek
French Comrades ....Win Mayo, Arthur Ulisse
Movie Director ....Paul Best
Assistant Director ....Lee Barry
Sonia ....Devra Kline
Grisha ....Forrest Green
Anna ....Alexandra Moss
Musicians ....Maurice Kogan, Leon Merian, Mervin Gold
Guard ....Edward Becker

Dancers: Estelle Aza, Barbara Bostock, Verna Cain, Geraldine Delaney, Devra Kline, Pat McBride, Carol Risser, Carol Stevens, Onna White; Martin Allen, Tommy Andrew, George Foster, Bruce Hoy, John Ray.

The action takes place in Paris and Moscow; the time is the present.

Staged by Cy Feuer; dances and musical numbers staged by Eugene Loring; settings and lighting by Jo Mielziner; costumes designed by Lucinda Ballard; additional costumes by Robert Mackintosh; musical direction and vocal arrangements by Herbert Greene; orchestrations by Don Walker; dance music arranged by Tommy Goodman; production stage manager for Feuer & Martin Productions, Henri Caubisens; stage manager, Terence Little.

Musical numbers—

ACT I

"Too Bad" ....Ivanov, Brankov, Bibinski and Hotel Staff
"Paris Loves Lovers" ....Canfield and Ninotchka
"Stereophonic Sound" ....Janice
"It's a Chemical Reaction, That's All" ....Ninotchka
"All of You" ....Canfield
"Satin and Silk" ....Janice
"Without Love" ....Ninotchka
Reprise: "All of You" ....Canfield

ACT II

"Hail, Bibinski" ....Ivanov, Brankov, Bibinski
                                        and French Comrades
"As On Through the Seasons We Sail" ....Canfield and Ninotchka
"Josephine" ....Janice and Chorus
"Siberia" ....Ivanov, Brankov, Bibinski
"Silk Stockings" ....Canfield
"The Red Blues" ....The Russians
Finale ....Entire Company

THE MASTER BUILDER

(40 performances)

Play in three acts by Henrik Ibsen, as adapted by Max Faber. Produced by the Phoenix Theatre (T. Edward Hambleton and Norris Houghton) at the Phoenix Theatre, March 1, 1955.

Cast of characters—

Kaia Fosli ....Muriel Berkson
Knut Brovik ....Art Smith
Ragnar Brovik ....Gene Saks
Halvard Solness ....Oscar Homolka
Aline Solness ....Margaret Barker
Dr. Herdal ....Joseph Foley
Hilda Wangel ....Joan Tetzel

Townspeople, visitors and workmen: Mack Bing, George Brenlin, Nat Burns, Prentiss Childs, Ethel Cunningham, Billy Harris, David Hooks, Charles Nelson, Peggy Pope, Michael Quinlivan, Simeon Saturn, Alan Ramsay, Barbara Woods.

The action takes place in Halvard Solness' house in Christiania, Norway. Act I.—Halvard Solness' office and drawing-office; late afternoon. Act II.—The sitting room; the following morning. Act III.—The veranda; the same evening.

Staged by Oscar Homolka, with the assistance of Ira Cirker; production designed by Boris Aronson; costumes by Alvin Colt; lighting by Lester Polakov; incidental music composed and arranged by Max Marlin; production stage manager, Robert Woods; company stage manager, George Quick.

(Closed April 3, 1955)

BUS STOP

(103 performances)
(Continued)

Play in three acts by William Inge. Produced by Robert Whitehead and Roger L. Stevens at the Music Box, March 2, 1955.

Cast of characters—

Elma Duckworth ....Phyllis Love
Grace ....Elaine Stritch
Will Masters ....Lou Polan
Cherie ....Kim Stanley
Dr. Gerald Lyman ....Anthony Ross
Carl ....Patrick McVey
Virgil Blessing ....Crahan Denton
Bo Decker ....Albert Salmi

The action takes place in a street-corner restaurant in a small town about thirty miles west of Kansas City. Act I.—A night in early March; 1:00 A.M. Act II.—A few minutes later. Act III.—Early morning; about 5:00 A.M.

Staged by Harold Clurman; setting by Boris Aronson; costumes and lighting by Paul Morrison; production stage manager, Frederic de Wilde.

See page 267.

CAT ON A HOT TIN ROOF

(79 performances)
(Continued)

Drama in three acts by Tennessee Williams. Produced by The Playwrights' Company at the Morosco Theatre, March 24, 1955.

Cast of characters—

Lacey ....Maxwell Glanville
Sookey ....Musa Williams
Margaret ....Barbara Bel Geddes
Brick ....Ben Gazzara
Mae, sometimes called Sister Woman ....Madeleine Sherwood
Gooper, sometimes called Brother Man ....Pat Hingle
Big Mama ....Mildred Dunnock
Dixie ....Pauline Hahn
Buster ....Darryl Richard
Sonny ....Seth Edwards
Trixie ....Janice Dunn
Big Daddy ....Burl Ives
Reverend Tooker ....Fred Stewart
Doctor Baugh ....R. G. Armstrong
Daisy ....Eva Vaughan Smith
Brightie ....Brownie McGhee
Small ....Sonny Terry

The action takes place in a bed-sitting room and section of the
gallery of a plantation home in the Mississippi Delta. The time, an
evening in summer; the action is continuous, with two intermissions.

Staged by Elia Kazan; scenery and lighting by Jo Mielziner; costumes by Lucinda Ballard and executed by Helene Pons; production
stage manager, Robert Downing; stage manager, Daniel S. Broun.

See page 288.

3 FOR TONIGHT

(63 performances)
(Continued)

A "diversion in song and dance" in two parts, with lyrics and special material by Robert Wells; original music by Walter Schumann;
arrangements by Nathan Scott. Produced by Paul Gregory at the
Plymouth Theatre, April 6, 1955.

Principals—

Marge and Gower Champion   Hiram Sherman
Harry Belafonte   Betty Benson
Voices of Walter Schumann

Chorus—John Bennett, Robert Brink, Andrew Case, Gina Christen,
Diane Doxee, Elaine Drew, Joyce L. Foss, Dorothy Gill, Nancy Harp,
Jimmy Harris, Mark Karl, Jerry Madison, Robert Miller, Ned Ro-
mero, Jack Steele, Brad Thomas, Robert Trevis, Karen Vonne,
Richard Wessler.

Staged and directed by Gower Champion; music conducted by Richard Pribor; guitarist for Mr. Belafonte, Millard Thomas; woodwinds:
Sherwin Lichtenfeld; percussion: Bob Morrison; bass: Milton Nadel;
pianist: John Williams; stage manager, Irving Sudrow.

Sketches and musical numbers—

PART I

We begin with our Story Teller ....Hiram Sherman
The sounds you will hear are
Impressions ....The Voices of Walter Schumann
And they will also sing
"All You Need Is a Song"

And now ....Marge and Gower Champion
"Dance, Dance, Dance"
"The Clock"
"By-Play for Drums"
Back to our Story Teller
Who introduces ....Harry Belafonte
With Millard Thomas and his guitar
"Jerry"
"Sylvie"
"Mark Twain"
"When the Saints Go Marching In"
On with our Story Teller
To ....Marge and Gower Champion
At   The Sunday Picnic Social
Featuring   "Summer in Fairview Falls"
"It Couldn't Be a Better Day"
"Here I Stand"
"The Auction"
Finale

PART II

Our Story Teller ....Hiram Sherman
Introduces ....Betty Benson and
The Voices of Walter Schumann
"Fly Bird"
We continue with ....Harry Belafonte and Millard Thomas
"Noah"
"Take My Mother Home"
"In That Great Gettin Up Mornin" *
And now we get very formal ....Hiram Sherman
Our Story Teller reads
"The Lecture"
Demonstrated by ....Marge and Gower Champion
We join ....Harry Belafonte
"Matilda"
"Scarlet Ribbons"
Our Story Teller takes us to
Yesterday
With ....Marge and Gower Champion
"By the Light of the Silvery Moon" †
"Shine on, Harvest Moon" †
"Troubles" ....Harry Belafonte
Finale ....The Entire Company

* Written by Jester Herston.
† Written by Jack Norworth.

CHAMPAGNE COMPLEX

(23 performances)

Farce in three acts by Leslie Stevens. Produced by Gayle Stine
at the Cort Theatre, April 12, 1955.

Cast of characters—

Helms Fell Harper ....John Dall
Allyn Macy ....Polly Bergen
Carter Bowen ....Donald Cook
The action takes place in Allyn Macy's apartment; the time is the
present. Act I.—Scene 1—Very early spring; late Friday night.
Scene 2—The next morning. Act II.—Two weeks later; Sunday
afternoon. Act III.—Later that evening.
Staged by Michael Gordon; production designed by Charles Elson;

overture and entr'acte music composed especially for the play by Jerry
Stevens; music arranged by Frank Beery; orchestra supervision by
Jack Eaton; stage manager, Peter Zeisler.

The fiancée of a prim young tycoon constantly gets high on champagne and proceeds to undress. Her worried beau calls in his psychoanalyst bachelor uncle; treatments first reveal that the girl doesn't love her fiancée, next that she does love her analyst (whom she marries).

(Closed April 30, 1955)

ANKLES AWEIGH

(50 performances)
(Continued)

Musical comedy in two acts, with book by Guy Bolton and Eddie Davis; music by Sammy Fain and lyrics by Dan Shapiro. Produced by Howard Hoyt, Reginald Hammerstein and Fred F. Finklehoffe at the Mark Hellinger Theatre, April 18, 1955.

Cast of characters—

Russ	Ed Hanley
Camera Man	Ray Mason
Tommy	Bill Costin
Pizza Cart Man	Frank Conville
Elsey	Betty Kean
Wynne	Jane Kean
Dinky	Lew Parker
Spud	Gabriel Dell
Lt. Bill Kelley	Mark Dawson
Native Girl	Nancy Walters
Captain Zimmerman	Mark Allen
Admiral Pottles	Will Hussung
Chipolata	Thelma Carpenter
Joe Mancinni	Mike Kellin
Tony	Herb Fields
Lucia	Betty George
The Duchess	Karen Shepard
Shore Patrol	Skeet Guenther

Dancers: Dick Alderson, Sandi Bonner, Gene Carrons, Patty Fitzsimmons, Marilyn Marsh, Meri Miller, Marianne Olsen, Marsha Rivers, Nina Starkey, Gloria Stevens, Patricia White, Ethel Winter, Hank Brunjes, Don Emmons, Skeet Guenther, Jack Purcell, John Smolko, Jack Timmers.

Singers: Marilynn Bradley, Thelma Dare, Virginia Martin, Ellen McCown, Janet Pavek, Karen Shepard, Nancy Walters, Herb Fields, Henry Hamilton, Warren Kemmerling, Michael King, Ray Mason, Jack Rains, Hobe Streiford.

The action takes place in Sicily and French Morocco, where an American movie company is on location; the time is the present. Act I.—Scene 1—Montefino; the piazza, afternoon. Scene 2—USS Alamo, below decks; that night. Scene 3—El Dahli night spot, Morocco; early the next morning. Scene 4—A bedroom in El Dahli. Scene 5—Montefino; the piazza. Act II.—Scene 1—Hotel Argento, Montefino; next day. Scene 2—A street in Montefino. Scene 3—Joe's room. Scene 4—Aboard the USS Alamo; the following night.

Staged by Fred F. Finklehoffe, with the assistance of Edward Clarke Lilley; choreography by Tony Charmoli; scenery and lighting by George Jenkins; costumes by Miles White; vocal and orchestral

arrangements by Don Walker; musical and choral director, Salvatore
dell'Isola; dance music devised by Roger Adams, with additional dance
music by Donald Pippin; stage managers, Neil Hartley and Herman
Shapiro.

Musical numbers—

ACT I
Scene 1
"Italy" ....Boys and Girls
"Old-Fashioned Mothers" ....Elsey and Wynne
"Skip the Build-Up" ....Elsey and Dinky
"Nothing at All" ....Wynne and Bill
"Walk Like a Sailor" ....Wynne, Dinky, Spud, Girls, Elsey,
                                    Hank Brunjes, Skeet Guenther

Scene 3
"Headin' for the Bottom" ....Chipolata, Girls and Patrons
                                              of night spot
"Nothing Can Replace a Man" ....Wynne and Boys
"Here's to Dear Old Us" ....Elsey, Dinky, Spud

Scene 4
"His and Hers" ....Wynne and Bill

Scene 5
"La Festa" ....Natives, Boys and Girls
                                     Soloist: Ray Mason

ACT II
Scene 1
"Ready Cash" ....Croupiers and Gamblers
"Kiss Me and Kill Me with Love" ....Wynne and Bill
"Honeymoon" ....Elsey and Girls
"The Villain Always Gets It" ....Boys and Girls

Scene 2
"The Code" ....Joe's Henchmen

Scene 4
"Walk Like a Sailor," Reprise ....Dancing Boys and Girls
"Eleven O'Clock Song" ....Elsey and Wynne
Finale ....Entire Company

ALL IN ONE

(47 performances)

A presentation comprising "Trouble in Tahiti," an opera in seven
scenes by Leonard Bernstein; a dance program by Paul Draper; and
"27 Wagons Full of Cotton," a one-act play by Tennessee Williams.
Produced by Charles Bowden and Richard Barr at The Playhouse,
April 19, 1955.

TROUBLE IN TAHITI

Cast of characters—
Dinah ....Alice Ghostley
Sam ....John Tyers
Trio:
    Constance Brigham
    John Taliaferro
    James Tushar

Scene 1—Sam and Dinah's house.   Scene 2—Sam's office.   Scene 3—The psychiatrist's office.   Scene 4—A street in the city.   Scene 5 —The gym.   Scene 6—The hat shop.   Scene 7—Sam and Dinah's house.

Staged by David Brooks; pianists: Joseph D. Lewis, Urey Krasnopolsky; drums: Max Rich; bass: Leonard Gaskin.

PAUL DRAPER

Accompanied by John Colman

PROGRAM

On the Beat ....Couperin
Alcina Suite ....Handel
  1. Menuet
  2. Sarabande
  3. Musette
  4. Tambourino
"Tea for Two" ....Youmans
Dance without Music
In a Dance Hall ....Porter
Satire on a Political Speech
Improvisation

27 WAGONS FULL OF COTTON

Cast of characters—

Flora Meighan ....Maureen Stapleton
Jake Meighan ....Myron McCormick
Silva Vicarro ....Felice Orlandi

The action takes place on the front porch of the Meighans' residence near Blue Mountain, Mississippi.   Scene 1—Early evening.   Scene 2—Noon, the next day.   Scene 3—Nine o'clock that evening.

Staged by Vincent J. Donehue; this presentation based upon recent production of the play by James S. Elliott.

For entire production of "All in One": settings and lighting by Eldon Elder; costumes by Pat Campbell; hats by Mr. John; stage manager, Barnett Owen.

(Closed May 28, 1955)

GUYS AND DOLLS

(16 performances)*
(Continued)

"Musical fable of Broadway," based on a story and characters by Damon Runyon, with music and lyrics by Frank Loesser; book by Jo Swerling and Abe Burrows.   Revived by the New York City Center Light Opera Company (William Hammerstein, General Director) at the New York City Center of Music and Drama, April 20,

* Includes reopening-night performance of May 31, 1955.

1955, for 15 performances.   Reopened at the New York City Center
of Music and Drama, May 31, 1955.

Cast of characters—

Nicely-Nicely Johnson .... Oggie Small
Benny Southstreet .... Al Nesor
Rusty Charlie .... Murray Vines
Sarah Brown .... Leila Martin
Arvide Abernathy .... Martin Wolfson
Mission Band .... Michelle Reiner, Paul Migan, Elaine Spaulding
Harry the Horse .... Tom Pedi
Lt. Brannigan .... Tom Ahearne
Nathan Detroit .... Walter Matthau
Angie the Ox .... Ralph Vucci
Miss Adelaide .... Helen Gallagher
Sky Masterson .... Ray Shaw
Joey Biltmore .... Joe Bernard
Mimi .... Norma Kaiser
General Matilda B. Cartwright .... Kate Tomlinson
Big Jule .... Lou Nova
Drunk .... Robert Karl
Waiter .... Seth Riggs
    Dancers: Ellen Beach, Sonya Besant, Louise Golden, Diana Hunter,
Norma Kaiser, Loys Lozano, Marcia Maier, Kirsten Valbor; Albert
Fiorella, Robert Karl, Frank Marasco, Tom Panko, Regis Powers,
Victor Reilley, Harry Lee Rogers, Marc West.
    Singers: Ken Emery, Clifford Fearl, Tom Powell, Seth Riggs, Bob
Rippy, Evans Thornton, Murray Vines, Ralph Vucci.
    Sightseers: Sheila Hayden, Rosemary Shein, Jane Wagner.
    Staged by Philip Mathias; musical director, Frederick Dvonch;
choreography by Onna White (after the original by Michael Kidd);
settings by Jo Mielziner; costumes by Alvin Colt; costume supervisor,
Frank Spencer; orchestral arrangements by George Bassman and Ted
Royal; vocal arrangements and direction by Herbert Greene; assistant
to William Hammerstein, Michael Shurtleff; production stage manager,
Bernard Gersten; stage manager, Richard Blofson.

Following cast changes in Reopening of May 31, 1955:

Nicely-Nicely Johnson .... John Dorman
Sarah Brown .... Patricia Northrop
Lt. Brannigan .... Wallace Rooney
Miss Adelaide .... Judy Johnson
Hot Box M.C. .... Robert Rippy
Waiter .... Ralph Vucci
    Dancers: Ana Baldwin, Ellen Beach, Jeanna Belkin, Sonya Besant,
Janet Gaylord, Norma Kaiser, Marcia Maier, Mary Martinet; Albert
Fiorella, Robert Karl, Frank Marasco, Bill McDonald, Tom Panko,
Regis Powers, Victor B. Reilley.
    Singers: Ken Emery, Clifford Fearl, Howard Lear, Tom Powell,
Robert Rippy, Evans Thornton, Murray Vines, Ralph Vucci.
    Sightseers: Alisa Dawson, Peg Shirley, Suzanne Sholes.
    Orchestra conducted by Julius Rudel.

Guys and Dolls was first produced November 24, 1950, by Feuer
and Martin at the Forty-Sixth Street Theatre for 1,200 performances.

INHERIT THE WIND

(46 performances)
(Continued)

Play in three acts by Jerome Lawrence and Robert E. Lee. Produced by Herman Shumlin, in association with Margo Jones, at the National Theatre, April 21, 1955.

Cast of characters—

Rachel Brown	Bethel Leslie
Meeker	Robert P. Lieb
Bertram Cates	Karl Light
Mr. Goodfellow	Salem Ludwig
Mrs. Krebs	Sara Floyd
The Rev. Jeremiah Brown	Staats Cotsworth
Corkin	Fred Herrick
Bollinger	Donald Elson
Platt	Fred Miller
Mr. Bannister	Charles Thompson
Melinda	Mary Kevin Kelly
Howard	Eric Berne
Mrs. Loomis	Rita Newton
Hot Dog Man	Howard Caine
Mrs. McClain	Margherita Sargent
Mrs. Blair	Ruth Newton
Elija	Charles Brin
E. K. Hornbeck	Tony Randall
Hurdy Gurdy Man	Harry Shaw
Timmy	Jack Banning
Mayor	James Maloney
Matthew Harrison Brady	Ed Begley
Mrs. Brady	Muriel Kirkland
Tom Davenport	William Darrid
Henry Drummond	Paul Muni
Judge	Louis Hector
Dunlap	Fred Miller
Sillers	Fred Herrick
Reuter's Man	Edmund Williams
Harry Y. Esterbrook	Perry Fiske

Townspeople, hawkers, reporters, jurors, spectators

Other cast members: Lou Adelman, Emmett Bradley, Joseph Brownstone, Michael Constantine, Michael Del Medico, James Greene, Ruth Hope, Sally Jessup, Julie Knox, Patricia Larson, Michael Lewin, Evelyn Mando, Sarah Meade, Gian Pace, Bee Peters, Richard Poston, Jack Riano, Gordon Russell, Carroll Saint, Robert Shannon, Maurice Shrog.

The action takes place in a small town; the time is summer, not too long ago.

Staged by Herman Shumlin; assistant director, Terese Hayden; scenery by Peter Larkin; lighting by Feder; costumes by Ruth Morley; production stage manager, Burry Fredrik; stage manager, David Clive.

See page 313.

PHOENIX '55

(43 performances)
(Continued)

Musical revue in two acts, with music by David Baker, lyrics by David Craig and sketches by Ira Wallach. Produced by the Phoenix

Theatre (T. Edward Hambleton and Norris Houghton) at the Phoenix Theatre, April 23, 1955.

Principals—

Nancy Walker	Harvey Lembeck
Gemze de Lappe	Marge Redmond
Kenneth Harvey	Elise Rhodes
Bill Heyer	Joshua Shelley
Louise Hoff	Elton Warren

Also—

Bob Bakanic	Dick Korthaze
Shellie Farrell	Ralph McWilliams
Jerry Fries	Cynthia Price
Jay Harnick	Rain Winslow

Pianists—

John Morris and Dorothy Freitag
Staged by Marc Daniels; choreography by Boris Runanin; musical direction by Buster Davis; scenery by Eldon Elder; costumes by Alvin Colt; ballet music by John Morris; orchestrations by Ralph Burns and Clare Grundman; lighting by Klaus Holm; production stage manager, Robert Woods; stage manager, Elliot Martin.

Musical numbers—

ACT I

Opening (Sketch by David Craig) ....Louise Hoff
"It Says Here" ....Bob Bakanic, Gemze de Lappe, Shellie Farrell, Jerry Fries, Jay Harnick, Kenneth Harvey, Bill Heyer, Dick Korthaze, Ralph McWilliams, Cynthia Price, Marge Redmond, Elise Rhodes, Joshua Shelley, Elton Warren, Rain Winslow
"Tomorrow Is Here" ....Nancy Walker and Company
Interviewer ....Harvey Lembeck
Handy Man Around the House
Nellie ....Louise Hoff
Viv ....Marge Redmond
Chuck ....Joshua Shelley
"All Around the World"
She ....Elise Rhodes
He ....Bill Heyer
First Prize
Dobberman ....Harvey Lembeck
Bradbury ....Kenneth Harvey
Millie Wubble ....Nancy Walker
Secretary ....Cynthia Price
Reporters ....Marge Redmond, Rain Winslow
Photographer ....Jay Harnick
"Never Wait for Love"
Sung by ....Elton Warren
Danced by ....Gemze de Lappe, Ralph McWilliams; Shellie Farrell, Jerry Fries; Rain Winslow, Bob Bakanic
"Down to the Sea" ....Nancy Walker
Utter Ecstasy
Clerk ....Harvey Lembeck
First Customer ....Rain Winslow
Second Customer ....Louise Hoff
Miss Lovelace ....Marge Redmond
The Trap (Libretto by Ira Wallach)
Narrator ....Kenneth Harvey
The Maiden ....Nancy Walker
The Young Dreamer ....Boris Runanin
The Father ....Harvey Lembeck
A Disreputable Element ....Rain Winslow
Friends, Relatives and Other Disreputable Elements ..The Company

ACT II

"This Tuxedo Is Mine!"
Sung by ....Bill Heyer
Danced by ....Bob Bakanic and Jerry Fries, Rain
Winslow and Shellie Farrell
The Ingenue
Wallingford Merkle ....Joshua Shelley
Clifford Bodmer ....Harvey Lembeck
Amanda Claxton ....Elise Rhodes
Chickie Popjoy ....Nancy Walker
"Just Him" (Sketch by David Craig)
Him ....Bill Heyer
Her ....Elise Rhodes
"The Charade of the Marionettes"
Sung by ....Elton Warren
Aerialist ....Gemze de Lappe
Lion-Tamer ....Ralph McWilliams
Clown ....A Clown
"A Funny Heart" ....Nancy Walker
"Suburban Retreat"
Brenda ....Louise Hoff
Harold ....Joshua Shelley
Upper Birth
Ted Morrow ....Kenneth Harvey
Annie Snodgrass ....Nancy Walker
Mike Snodgrass ....Harvey Lembeck
Uncle Willie ....Bob Bakanic
Delivery Man ....Jay Harnick
"Finale" ....Entire Company

THE HONEYS

(36 performances)

Farce comedy in three acts by Roald Dahl. Produced by **Cheryl**
Crawford at the Longacre Theatre, April 28, 1955.

Cast of characters—

Maggie (Mrs. Curtis Honey) ....Dorothy Stickney
Mary (Mrs. Bennett Honey) ....Jessica Tandy
Bennett Honey }
Curtis Honey (Bennett's Twin Brother) } ....Hume Cronyn
Nellie Fleischman ....Mary Finney
Potts ....Dana Elcar

Act I.—The living room of Bennett Honey's house, in New York
City; at breakfast time, the day before New Year's Eve. Act II.—
Scene 1—The living room of Curtis Honey's house, in the suburbs of
Boston; late afternoon, the same day. Scene 2—The same; lunch time
the next day. Scene 3—The same; four hours later. Act III.—
Scene 1—Same as Act II; twenty minutes later. Scene 2—The same;
just before midnight.

Staged by Frank Corsaro; settings by Ben Edwards; costumes by
Motley; stage manager, Paul A. Foley.

Bennett and Curtis Honey are despotic irascible twin brothers
married to pleasant, long-suffering wives. Seeing what a delightful
life a recently widowed friend of theirs is leading is all the two Mrs.
Honeys need to make widows of themselves. Disposing of their husbands requires a stalled elevator, tainted oyster juice, a skull-bopping

with a frozen leg of lamb, and a medicinal drink containing tiger's whiskers; but the job is ultimately effected.

(Closed May 28, 1955)

SOUTH PACIFIC

(15 performances)

Musical in two acts, adapted from *Tales of the South Pacific* by James M. Michener, with music by Richard Rodgers; lyrics by Oscar Hammerstein 2nd; book by Oscar Hammerstein 2nd and Joshua Logan. Revived by the New York City Center Light Opera Company (William Hammerstein, General Director) at the New York City Center of Music and Drama, May 4, 1955.

Cast of characters—

Ngana	Margaret Sokal
Jerome	Antonio Obregon
Henry	Richard Silvera
Ensign Nellie Forbush	Sandra Deel
Emile de Becque	Richard Collett
Bloody Mary	Sylvia Syms
Bloody Mary's Assistant	Julie Winston
Abner	J. J. Riley
Stewpot	Frank Maxwell
Luther Billis	Henry Slate
Professor	Gene Saks
Lt. Joseph Cable, U.S.M.C.	Herb Banke
Capt. George Brackett, U.S.N.	Martin Wolfson
Cmdr. William Harbison, U.S.N.	Warren J. Brown
Yeoman Herbert Quale	Seth Riggs
Sgt. Kenneth Johnson	Howard Lear
Marine Cpl. Richard West	Evans Thornton
Seabee Morton Wise	Murray Vines
Seaman Tom O'Brien	Dick Armbrust
Radio Operator Bob McCaffrey	Clifford Fearl
Staff Sgt. Thomas Hassinger	Ralph Vucci
Lt. Genevieve Marshall	Eileen Moran
Ensign Dinah Murphy	Edith Lane
Ensign Janet MacGregor	Janice Samarie
Ensign Cora MacRae	Louise Pearl
Ensign Bessie Noonan	Michelle Reiner
Ensign Connie Walewska	Helen Baisley
Ensign Pamela Whitmore	Elaine Spaulding
Ensign Sue Yaeger	Theresa Mari
Michel	Balentin Obregon
Liat	Carol Lawrence
Marcel, Henry's Assistant	Nick Gentile
Lt. Buzz Adams	Don Fellows
Shore Patrol Officer	Bob Rippy
Sailors	Richard Hildebrandt, Raymond Wearer
Islander	Emy Boselli

Staged by Charles Atkin; musical director, Frederick Dvonch; costumes by Motley; scenery by Jo Mielziner; orchestrations by Robert Russell Bennett; costume supervisor, Frank Spencer; assistant to William Hammerstein, Michael Shurtleff; production stage manager, Bernard Gersten; stage manager, Richard Blofson.

South Pacific was first produced April 7, 1949, by Richard Rodgers, Oscar Hammerstein 2nd, Leland Hayward and Joshua Logan at the Majestic Theatre for 1,925 performances.

(Closed May 15, 1955)

DAMN YANKEES

(30 performances)
(Continued)

Musical comedy in two acts, based on the novel, *The Year the Yankees Lost the Pennant*, by Douglass Wallop. Book by George Abbott and Douglass Wallop; music and lyrics by Richard Adler and Jerry Ross. Produced by Frederick Brisson, Robert E. Griffith and Harold S. Prince, in association with Albert B. Taylor, at the Forty-Sixth Street Theatre, May 5, 1955.

Cast of characters—

```
Meg .............................................Shannon  Bolin
Joe Boyd ........................................Robert Shafer
Applegate .......................................Ray Walston
Sister ..........................................Jean Stapleton
Doris ...........................................Elizabeth Howell
Joe Hardy .......................................Stephen  Douglass
Henry ...........................................Al Lanti
Sohovik .........................................Eddie Phillips
Smokey ..........................................Nathaniel Frey
Vernon ..........................................Albert Linville
Van Buren .......................................Russ Brown
Rocky ...........................................Jimmie Komack
Gloria ..........................................Rae Allen
Teen-Ager .......................................Cherry Davis
Lynch ...........................................Del Horstmann
Welch ...........................................Richard Bishop
Lola ............................................Gwen Verdon
Miss Weston .....................................Janie Janvier
Guard ...........................................George Marcy
Commissioner ....................................Del Horstmann
Postmaster ......................................Albert Linville
```
    Dancers: Betty Carr, Patricia Ferrier, Marlyn Greer, Marie Kolin, Julia Marlowe, Svetlana McLee; Robert Evans, Timmy Everett, William Joyce, Harvey Jung, Al Lanti, George Marcy, Eddie Phillips, Mark Ward.
    Singers: Cherry Davis, Jeanne Grant, Janet Hayes, Janie Janvier, Joan Keenan, Suzanne Lovell; Frank Bouley, Fred Bryan, Del Horstmann, Ralph Lowe, Albert Linville, Ralph Strane.
    Children: Ronn Cummins, Jackie Scholle.
    The action takes place some time in the future—Washington, D. C.
    Staged by George Abbott; dances and musical numbers staged by Bob Fosse; scenery and costumes designed by William and Jean Eckart; musical direction by Hal Hastings; orchestrations by Don Walker; dance music arrangements by Roger Adams; stage managers, James Hammerstein, Fred Hearn and Robert Evans.

Musical numbers—
ACT I
"Six Months Out of Every Year" .....Shannon Bolin, Robert Shafer, Baseball Fans, Baseball Widows

"Goodbye, Old Girl" ....Robert Shafer, Stephen Douglass
"Heart" ....Russ Brown, Jimmie Komack,
                                        Nathaniel Frey, Albert Linville
"Shoeless Joe from Hannibal, Mo." ...Rae Allen and Baseball Players
"A Man Doesn't Know" ....Stephen Douglass
"A Little Brains—A Little Talent" ....Gwen Verdon
"A Man Doesn't Know" (Reprise) ....Stephen Douglass,
                                                        Shannon Bolin
"Whatever Lola Wants" ....Gwen Verdon
"Not Meg" ....Ray Wolston and Gossips
"Who's Got the Pain?" ....Gwen Verdon and Eddie Phillips
            (Dance staged by Bob Fosse and Gwen Verdon)
"The American League" ....The Downtown Fan Club

ACT II

"The Game" ....Jimmie Komack, Nathaniel
                                        Frey, and Baseball Players
"Heart" (Reprise) ....Jean Stapleton, Ronn Cummins,
                                        Jackie Scholle, Cherry Davis
"Near to You" ....Stephen Douglass, Shannon Bolin
"Those Were the Good Old Days" ....Ray Walston
"Two Lost Souls" ....Gwen Verdon, Stephen Douglass,
                                        and Guys and Dolls
"A Man Doesn't Know" (Reprise) ....Shannon Bolin, Robert Shafer

FINIAN'S RAINBOW

(15 performances)

Musical comedy in two acts, with book by E. Y. Harburg and Fred Saidy, lyrics by E. Y. Harburg and music by Burton Lane. Revived by the New York City Center Light Opera Company (William Hammerstein, General Director) at the New York City Center of Music and Drama, May 18, 1955.

Cast of characters—

Buzz Collins ....Eddie Bruce
Sheriff ....Jack Bryan
First Sharecropper ....Evans Thornton
Second Sharecropper ....Seth Riggs
Susan Mahoney ....Anita Alvarez
Henry ....Michael Gilford
Third Sharecropper ....Rosetta LeNoire
Finian McLonergan ....Will Mahoney
Sharon McLonergan ....Helen Gallagher
Woody Mahoney ....Merv Griffin
Og (a Leprechaun) ....Donn Driver
Howard ....Terry Carter
Senator Billboard Rawkins ....Frank Borgman
First Geologist ....Walter P. Brown
Second Geologist ....Emory Knight
Diane ....Lynn-Rose Kohan
Honey Lou ....Jonelle Allen
John (The Preacher) ....Rodester Timmons
Mr. Robust ....Oggie Small
Mr. Shears ....James Elward
First Passion Pilgrim Gospeleer ....John Bouie
Second Passion Pilgrim Gospeleer ....Elwood Smith
Third Passion Pilgrim Gospeleer ....Jay J. Riley
First Deputy ....Howard Lear
Second Deputy ....Richard Blofson
Third Deputy ....Emory Knight

Dancers—Boys: Albert Fiorella, Robert Karl, Tom Panko, Charles Queenan, Jay J. Riley, Harry Lee Rogers, Marc West. Girls: Erona Harris, Norma Kaiser, Loys Lozano, Mary Martinet, Vera McNichols, Nadine Revene, Kirsten Valbor, Elizabeth Williamson.

Singers—Boys: John Bouie, Walter P. Brown, Clifford Fearl, Howard Lear, Seth Riggs, Jay J. Riley, Robert Rippy, Elwood Smith, Evans Thornton, Rodester Timmons, Murray Vines. Girls: Helen Baisley, Theresa Mari, Rosalie Maxwell, Eileen Moran, Louise Pearl, Michelle Reiner, Janice Samarie, Christine Spencer.

Staged by William Hammerstein; choreography by Onna White (after the original by Michael Kidd); scenery by Howard Bay; costumes by Alvin Colt; orchestrations by Robert Russell Bennett and Don Walker; conductor, Julius Rudel; costume supervisor, Frank Spencer; assistant to William Hammerstein, Michael Shurtleff; musical director, Frederick Dvonch; production stage manager, Bernard Gersten; stage manager, Richard Blofson.

Finian's Rainbow was first produced January 10, 1947, by Lee Sabison and William R. Katzell at the Forty-Sixth Street Theatre for 725 performances.

(Closed May 29, 1955)

ONCE UPON A TAILOR

(8 performances)

Play in three acts by Baruch Lumet, adapted by Henry Sherman. Produced by The Playwrights' Company and George Boroff at the Cort Theatre, May 23, 1955.

Cast of characters—

Sheindel	Anita Cooper
Sorelle	Anne Hegira
Frenzl	Oscar Karlweis
Leibel	Jimmy Oster
Chana Bayle	Adelaide Klein
Bertzi	Peter Fernandez
Elka	Rebecca Darke
Mechel	Milton Selzer

The action takes place in Tarnoff, Galicia, a province of Austria, seventy-five years ago. Act I.—Frenzl's cottage, between the woods and the village; early morning. Act II.—Scene 1—A week later. Scene 2—Later, the same day. Scene 3—In the woods; early evening. Act III.—Scene 1—Late in the evening. Scene 2—The next morning at sunrise.

Staged by Joseph Anthony; scenery by Boris Aronson; lighting and costumes by Paul Morrison; music by Sol Kaplan; production stage manager, James Gelb; stage manager, Theodore Mann.

Limp, feckless folk-comedy about a hard-up Lithuanian tailor who in desperation turns matchmaker and arranges to marry off a village girl to the well-to-do young man who is secretly courting the tailor's own daughter. There are further complications and a happy ending.

(Closed May 28, 1955)

SEVENTH HEAVEN

(6 performances)
(Continued)

Musical play in two acts, based upon the play *Seventh Heaven* written by Austin Strong and produced by John Golden. Book by Victor Wolfson and Stella Unger; music by Victor Young; lyrics by Stella Unger. Produced by Gant Gaither and William Bacher at the ANTA Theatre, May 26, 1955.

Cast of characters—

Boule	Kurt Kasznar
Camille	Gerrianne Raphael
Collette	Patricia Hammerlee
Fifi	Chita Rivera
Mme. Suze	Beatrice Arthur
Father Chevillon	Malcolm Lee Beggs
Diane	Gloria DeHaven
First Sailor	Philip Cook
Second Sailor	Leo Kayworth
Policeman	Walter Brandin
First Nun	Nanette Vezina
Second Nun	Joy Marlene
Street Cleaner	Ralph Quist
Organ Grinder	William Carson
First Senegalese	Ray Saint Jacques
Second Senegalese	James E. Wall
Dandy	John Carter
Baker Boy	Joseph Flynn
Housewife	Jeanne Schlegel
Artist	Jimmy White
Streetwalkers	Lee Becker, Bonnie Evans, Helena Seroy
Midinette	Nancy Lynch
Fleegle (The Rat)	Robert Clary
Inspector	Scott Merrill
Gobin	David Collyer
Vulmir	Ferdi Hoffman
Chico	Ricardo Montalban
Children	Betty Jane Seagle, Barbara Stabile, Barclay Hodges
French Official	George Burles
Flower Vendor	Winifred Ainslee
First French Soldier	Ray Saint Jacques
Second French Soldier	James E. Wall
First American Soldier	Ralph Quist
Second American Soldier	Joseph Flynn
Apaches	Edmund Hall, Ralph Wayne
Accordionist	Dominic Cortese

Dancers: Lee Becker, Bonnie Evans, Nancy Lynch, Helena Seroy, Rebecca Vorno; Philip Cook, Victor Duntiere, William Guske, Philip Salem, Jimmy White.

Singers: Winifred Ainslee, Gwen Harmon, Joy Marlene, Alexandra Moss, Jeanne Schlegel, Nanette Vezina; Walter Brandin, George Burles, William Carson, John Carter, Joseph Flynn, Edmund Hall, Leo Kayworth, Ralph Quist, Ray Saint Jacques, James E. Wall, Ralph Wayne.

The action takes place in and around Paris, France; the time is 1914-1918. Act I.—Scene 1—A cul-de-sac. Scene 2—A street in Paris. Scene 3—Chico's sewer. Scene 4—Rue Notre Dame de Lorette. Scene 5—Chico's attic. Scene 6—The street. Scene 7—"Heaven" —four days later. Scene 8—Rue Notre Dame de Lorette. Scene 9— Fête Montmartre. Act II.—Scene 1—Railroad station. Scene 2— The street. Scene 3—In the trenches. Scene 4—No Man's Land. Scene 5—Behind the lines—a canteen. Scene 6—The search. Scene 7—The cul-de-sac.

Staged by John C. Wilson; scenery and costumes by Marcel Vertes; choreography by Peter Gennaro; lighting by Feder; musical director, Max Meth; orchestral arrangements, David Terry; choral director, Crane Calder; production stage manager, Ward Bishop; stage managers, Earl J. Brisgal and Ernestine Perrie.

Musical numbers—

ACT I

"C'est la Vie" ....Fleegle, Boule, Suze and Company
"Where Is That Someone for Me?" ....Diane
"Camille, Collette, Fifi" ....Fifi, Collette and Camille
"Man with a Dream" ....Chico and Company
"Remarkable Fellow" ....Chico, Fifi, Inspector and Company
"If It's a Dream" ....Diane
"Happy Little Crook" ....Fleegle
"Sun at My Window, Love at My Door" ....Diane, Chico
and Company
Reprise: "Where Is That Someone for Me?" ....Diane
"Glove Dance" ....Bonnie Evans, Nancy Lynch, Helena Seroy,
Rebecca Vorno, Philip Cook, Victor
Duntiere, Philip Salem, Jimmy White

ACT II

"A Miss You Kiss" ....Chico and Company
Reprise: "Camille, Collette, Fifi" ....Fifi, Collette, Camille
"Chico's Reverie" (White and Gold Ballet) ....Company
"Love, Love, Love" ....Camille, Collette, Fifi and Jimmy White
Reprise: "If It's a Dream" ....Diane
"Love Sneaks Up on You" ....Fleegle and Collette
Finale ....Entire Company

FACTS AND FIGURES

HIT TUNES OF THE SEASON

WHATEVER LOLA WANTS from *Damn Yankees*

Words and music by Richard Adler and Jerry Ross

What - ev - er Lo - la Wants_____   Lo - la gets,_____

— And lit - tle man,   lit - tle Lo - la wants you.

TWO LADIES IN DE SHADE OF DE BANANA TREE

from *House of Flowers*

Music by Harold Arlen

Lyrics by Truman Capote and Harold Arlen

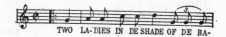

TWO LA-DIES IN DE SHADE OF DE BA-

NA- NA TREE. How de - lec - ta - ble, de - sir - ous they can be,___ in de

black,black shade of de Ba - na - na tree. _____

421

VARIETY'S TABULATION
OF FINANCIAL HITS AND FLOPS *

HITS

Anastasia

Bad Seed

The Boy Friend

Bus Stop

Cat on a Hot Tin Roof

Fanny

Lunatics and Lovers

A Midsummer Night's Dream

Peter Pan

The Rainmaker

Ruth and Paul Draper

The Tender Trap

3 for Tonight

Witness for the Prosecution

STATUS NOT YET DEFINITE

Ankles Aweigh

Damn Yankees

The Desperate Hours

Inherit the Wind

Plain and Fancy

Seventh Heaven

Silk Stockings

FAILURES

Abie's Irish Rose

All in One

All Summer Long

Black-Eyed Susan

Champagne Complex

The Dark Is Light Enough

Dear Charles

Festival

The Flowering Peach

Fragile Fox

The Grand Prize

Hit the Trail

Home Is the Hero

The Honeys

House of Flowers

The Living Room

Mrs. Patterson

On Your Toes

Once Upon a Tailor

One Eye Closed

Portrait of a Lady

Quadrille

Reclining Figure

The Saint of Bleecker Street

The Southwest Corner

Tonight in Samarkand

The Traveling Lady

The Wayward Saint

Wedding Breakfast

* The criterion here is not **how** long a play ran, or how well it was regarded, but only whether it proved a profitable investment.

NON-COMMERCIAL

Carousel
The Doctor's Dilemma
Finian's Rainbow
The Fourposter
Guys and Dolls
The Master Builder
Phoenix '55

Sandhog
Sing Me No Lullaby
South Pacific
The Time of Your Life
What Every Woman Knows
The Wisteria Trees

CLOSED OUT OF TOWN

Hello, Paree
Put Them All Together

Sailor's Delight
Saint Joan

Holdovers from 1953-54 Season, Since Clarified

HITS

Anniversary Waltz
Kismet
Oh, Men! Oh, Women!

Ondine
Pajama Game

FAILURES

By the Beautiful Sea
The Girl in Pink Tights
The Golden Apple
John Murray Anderson's Almanac

King of Hearts
The Remarkable Mr. Pennypacker

STATISTICAL SUMMARY

(LAST SEASON PLAYS WHICH ENDED RUNS AFTER JUNE 1, 1954)

Plays	Number Performances	
The Fifth Season	654	(Closed October 23, 1954)
Kismet	583	(Closed April 23, 1955)
Wonderful Town	559	(Closed July 3, 1954)
The Solid Gold Cadillac	526	(Closed February 12, 1955)
The Caine Mutiny Court Martial	415	(Closed January 15, 1955)
Oh, Men! Oh, Women!	382	(Closed November 13, 1954)
Sabrina Fair	318	(Closed August 21, 1954)
King of Hearts	279	(Closed November 27, 1954)
By the Beautiful Sea	270	(Closed November 27, 1954)
John Murray Anderson's Almanac	229	(Closed June 26, 1954)
The Remarkable Mr. Pennypacker	221	(Closed July 10, 1954)
Ondine	157	(Closed July 3, 1954)
The Golden Apple	125	(Closed August 7, 1954)
The Girl in Pink Tights	115	(Closed June 12, 1954)
The Sea Gull	40	(Closed June 13, 1954)

LONG RUNS ON BROADWAY

To June 1, 1955

(Plays marked with asterisk were still playing June 1, 1955)

Plays	Number Performances	Plays	Number Performances
Life with Father	3,224	You Can't Take It with You	837
Tobacco Road	3,182	Three Men on a Horse	835
Abie's Irish Rose	2,327	Where's Charlie?	792
Oklahoma!	2,248	The Ladder	789
South Pacific	1,925	State of the Union	765
Harvey	1,775	The First Year	760
Born Yesterday	1,642	Death of a Salesman	742
The Voice of the Turtle	1,557	Sons o' Fun	742
Arsenic and Old Lace	1,444	The Man Who Came to Dinner	739
Hellzapoppin	1,404	Call Me Mister	734
Angel Street	1,295	High Button Shoes	727
Lightnin'	1,291	Finian's Rainbow	725
The King and I	1,246	Claudia	722
Guys and Dolls	1,200	The Gold Diggers	720
Mister Roberts	1,157	I Remember Mama	714
Annie Get Your Gun	1,147	Junior Miss	710
Pins and Needles	1,108	Seventh Heaven	704
Kiss Me, Kate	1,070	Peg o' My Heart	692
* The Seven Year Itch	1,058	* Tea and Sympathy	691
Anna Lucasta	957	The Children's Hour	691
Kiss and Tell	957	Dead End	687
The Moon Is Blue	924	The Lion and the Mouse	686
Carousel	890	* The Teahouse of the August Moon	684
Hats Off to Ice	889	Dear Ruth	683
Follow the Girls	882	East Is West	680
The Bat	867	The Doughgirls	671
* Can-Can	865	Irene	670
My Sister Eileen	865	Boy Meets Girl	669
White Cargo	864		
Song of Norway	860		
A Streetcar Named Desire	855		

Plays	*Number Performances*	*Plays*	*Number Performances*
Blithe Spirit	657	The Glass Menagerie	561
The Women	657	Wonderful Town	559
A Trip to Chinatown	657	Rose Marie	557
Bloomer Girl	654	Strictly Dishonorable	557
The Fifth Season	654	Ziegfeld Follies	553
* Comedy in Music	652	Floradora	553
Rain	648	Dial "M" for Murder	552
Call Me Madam	644	Good News	551
Janie	642	Let's Face It	547
The Green Pastures	640	Within the Law	541
The Fourposter	632	The Music Master	540
Is Zat So?	618	Pal Joey	540
The Happy Time	614	What a Life	538
Separate Rooms	613	The Red Mill	531
Affairs of State	610	The Solid Gold Cadillac	526
Star and Garter	609	The Boomerang	522
The Student Prince	608	Rosalinda	521
Broadway	603	Chauve Souris	520
Adonis	603	Blackbirds	518
Street Scene	601	Sunny	517
Kiki	600	Victoria Regina	517
Wish You Were Here	598	The Vagabond King	511
A Society Circus	596	The New Moon	509
Blossom Time	592	Shuffle Along	504
The Two Mrs. Carrolls	585	Up in Central Park	504
Kismet	583	Carmen Jones	503
Detective Story	581	The Member of the Wedding	501
Brigadoon	581	Personal Appearance	501
Brother Rat	577	Panama Hattie	501
Show Boat	572	Bird in Hand	500
The Show-Off	571	Sailor, Beware!	500
Sally	570	Room Service	500
One Touch of Venus	567	Tomorrow the World	500
Happy Birthday	564		

NEW YORK DRAMA CRITICS CIRCLE AWARDS

At their annual Spring meeting, the New York Drama Critics Circle chose Tennessee Williams' *Cat on a Hot Tin Roof* as the best new American play of the season, with William Inge's *Bus Stop* as runner-up. As the best foreign play the Circle chose Agatha Christie's *Witness for the Prosecution,* and as the best musical, Gian-Carlo Menotti's opera, *The Saint of Bleecker Street.*

Circle awards have been—

1935-36—Winterset, by Maxwell Anderson
1936-37—High Tor, by Maxwell Anderson
1937-38—Of Mice and Men, by John Steinbeck
1938-39—No award.
1939-40—The Time of Your Life, by William Saroyan
1940-41—Watch on the Rhine, by Lillian Hellman
1941-42—No award.
1942-43—The Patriots, by Sidney Kingsley
1943-44—No award.
1944-45—The Glass Menagerie, by Tennessee Williams
1945-46—No award.
1946-47—All My Sons, by Arthur Miller
1947-48—A Streetcar Named Desire, by Tennessee Williams
1948-49—Death of a Salesman, by Arthur Miller
1949-50—The Member of the Wedding, by Carson McCullers
1950-51—Darkness at Noon, by Sidney Kingsley
1951-52—I Am a Camera, by John van Druten
1952-53—Picnic, by William Inge
1953-54—The Teahouse of the August Moon, by John Patrick
1954-55—Cat on a Hot Tin Roof, by Tennessee Williams

PULITZER PRIZE WINNERS

For the third successive season, the Pulitzer Prize went to the same play as the Critics Circle award—in this case, Tennessee Williams' *Cat on a Hot Tin Roof.*

Pulitzer awards have been—

1917-18—Why Marry?, by Jesse Lynch Williams
1918-19—No award.
1919-20—Beyond the Horizon, by Eugene O'Neill
1920-21—Miss Lulu Bett, by Zona Gale
1921-22—Anna Christie, by Eugene O'Neill
1922-23—Icebound, by Owen Davis
1923-24—Hell-bent fer Heaven, by Hatcher Hughes
1924-25—They Knew What They Wanted, by Sidney Howard
1925-26—Craig's Wife, by George Kelly
1926-27—In Abraham's Bosom, by Paul Green
1927-28—Strange Interlude, by Eugene O'Neill
1928-29—Street Scene, by Elmer Rice
1929-30—The Green Pastures, by Marc Connelly
1930-31—Alison's House, by Susan Glaspell
1931-32—Of Thee I Sing, by George S. Kaufman, Morrie Ryskind, Ira and George Gershwin
1932-33—Both Your Houses, by Maxwell Anderson
1933-34—Men in White, by Sidney Kingsley
1934-35—The Old Maid, by Zoë Akins
1935-36—Idiot's Delight, by Robert E. Sherwood
1936-37—You Can't Take It with You, by Moss Hart and George S. Kaufman
1937-38—Our Town, by Thornton Wilder
1938-39—Abe Lincoln in Illinois, by Robert E. Sherwood
1939-40—The Time of Your Life, by William Saroyan
1940-41—There Shall Be No Night, by Robert E. Sherwood
1941-42—No award.
1942-43—The Skin of Our Teeth, by Thornton Wilder
1943-44—No award.
1944-45—Harvey, by Mary Coyle Chase
1945-46—State of the Union, by Howard Lindsay and Russel Crouse

1946-47—No award.
1947-48—A Streetcar Named Desire, by Tennessee Williams
1948-49—Death of a Salesman, by Arthur Miller
1949-50—South Pacific, by Richard Rodgers, Oscar Hammer-
          stein II and Joshua Logan
1950-51—No award.
1951-52—The Shrike, by Joseph Kramm
1952-53—Picnic, by William Inge
1953-54—The Teahouse of the August Moon, by John Patrick
1954-55—Cat on a Hot Tin Roof, by Tennessee Williams

BOOKS ON THE THEATRE

1954-1955

Abbott, George, and Bissell, Richard. *The Pajama Game.* (Music and lyrics by Richard Adler and Jerry Ross.) Random House. $2.75.

Aldrich, Richard. *Gertrude Lawrence as Mrs. A.* Greystone Press. $4.95.

Allen, Fred. *Treadmill to Oblivion.* Little, Brown. $4.00.

Anderson, John Murray. *Out without My Rubbers.* Library Publishers. $3.95.
Memoirs as told to Abercrombie Anderson.

Anderson, Maxwell. *Bad Seed.* Dodd, Mead. $3.00.

Bailey, Howard. *The ABC's of Play Producing.* David McKay. $3.50.
A handbook for the non-professional.

Barnes, Eric Wollencott. *The Lady of Fashion: The Life and the Theatre of Anna Cora Mowatt.* Scribner's. $4.75.

Barrymore, Ethel. *Memories.* Harper's. $4.00.

Bentley, Eric. *The Dramatic Event.* Horizon Press. $3.50.

Bentley, Eric (Editor). *The Modern Theatre* (3 volumes). Anchor Books. $.95 each.
A series of volumes containing plays from Musset to Brecht, Giraudoux and Anouilh.

Blum, Daniel (Editor). *Theatre World.* Greenberg. $4.50.

Chapman, John (Editor). *Theatre '54.* Random House. $5.00.

Chapman, John, and Sherwood, Garrison. *The Best Plays of 1894-1899.* Dodd, Mead. $5.00.
The Little Minister, The Heart of Maryland, Trelawny of the Wells, etc.

Chayefsky, Paddy. *Television Plays*. Simon & Schuster. $3.75.

Courtney, Marguerite. *Laurette*. Rinehart. $5.00.
The life of Laurette Taylor, written by her daughter.

Dekker, Thomas (Fredson Bowers, Editor). *Dramatic Works*, Vol. II. Cambridge University Press. $7.50.

Euripides. *Alcestis; The Medea; The Heracleidae; Hippolytus*. Variously translated into English, and with a general introduction by Richard Lattimore. University of Chicago Press. $3.75.

Fitts, Dudley (Editor). *Six Greek Plays in Modern Translation*. Dryden Press. $1.95.

Fry, Christopher. *The Dark Is Light Enough*. Oxford University Press. $2.75.

Gassner, John. *Masters of the Drama*. Dover. $5.95.
Third revised edition.

Hayes, Joseph. *The Desperate Hours*. Random House. $2.75.

Hellman, Lillian (Editor). *The Selected Letters of Anton Chekhov*. (Translated by Sidonie K. Lederer.) Farrar, Straus. $4.00.

Inge, William. *Bus Stop*. Random House. $2.75.

Kronenberger, Louis (Editor). *The Best Plays of 1953-1954*. Dodd, Mead. $5.00.

Logan, Joshua, and Behrman, S. N. *Fanny*. Random House. $2.75.

Mander, Raymond, and Mitchenson, Joe. *Theatrical Companion to Shaw*. Pitman Publishing Company. $9.00.
A pictorial record of first performances of Shaw's plays.

McCarthy, Desmond. *Theatre*. Oxford University Press. $3.50.
Essays on dramatists and drama.

Nash, N. Richard. *The Rainmaker*. Random House. $2.75.

Nicoll, Allardyce (Editor). *Shakespeare Survey: 8*. Cambridge University Press. $3.75.

Samachson, Dorothy and Joseph. *The Dramatic Story of the Theatre*. Abelard-Schuman. $4.00.

Schoenbaum, Samuel. *Middleton's Tragedies*. Columbia University Press. $4.50.
A critical study of the Elizabethan playwright.

Shakespeare, William. *Facsimile Edition of the First Folio.* Yale University Press. $12.50.

Shaw, Bernard. *Plays and Players: Theatre Essays by G.B.S.* World's Classics. $1.35.

Shulman, Max, and Smith, Robert Paul. *The Tender Trap.* Random House. $2.75.

Sievers, W. David. *Freud on Broadway.* Hermitage House. $5.00. A survey of psychoanalysis in relation to American drama.

Stevenson, Burton E. *A King in Babylon:* A Romantic Melodrama in Three Acts. Baker and Taylor. $3.50.

Teichman, Howard, and Kaufman, George S. *The Solid Gold Cadillac.* Random House. $2.75.

PREVIOUS VOLUMES OF BEST PLAYS

Plays chosen to represent the theatre seasons from 1899 to 1954 are as follows:

1899-1909

BARBARA FRIETCHIE, by Clyde Fitch. Life Publishing Co.
THE CLIMBERS, by Clyde Fitch. Macmillan.
If I WERE KING, by Justin Huntly McCarthy. Samuel French.
THE DARLING OF THE GODS, by David Belasco. Little, Brown.
THE COUNTY CHAIRMAN, by George Ade. Samuel French.
LEAH KLESCHNA, by C. M. S. McLellan. Samuel French.
THE SQUAW MAN, by Edwin Milton Royle.
THE GREAT DIVIDE, by William Vaughn Moody. Samuel French.
THE WITCHING HOUR, by Augustus Thomas. Samuel French.
THE MAN FROM HOME, by Booth Tarkington and Harry Leon Wilson. Samuel French.

1909-1919

THE EASIEST WAY, by Eugene Walter. G. W. Dillingham and Houghton Mifflin.
MRS. BUMPSTEAD-LEIGH, by Harry James Smith. Samuel French.
DISRAELI, by Louis N. Parker. Dodd, Mead.
ROMANCE, by Edward Sheldon. Macmillan.
SEVEN KEYS TO BALDPATE, by George M. Cohan. Published by Bobbs-Merrill as a novel by Earl Derr Biggers; as a play by Samuel French.
ON TRIAL, by Elmer Reizenstein. Samuel French.
THE UNCHASTENED WOMAN, by Louis Kaufman Anspacher. Harcourt, Brace and Howe.
GOOD GRACIOUS ANNABELLE, by Clare Kummer. Samuel French.
WHY MARRY?, by Jesse Lynch Williams. Scribner.
JOHN FERGUSON, by St. John Ervine. Macmillan.

1919-1920

ABRAHAM LINCOLN, by John Drinkwater. Houghton Mifflin.
CLARENCE, by Booth Tarkington. Samuel French.
BEYOND THE HORIZON, by Eugene G. O'Neill. Boni & Liveright.

Déclassée, by Zoë Akins. Liveright, Inc.
The Famous Mrs. Fair, by James Forbes. Samuel French.
The Jest, by Sem Benelli. (American adaptation by Edward Sheldon.)
Jane Clegg, by St. John Ervine. Henry Holt.
Mamma's Affair, by Rachel Barton Butler. Samuel French.
Wedding Bells, by Salisbury Field. Samuel French.
Adam and Eva, by George Middleton and Guy Bolton. Samuel French.

1920-1921

Deburau, adapted from the French of Sacha Guitry by H. Granville Barker. Putnam.
The First Year, by Frank Craven. Samuel French.
Enter Madame, by Gilda Varesi and Dolly Byrne. Putnam.
The Green Goddess, by William Archer. Knopf.
Liliom, by Ferenc Molnar. Boni & Liveright.
Mary Rose, by James M. Barrie. Scribner.
Nice People, by Rachel Crothers. Scribner.
The Bad Man, by Porter Emerson Browne. Putnam.
The Emperor Jones, by Eugene G. O'Neill. Boni & Liveright.
The Skin Game, by John Galsworthy. Scribner.

1921-1922

Anna Christie, by Eugene G. O'Neill. Boni & Liveright.
A Bill of Divorcement, by Clemence Dane. Macmillan.
Dulcy, by George S. Kaufman and Marc Connelly. Putnam.
He Who Gets Slapped, adapted from the Russian of Leonid Andreyev by Gregory Zilboorg. Brentano's.
Six Cylinder Love, by William Anthony McGuire.
The Hero, by Gilbert Emery.
The Dover Road, by Alan Alexander Milne. Samuel French.
Ambush, by Arthur Richman.
The Circle, by William Somerset Maugham.
The Nest, by Paul Geraldy and Grace George.

1922-1923

Rain, by John Colton and Clemence Randolph. Liveright, Inc.
Loyalties, by John Galsworthy. Scribner.
Icebound, by Owen Davis. Little, Brown.
You and I, by Philip Barry. Brentano's.
The Fool, by Channing Pollock. Brentano's.

MERTON OF THE MOVIES, by George Kaufman and Marc Connelly, based on the novel of the same name by Harry Leon Wilson.

WHY NOT? by Jesse Lynch Williams. Walter H. Baker Co.

THE OLD SOAK, by Don Marquis. Doubleday, Page.

R.U.R., by Karel Capek. Translated by Paul Selver. Doubleday, Page.

MARY THE 3D, by Rachel Crothers. Brentano's.

1923-1924

THE SWAN, translated from the Hungarian of Ferenc Molnar by Melville Baker. Boni & Liveright.

OUTWARD BOUND, by Sutton Vane. Boni & Liveright.

THE SHOW-OFF, by George Kelly. Little, Brown.

THE CHANGELINGS, by Lee Wilson Dodd. Dutton.

CHICKEN FEED, by Guy Bolton. Samuel French.

SUN-UP, by Lula Vollmer. Brentano's.

BEGGAR ON HORSEBACK, by George Kaufman and Marc Connelly. Boni & Liveright.

TARNISH, by Gilbert Emery. Brentano's.

THE GOOSE HANGS HIGH, by Lewis Beach. Little, Brown.

HELL-BENT FER HEAVEN, by Hatcher Hughes. Harper.

1924-1925

WHAT PRICE GLORY? by Laurence Stallings and Maxwell Anderson. Harcourt, Brace.

THEY KNEW WHAT THEY WANTED, by Sidney Howard. Doubleday, Page.

DESIRE UNDER THE ELMS, by Eugene G. O'Neill. Boni & Liveright.

THE FIREBRAND, by Edwin Justus Mayer. Boni & Liveright.

DANCING MOTHERS, by Edgar Selwyn and Edmund Goulding.

MRS. PARTRIDGE PRESENTS, by Mary Kennedy and Ruth Warren. Samuel French.

THE FALL GUY, by James Gleason and George Abbott. Samuel French.

THE YOUNGEST, by Philip Barry. Samuel French.

MINICK, by Edna Ferber and George S. Kaufman. Doubleday, Page.

WILD BIRDS, by Dan Totheroh. Doubleday, Page.

1925-1926

CRAIG'S WIFE, by George Kelly. Little, Brown.
THE GREAT GOD BROWN, by Eugene G. O'Neill. Boni & Liveright.
THE GREEN HAT, by Michael Arlen.
THE DYBBUK, by S. Ansky, Henry G. Alsberg-Winifred Katzin translation. Boni & Liveright.
THE ENEMY, by Channing Pollock. Brentano's.
THE LAST OF MRS. CHEYNEY, by Frederick Lonsdale. Samuel French.
BRIDE OF THE LAMB, by William Hurlbut. Boni & Liveright.
THE WISDOM TOOTH, by Marc Connelly. George H. Doran.
THE BUTTER AND EGG MAN, by George Kaufman. Boni & Liveright.
YOUNG WOODLEY, by John van Druten. Simon & Schuster.

1926-1927

BROADWAY, by Philip Dunning and George Abbott. George H. Doran.
SATURDAY'S CHILDREN, by Maxwell Anderson. Longmans, Green.
CHICAGO, by Maurine Watkins. Knopf.
THE CONSTANT WIFE, by William Somerset Maugham. George H. Doran.
THE PLAY'S THE THING, by Ferenc Molnar and P. G. Wodehouse. Brentano's.
THE ROAD TO ROME, by Robert Emmet Sherwood. Scribner.
THE SILVER CORD, by Sidney Howard. Scribner.
THE CRADLE SONG, translated from the Spanish of G. Martinez Sierra by John Garrett Underhill. Dutton.
DAISY MAYME, by George Kelly. Little, Brown.
IN ABRAHAM'S BOSOM, by Paul Green. McBride.

1927-1928

STRANGE INTERLUDE, by Eugene G. O'Neill. Boni & Liveright.
THE ROYAL FAMILY, by Edna Ferber and George Kaufman. Doubleday, Doran.
BURLESQUE, by George Manker Watters and Arthur Hopkins. Doubleday, Doran.
COQUETTE, by George Abbott and Ann Bridgers. Longmans, Green.
BEHOLD THE BRIDEGROOM, by George Kelly. Little, Brown.
PORGY, by DuBose Heyward. Doubleday, Doran.
PARIS BOUND, by Philip Barry. Samuel French.
ESCAPE, by John Galsworthy. Scribner.

THE RACKET, by Bartlett Cormack. Samuel French.
THE PLOUGH AND THE STARS, by Sean O'Casey. Macmillan.

1928-1929

STREET SCENE, by Elmer Rice. Samuel French.
JOURNEY'S END, by R. C. Sherriff. Brentano's.
WINGS OVER EUROPE, by Robert Nichols and Maurice Browne. Co-
    vici-Friede.
HOLIDAY, by Philip Barry. Samuel French.
THE FRONT PAGE, by Ben Hecht and Charles MacArthur. Covici-
    Friede.
LET US BE GAY, by Rachel Crothers. Samuel French.
MACHINAL, by Sophie Treadwell.
LITTLE ACCIDENT, by Floyd Dell and Thomas Mitchell.
GYPSY, by Maxwell Anderson.
THE KINGDOM OF GOD, by G. Martinez Sierra; English version by
    Helen and Harley Granville-Barker. Dutton.

1929-1930

THE GREEN PASTURES, by Marc Connelly (adapted from "Ol' Man
    Adam and His Chillun," by Roark Bradford). Farrar & Rine-
    hart.
THE CRIMINAL CODE, by Martin Flavin. Horace Liveright.
BERKELEY SQUARE, by John Balderston.
STRICTLY DISHONORABLE, by Preston Sturges. Horace Liveright.
THE FIRST MRS. FRASER, by St. John Ervine. Macmillan.
THE LAST MILE, by John Wexley. Samuel French.
JUNE MOON, by Ring W. Lardner and George S. Kaufman. Scribner.
MICHAEL AND MARY, by A. A. Milne. Chatto & Windus.
DEATH TAKES A HOLIDAY, by Walter Ferris (adapted from the Ital-
    ian of Alberto Casella). Samuel French.
REBOUND, by Donald Ogden Stewart. Samuel French.

1930-1931

ELIZABETH THE QUEEN, by Maxwell Anderson. Longmans, Green.
TOMORROW AND TOMORROW, by Philip Barry. Samuel French.
ONCE IN A LIFETIME, by George S. Kaufman and Moss Hart. Far-
    rar & Rinehart.
GREEN GROW THE LILACS, by Lynn Riggs. Samuel French.
AS HUSBANDS GO, by Rachel Crothers. Samuel French.

ALISON'S HOUSE, by Susan Glaspell. Samuel French.

FIVE-STAR FINAL, by Louis Weitzenkorn. Samuel French.

OVERTURE, by William Bolitho. Simon & Schuster.

THE BARRETTS OF WIMPOLE STREET, by Rudolf Besier. Little, Brown.

GRAND HOTEL, adapted from the German of Vicki Baum by W. A. Drake.

1931-1932

OF THEE I SING, by George S. Kaufman and Morrie Ryskind; music and lyrics by George and Ira Gershwin. Knopf.

MOURNING BECOMES ELECTRA, by Eugene G. O'Neill. Horace Liveright.

REUNION IN VIENNA, by Robert Emmet Sherwood. Scribner.

THE HOUSE OF CONNELLY, by Paul Green. Samuel French.

THE ANIMAL KINGDOM, by Philip Barry. Samuel French.

THE LEFT BANK, by Elmer Rice. Samuel French.

ANOTHER LANGUAGE, by Rose Franken. Samuel French.

BRIEF MOMENT, by S. N. Behrman. Farrar & Rinehart.

THE DEVIL PASSES, by Benn W. Levy. Martin Secker.

CYNARA, by H. M. Harwood and R. F. Gore-Browne. Samuel French.

1932-1933

BOTH YOUR HOUSES, by Maxwell Anderson. Samuel French.

DINNER AT EIGHT, by George S. Kaufman and Edna Ferber. Doubleday, Doran.

WHEN LADIES MEET, by Rachel Crothers. Samuel French.

DESIGN FOR LIVING, by Noel Coward. Doubleday, Doran.

BIOGRAPHY, by S. N. Behrman. Farrar & Rinehart.

ALIEN CORN, by Sidney Howard. Scribner.

THE LATE CHRISTOPHER BEAN, adapted from the French of René Fauchois by Sidney Howard. Samuel French.

WE, THE PEOPLE, by Elmer Rice. Coward-McCann.

PIGEONS AND PEOPLE, by George M. Cohan.

ONE SUNDAY AFTERNOON, by James Hagan. Samuel French.

1933-1934

MARY OF SCOTLAND, by Maxwell Anderson. Doubleday, Doran.

MEN IN WHITE, by Sidney Kingsley. Covici-Friede.

DODSWORTH, by Sinclair Lewis and Sidney Howard. Harcourt, Brace.

AH, WILDERNESS, by Eugene O'Neill. Random House.
THEY SHALL NOT DIE, by John Wexley. Knopf.
HER MASTER'S VOICE, by Clare Kummer. Samuel French.
NO MORE LADIES, by A. E. Thomas.
WEDNESDAY'S CHILD, by Leopold Atlas. Samuel French.
THE SHINING HOUR, by Keith Winter. Doubleday, Doran.
THE GREEN BAY TREE, by Mordaunt Shairp. Baker International
    Play Bureau.

1934-1935

THE CHILDREN'S HOUR, by Lillian Hellman. Knopf.
VALLEY FORGE, by Maxwell Anderson. Anderson House.
THE PETRIFIED FOREST, by Robert Sherwood. Scribner.
THE OLD MAID, by Zoë Akins. Appleton-Century.
ACCENT ON YOUTH, by Samson Raphaelson. Samuel French.
MERRILY WE ROLL ALONG, by George S. Kaufman and Moss Hart.
    Random House.
AWAKE AND SING, by Clifford Odets. Random House.
THE FARMER TAKES A WIFE, by Frank B. Elser and Marc Connelly.
LOST HORIZONS, by John Hayden.
THE DISTAFF SIDE, by John van Druten. Knopf.

1935-1936

WINTERSET, by Maxwell Anderson. Anderson House.
IDIOT'S DELIGHT, by Robert Emmet Sherwood. Scribner.
END OF SUMMER, by S. N. Behrman. Random House.
FIRST LADY, by Katharine Dayton and George S. Kaufman. Ran-
    dom House.
VICTORIA REGINA, by Laurence Housman. Samuel French.
BOY MEETS GIRL, by Bella and Samuel Spewack. Random House.
DEAD END, by Sidney Kingsley. Random House.
CALL IT A DAY, by Dodie Smith. Samuel French.
ETHAN FROME, by Owen Davis and Donald Davis. Scribner.
PRIDE AND PREJUDICE, by Helen Jerome. Doubleday, Doran.

1936-1937

HIGH TOR, by Maxwell Anderson. Anderson House.
YOU CAN'T TAKE IT WITH YOU, by Moss Hart and George S. Kauf-
    man. Farrar & Rinehart.
JOHNNY JOHNSON, by Paul Green. Samuel French.
DAUGHTERS OF ATREUS, by Robert Turney. Knopf.

STAGE DOOR, by Edna Ferber and George S. Kaufman. Doubleday, Doran.

THE WOMEN, by Clare Boothe. Random House.

ST. HELENA, by R. C. Sherriff and Jeanne de Casalis. Samuel French.

YES, MY DARLING DAUGHTER, by Mark Reed. Samuel French.

EXCURSION, by Victor Wolfson. Random House.

TOVARICH, by Jacques Deval and Robert E. Sherwood. Random House.

1937-1938

OF MICE AND MEN, by John Steinbeck. Covici-Friede.

OUR TOWN, by Thornton Wilder. Coward-McCann.

SHADOW AND SUBSTANCE, by Paul Vincent Carroll. Random House.

ON BORROWED TIME, by Paul Osborn. Knopf.

THE STAR-WAGON, by Maxwell Anderson. Anderson House.

SUSAN AND GOD, by Rachel Crothers. Random House.

PROLOGUE TO GLORY, by E. P. Conkle. Random House.

AMPHITRYON 38, by S. N. Behrman. Random House.

GOLDEN BOY, by Clifford Odets. Random House.

WHAT A LIFE, by Clifford Goldsmith. Dramatists' Play Service.

1938-1939

ABE LINCOLN IN ILLINOIS, by Robert E. Sherwood. Scribner.

THE LITTLE FOXES, by Lillian Hellman. Random House.

ROCKET TO THE MOON, by Clifford Odets. Random House.

THE AMERICAN WAY, by George S. Kaufman and Moss Hart. Random House.

NO TIME FOR COMEDY, by S. N. Behrman. Random House.

THE PHILADELPHIA STORY, by Philip Barry. Coward-McCann.

THE WHITE STEED, by Paul Vincent Carroll. Random House.

HERE COME THE CLOWNS, by Philip Barry. Coward-McCann.

FAMILY PORTRAIT, by Lenore Coffee and William Joyce Cowen. Random House.

KISS THE BOYS GOOD-BYE, by Clare Boothe. Random House.

1939-1940

THERE SHALL BE NO NIGHT, by Robert E. Sherwood. Scribner.

KEY LARGO, by Maxwell Anderson. Anderson House.

THE WORLD WE MAKE, by Sidney Kingsley.

LIFE WITH FATHER, by Howard Lindsay and Russel Crouse. Knopf.

THE MAN WHO CAME TO DINNER, by George S. Kaufman and Moss Hart. Random House.

THE MALE ANIMAL, by James Thurber and Elliott Nugent. Random House, New York, and MacMillan Co., Canada.

THE TIME OF YOUR LIFE, by William Saroyan. Harcourt, Brace.

SKYLARK, by Samson Raphaelson. Random House.

MARGIN FOR ERROR, by Clare Boothe. Random House.

MORNING'S AT SEVEN, by Paul Osborn. Samuel French.

1940-1941

NATIVE SON, by Paul Green and Richard Wright. Harper.

WATCH ON THE RHINE, by Lillian Hellman. Random House.

THE CORN IS GREEN, by Emlyn Williams. Random House.

LADY IN THE DARK, by Moss Hart. Random House.

ARSENIC AND OLD LACE, by Joseph Kesselring. Random House.

MY SISTER EILEEN, by Joseph Fields and Jerome Chodorov. Random House.

FLIGHT TO THE WEST, by Elmer Rice. Coward-McCann.

CLAUDIA, by Rose Franken Meloney. Farrar & Rinehart.

MR. AND MRS. NORTH, by Owen Davis. Samuel French.

GEORGE WASHINGTON SLEPT HERE, by George S. Kaufman and Moss Hart. Random House.

1941-1942

IN TIME TO COME, by Howard Koch. Dramatists' Play Service.

THE MOON IS DOWN, by John Steinbeck. Viking.

BLITHE SPIRIT, by Noel Coward. Doubleday, Doran.

JUNIOR MISS, by Jerome Chodorov and Joseph Fields. Random House.

CANDLE IN THE WIND, by Maxwell Anderson. Anderson House.

LETTERS TO LUCERNE, by Fritz Rotter and Allen Vincent. Samuel French.

JASON, by Samson Raphaelson. Random House.

ANGEL STREET, by Patrick Hamilton. Constable & Co., under the title "Gaslight."

UNCLE HARRY, by Thomas Job. Samuel French.

HOPE FOR A HARVEST, by Sophie Treadwell. Samuel French.

1942-1943

THE PATRIOTS, by Sidney Kingsley. Random House.

THE EVE OF ST. MARK, by Maxwell Anderson. Anderson House.

THE SKIN OF OUR TEETH, by Thornton Wilder. Harper.

WINTER SOLDIERS, by Dan James.

TOMORROW THE WORLD, by James Gow and Arnaud d'Usseau. Scribner.

HARRIET, by Florence Ryerson and Colin Clements. Scribner.

THE DOUGHGIRLS, by Joseph Fields. Random House.

THE DAMASK CHEEK, by John van Druten and Lloyd Morris. Random House.

KISS AND TELL, by F. Hugh Herbert. Coward-McCann.

OKLAHOMA!, by Oscar Hammerstein 2nd and Richard Rodgers. Random House.

1943-1944

WINGED VICTORY, by Moss Hart. Random House.

THE SEARCHING WIND, by Lillian Hellman. Viking.

THE VOICE OF THE TURTLE, by John van Druten. Random House.

DECISION, by Edward Chodorov.

OVER 21, by Ruth Gordon. Random House.

OUTRAGEOUS FORTUNE, by Rose Franken. Samuel French.

JACOBOWSKY AND THE COLONEL, by S. N. Behrman. Random House.

STORM OPERATION, by Maxwell Anderson. Anderson House.

PICK-UP GIRL, by Elsa Shelley.

THE INNOCENT VOYAGE, by Paul Osborn.

1944-1945

A BELL FOR ADANO, by Paul Osborn. Knopf.

I REMEMBER MAMA, by John van Druten. Harcourt, Brace.

THE HASTY HEART, by John Patrick. Random House.

THE GLASS MENAGERIE, by Tennessee Williams. Random House.

HARVEY, by Mary Chase.

THE LATE GEORGE APLEY, by John P. Marquand and George S. Kaufman.

SOLDIER'S WIFE, by Rose Franken. Samuel French.

ANNA LUCASTA, by Philip Yordan. Random House.

FOOLISH NOTION, by Philip Barry.

DEAR RUTH, by Norman Krasna. Random House.

1945-1946

STATE OF THE UNION, by Howard Lindsay and Russel Crouse. Random House.

HOME OF THE BRAVE, by Arthur Laurents. Random House.

Deep Are the Roots, by Arnaud d'Usseau and James Gow. Scribner.

The Magnificent Yankee, by Emmet Lavery. Samuel French.

Antigone, by Lewis Galantière (from the French of Jean Anouilh). Random House.

O Mistress Mine, by Terence Rattigan. Published and revised by the author.

Born Yesterday, by Garson Kanin. Viking.

Dream Girl, by Elmer Rice. Coward-McCann.

The Rugged Path, by Robert E. Sherwood. Scribner.

Lute Song, by Will Irwin and Sidney Howard. Published version by Will Irwin and Leopoldine Howard.

1946-1947

All My Sons, by Arthur Miller. Reynal & Hitchcock.

The Iceman Cometh, by Eugene G. O'Neill. Random House.

Joan of Lorraine, by Maxwell Anderson. Published by Maxwell Anderson.

Another Part of the Forest, by Lillian Hellman. Viking.

Years Ago, by Ruth Gordon. Viking.

John Loves Mary, by Norman Krasna. Copyright by Norman Krasna.

The Fatal Weakness, by George Kelly. Samuel French.

The Story of Mary Surratt, by John Patrick. Dramatists' Play Service.

Christopher Blake, by Moss Hart. Random House.

Brigadoon, by Alan Jay Lerner and Frederick Loewe. Coward-McCann.

1947-1948

A Streetcar Named Desire, by Tennessee Williams. New Directions.

Mister Roberts, by Thomas Heggen and Joshua Logan. Houghton Mifflin.

Command Decision, by William Wister Haines. Random House.

The Winslow Boy, by Terence Rattigan.

The Heiress, by Ruth and Augustus Goetz.

Allegro, by Richard Rodgers and Oscar Hammerstein 2d. Knopf. Music published by Williamson Music, Inc.

Eastward in Eden, by Dorothy Gardner. Longmans, Green.

Skipper Next to God, by Jan de Hartog.

AN INSPECTOR CALLS, by J. B. Priestley.
ME AND MOLLY, by Gertrude Berg.

1948-1949

DEATH OF A SALESMAN, by Arthur Miller. Viking.
ANNE OF THE THOUSAND DAYS, by Maxwell Anderson. Sloane.
THE MADWOMAN OF CHAILLOT, by Maurice Valency, adapted from the French of Jean Giraudoux. Random House.
DETECTIVE STORY, by Sidney Kingsley. Random House.
EDWARD, MY SON, by Robert Morley and Noel Langley. Random House, New York, and Samuel French, London.
LIFE WITH MOTHER, by Howard Lindsay and Russel Crouse. Knopf.
LIGHT UP THE SKY, by Moss Hart. Random House.
THE SILVER WHISTLE, by Robert Edward McEnroe. Dramatists' Play Service.
TWO BLIND MICE, by Samuel Spewack. Dramatists' Play Service.
GOODBYE, MY FANCY, by Fay Kanin. Samuel French.

1949-1950

THE COCKTAIL PARTY, by T. S. Eliot. Harcourt, Brace.
THE MEMBER OF THE WEDDING, by Carson McCullers. Houghton Mifflin.
THE INNOCENTS, by William Archibald. Coward-McCann.
LOST IN THE STARS, by Maxwell Anderson and Kurt Weill. Sloane.
COME BACK, LITTLE SHEBA, by William Inge. Random House.
THE HAPPY TIME, by Samuel Taylor. Random House.
THE WISTERIA TREES, by Joshua Logan. Random House.
I KNOW MY LOVE, by S. N. Behrman. Random House.
THE ENCHANTED, by Maurice Valency, adapted from a play by Jean Giraudoux. Random House.
CLUTTERBUCK, by Benn W. Levy. Dramatists' Play Service.

1950-1951

GUYS AND DOLLS, by Jo Swerling, Abe Burrows and Frank Loesser.
DARKNESS AT NOON, by Sidney Kingsley and Arthur Koestler. Random House.
BILLY BUDD, by Louis O. Coxe and Robert Chapman. Princeton University Press.
THE AUTUMN GARDEN, by Lillian Hellman. Little, Brown & Co.

BELL, BOOK AND CANDLE, by John van Druten. Random House.
THE COUNTRY GIRL, by Clifford Odets. Viking Press.
THE ROSE TATTOO, by Tennessee Williams. New Directions.
SEASON IN THE SUN, by Wolcott Gibbs. Random House.
AFFAIRS OF STATE, by Louis Verneuil.
SECOND THRESHOLD, by Philip Barry. Harper & Bros.

1951-1952

MRS. MCTHING, by Mary Coyle Chase.
THE SHRIKE, by Joseph Kramm. Random House.
I AM A CAMERA, by John van Druten. Random House.
THE FOURPOSTER, by Jan de Hartog.
POINT OF NO RETURN, by Paul Osborn. Random House.
BAREFOOT IN ATHENS, by Maxwell Anderson. Sloane.
VENUS OBSERVED, by Christopher Fry. Oxford.
JANE, by S. N. Behrman and Somerset Maugham. Random House.
GIGI, by Anita Loos and Colette. Random House.
REMAINS TO BE SEEN, by Howard Lindsay and Russel Crouse.
    Random House.

1952-1953

THE TIME OF THE CUCKOO, by Arthur Laurents. Random House.
BERNARDINE, by Mary Coyle Chase.
DIAL "M" FOR MURDER, by Frederick Knott. Random House.
THE CLIMATE OF EDEN, by Moss Hart. Random House.
THE LOVE OF FOUR COLONELS, by Peter Ustinov.
THE CRUCIBLE, by Arthur Miller. Viking.
THE EMPEROR'S CLOTHES, by George Tabori. Samuel French.
PICNIC, by William Inge. Random House.
WONDERFUL TOWN, by Joseph Fields, Jerome Chodorov, Betty
    Comden and Adolph Green. Random House.
MY 3 ANGELS, by Sam and Bella Spewack.

1953-1954

THE CAINE MUTINY COURT-MARTIAL, by Herman Wouk. Double-
    day & Company, Inc.
IN THE SUMMER HOUSE, by Jane Bowles. Random House.
THE CONFIDENTIAL CLERK, by T. S. Eliot. Harcourt, Brace and
    Company, Inc.
TAKE A GIANT STEP, by Louis Peterson. Louis S. Peterson.
THE TEAHOUSE OF THE AUGUST MOON, by John Patrick. G. P.
    Putnam's Sons.

THE IMMORALIST, by Ruth and Augustus Goetz. Ruth and Augustus Goetz.

TEA AND SYMPATHY, by Robert Anderson. Robert Anderson and Random House.

THE GIRL ON THE VIA FLAMINIA, by Alfred Hayes. Alfred Hayes.

THE GOLDEN APPLE, by John Latouche and Jerome Moross. Random House.

THE MAGIC AND THE LOSS, by Julian Funt. Julian Funt.

WHERE AND WHEN THEY WERE BORN

(Compiled from the most authentic records available)

Abbott, George	Forestville, N. Y.	1889
Abel, Walter	St. Paul, Minn.	1898
Addy, Wesley	Omaha, Neb.	1912
Aherne, Brian	King's Norton, England	1902
Aldrich, Richard	Boston, Mass.	1902
Anders, Glenn	Los Angeles, Cal.	1890
Anderson, Judith	Australia	1898
Anderson, Maxwell	Atlantic City, Pa.	1888
Arthur, Jean	New York City	1905
Ashcroft, Peggy	Croydon, England	1907
Bainter, Fay	Los Angeles, Cal.	1892
Bankhead, Tallulah	Huntsville, Ala.	1902
Barrymore, Ethel	Philadelphia, Pa.	1879
Barton, James	Gloucester, N. J.	1890
Behrman, S. N.	Worcester, Mass.	1893
Bellamy, Ralph	Chicago, Ill.	1904
Bergman, Ingrid	Stockholm	1917
Bergner, Elisabeth	Vienna	1900
Berlin, Irving	Russia	1888
Best, Edna	Hove, England	1900
Blackmer, Sidney	Salisbury, N. C.	1898
Bolger, Ray	Dorchester, Mass.	1904
Bondi, Beulah	Chicago, Ill.	1892
Bourneuf, Philip	Boston, Mass.	1912
Boyer, Charles	Figeac, France	1899
Brando, Marlon	Omaha, Neb.	1924
Brent, Romney	Saltillo, Mex.	1902
Brown, Joe E.	Holgate, Ohio	1892
Burke, Billie	Washington, D. C.	1885
Byington, Spring	Colorado Springs, Colo.	1898
Cagney, James	New York City	1904
Cagney, Jeanne	New York City	1920
Calhern, Louis	New York City	1895

Cantor, Eddie .... New York City 1892
Carnovsky, Morris .... St. Louis, Mo. 1898
Carradine, John .... New York City 1906
Carroll, Leo G. .... Weedon, England 1892
Carroll, Madeleine .... West Bromwich, England 1906
Chase, Ilka .... New York City 1905
Chatterton, Ruth .... New York City 1893
Claire, Ina .... Washington, D. C. 1895
Clark, Bobby .... Springfield, Ohio 1888
Clift, Montgomery .... Omaha, Neb. 1921
Clive, Colin .... St. Malo, France 1900
Clurman, Harold .... New York City 1901
Cobb, Lee .... New York City 1911
Coburn, Charles .... Macon, Ga. 1877
Collinge, Patricia .... Dublin 1894
Collins, Russell .... New Orleans, La. 1897
Colt, Ethel Barrymore ...... Mamaroneck, N. Y. 1911
Colt, John Drew .... New York City 1914
Conroy, Frank .... London, England 1885
Cook, Donald .... Portland, Ore. 1902
Cook, Joe .... Evansville, Ind. 1890
Cooper, Melville .... Birmingham, England 1896
Corbett, Leonora .... London, England 1908
Cornell, Katharine .... Berlin, Germany 1898
Coulouris, George .... Manchester, England 1906
Coward, Noel .... Teddington, England 1899
Cromwell, John .... Toledo, Ohio 1888
Cronyn, Hume .... London, Ontario 1912
Crothers, Rachel .... Bloomington, Ill. 1878
Crouse, Russel .... Findlay, Ohio 1893
Cummings, Constance ...... Seattle, Wash. 1911

Dale, Margaret .... Philadelphia, Pa. 1880
Dana, Leora .... New York City 1923
Daniell, Henry .... London, England 1894
Davis, Owen .... Portland, Me. 1874
Derwent, Clarence .... London, England 1884
Dixon, Jean .... Waterbury, Conn. 1905
Douglas, Melvyn .... Macon, Ga. 1901
Dowling, Eddie .... Woonsocket, R. I. 1894
Drake, Alfred .... New York City 1914
Duncan, Todd .... Danville, Ky. 1900

Dunning, Philip .... Meriden, Conn. 1890
Durante, Jimmy .... New York City 1893

Eldridge, Florence .... Brooklyn, N. Y. 1901
Elsom, Isobel .... Cambridge, England 1893
Evans, Edith .... London, England 1888
Evans, Maurice .... Dorchester, England 1901
Evans, Wilbur .... Philadelphia, Pa. 1908
Evelyn, Judith .... Seneca, S. Dak. 1913
Ewell, Tom .... Owensboro, Ky. 1912

Fabray, Nanette .... New Orleans, La. 1921
Fay, Frank .... San Francisco, Cal. 1897
Ferber, Edna .... Kalamazoo, Mich. 1887
Ferrer, José .... Puerto Rico 1912
Field, Betty .... Boston, Mass. 1918
Field, Virginia .... London 1917
Fields, Gracie .... Rochdale, England 1898
Fitzgerald, Barry .... Dublin, Ireland 1888
Fitzgerald, Geraldine .... Dublin, Ireland 1914
Flemyng, Robert .... Liverpool 1912
Fletcher, Bramwell ...... Bradford, Yorkshire, Eng. ... 1904
Fonda, Henry .... Grand Island, Neb. 1905
Fontanne, Lynn .... London, England 1887
Forbes, Brenda .... London, England 1909
Foy, Eddie, Jr. .... New Rochelle, N. Y. 1907
Francis, Arlene .... Boston, Mass. 1908
Fry, Christopher .... England 1907

Gahagan, Helen .... Boonton, N. J. 1900
Gaxton, William .... San Francisco, Cal. 1893
Geddes, Barbara Bel ...... New York City 1922
Geddes, Norman Bel ...... Adrian, Mich. 1893
George, Grace .... New York City 1879
Gershwin, Ira .... New York City 1896
Gielgud, Sir John .... London, England 1904
Gillmore, Margalo .... England 1901
Gilmore, Virginia .... El Monte, Cal. 1919
Gish, Dorothy .... Massillon, Ohio 1898
Gish, Lillian .... Springfield, Ohio 1896
Golden, John .... New York City 1874
Goodner, Carol .... New York City 1904

Gordon, Ruth . . . . Wollaston, Mass. 1896
Greaza, Walter . . . . St. Paul, Minn. 1900
Green, Martyn . . . . London, England 1899
Greenwood, Joan . . . . London, England 1921
Guinness, Alec . . . . London 1914
Gwenn, Edmund . . . . Glamorgan, Wales 1875

Hagen, Uta . . . . Göttingen, Germany 1919
Hammerstein, Oscar, II . . . . . New York City 1895
Hampden, Walter . . . . Brooklyn, N. Y. 1879
Hardie, Russell . . . . Griffin Mills, N. Y. 1906
Hardwicke, Sir Cedric . . . . . . Lye, Stourbridge, England . . . 1893
Harris, Julie . . . . Grosse Point, Mich. 1925
Harrison, Rex . . . . Huyton, Lancashire, England . . 1908
Hart, Moss . . . . New York City 1904
Havoc, June . . . . Seattle, Wash. 1916
Haydon, Julie . . . . Oak Park, Ill. 1910
Hayes, Helen . . . . Washington, D. C. 1900
Hayward, Leland . . . . Nebraska City, Neb. 1902
Heflin, Frances . . . . Oklahoma City, Okla. 1924
Heineman, Eda . . . . Japan 1891
Hellman, Lillian . . . . New Orleans, La. 1905
Helmore, Tom . . . . London, England 1912
Helpmann, Robert . . . . South Australia 1911
Henie, Sonja . . . . Oslo, Norway 1913
Hepburn, Audrey . . . . Brussels 1929
Hepburn, Katharine . . . . Hartford, Conn. 1909
Hiller, Wendy . . . . Bramhall, England 1912
Holliday, Judy . . . . New York City 1924
Holm, Celeste . . . . New York City 1919
Homolka, Oscar . . . . Vienna 1898
Hull, Josephine . . . . Newtonville, Mass. 1886
Hull, Henry . . . . Louisville, Ky. 1890
Hunt, Martita . . . . Argentine Republic 1900
Hunter, Kim . . . . Detroit, Mich. 1922
Hussey, Ruth . . . . Providence, R. I. 1917

Inescort, Frieda . . . . Hitchin, Scotland 1901
Ives, Burl . . . . Hunt Township, Ill. 1909

Johnson, Harold J. (Chic) . . . Chicago, Ill. 1891
Joy, Nicholas . . . . Paris, France 1889

Kane, Whitford .... Larne, Ireland 1882
Kanin, Garson .... Rochester, N. Y. 1912
Karloff, Boris .... Dulwich, England 1887
Kaufman, George S. .... Pittsburgh, Pa. 1889
Kaye, Danny .... New York City 1914
Kazan, Elia .... Constantinople 1909
Keith, Robert .... Fowler, Ind. 1898
Kennedy, Arthur .... Worcester, Mass. 1914
Kerr, Deborah .... Helensburgh, Scotland 1921
Kerr, John .... New York City 1931
Kilbride, Percy .... San Francisco, Cal. 1880
King, Dennis .... Coventry, England 1897
Kingsley, Sidney .... New York City 1906
Kirkland, Patricia .... New York City 1927
Knox, Alexander .... Ontario 1907
Kruger, Otto .... Toledo, Ohio 1885

Lahr, Bert .... New York City 1895
Landis, Jessie Royce .... Chicago, Ill. 1904
Laughton, Charles .... Scarborough, England 1899
LeGallienne, Eva .... London 1899
Leigh, Vivien .... Darjeeling, India 1913
Leighton, Margaret .... Barnt Green, England 1922
Lillie, Beatrice .... Toronto, Canada 1898
Lindsay, Howard .... Waterford, N. Y. 1899
Linn, Bambi .... Brooklyn, N. Y. 1926
Lockhart, Gene .... Ontario 1892
Loeb, Philip .... Philadelphia, Pa. 1892
Logan, Joshua .... Texarkana, Tex. 1908
Lonergan, Lenore .... Toledo, Ohio 1928
Lukas, Paul .... Budapest, Hungary 1891
Lunt, Alfred .... Milwaukee, Wis. 1893
Lytell, Bert .... New York City 1885

MacMahon, Aline .... McKeesport, Pa. 1899
Mamoulian, Rouben .... Tiflis, Russia 1898
Mann, Iris .... Brooklyn, N. Y. 1939
March, Fredric .... Racine, Wis. 1897
Martin, Mary .... Weatherford, Texas 1913
Mason, James .... Huddersfield, England 1909
Massey, Raymond .... Toronto, Canada 1896
Matteson, Ruth .... San Jose, Cal. 1905

Maugham, W. Somerset ...... England 1874
McClintic, Guthrie .... Seattle, Wash. 1893
McCormick, Myron .... Albany, Ind. 1907
McCracken, Joan .... Philadelphia, Pa. 1923
McGrath, Paul .... Chicago, Ill. 1900
McGuire, Dorothy .... Omaha, Neb. 1918
Menotti, Gian-Carlo .... Italy 1912
Meredith, Burgess .... Cleveland, Ohio 1908
Merman, Ethel .... Astoria, L. I. 1909
Middleton, Ray .... Chicago, Ill. 1907
Mielziner, Jo .... Paris, France 1901
Miller, Arthur .... New York City 1915
Miller, Gilbert .... New York City 1884
Mitchell, Thomas .... Elizabeth, N. J. 1892
Moore, Victor .... Hammonton, N. J. 1876
Moorehead, Agnes .... Clinton, Mass. 1906
Morgan, Claudia .... New York City 1912
Morley, Robert .... Semley, England 1908
Moss, Arnold .... Brooklyn, N. Y. 1910
Muni, Paul .... Lemberg, Austria 1895

Nagel, Conrad .... Keokuk, Iowa 1897
Natwick, Mildred .... Baltimore, Md. 1908
Neal, Patricia .... Packard, Ky. 1926
Nesbitt, Cathleen .... Cheshire, England 1889
Nugent, Elliott .... Dover, Ohio 1900

Odets, Clifford .... Philadelphia, Pa. 1906
Oenslager, Donald .... Harrisburg, Pa. 1902
Olivier, Sir Laurence .... Dorking, Surrey, England 1907
Olsen, John Siguard (Ole) ... Peru, Ind. 1892
O'Malley, Rex .... London, England 1906
O'Neal, Frederick .... Brookville, Miss. 1905

Page, Geraldine .... Kirksville, Mo. 1925
Palmer, Lilli .... Posen, Austria 1914
Petina, Irra .... Leningrad, Russia 1900
Picon, Molly .... New York City 1898
Pinza, Ezio .... Rome, Italy 1895
Porter, Cole .... Peru, Ind. 1892
Price, Vincent .... St. Louis, Mo. 1914

Rains, Claude .... London, England 1889
Raitt, John .... Santa Ana, Cal. 1917
Rathbone, Basil .... Johannesburg 1892
Redman, Joyce .... Newcastle, Ireland 1918
Reed, Florence .... Philadelphia, Pa. 1883
Rennie, James .... Toronto, Canada 1890
Rice, Elmer .... New York City 1892
Richardson, Sir Ralph .... Cheltenham, England 1902
Roberts, Joan .... New York City 1918
Rodgers, Richard .... New York City 1902
Ross, Anthony .... New York City 1906
Royle, Selena .... New York City 1905

Sarnoff, Dorothy .... Brooklyn, N. Y. 1919
Saroyan, William .... Fresno, Cal. 1908
Scott, Martha .... Jamesport, Mo. 1914
Segal, Vivienne .... Philadelphia, Pa. 1897
Sherman, Hiram .... Boston, Mass. 1908
Sherwood, Robert Emmet .... New Rochelle, N. Y. 1896
Shumlin, Herman .... Atwood, Colo. 1898
Silvers, Phil .... Brooklyn, N. Y. 1911
Simms, Hilda .... Minneapolis, Minn. 1920
Skinner, Cornelia Otis ...... Chicago, Ill. 1902
Slezak, Walter .... Vienna, Austria 1902
Smith, Kent .... Smithfield, Me. 1910
Stapleton, Maureen .... Troy, N. Y. 1926
Starr, Frances .... Oneonta, N. Y. 1886
Stickney, Dorothy .... Dickinson, N. D. 1903
Stoddard, Haila .... Great Falls, Mont. 1914
Stone, Carol .... New York City 1917
Stone, Dorothy .... New York City 1905
Stone, Ezra .... New Bedford, Mass. 1918
Stone, Fred .... Denver, Colo. 1873
Straight, Beatrice .... Old Westbury, N. Y. 1918
Sullavan, Margaret .... Norfolk, Va. 1910
Sullivan, Francis L. .... London 1903

Tandy, Jessica .... London, England 1909
Tetzel, Joan .... New York City 1923
Thorndike, Sybil .... Gainsborough, England 1882
Tozere, Frederick .... Brookline, Mass. 1901

Tracy, Lee .... Atlanta, Ga. 1898
Truex, Ernest .... Red Hill, Mo. 1890

van Druten, John .... London, England 1902
Van Patten, Dick .... New York City 1929
Varden, Evelyn .... Venita, Okla. 1893

Walker, June .... New York City 1904
Walker, Nancy .... Philadelphia, Pa. 1922
Wallach, Eli .... Brooklyn, N. Y. 1915
Wanamaker, Sam .... Chicago, Ill. 1919
Ward, Penelope .... London, England 1914
Waring, Richard .... Buckinghamshire, England ... 1912
Waters, Ethel .... Chester, Pa. 1900
Watson, Douglas .... Jackson, Ga. 1921
Watson, Lucile .... Quebec, Canada 1879
Wayne, David .... Travers City, Mich. 1914
Webb, Alan .... York, England 1906
Webb, Clifton .... Indiana 1891
Webster, Margaret .... New York City 1905
Welles, Orson .... Kenosha, Wis. 1915
West, Mae .... Brooklyn, N. Y. 1892
Weston, Ruth .... Boston, Mass. 1911
Widmark, Richard .... Sunrise, Minn. 1914
Wilder, Thornton .... Madison, Wis. 1897
Willard, Catherine .... Dayton, Ohio 1895
Williams, Emlyn .... Wales 1905
Williams, Rhys .... Wales 1903
Williams, Tennessee .... Columbus, Miss. 1914
Winwood, Estelle .... England 1883
Wood, Peggy .... Brooklyn, N. Y. 1894
Wyatt, Jane .... Campgaw, N. J. 1912
Wynn, Ed .... Philadelphia, Pa. 1886
Wynn, Keenan .... New York City 1917

Yurka, Blanche .... Bohemia 1893

NECROLOGY

June 1, 1954—May 31, 1955

Arnold, Seth, 70, actor. He began his career with a one-line role in "Quo Vadis" with Boston's Castle Square Stock Company in 1901. His other appearances include roles in "Nightmare," "Quicksand," "Mourning Becomes Electra," "Pursuit of Happiness" and "Ah, Wilderness!". He was also with Helen Hayes in "What Every Woman Knows" and "Harriet." In 1950 he appeared in "Arms and the Girl." Born London; died New York, January 3, 1955.

Bara, Theda, about 70, actress. Born Theodosia Goodman. As Theodosia de Coppet she supported Edwin Stevens in "The Devil" in 1908. She then went into the movies and became William Fox's first great star. She was both a symbol and a personality—the "vampire" type—the ageless siren. Her magnetism at the box office was tremendous. She starred on Broadway in 1921 in "The Blue Flame." For the past several years she had been in retirement. Born Cincinnati; died Los Angeles, April 7, 1955.

Barrymore, Lionel, 76, actor. Made his stage debut at the age of six when a child actor became ill and he was pressed into service. At 15 he appeared with his grandmother, Louisa (Mrs. John) Drew, in "The Rivals." He then left the stage for three years to study painting. When he returned he was in "Squire Kate" and several plays with Nance O'Neil. He made silent movies with Mary Pickford, the Gish sisters and others. One of his most famous roles was in 1917 as Col. Ibbetson in "Peter Ibbetson." Then followed "The Copperhead," "The Jest," "Macbeth" and "The Claw." After "Laugh, Clown, Laugh," "The Piker" and "Man or Devil" he went to Hollywood, where he became one of the movie greats. He wrote his memoirs, as well as a novel, "Mr. Cantonwine: A Moral Tale." His yearly radio interpretation of Scrooge in Dickens' "Christmas Carol" became traditional. He was the eldest of Maurice Barrymore's three famous children. Born Philadelphia; died Los Angeles, November 15, 1954.

Belmore, Daisy, 80, actress. At six she was seen in Shakespearean roles in her native England. Charles Frohman brought her to the United States in 1910 to appear in "Our Miss Gibbs." She later supported such stars as Laurette Taylor, Mrs. Leslie Carter, the Lunts, Leslie Howard and George M. Cohan. In motion pictures she was seen with Gary Cooper, Ben Lyons, Bebe Daniels and others. She was the last of the widely known theatrical Belmore family. Born England; died New York, December 12, 1954.

Benavente y Martinez, Jacinto, 87, playwright. Spain's greatest contemporary playwright and the 1922 Nobel prizewinner had his first theatrical work produced in 1894 and has written 170 plays since that time. He is best known in the United States for his "Bonds of Interest," the Theatre Guild's first production, and for "The Passion Flower," in which Nance O'Neil starred for years. Born Madrid; died Madrid, July 14, 1954.

Browne, Maurice, 74, actor, producer. After fighting in the Boer War he came to the United States and with Ellen Van Volkenburgh founded the Chicago Little Theatre in 1912. This was the father of Little Theatres that sprang up all over the country. He had considerable success as an actor in London and made a fortune out of his many productions of "Journey's End," one of the greatest successes of all time. He also produced the first Paul Robeson "Othello." Born Reading, Eng.; died Torquay, Devon, January 21, 1955.

Burt, William P., 88, actor, director. As a youth he performed in minstrel and medicine shows, vaudeville, repertory, stock and later on Broadway and in films. From 1917 to 1921 he produced motion picture serials with George B. Seitz. His acting credits in pictures include "Danger Signals," "King of Kings" and "Cimarron." He also wrote radio scripts. Died Denver, February 23, 1955.

Claudel, Paul, 86, playwright, poet, diplomat. After a Paris education he entered the diplomatic service, his first post being as assistant consul in New York. During a long diplomatic career which included his being French Ambassador to the United States from 1927 to 1933 he managed to write, and devoted himself to literature after retiring from diplomacy in 1935. He wrote much poetry, translated Aeschylus, did a libretto for Darius Milhaud's "Christophe Colomb" and in addition to other plays wrote "The Tidings Brought to Mary," a contemporary classic that was revived by the Comédie Française just before his death. In 1946 he was made a member of the

French Academy. Born Villeneuve-sur-Fère; died Paris, February 23, 1955.

Colette, Sidonie Gabrielle, 81, writer. One of the most famous of modern French writers, she was the first woman president of the distinguished Goncourt Academy and the second woman in history to be made a grand officer in the Legion of Honor. After writing the famous "Claudine" novels—which her husband published under his name—she divorced him and became a music hall dancer. In 1920 she wrote "Chéri," adapted it into a play and played the principal role herself. Although she was famous in her native France she was not widely known in this country. She is best remembered here for her "Gigi," which she wrote as a novel and which was dramatized for Broadway by Anita Loos. It made a star out of Audrey Hepburn, whom Colette personally selected to play the leading role. Born Saint-Sauveur-en-Puisaye in Burgundy; died Paris, August 3, 1954.

Collier, Constance, 77, actress. She began her career in the provinces in England as a fairy in "A Midsummer Night's Dream" at the age of four. She was in the chorus of light opera and made an appearance with the Gaiety Girls. For a time she studied in Paris with Coquelin. In 1902 she began a seven-year association with H. Beerbohm Tree's company and her Broadway debut was in "Samson" in support of William Gillette. Thereafter she moved back and forth across the Atlantic appearing in many productions. D. W. Griffith brought her to Hollywood in 1915 and she made her motion picture debut in his "Intolerance." She was with John and Lionel Barrymore in "Peter Ibbetson" and later collaborated with Deems Taylor on the libretto for the opera. In late years she coached many famous stars, particularly in Shakespearean roles. Born Windsor, England; died New York, April 25, 1955.

Cotopouli, Marika, 68, actress. This Greek actress was called the Sarah Bernhardt of Athens, where she had her own theatre for many years. In 1930 she brought her company to New York. Born Greece; died Athens, September 11, 1954.

de Mille, William C., 76, playwright. A Columbia University graduate, he wrote such plays as "Strongheart," "Classmates," "The Warrens of Virginia," "The Woman" and "After Five" (this last with his brother Cecil). He was a director and producer of many fine motion pictures, including "Craig's Wife," "Tenth Avenue," "The Idle Rich" and "The Fast Set." He was once president of The Motion Picture Academy of Arts and Sciences.

In 1941 he joined the University of Southern California and founded the school's drama department. He retired in 1953. Born Washington, N. C.; died Los Angeles, March 5, 1955.

Flexner, Anne Crawford, 80, playwright. Minnie Maddern Fiske produced and appeared in her first play "Miranda of the Balcony." Two years later her "Mrs. Wiggs of the Cabbage Patch" was seen on Broadway with great success. Other plays include "The Marriage Game" and "A Lucky Star." Her most recent play was "Aged 26," produced in 1936. Born Georgetown, Ky.; died Providence, R. I., January 11, 1955.

Friganza, Trixie, 83, comedienne. For more than half a century she was one of musical comedy's and vaudeville's bright stars and was also a success in motion pictures. Made her first stage appearance in 1889 in "The Pearl of Pekin." This was followed by a long string of hits, among them "The Little Trouper," "La Poupée," "The Belle of Bohemia" (in which she went to London), "A Trip to Chinatown" on down to "The Sweetest Girl in Paris" and "John Murray Anderson's Almanac." She was known as the "Champagne Girl." Her real name was O'Callaghan. Born Cincinnati; died Pasadena, February 27, 1955.

Gallagher, Richard S. (Skeets), 64, actor. He set out to be a civil engineer, switched to law and finally ended up an entertainer. He began in vaudeville where he became a headliner. In 1921 he made his New York debut in "Up in the Clouds" and the following year was starred in "Up She Goes." He appeared in such hits as "No, No, Nanette," "Marjorie," "The City Chap" and "Lucky" before going to Hollywood where he made twenty-five films in ten years. His last and best-known picture was "Idiot's Delight" with Norma Shearer in 1939. Born Terre Haute, Ind.; died Santa Monica, Calif., May 22, 1955.

George, Gladys, 50, actress. She made her stage debut at the age of three. She played many stock engagements and reached Broadway stardom in "Personal Appearance." She received Motion Picture Academy recognition in 1936 for her role in "Valiant Is the Word for Carrie." This was followed by a busy motion picture career. Born Patten, Maine; died Hollywood, December 8, 1954.

Gill, Basil, 78, actor. Made his stage debut at twenty in a provincial theatre in "The Sign of the Cross," followed by a London appearance in "The Daughter of Babylon." From 1903 to 1907 he was with Beerbohm Tree's company in London and in 1912 he came to New York in "The Daughter of Heaven."

A year later he was seen here in "The Secret." In 1925 he supported Florence Reed and Lyn Harding in "Macbeth" on Broadway. His career extended over fifty years. Born Birkenhead, Cheshire, England; died Hove, England, April 23, 1955.

Goetz, E. Ray, 68, producer, songwriter. Back in the 'teens he was associated with Raymond Hitchcock, producing and writing the lyrics for "Hitchy-Koo." In 1923 he wrote lyrics for George White's "Scandals." He was both author and producer of "The Lady of the Orchids," which played on Broadway in 1928. He produced "Fifty Million Frenchmen" and "The New Yorkers." Born Buffalo; died Greenwich, Conn., June 12, 1954.

Harrington, Alice, 81, actress. A graduate of the American Academy of Dramatic Arts, she made her professional debut in 1900 with the Ben Greet Players. From 1905 to 1908 she was with the Shakespearean troupe of Sothern and Marlowe, and for the next four years with the Castle Square Stock Company of Boston. In 1930 she joined the faculty of the American Academy of Dramatic Arts where she taught and directed until 1951. Born Marlboro, Mass.; died Greenwich, Conn., June 6, 1954.

Hilton, James, 54, writer. He wrote fourteen novels, many of them best sellers. His "Goodbye, Mr. Chips" and "Lost Horizon," both of which sold over three million copies, were made into fine and popular motion pictures. His motion picture script of "Mrs. Miniver" won him an Academy Award. Born Lancashire, England; died Long Beach, Calif., December 20, 1954.

Howard, Tom, 69, comedian. He was clerk in a grocery store when, in 1905, he got his first job in show business. In his early career he played in vaudeville and burlesque and later was featured in many Broadway musicals and revues. He was in "Smiles" with Marilyn Miller, "Keep Moving," "The Gang's All Here" and "Rain or Shine" with Joe Cook. In recent years he became familiar to radio listeners as the quizmaster on "It Pays to Be Ignorant." Born in County Tyrone, Ireland; died Red Bank, N. J., February 27, 1955.

Hubbel, Raymond, 75, composer. He wrote the music for thirty-eight Broadway shows, among them seven editions of the Ziegfeld Follies. Others include "Fantana," "The Runaways," "Yours Truly" and "Here and There." "Poor Butterfly" was one of his most famous songs. Born Urbana, Ohio; died Miami, Fla., December 13, 1954.

Jerrold, Mary, 77, actress. Made her stage debut with Sir George Alexander in "Mary Pennington, Spinster." She was also in "Mary Rose," "Quality Street" and "Milestones." She is remembered in New York for her fine performance in Maugham's "The Sacred Flame," and recently appeared in London in "A Day by the Sea" with John Gielgud and Ralph Richardson. Born London; died London, March 3, 1955.

Jones, Robert Edmond, 67, scenic designer. For nearly thirty years he was one of the theatre's foremost designers and most influential forces. After graduating from Harvard in 1910 he stayed on for two years as instructor in Fine Arts and became interested in theatre. For a time he was costume designer for Comstock and Gest. In 1913 he went to Europe and was with Max Reinhardt's Deutsches Theatre for a year. When he returned to New York he did the settings for Anatole France's "The Man Who Married a Dumb Wife" and audiences gasped with admiration. Thereafter his reputation was secure. He tried always to design sets which would more fully project the playwright's thought. In a five-year period beginning in 1915 he designed the sets for seventeen plays, two ballets and five masques. In 1921 he began working with Eugene O'Neill and designed the productions for many of his plays. He received Yale University's Howland Memorial Prize and in 1933 the Fine Arts Medal of the American Institute of Architects. His most recent work was for the revival of "Green Pastures" in 1950. Its original success was in part attributed to Mr. Jones' sets. Born Milton, N. H.; died Milton, N. H., November 26, 1954.

Karson, Nat, 46, scenic designer. He won a scholarship to the Chicago Art Institute and later came to New York. He entered the theatre world via the Federal Theatre Project. He was then for seven years at Radio City Music Hall but during that time managed to sandwich in some Broadway shows, among them "Life with Father." His greatest success was a presentation of "Hamlet" at the Kronborg Festival, Elsinore, Denmark, in 1949. Born Zurich, Switzerland; died New York, September 27, 1954.

Kinnell, Murray, 65, actor. Made his first stage appearance in London in 1907 in Shakespearean repertory. After appearing with Sir Frank Benson's company he came to New York in 1912 in "Pomander Walk." He supported Doris Keane, Sothern and Marlowe and George Arliss. Born England; died Santa Barbara, Calif., August 14, 1954.

Levey, Ethel, 72, actress. First appeared on the stage in "A Milk White Flag" in 1897 in San Francisco. She was first seen in New York at Weber and Fields' Music Hall. She later became associated with (and married to) George M. Cohan. For many years she played the leading music halls of the United States, England and the continent. Recently in New York she was featured in "Sunny River" and "Marinka." Born San Francisco; died New York, February 27, 1955.

Lorraine, Lillian, 63, actress. Known as "The American Beauty of Broadway" and described by Ziegfeld as "the most beautiful actress in the world," she was first seen in New York in the Ziegfeld Follies of 1909. She was in many succeeding Follies and rose to stardom in "The Blue Kitten" in 1922. Her career was cut short that year when she fell on an icy pavement and suffered spinal injuries. Born San Francisco; died New York, April 17, 1955.

Lytell, Bert, 69, actor. He had a walk-on part with his parents at the age of three. His first regular part came when he was seventeen, in a stock company in Newark, N. J. For the next twelve years he was in stock and at one time managed his own company. From 1914 to 1919 he was on Broadway and later toured in vaudeville for two years in "The Valiant." Later he became a star in motion pictures, among them "The Lone Wolf," "Alias Jimmy Valentine" and "Lady Windermere's Fan." Among his best-remembered plays are "Brothers," "First Legion" and "Margin for Error." He was president of Actors' Equity for six years. Born New York; died New York, September 28, 1954.

McCormick, Arthur L., 81, playwright. Among his plays are "The Life of an Actress," "The Storm," "The Gulf" and "The Burglar and the Lady." He depended heavily on spectacular scenic effects. His last Broadway play was "Shipwrecked" in 1924, in which a ship burned and sank on stage. Born Port Huron, Mich.; died New York, June 25, 1954.

McGee, Harold J., 55, actor. After graduating from Union College in 1920 he was a student with the original Provincetown Theatre Group, later serving on their board of directors. He was in a number of the early Eugene O'Neill plays. Most recently he was in "Anne of the Thousand Days" and "The Shrike." Born Schenectady; died New York, February 23, 1955.

Major, Clare Tree, 74, producer. An actress in her native England, she came to New York in 1914 and soon established the Children's Theatre that bears her name. In 1948 she had as many as six companies on tour at the same time. She prepared most of the dramatizations of her plays as well as supervising their production. Her name has become synonymous with children's theatre. Born England; died New York, October 9, 1954.

Miles, Carlton (age not recorded), playwright. A graduate of the University of Minnesota, he was with the Minneapolis *Journal* for twenty years, fifteen of them as drama critic. He was represented on Broadway by "Portrait of Gilbert" and "The Eldest." For his last fifteen years he was associated with the Lunts as press-agent. Born Fergus Falls, Minn.; died New York, September 18, 1954.

Moore, Tom, 71, actor. He came from Ireland and went to Hollywood in 1917. He played opposite many of the female stars of the silent era. His pictures include "Manhandled," "A Kiss for Cinderella," "Song and Dance Man," "The Last Parade" and "The Wise Wife." In recent years he appeared with Billie Burke in a touring company of "Life with Mother" and later in TV with Doris Kenyon. Born Ireland; died Santa Monica, Calif., February 12, 1955.

Munson, Ona, 49, actress. Her career began in vaudeville in 1922. This was followed by leads in "No, No, Nanette," on tour, and on Broadway in "Twinkle, Twinkle," "Manhattan Mary," "Hold Everything" and "Ghosts" with Nazimova. She appeared in several motion pictures, among them "Gone with the Wind." Recently she was in the revival of "First Lady" at the City Center. Born Portland, Ore.; died New York, February 11, 1955.

Pallette, Eugene, 65, actor. He started as an extra in early movies but by 1916 was playing much more important roles. Among his many pictures were "The Virginian," "The Mark of Zorro," "The Ghost Goes West" and "The Male Animal." He also played stock but never appeared on Broadway. Born Winfield, Kansas; died Los Angeles, September 3, 1954.

Perlman, William, 72, playwright. In 1927 his "My Country" was produced on Broadway and later his "Broken Chain." He was co-owner and manager of the Mayfair Theatre from 1924 to 1928 and was one of the producers of "Juno and the Paycock" there in 1926. Died New York, November 18, 1954.

Pichel, Irving, 63, actor, director. Graduated from Harvard in 1914, he made his stage debut with the old Castle Square Theatre Company of Boston. He entered the little theatre movement and organized community playhouses in St. Louis, Detroit, St. Paul and Minneapolis. He directed many O'Neill plays on the West Coast. As an actor he was seen in such motion pictures as "The Cheat," "Oliver Twist" and "Cleopatra." Films he directed include "Mr. Peabody and the Mermaid," "The Miracle of the Bells" and "The Moon Is Down." He recently completed "Day of Triumph." Born Pittsburgh; died Los Angeles, July 13, 1954.

Polgar, Alfred, 81, playwright. After attending the University of Vienna he became a reporter and later drama critic for several European papers. He held a position in the German language press similar to that of Alexander Woollcott here. He came to the United States in 1940 and worked for two years at MGM studios in Hollywood. One of his better-known plays is "The Absconders." He successfully translated John van Druten's "The Voice of the Turtle" and "Bell, Book and Candle" into German. Born Vienna; died Zurich, Switzerland, April 24, 1955.

Riggs, Lynn, 54, playwright. His first New York production was "The Big Lake," which led to a Guggenheim Fellowship. His "Green Grow the Lilacs" was produced by the Theatre Guild in 1931 and became the basis, years later, for Rodgers and Hammerstein's "Oklahoma!". Other plays include "Roadside," "Russet Mantle," "The Cream in the Well." Born Oklahoma; died New York, June 30, 1954.

Robey, Sir George, 85, comedian. Known in England as the Prime Minister of Mirth, he began his theatrical career in 1891. He was one of the greats of the English music halls. Two of his famous numbers were "If You Were the Only Girl in the World" and "Another Little Drink Won't Do Us Any Harm." He played a wide variety of roles, from a revue appearance in "The Bing Boys Are Here" in 1916 to Falstaff in "Henry IV" in 1935. Born England; died London, November 29, 1954.

Royle, Selena Fetter, 95, actress. As Selena Fetter she made her theatrical debut in Louisville, Ky., at McCauley's Theatre as Juliet. She later supported such stars as Stuart Robson, William H. Crane and Lionel Barrymore, and appeared in several plays with and by her husband, Edwin Milton Royle. Born Kentucky; died Van Nuys, Calif., May 10, 1955.

Sakall, S. Z., 67, actor. He was a principal on the stage and screen in Vienna and Berlin before fleeing Hitler's regime and coming to the United States in 1939. He was in a long list of Hollywood films and became known by the nickname of "Cuddles." He appeared in the famous European film "Two Hearts in Waltz Time." Here he played in "The Dolly Sisters," "Lullaby of Broadway" and "April Showers." Born Budapest; died Hollywood, February 12, 1955.

Schuenzel, Reinhold, 65, actor, director. He began his stage career
in 1915 in Berlin and was one of Germany's best-known silent
film stars. His American career began in 1937 in Hollywood,
and among the films he directed are "New Wine" and "Bala-
laika." Made his Broadway debut in 1945 in "Marinka" and
was later in the revival of "He Who Gets Slapped" and in
"Monserrat." Born Germany; died Munich, Germany, September 11, 1954.

Selwyn, Ruth, 49, producer, actress. Made her theatrical debut as
a singer and dancer in George White's "Scandals." In 1929 she
became one of New York's first woman producers with "The
9:15 Revue." She later went to Hollywood and appeared in
motion pictures. Died Hollywood, December 13, 1954.

Shannon, Effie, 87, actress. She first appeared at seven in Boston
as Eva in "Uncle Tom's Cabin" and made her Broadway debut
in 1886 in "Tangled Lives." She played for Augustin Daly and
David Belasco. She and her husband, Herbert Kelcey, starred
in such plays as "The Moth and the Flame," "Her Lord and
Master" and "The Lightning Conductor." More recently she
was in "Parnell," "Wingless Victory" and (her last appearance
on Broadway) "Arsenic and Old Lace." She was active in the
theatre for 68 years. Born Cambridge, Mass.; died Bay Shore,
L. I., July 23, 1954.

Spong, Hilda, 80, actress. In her sixty-five years on the stage she
played everything from Shakespeare to farce. She spent most
of her early days playing in Australia and later made a tremendous hit in London as Imogene Parrott in Pinero's "Trelawny of the Wells." It was in this same role that she made
her American debut in 1898. Among her many other plays in
this country were: "The High Road," "Evensong," "The
Swan," "Only the Young" and "The Lady Has a Heart." Born
London; died Ridgefield, Conn., May 16, 1955.

Starling, Lynn, 67, playwright. Originally a teacher of languages
at the Lawrenceville, N. J., school, he later studied at a drama
school and was in the original production of "The Better 'Ole."
Among his many plays are "In His Arms," "Weak Sisters,"
"Cup of Sugar," "First Apple" and his biggest hit, "Meet the
Wife." He also wrote for motion pictures. Born Hopkinsville,
Ky.; died Hollywood, March 1955.

Vollmer, Lula, 57, playwright. She attended what is now Asheville
(N. C.) College and wrote several plays which were produced
on Broadway during the twenties, among them "The Shame
Woman," "Sentinels" and "Trigger." She is best known, how-

ever, for "Sun-Up," which ran for two years on Broadway. By waiving royalties, she raised about $40,000 from tours of this play for educational work in the mountain areas of the south. Born Keyser, N. C.; died New York, May 2, 1955.

Weeks, Barbara, 47, actress. For eighteen years she was prominent on radio shows, and during the twenties and early thirties was in several Broadway productions—the last of them "Double Dummy" in 1937. Born Binghamton, N. Y.; died New York, July 4, 1954.

Weiman, Rita (age not recorded), playwright. She was the author of many magazine stories, several of which found their way to the screen. In 1920 her play "The Acquittal" was a great success on Broadway; she also wrote "The Backdrop," "The Lizard" and "Vengeance Is Mine." Born Philadelphia; died Hollywood, June 23, 1954.

Weller, Carrie, 66, actress. She made her stage debut in a Chicago stock company at the age of fourteen. She came to Broadway in the twenties and was in such plays as "Henry—Behave," "The Front Page," "The Bat," "Music in the Air," "Our Town" and "The Merchant of Yonkers." Born La Porte, Ind.; died Long Island, June 6, 1954.

Willard, Catherine, 54, actress. A leading woman for twenty-five years, she made her first appearance in Exeter, England, in 1915 with Frank Benson in "The Taming of the Shrew" and later was at the Old Vic. In 1921 she appeared with the Henry Jewett Company in Boston where she remained for several years playing eighty-six roles, in Ibsen, Shaw, Galsworthy, Pinero, etc. In New York she was seen in such hits as "The Great Gatsby," "Young Love," "Topaze" and "The Deep Mrs. Sykes." Her last Broadway appearance was in "I Am a Camera" in 1952. Born Dayton, Ohio; died New York, November 4, 1954.

THE DECADES' TOLL

(Prominent Theatrical Figures Who Have Died
in Recent Years)

	Born	Died
Adams, Maude	1872	1953
Anderson, John Murray	1886	1954
Arliss, George	1869	1946
Bennett, Richard	1873	1944
Bernstein, Henri	1876	1953
Carroll, Earl	1893	1948
Carte, Rupert D'Oyly	1876	1948
Christians, Mady	1900	1951
Cochran, Charles B.	1872	1951
Collier, Willie	1866	1943
Cowl, Jane	1884	1950
Craven, Frank	1890	1945
Crosman, Henrietta	1865	1944
Digges, Dudley	1879	1947
Duncan, Augustin	1872	1954
Errol, Leon	1881	1951
Fields, W. C.	1879	1946
Garfield, John	1913	1952
Gaige, Crosby	1883	1949
Hart, Lorenz	1895	1943
Hart, William S.	1870	1946
Hooker, Brian	1881	1947
Howard, Willie	1883	1949
Jolson, Al.	1886	1950
Jouvet, Louis	1887	1951
Kern, Jerome D.	1885	1945
Lawrence, Gertrude	1898	1952
Lehar, Franz	1870	1948
Loftus, Cecilia	1876	1943
Lord, Pauline	1890	1950
Mantle, Burns	1873	1948
Marlowe, Julia	1866	1950
Merivale, Philip	1886	1946

	Born	Died
Molnar, Ferenc	1878	1952
Moore, Grace	1901	1947
Nazimova, Alla	1879	1945
Nethersole, Olga	1870	1951
O'Neill, Eugene	1888	1953
Patterson, Joseph Medill	1879	1946
Perry, Antoinette	1888	1946
Powers, James T.	1862	1943
Reinhardt, Max	1873	1943
Romberg, Sigmund	1887	1951
Scheff, Fritzi	1879	1954
Selwyn, Edgar	1875	1944
Shaw, G. B.	1856	1950
Sheldon, Edward	1886	1946
Shubert, Lee	1875	1953
Tarkington, Booth	1869	1946
Tauber, Richard	1890	1948
Tyler, George C.	1867	1946
Ward, Fannie	1872	1952
Warfield, David	1866	1951
Webster, Ben	1864	1947
Whitty, Dame May	1865	1948
Woods, Al H.	1870	1951
Woollcott, Alexander	1887	1943
Youmans, Vincent	1899	1946

INDICES

INDICES

INDEX OF AUTHORS AND PLAYWRIGHTS

INDEX OF PLAYS AND CASTS

Bold face page numbers refer to pages on which
Cast of Characters may be found.

476

INDEX OF PRODUCERS, DIRECTORS,
DESIGNERS, STAGE MANAGERS,
COMPOSERS, AND CHOREOGRAPHERS